THE LAST MAN —
WHYS AND WHEREFORES

Brian K. Vaughan Writer

Pia Guerra Penciller

José Marzán, Jr. Inker

Zylonol Colorist

Clem Robins Letterer

Massimo Carnevale Original series covers

Y: THE LAST MAN created by Brian K. Vaughan and Pia Guerra

Cover illustrations by Massimo Carnevale.
Logo designs by Terry Marks.

Y: THE LAST MAN — WHYS AND WHEREFORES. Published by DC Comics.
Cover and compilation Copyright © 2008 DC Comics. All Rights Reserved.
Originally published in single magazine form as Y: THE LAST MAN 55-60.
Copyright © 2007, 2008 Brian K. Vaughan and Pia Guerra. All Rights Reserved.
All characters, their distinctive likenesses and related elements featured in
this publication are trademarks of Brian K. Vaughan and Pia Guerra. VERTIGO
is a trademark of DC Comics. The stories, characters and incidents featured
in this publication are entirely fictional. DC Comics does not read or
accept unsolicited submissions of ideas, stories or artwork. DC Comics,
1700 Broadway, New York, NY 10019. A Warner Bros. Entertainment Company.
Printed in Canada. Second Printing. ISBN: 978-1-4012-1813-3

Y THE LAST MAN — Contents

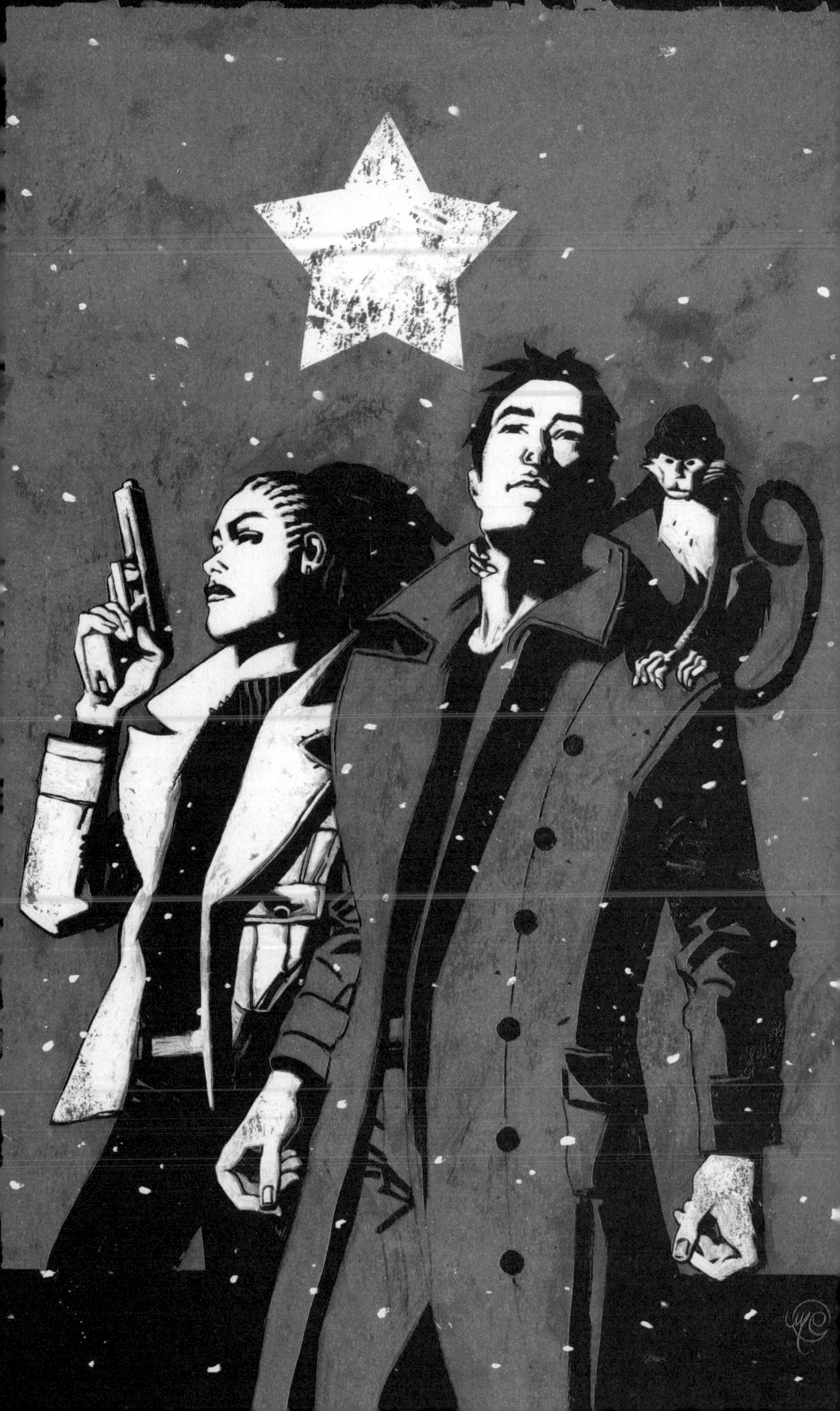

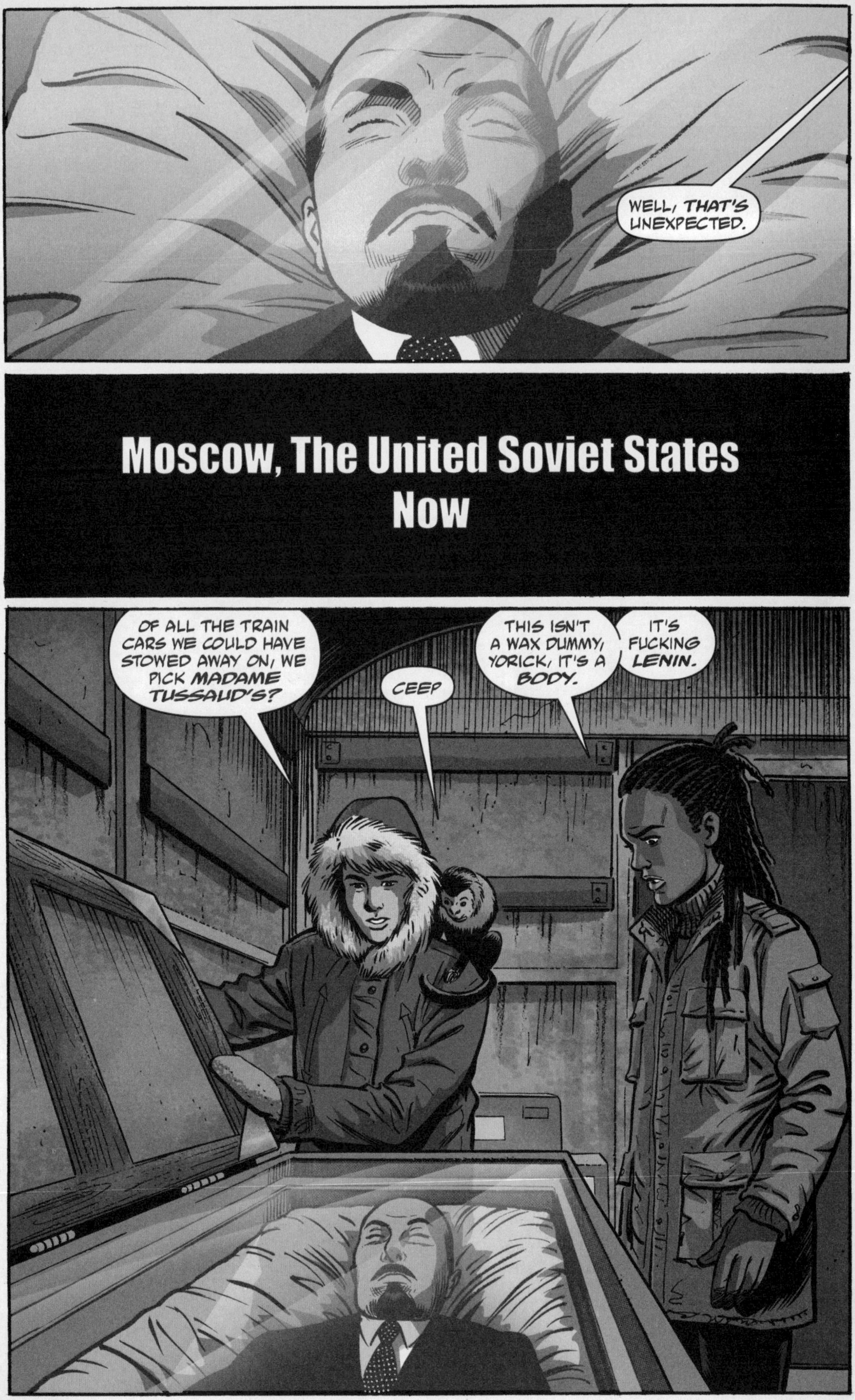
WELL, THAT'S UNEXPECTED.
Moscow, The United Soviet States
Now
OF ALL THE TRAIN CARS WE COULD HAVE STOWED AWAY ON, WE PICK MADAME TUSSAUD'S?
CEEP
THIS ISN'T A WAX DUMMY, YORICK, IT'S A BODY.
IT'S FUCKING LENIN.

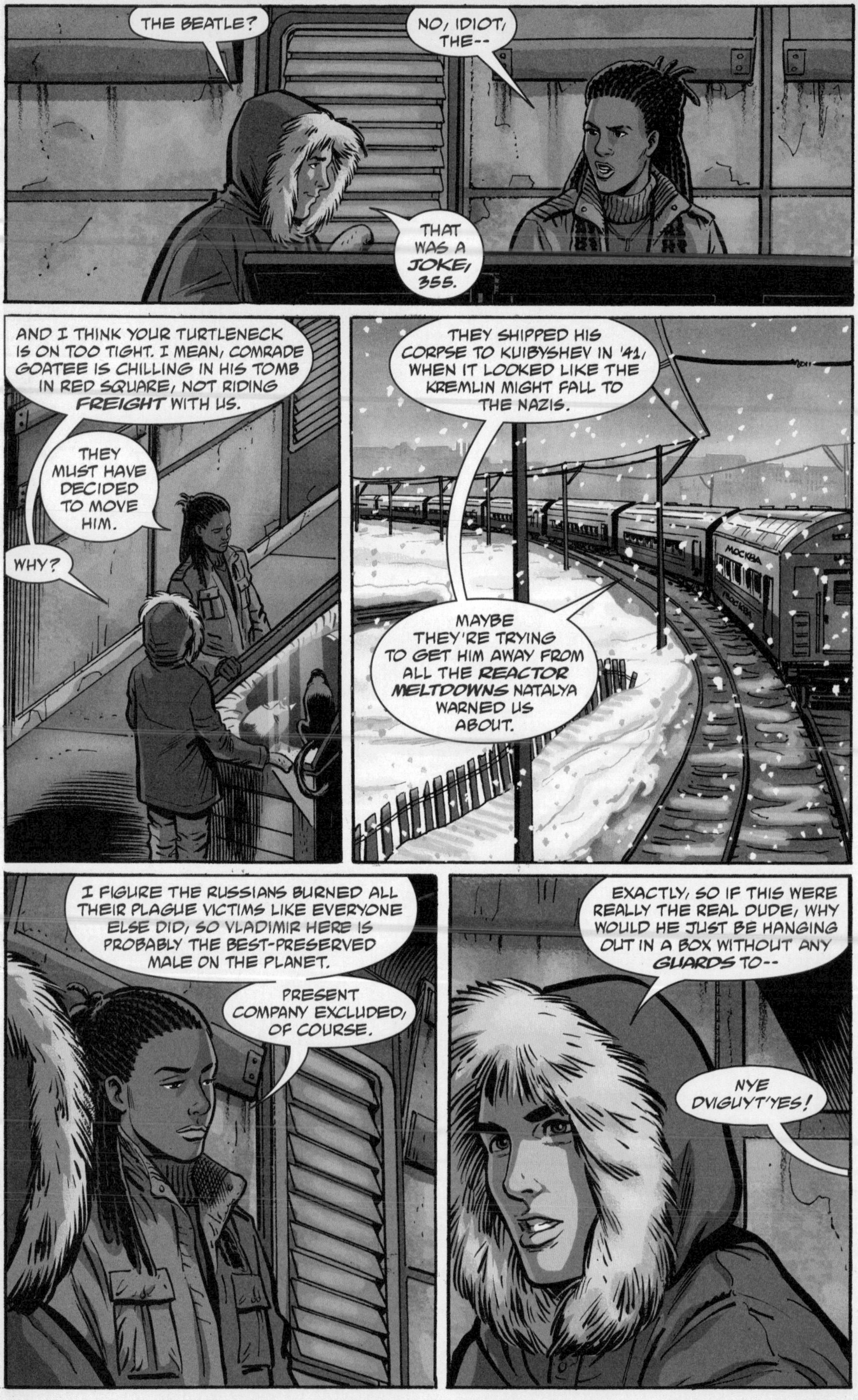
THE BEATLE?
NO, IDIOT, THE--
THAT WAS A JOKE, 355.
AND I THINK YOUR TURTLENECK IS ON TOO TIGHT. I MEAN, COMRADE GOATEE IS CHILLING IN HIS TOMB IN RED SQUARE, NOT RIDING FREIGHT WITH US.
THEY MUST HAVE DECIDED TO MOVE HIM.
WHY?
THEY SHIPPED HIS CORPSE TO KUIBYSHEV IN '41, WHEN IT LOOKED LIKE THE KREMLIN MIGHT FALL TO THE NAZIS.
МОСКВА
MAYBE THEY'RE TRYING TO GET HIM AWAY FROM ALL THE REACTOR MELTDOWNS NATALYA WARNED US ABOUT.
I FIGURE THE RUSSIANS BURNED ALL THEIR PLAGUE VICTIMS LIKE EVERYONE ELSE DID, SO VLADIMIR HERE IS PROBABLY THE BEST-PRESERVED MALE ON THE PLANET.
PRESENT COMPANY EXCLUDED, OF COURSE.
EXACTLY, SO IF THIS WERE REALLY THE REAL DUDE, WHY WOULD HE JUST BE HANGING OUT IN A BOX WITHOUT ANY GUARDS TO--
NYE DVIGUYT'YES!

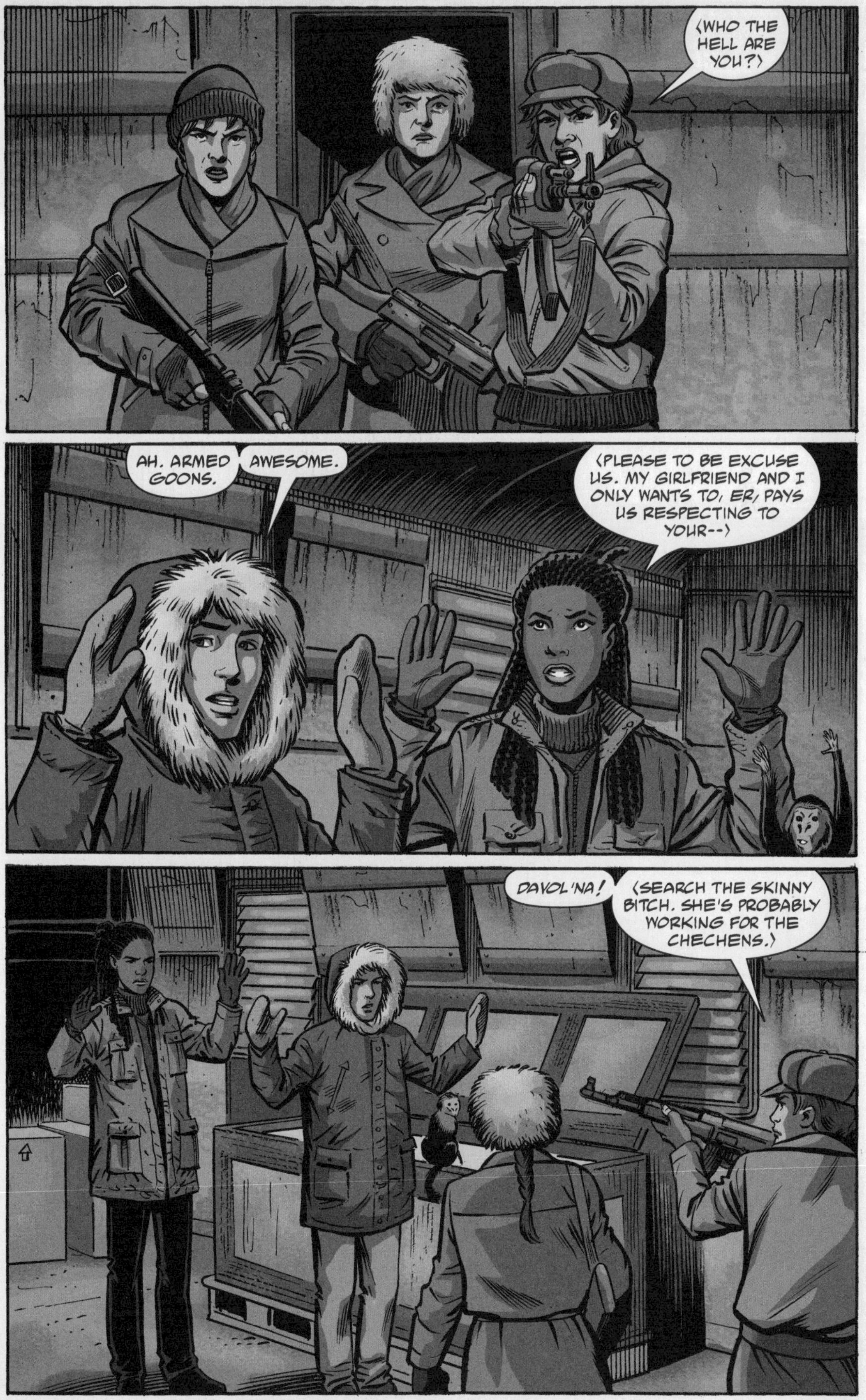
⟨WHO THE HELL ARE YOU?⟩
AH. ARMED GOONS.
AWESOME.
⟨PLEASE TO BE EXCUSE US. MY GIRLFRIEND AND I ONLY WANTS TO, ER, PAYS US RESPECTING TO YOUR--⟩
DAVOL'NA!
⟨SEARCH THE SKINNY BITCH. SHE'S PROBABLY WORKING FOR THE CHECHENS.⟩

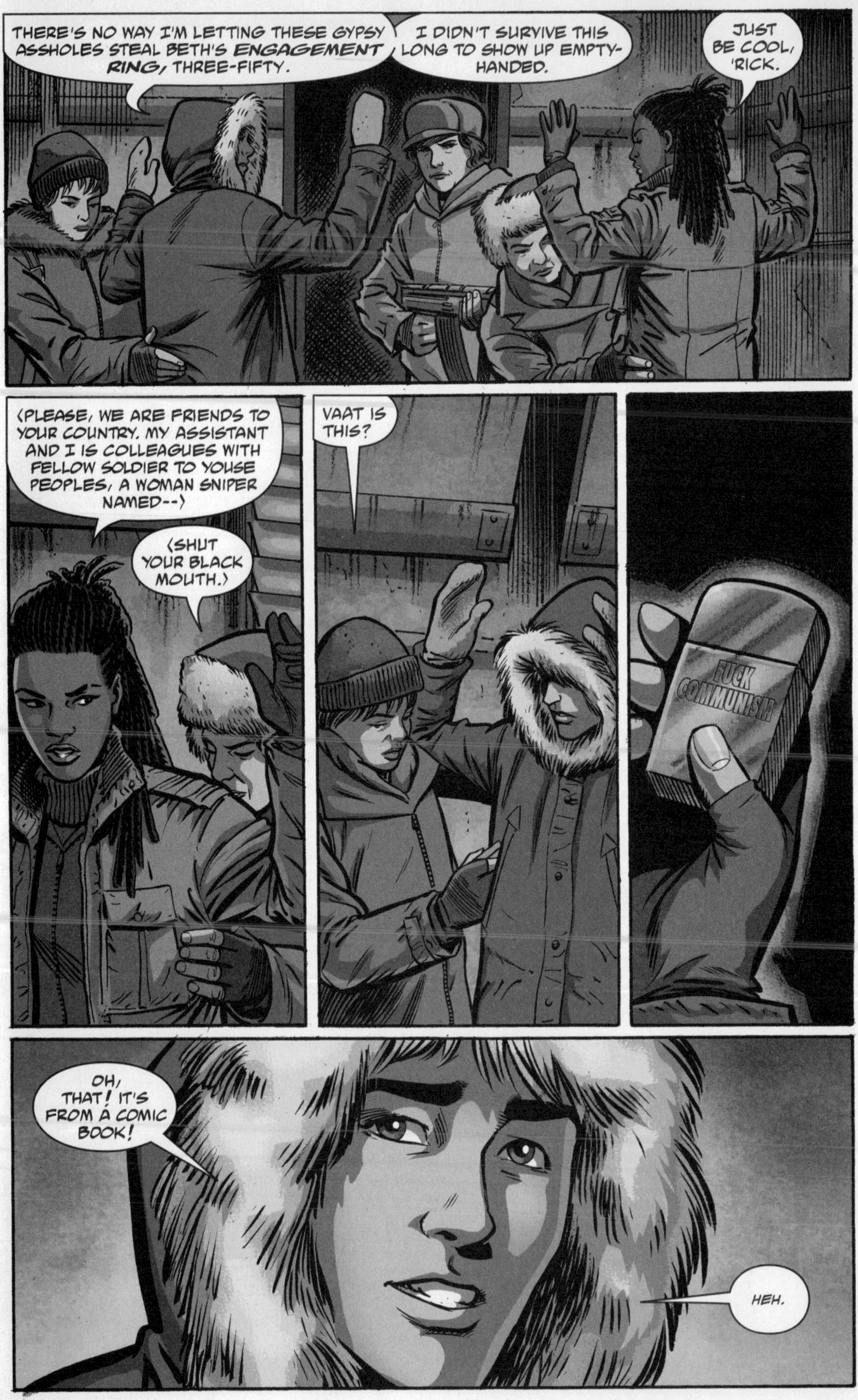
THERE'S NO WAY I'M LETTING THESE GYPSY ASSHOLES STEAL BETH'S ENGAGEMENT RING, THREE-FIFTY.
I DIDN'T SURVIVE THIS LONG TO SHOW UP EMPTY-HANDED.
JUST BE COOL, 'RICK.
‹PLEASE, WE ARE FRIENDS TO YOUR COUNTRY. MY ASSISTANT AND I IS COLLEAGUES WITH FELLOW SOLDIER TO YOUSE PEOPLES, A WOMAN SNIPER NAMED--›
‹SHUT YOUR BLACK MOUTH.›
VAAT IS THIS?
FUCK COMMUNISM
OH, THAT! IT'S FROM A COMIC BOOK!
HEH.

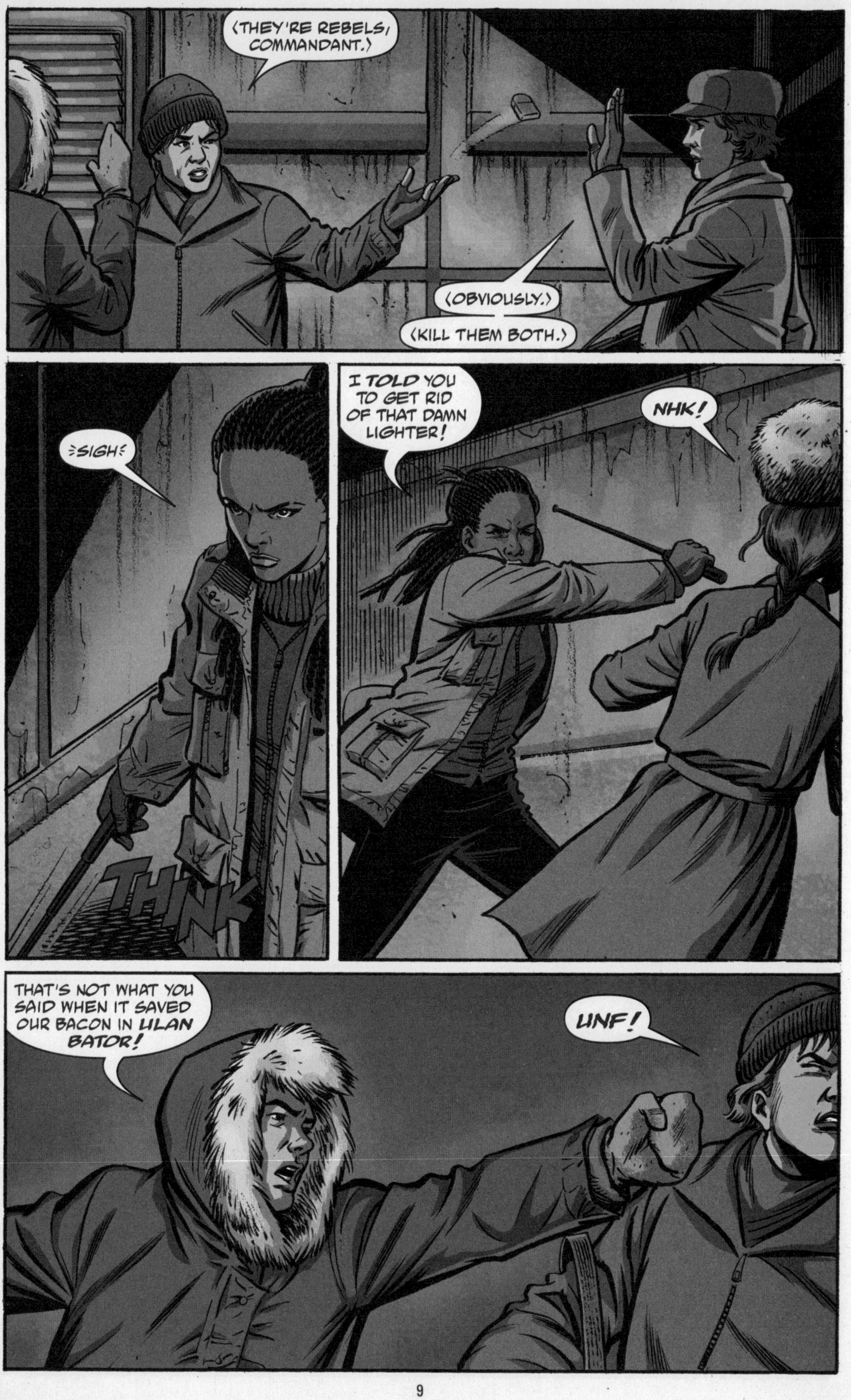

‹THEY'RE REBELS, COMMANDANT.›
‹OBVIOUSLY.›
‹KILL THEM BOTH.›
≶SIGH≶
THINK
I TOLD YOU TO GET RID OF THAT DAMN LIGHTER!
NHK!
THAT'S NOT WHAT YOU SAID WHEN IT SAVED OUR BACON IN ULAN BATOR!
UNF!

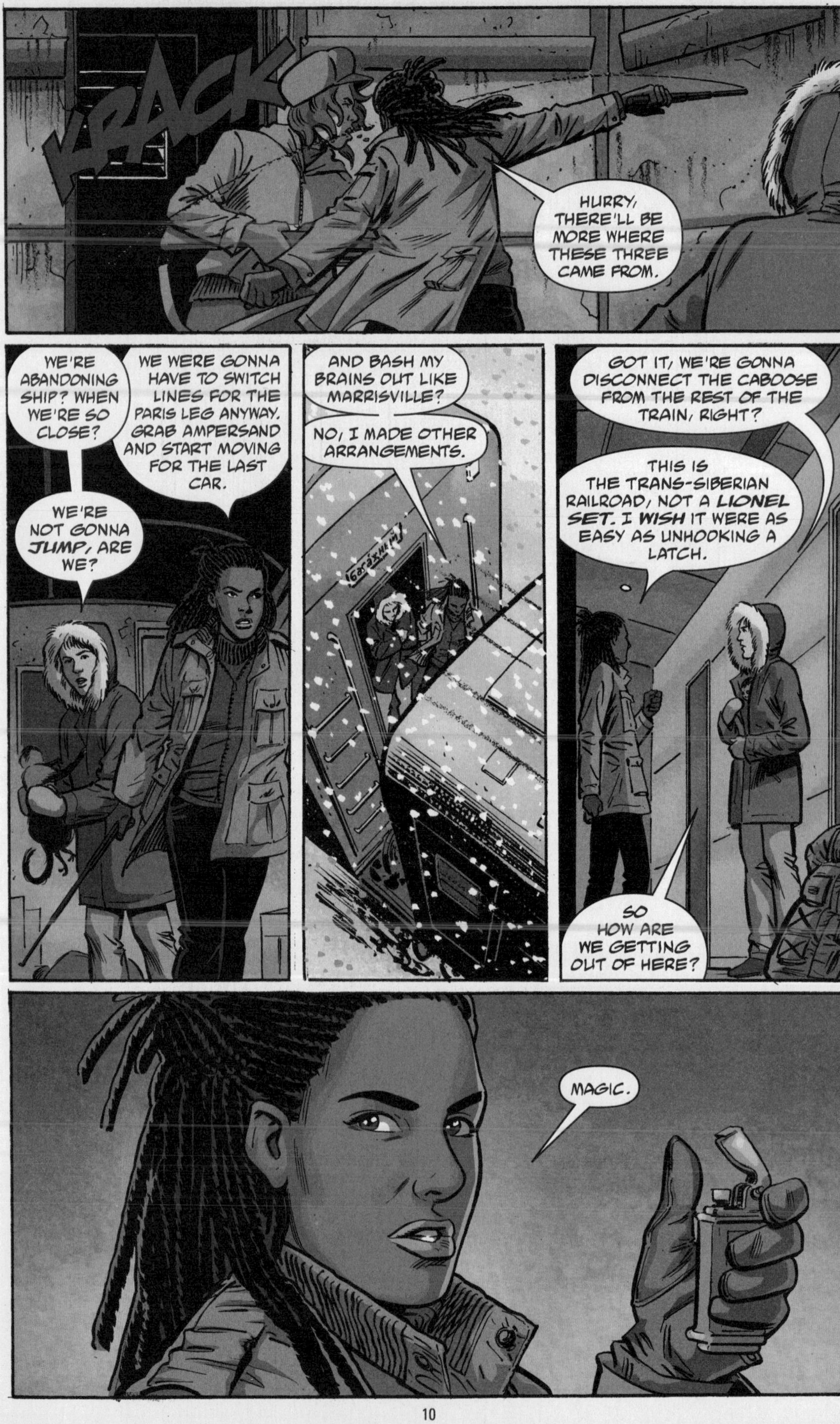
KRACK
HURRY, THERE'LL BE MORE WHERE THESE THREE CAME FROM.
WE'RE ABANDONING SHIP? WHEN WE'RE SO CLOSE?
WE WERE GONNA HAVE TO SWITCH LINES FOR THE PARIS LEG ANYWAY. GRAB AMPERSAND AND START MOVING FOR THE LAST CAR.
WE'RE NOT GONNA JUMP, ARE WE?
AND BASH MY BRAINS OUT LIKE MARRISVILLE?
NO, I MADE OTHER ARRANGEMENTS.
GOT IT, WE'RE GONNA DISCONNECT THE CABOOSE FROM THE REST OF THE TRAIN, RIGHT?
THIS IS THE TRANS-SIBERIAN RAILROAD, NOT A LIONEL SET. I WISH IT WERE AS EASY AS UNHOOKING A LATCH.
SO HOW ARE WE GETTING OUT OF HERE?
MAGIC.

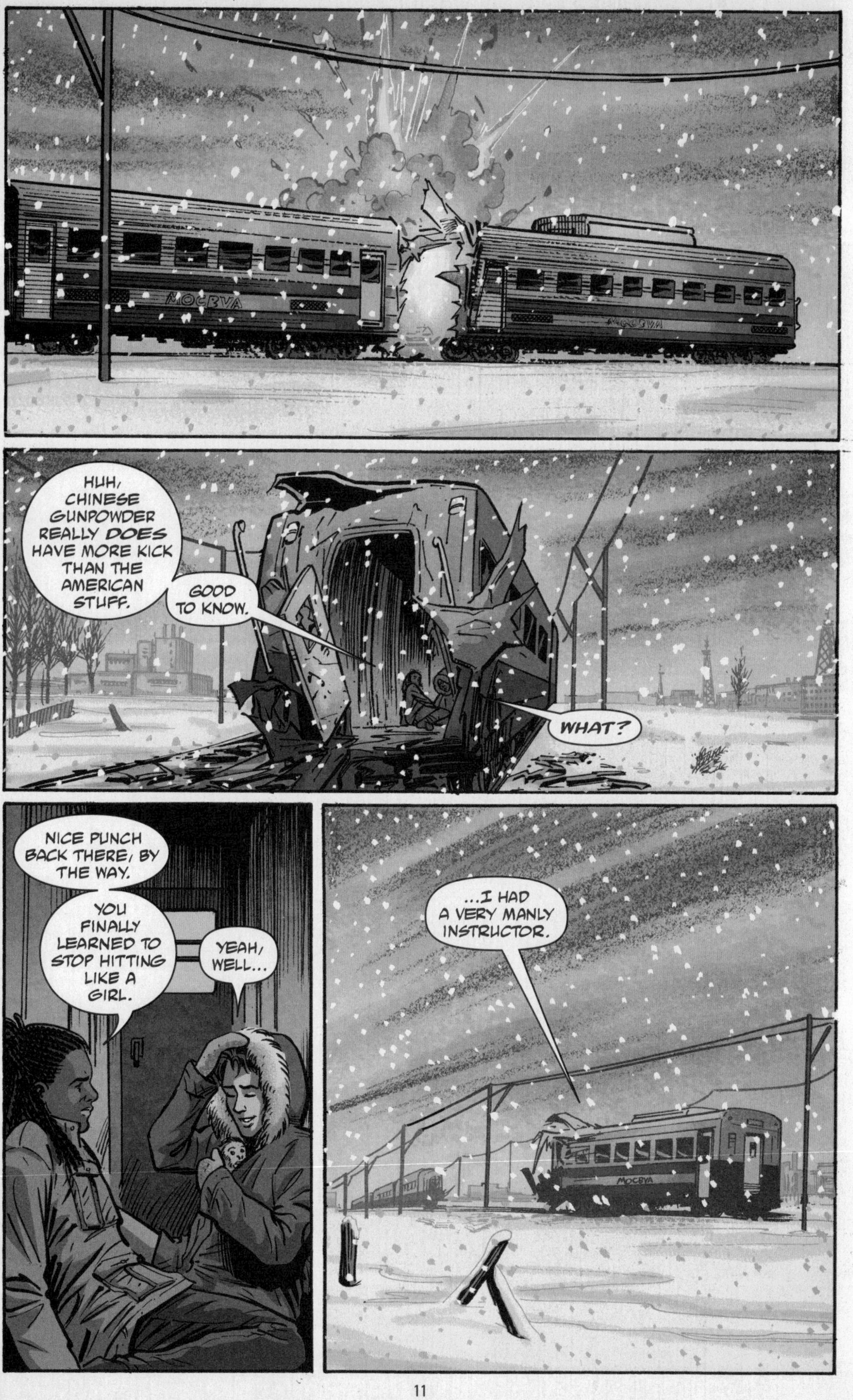
HUH, CHINESE GUNPOWDER REALLY *DOES* HAVE MORE KICK THAN THE AMERICAN STUFF.
GOOD TO KNOW.
WHAT?
NICE PUNCH BACK THERE, BY THE WAY.
YOU FINALLY LEARNED TO STOP HITTING LIKE A GIRL.
YEAH, WELL...
...I HAD A VERY MANLY INSTRUCTOR.

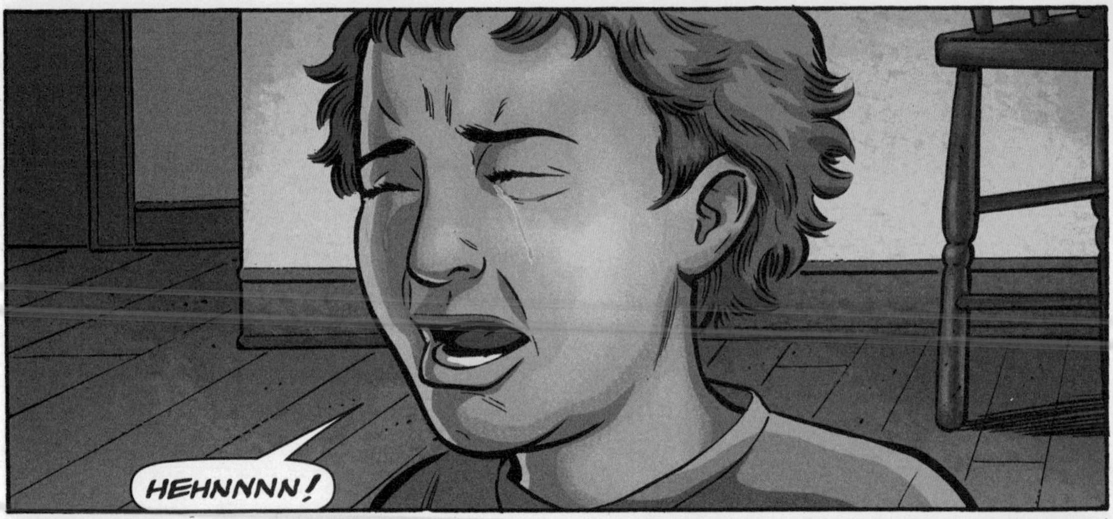
HEHNNNN!

Paris, France
Now

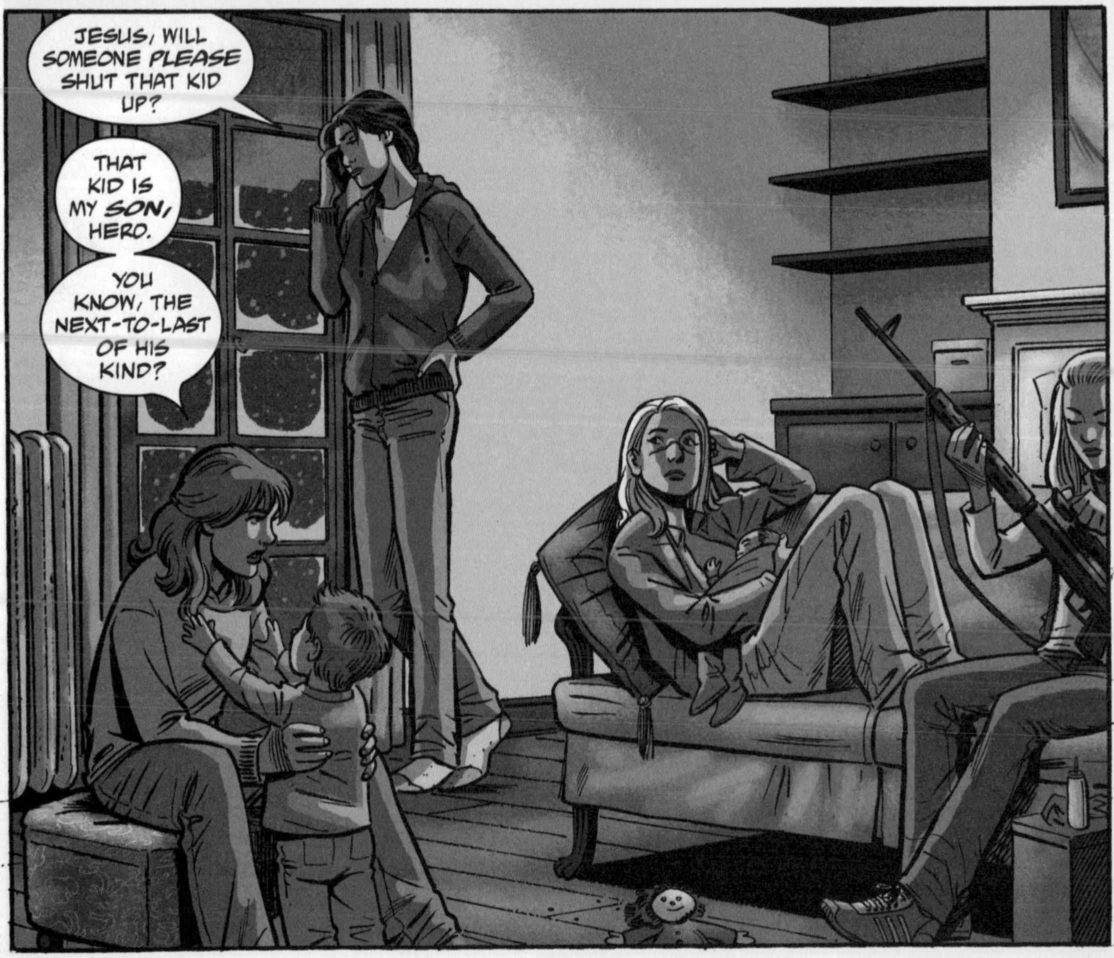
JESUS, WILL SOMEONE PLEASE SHUT THAT KID UP?
THAT KID IS MY SON, HERO.
YOU KNOW, THE NEXT-TO-LAST OF HIS KIND?

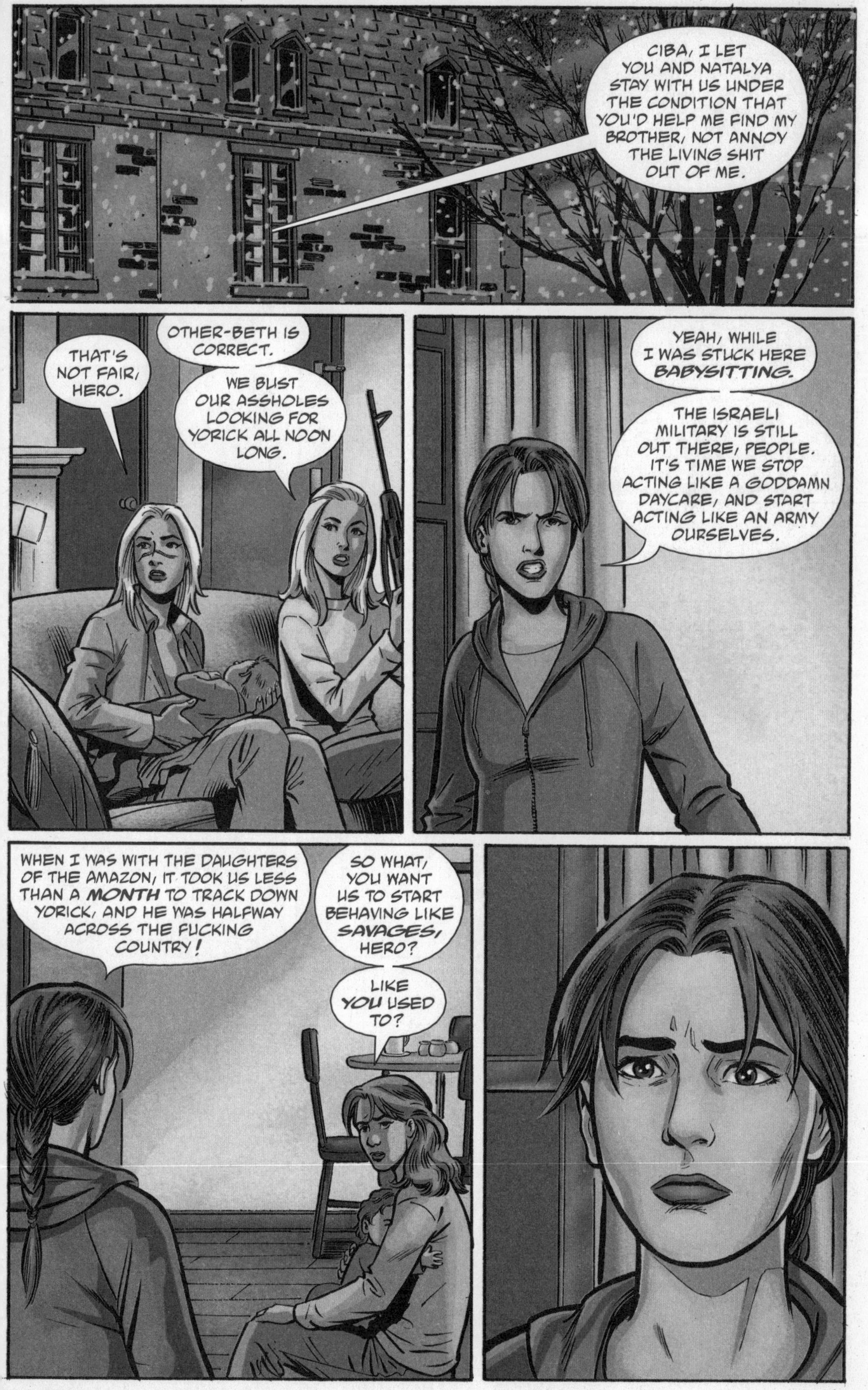
CIBA, I LET YOU AND NATALYA STAY WITH US UNDER THE CONDITION THAT YOU'D HELP ME FIND MY BROTHER, NOT ANNOY THE LIVING SHIT OUT OF ME.
THAT'S NOT FAIR, HERO.
OTHER-BETH IS CORRECT.
WE BUST OUR ASSHOLES LOOKING FOR YORICK ALL NOON LONG.
YEAH, WHILE I WAS STUCK HERE *BABYSITTING*.
THE ISRAELI MILITARY IS STILL OUT THERE, PEOPLE. IT'S TIME WE STOP ACTING LIKE A GODDAMN DAYCARE, AND START ACTING LIKE AN ARMY OURSELVES.
WHEN I WAS WITH THE DAUGHTERS OF THE AMAZON, IT TOOK US LESS THAN A *MONTH* TO TRACK DOWN YORICK, AND HE WAS HALFWAY ACROSS THE FUCKING COUNTRY!
SO WHAT, YOU WANT US TO START BEHAVING LIKE *SAVAGES*, HERO?
LIKE *YOU* USED TO?

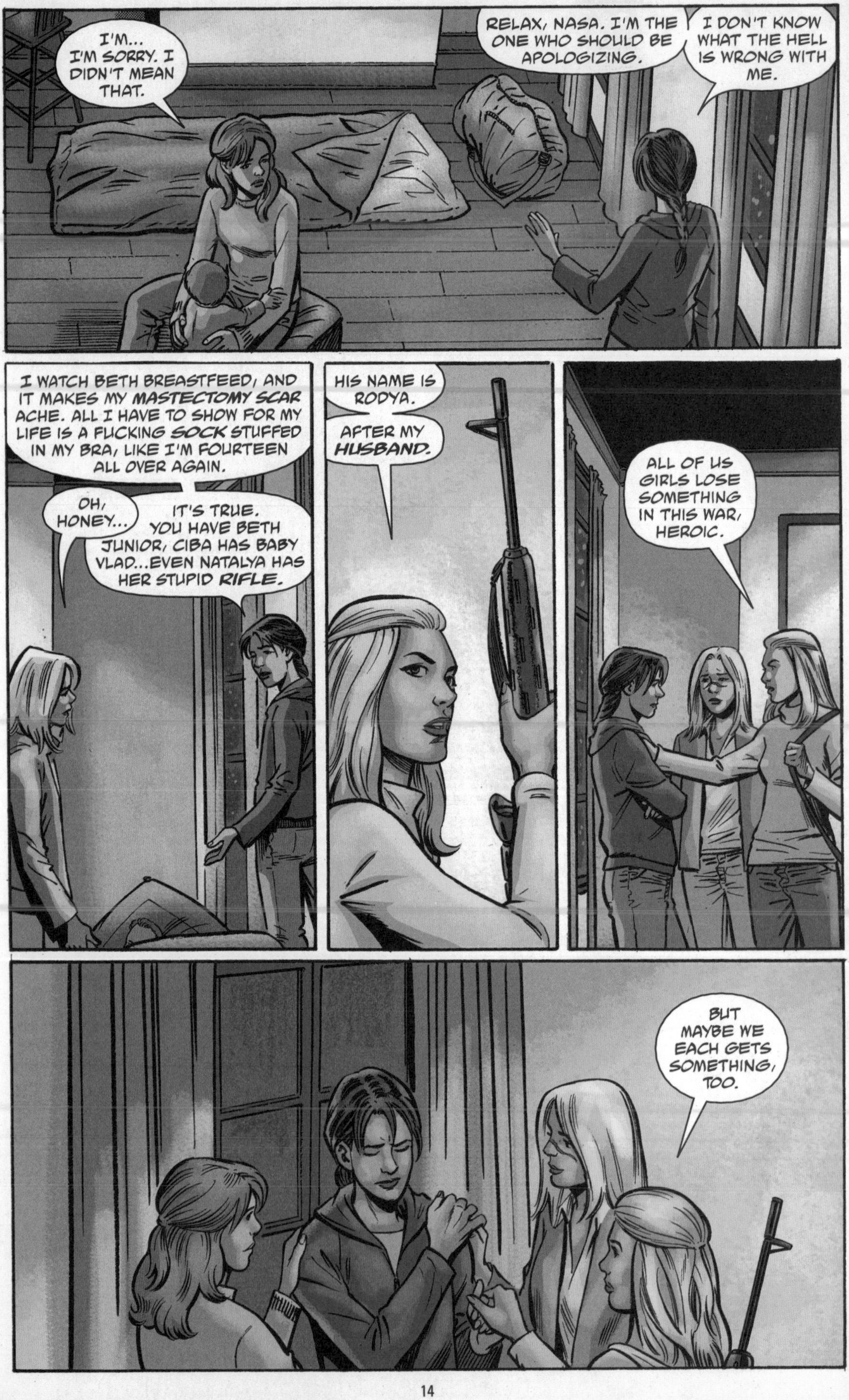

I'M... I'M SORRY. I DIDN'T MEAN THAT.
RELAX, NASA. I'M THE ONE WHO SHOULD BE APOLOGIZING.
I DON'T KNOW WHAT THE HELL IS WRONG WITH ME.
I WATCH BETH BREASTFEED, AND IT MAKES MY MASTECTOMY SCAR ACHE. ALL I HAVE TO SHOW FOR MY LIFE IS A FUCKING SOCK STUFFED IN MY BRA, LIKE I'M FOURTEEN ALL OVER AGAIN.
OH, HONEY...
IT'S TRUE. YOU HAVE BETH JUNIOR, CIBA HAS BABY VLAD...EVEN NATALYA HAS HER STUPID RIFLE.
HIS NAME IS RODYA.
AFTER MY HUSBAND.
ALL OF US GIRLS LOSE SOMETHING IN THIS WAR, HEROIC.
BUT MAYBE WE EACH GETS SOMETHING, TOO.

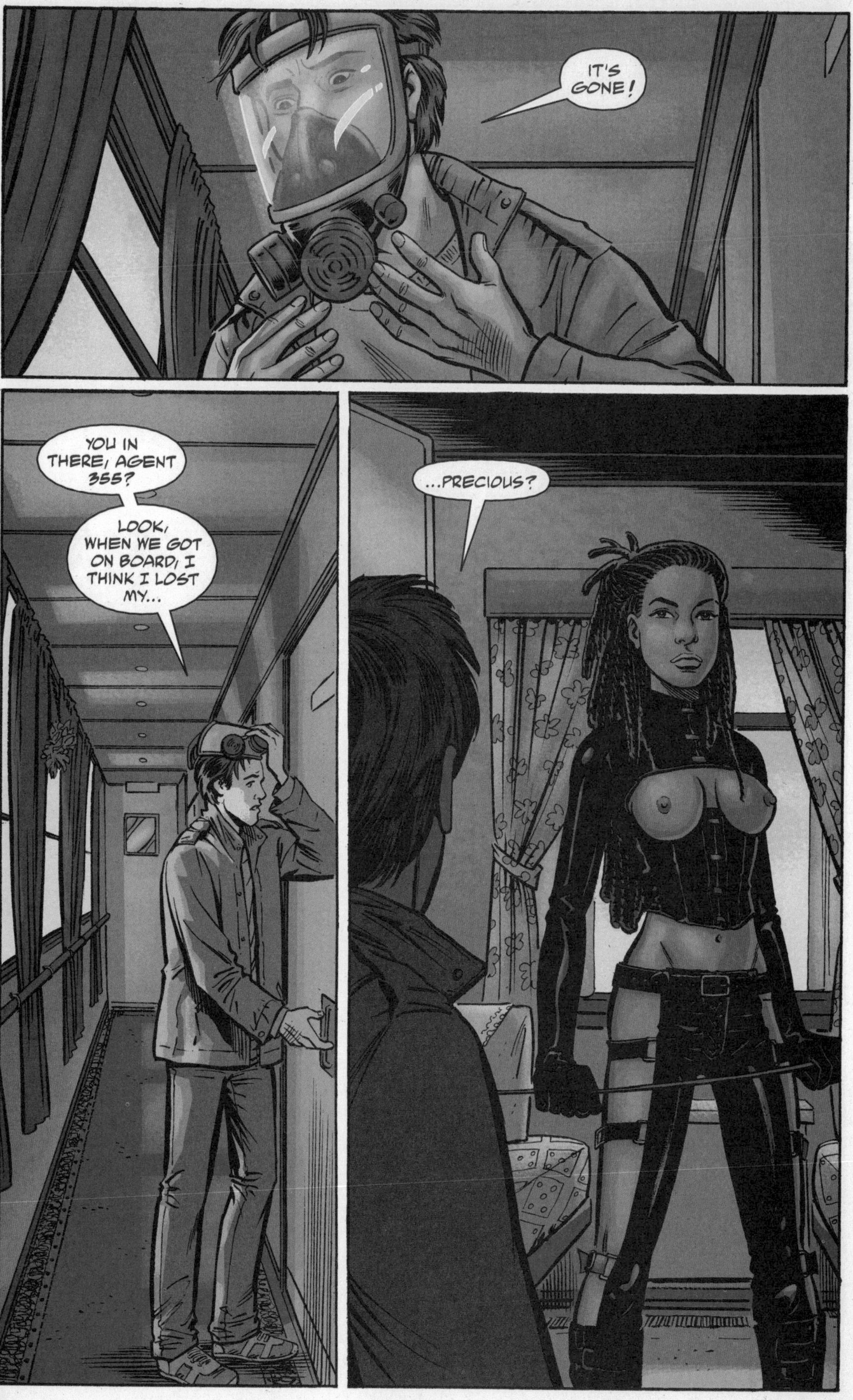

IT'S GONE!
YOU IN THERE, AGENT 355?
LOOK, WHEN WE GOT ON BOARD, I THINK I LOST MY...
...PRECIOUS?

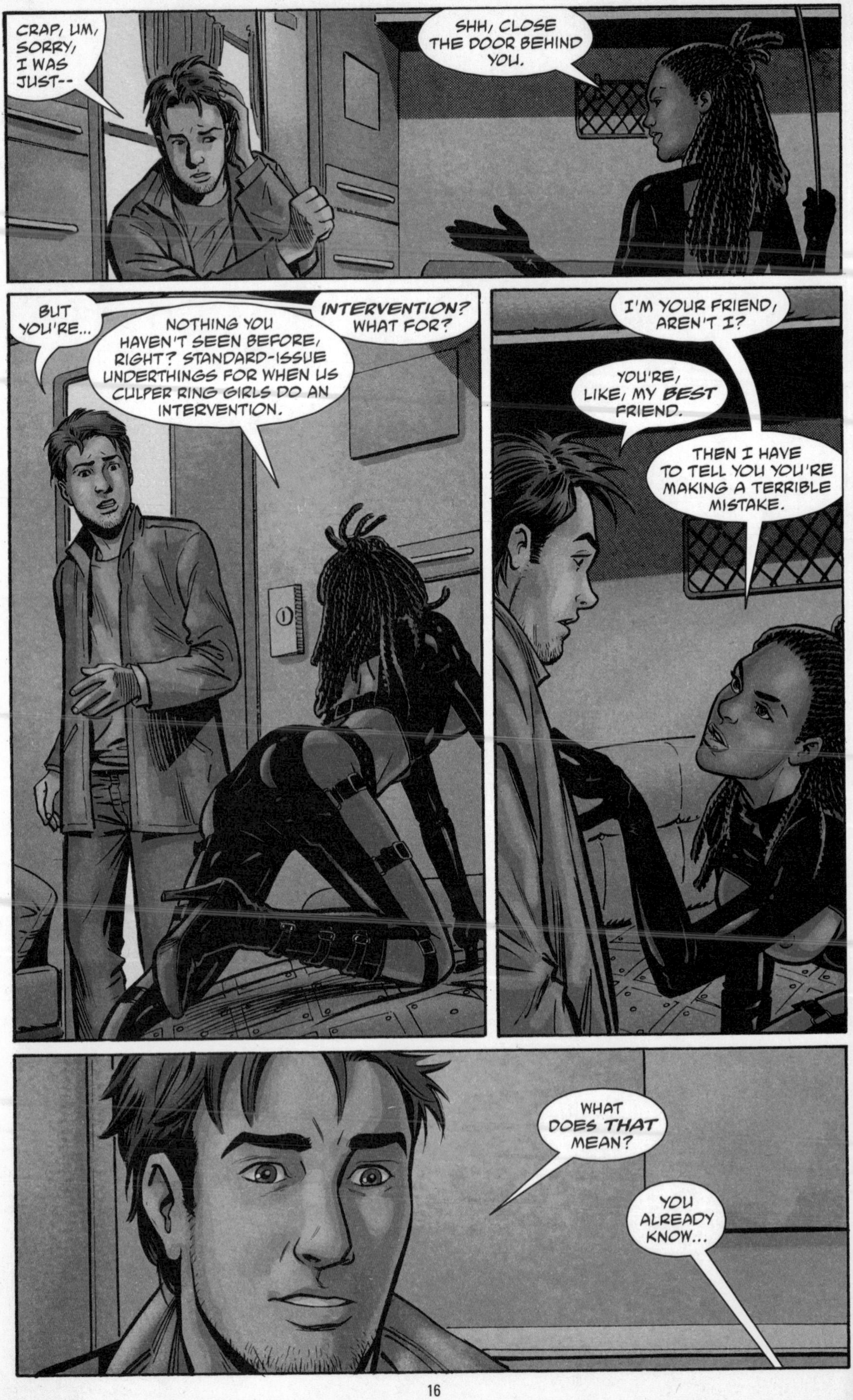
CRAP, UM, SORRY, I WAS JUST--
SHH, CLOSE THE DOOR BEHIND YOU.
BUT YOU'RE...
NOTHING YOU HAVEN'T SEEN BEFORE, RIGHT? STANDARD-ISSUE UNDERTHINGS FOR WHEN US CULPER RING GIRLS DO AN INTERVENTION.
INTERVENTION? WHAT FOR?
I'M YOUR FRIEND, AREN'T I?
YOU'RE, LIKE, MY **BEST** FRIEND.
THEN I HAVE TO TELL YOU YOU'RE MAKING A TERRIBLE MISTAKE.
WHAT **DOES *THAT*** MEAN?
YOU ALREADY KNOW...

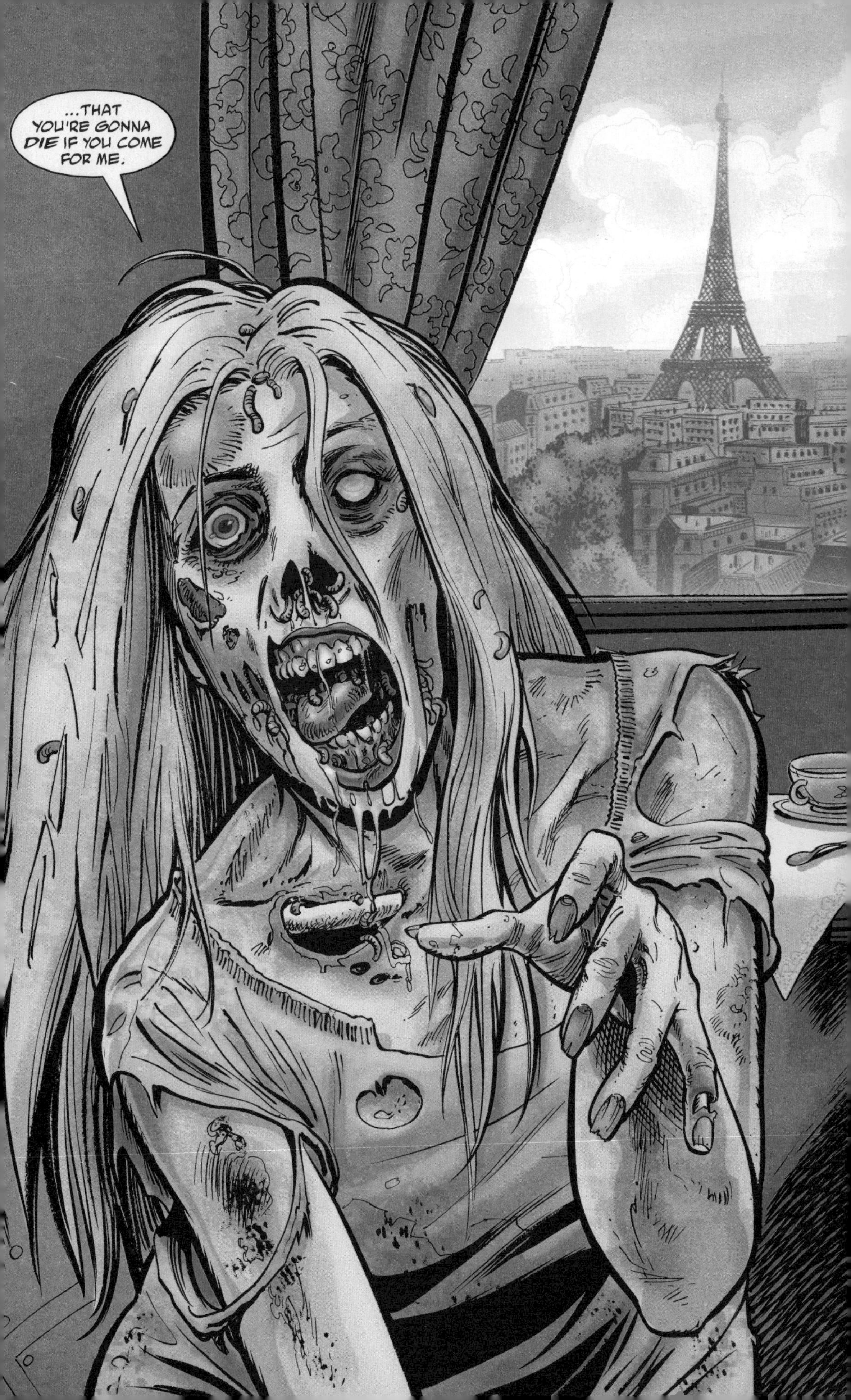
...THAT YOU'RE GONNA DIE IF YOU COME FOR ME.

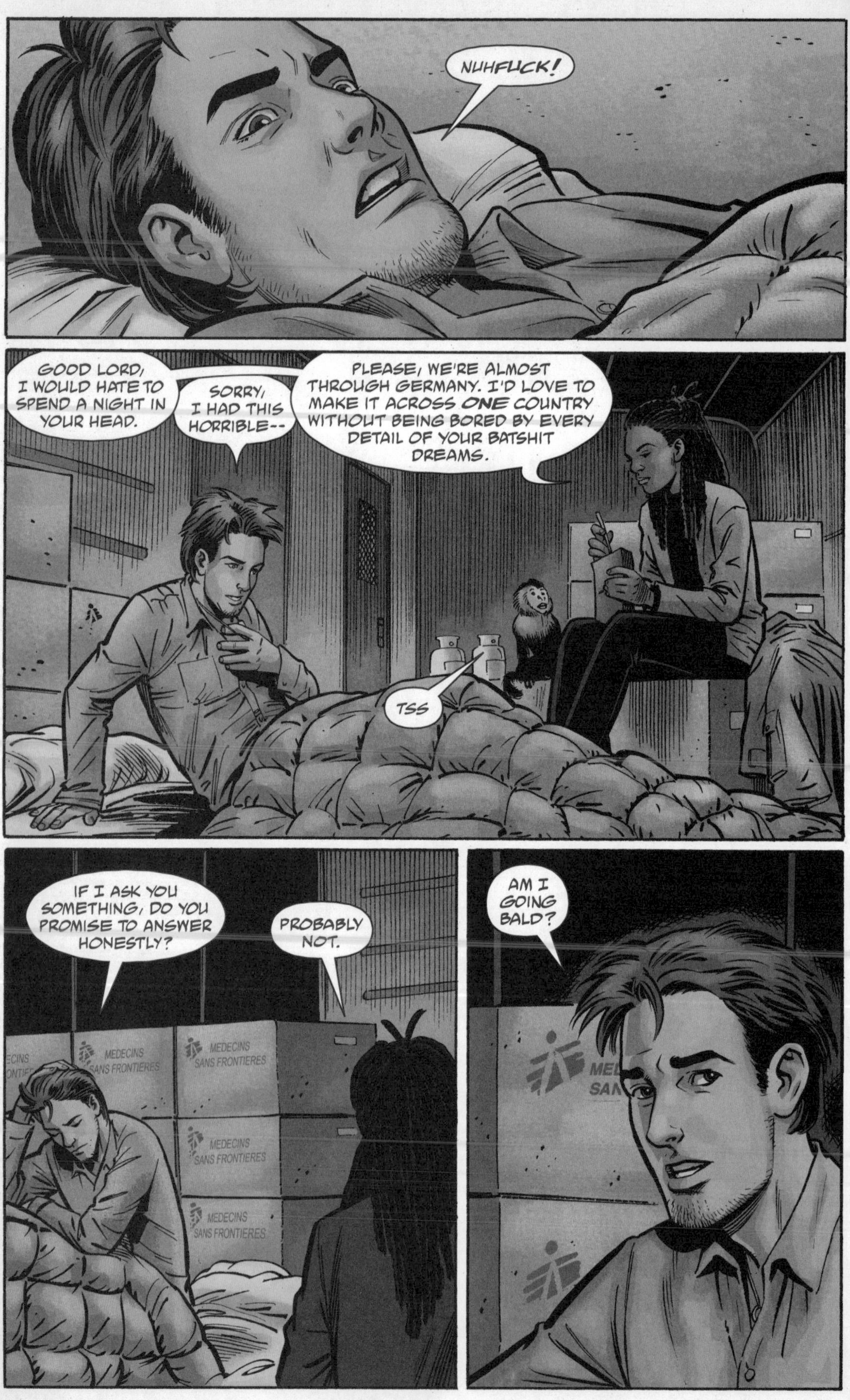
NUHFUCK!
GOOD LORD, I WOULD HATE TO SPEND A NIGHT IN YOUR HEAD.
SORRY, I HAD THIS HORRIBLE--
PLEASE, WE'RE ALMOST THROUGH GERMANY. I'D LOVE TO MAKE IT ACROSS ONE COUNTRY WITHOUT BEING BORED BY EVERY DETAIL OF YOUR BATSHIT DREAMS.
TSS
IF I ASK YOU SOMETHING, DO YOU PROMISE TO ANSWER HONESTLY?
PROBABLY NOT.
MEDECINS SANS FRONTIERES
MEDECINS SANS FRONTIERES
MEDECINS SANS FRONTIERES
MEDECINS SANS FRONTIERES
AM I GOING BALD?

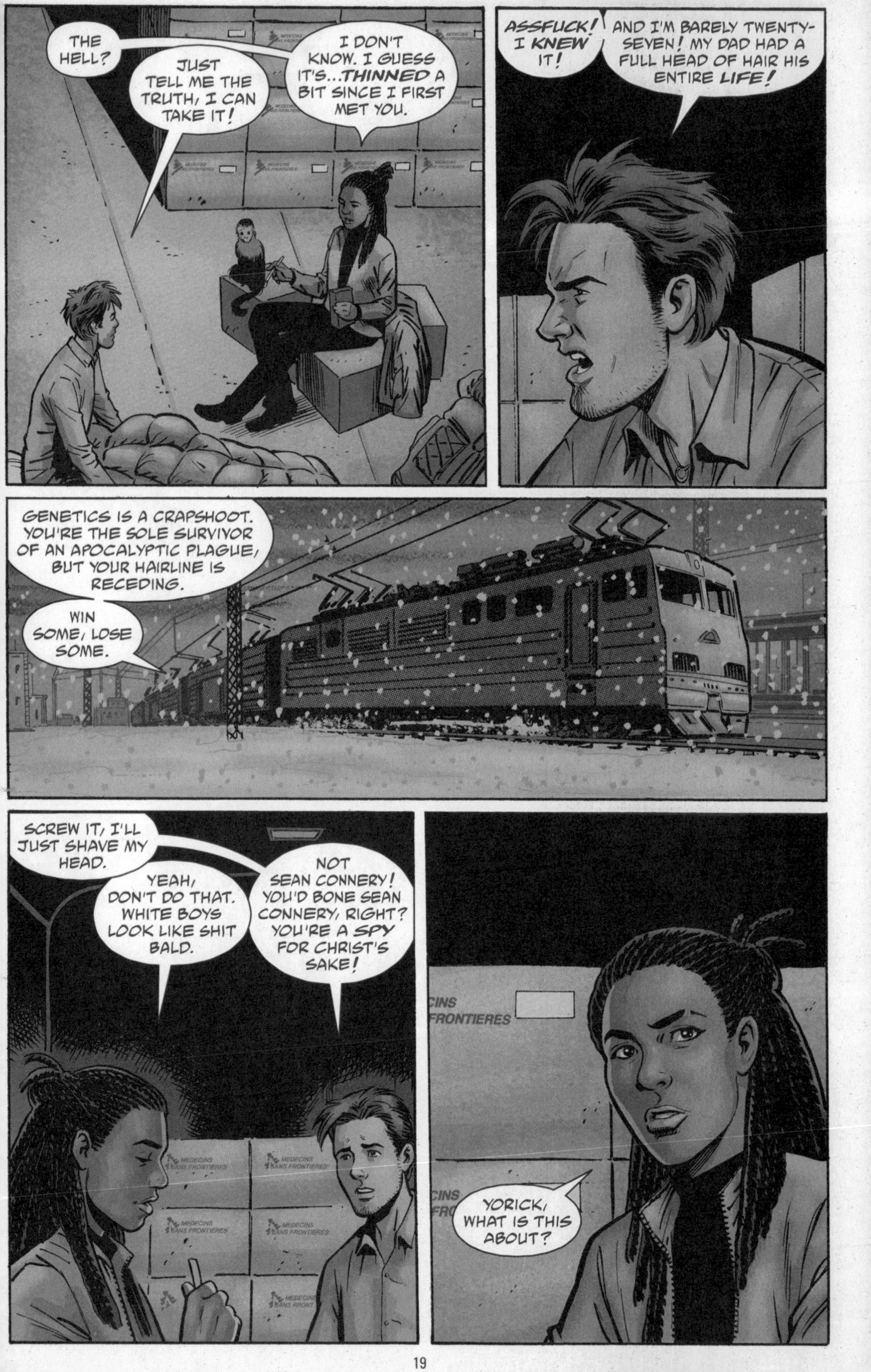
THE HELL?
JUST TELL ME THE TRUTH, I CAN TAKE IT!
I DON'T KNOW. I GUESS IT'S...THINNED A BIT SINCE I FIRST MET YOU.
ASSFUCK! I KNEW IT!
AND I'M BARELY TWENTY-SEVEN! MY DAD HAD A FULL HEAD OF HAIR HIS ENTIRE LIFE!
GENETICS IS A CRAPSHOOT. YOU'RE THE SOLE SURVIVOR OF AN APOCALYPTIC PLAGUE, BUT YOUR HAIRLINE IS RECEDING.
WIN SOME, LOSE SOME.
SCREW IT, I'LL JUST SHAVE MY HEAD.
YEAH, DON'T DO THAT. WHITE BOYS LOOK LIKE SHIT BALD.
NOT SEAN CONNERY! YOU'D BONE SEAN CONNERY, RIGHT? YOU'RE A SPY FOR CHRIST'S SAKE!
MEDECINS SANS FRONTIERES
YORICK, WHAT IS THIS ABOUT?

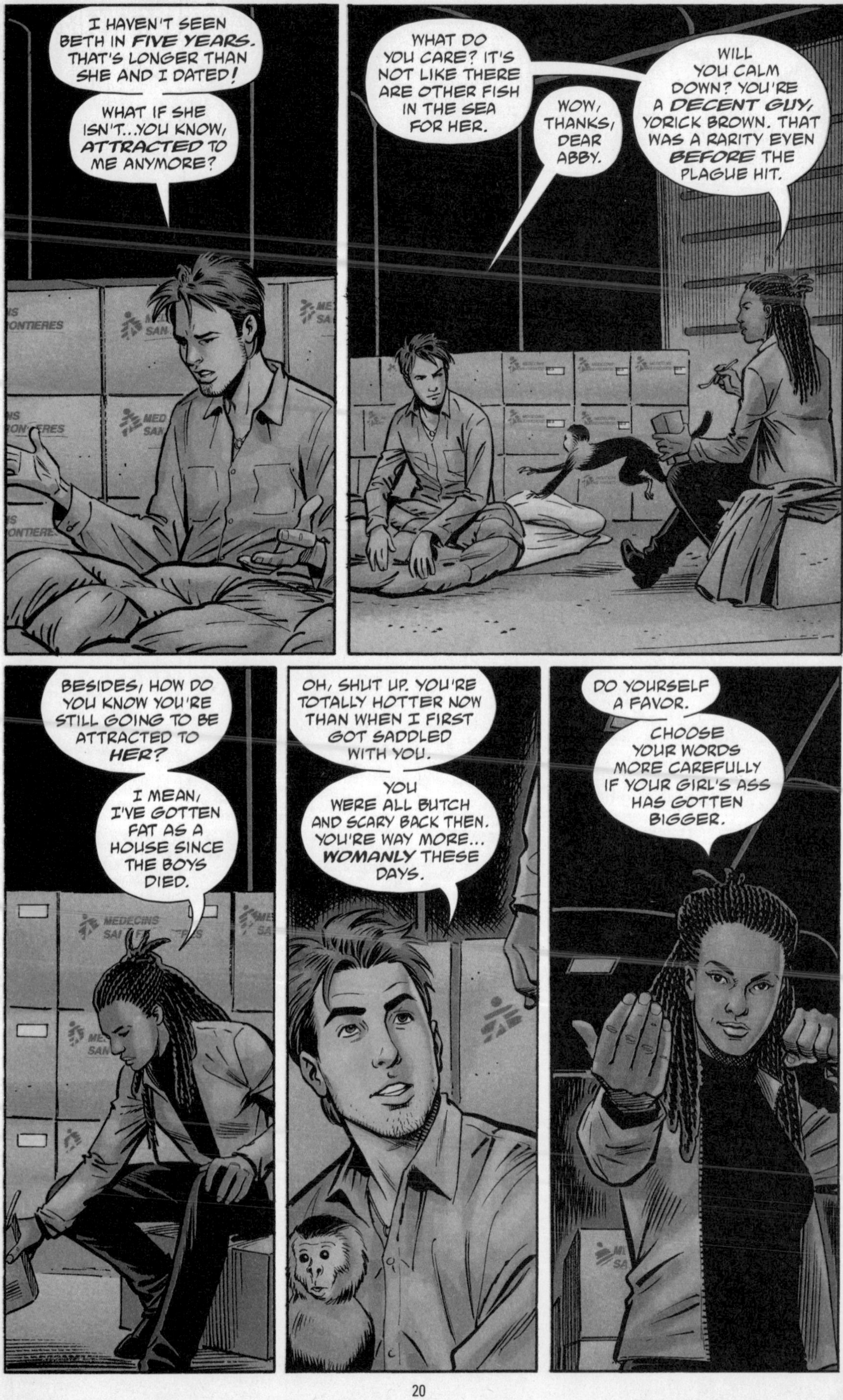
I HAVEN'T SEEN BETH IN FIVE YEARS. THAT'S LONGER THAN SHE AND I DATED!
WHAT IF SHE ISN'T...YOU KNOW, ATTRACTED TO ME ANYMORE?
WHAT DO YOU CARE? IT'S NOT LIKE THERE ARE OTHER FISH IN THE SEA FOR HER.
WOW, THANKS, DEAR ABBY.
WILL YOU CALM DOWN? YOU'RE A DECENT GUY, YORICK BROWN. THAT WAS A RARITY EVEN BEFORE THE PLAGUE HIT.
BESIDES, HOW DO YOU KNOW YOU'RE STILL GOING TO BE ATTRACTED TO HER?
I MEAN, I'VE GOTTEN FAT AS A HOUSE SINCE THE BOYS DIED.
OH, SHUT UP. YOU'RE TOTALLY HOTTER NOW THAN WHEN I FIRST GOT SADDLED WITH YOU.
YOU WERE ALL BUTCH AND SCARY BACK THEN. YOU'RE WAY MORE... WOMANLY THESE DAYS.
DO YOURSELF A FAVOR.
CHOOSE YOUR WORDS MORE CAREFULLY IF YOUR GIRL'S ASS HAS GOTTEN BIGGER.

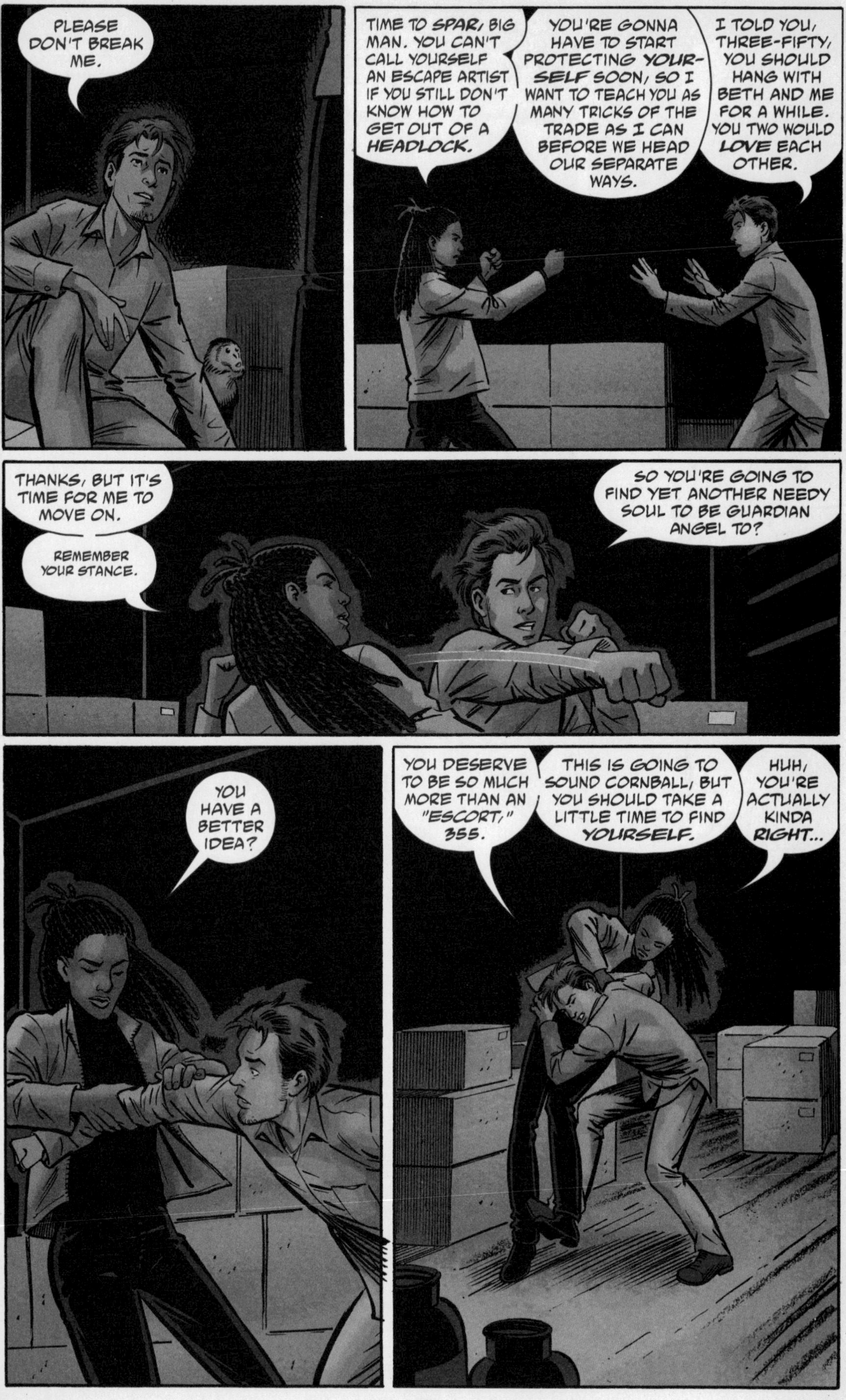
PLEASE DON'T BREAK ME.
TIME TO SPAR, BIG MAN. YOU CAN'T CALL YOURSELF AN ESCAPE ARTIST IF YOU STILL DON'T KNOW HOW TO GET OUT OF A HEADLOCK.
YOU'RE GONNA HAVE TO START PROTECTING YOURSELF SOON, SO I WANT TO TEACH YOU AS MANY TRICKS OF THE TRADE AS I CAN BEFORE WE HEAD OUR SEPARATE WAYS.
I TOLD YOU, THREE-FIFTY, YOU SHOULD HANG WITH BETH AND ME FOR A WHILE. YOU TWO WOULD LOVE EACH OTHER.
THANKS, BUT IT'S TIME FOR ME TO MOVE ON.
REMEMBER YOUR STANCE.
SO YOU'RE GOING TO FIND YET ANOTHER NEEDY SOUL TO BE GUARDIAN ANGEL TO?
YOU HAVE A BETTER IDEA?
YOU DESERVE TO BE SO MUCH MORE THAN AN "ESCORT," 355.
THIS IS GOING TO SOUND CORNBALL, BUT YOU SHOULD TAKE A LITTLE TIME TO FIND YOURSELF.
HUH, YOU'RE ACTUALLY KINDA RIGHT...

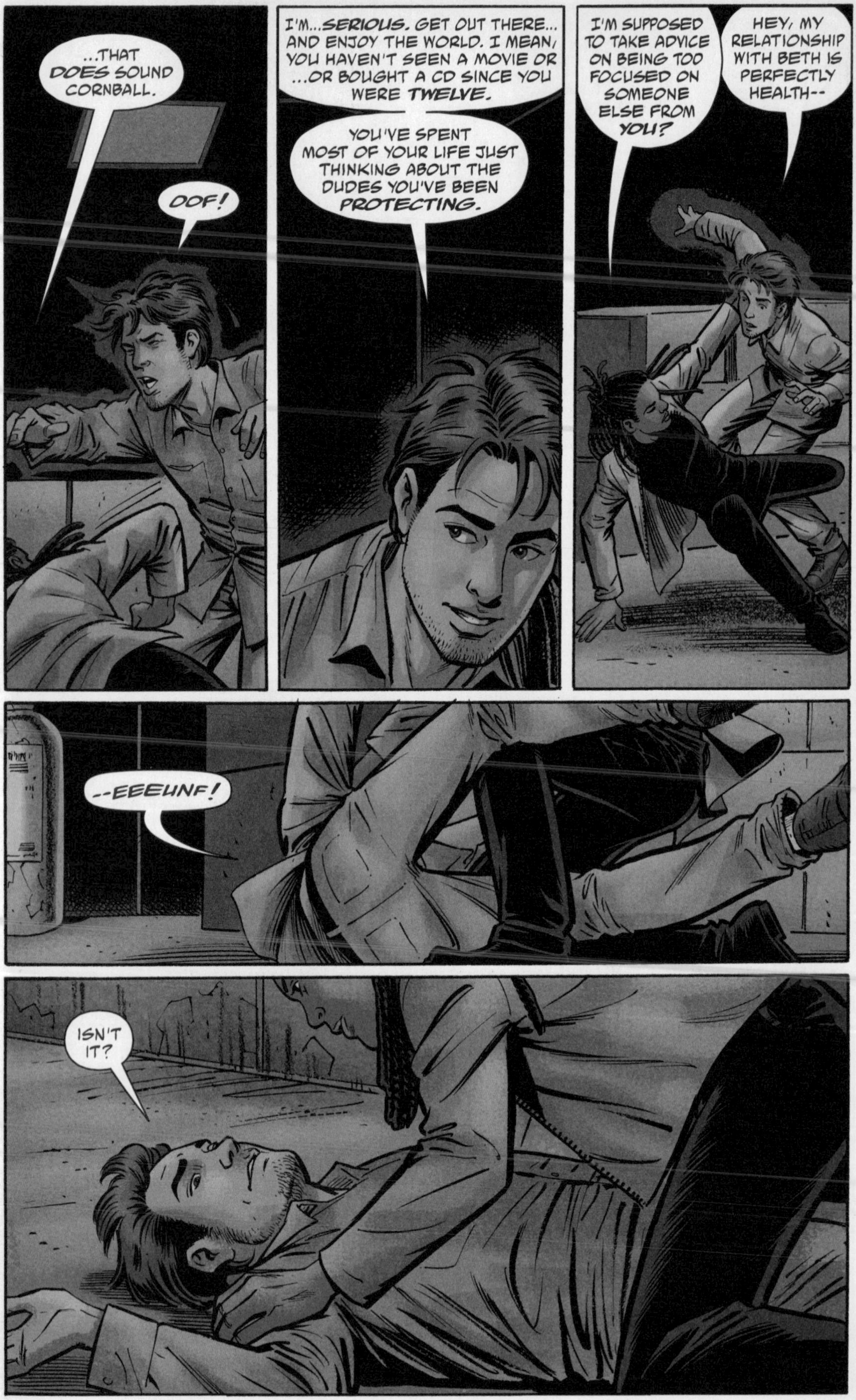
...THAT DOES SOUND CORNBALL.
OOF!
I'M...SERIOUS. GET OUT THERE... AND ENJOY THE WORLD. I MEAN, YOU HAVEN'T SEEN A MOVIE OR ...OR BOUGHT A CD SINCE YOU WERE TWELVE.
YOU'VE SPENT MOST OF YOUR LIFE JUST THINKING ABOUT THE DUDES YOU'VE BEEN PROTECTING.
I'M SUPPOSED TO TAKE ADVICE ON BEING TOO FOCUSED ON SOMEONE ELSE FROM YOU?
HEY, MY RELATIONSHIP WITH BETH IS PERFECTLY HEALTH--
--EEEUNF!
ISN'T IT?

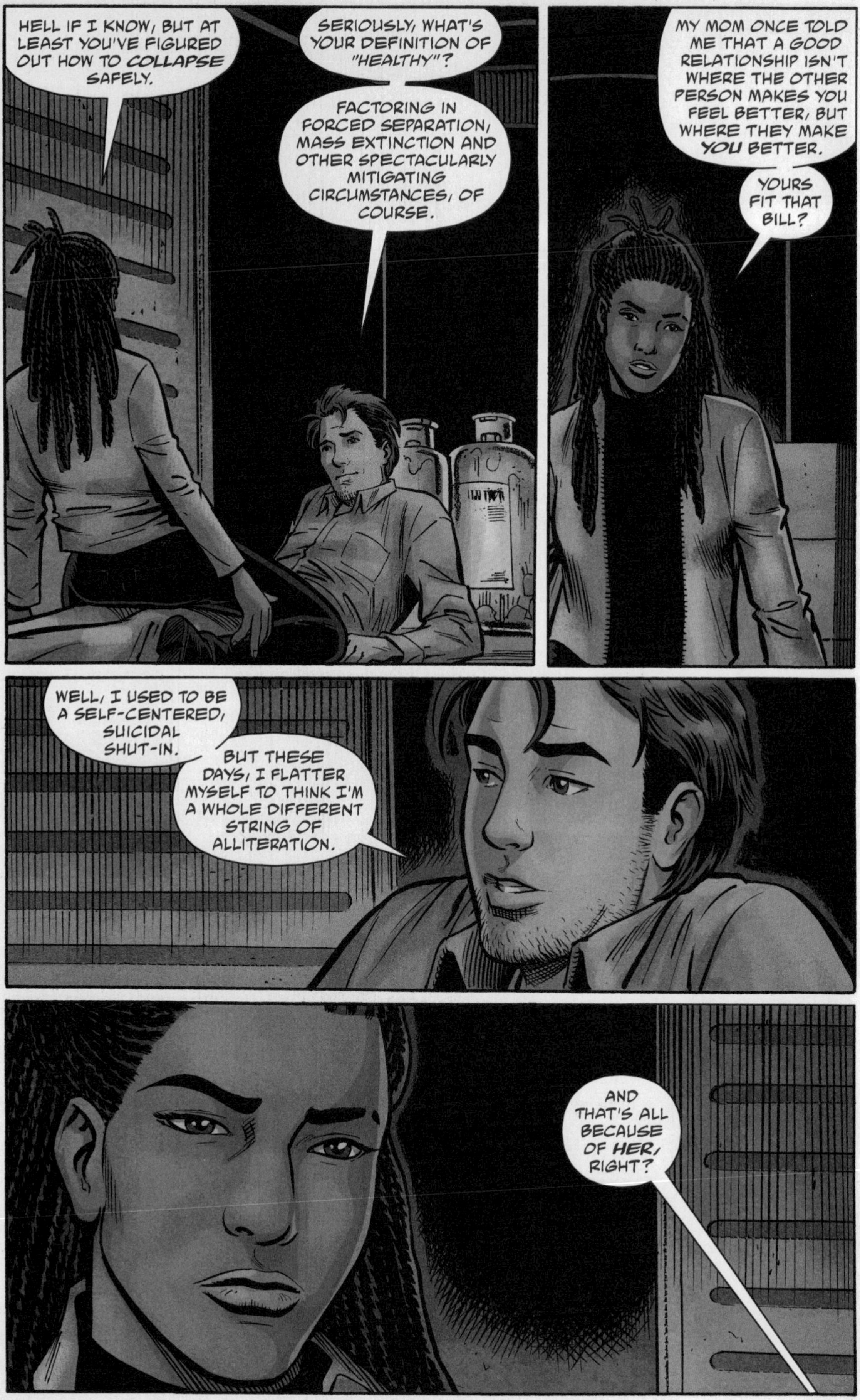
HELL IF I KNOW, BUT AT LEAST YOU'VE FIGURED OUT HOW TO COLLAPSE SAFELY.
SERIOUSLY, WHAT'S YOUR DEFINITION OF "HEALTHY"?
FACTORING IN FORCED SEPARATION, MASS EXTINCTION AND OTHER SPECTACULARLY MITIGATING CIRCUMSTANCES, OF COURSE.
MY MOM ONCE TOLD ME THAT A GOOD RELATIONSHIP ISN'T WHERE THE OTHER PERSON MAKES YOU FEEL BETTER, BUT WHERE THEY MAKE YOU BETTER.
YOURS FIT THAT BILL?
WELL, I USED TO BE A SELF-CENTERED, SUICIDAL SHUT-IN.
BUT THESE DAYS, I FLATTER MYSELF TO THINK I'M A WHOLE DIFFERENT STRING OF ALLITERATION.
AND THAT'S ALL BECAUSE OF HER, RIGHT?

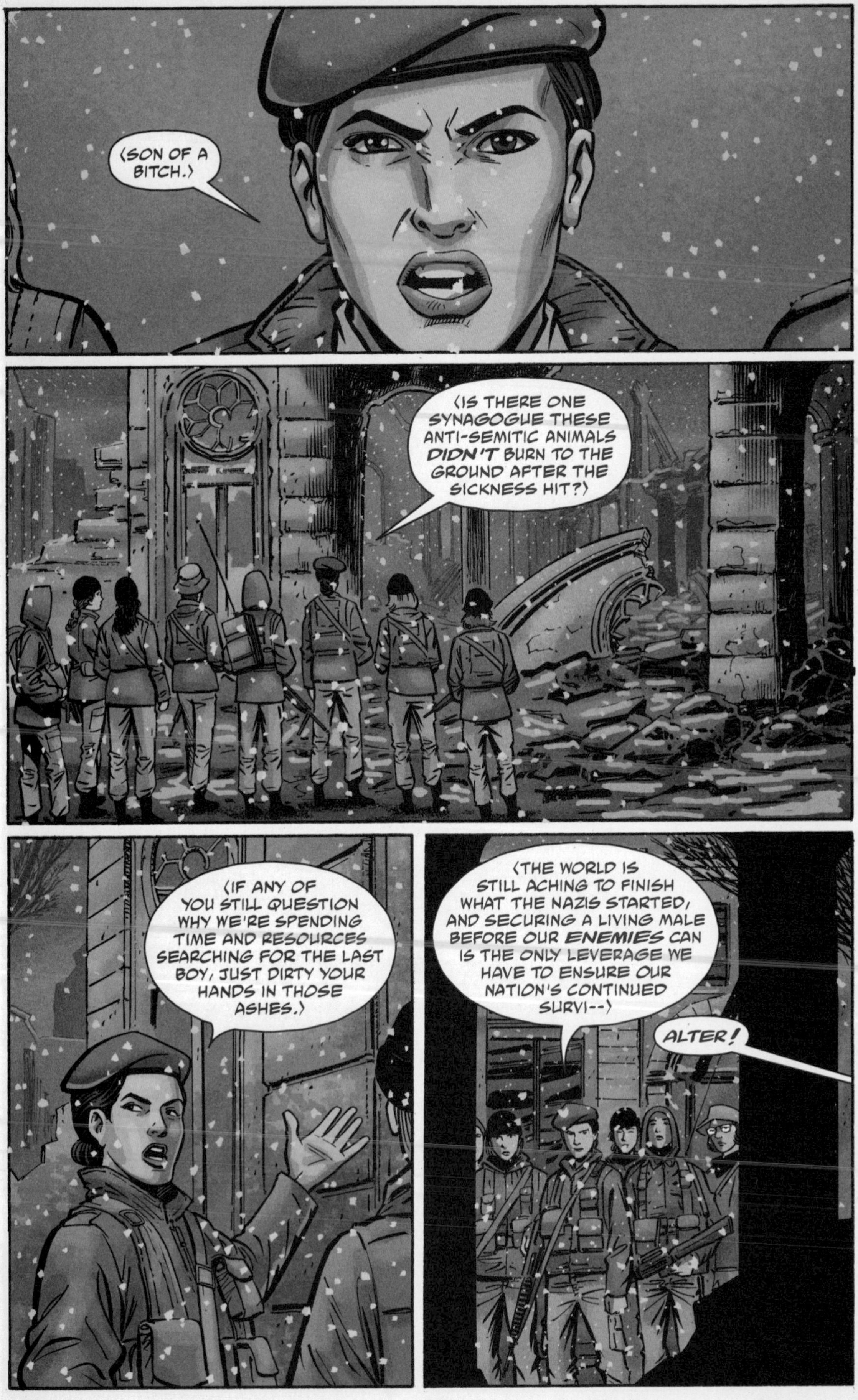

⟨SON OF A BITCH.⟩
⟨IS THERE ONE SYNAGOGUE THESE ANTI-SEMITIC ANIMALS DIDN'T BURN TO THE GROUND AFTER THE SICKNESS HIT?⟩
⟨IF ANY OF YOU STILL QUESTION WHY WE'RE SPENDING TIME AND RESOURCES SEARCHING FOR THE LAST BOY, JUST DIRTY YOUR HANDS IN THOSE ASHES.⟩
⟨THE WORLD IS STILL ACHING TO FINISH WHAT THE NAZIS STARTED, AND SECURING A LIVING MALE BEFORE OUR ENEMIES CAN IS THE ONLY LEVERAGE WE HAVE TO ENSURE OUR NATION'S CONTINUED SURVI--⟩
ALTER!

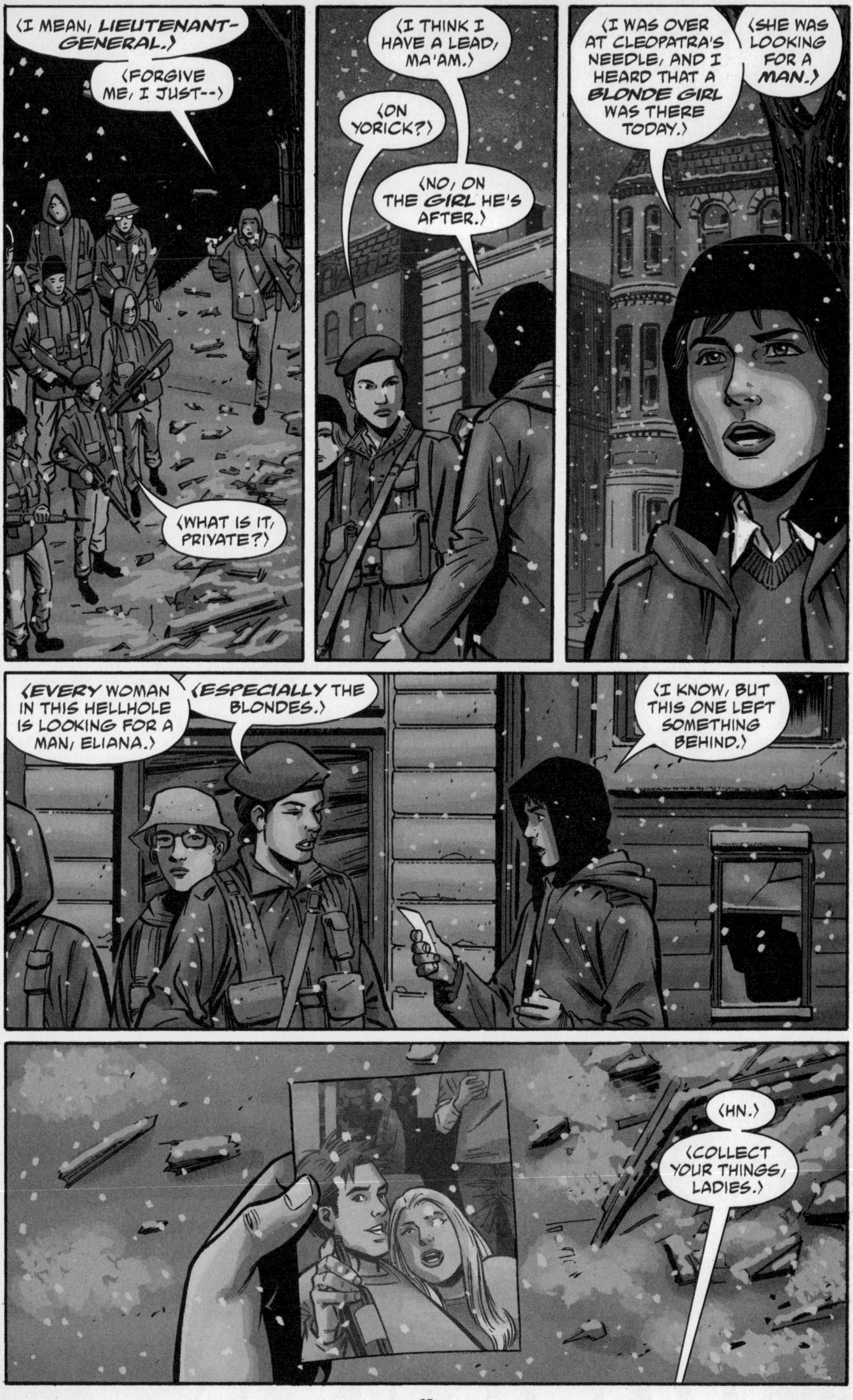

⟨I MEAN, LIEUTENANT-GENERAL.⟩
⟨FORGIVE ME, I JUST--⟩
⟨WHAT IS IT, PRIVATE?⟩
⟨I THINK I HAVE A LEAD, MA'AM.⟩
⟨ON YORICK?⟩
⟨NO, ON THE GIRL HE'S AFTER.⟩
⟨I WAS OVER AT CLEOPATRA'S NEEDLE, AND I HEARD THAT A BLONDE GIRL WAS THERE TODAY.⟩
⟨SHE WAS LOOKING FOR A MAN.⟩
⟨EVERY WOMAN IN THIS HELLHOLE IS LOOKING FOR A MAN, ELIANA.⟩
⟨ESPECIALLY THE BLONDES.⟩
⟨I KNOW, BUT THIS ONE LEFT SOMETHING BEHIND.⟩
⟨HN.⟩
⟨COLLECT YOUR THINGS, LADIES.⟩

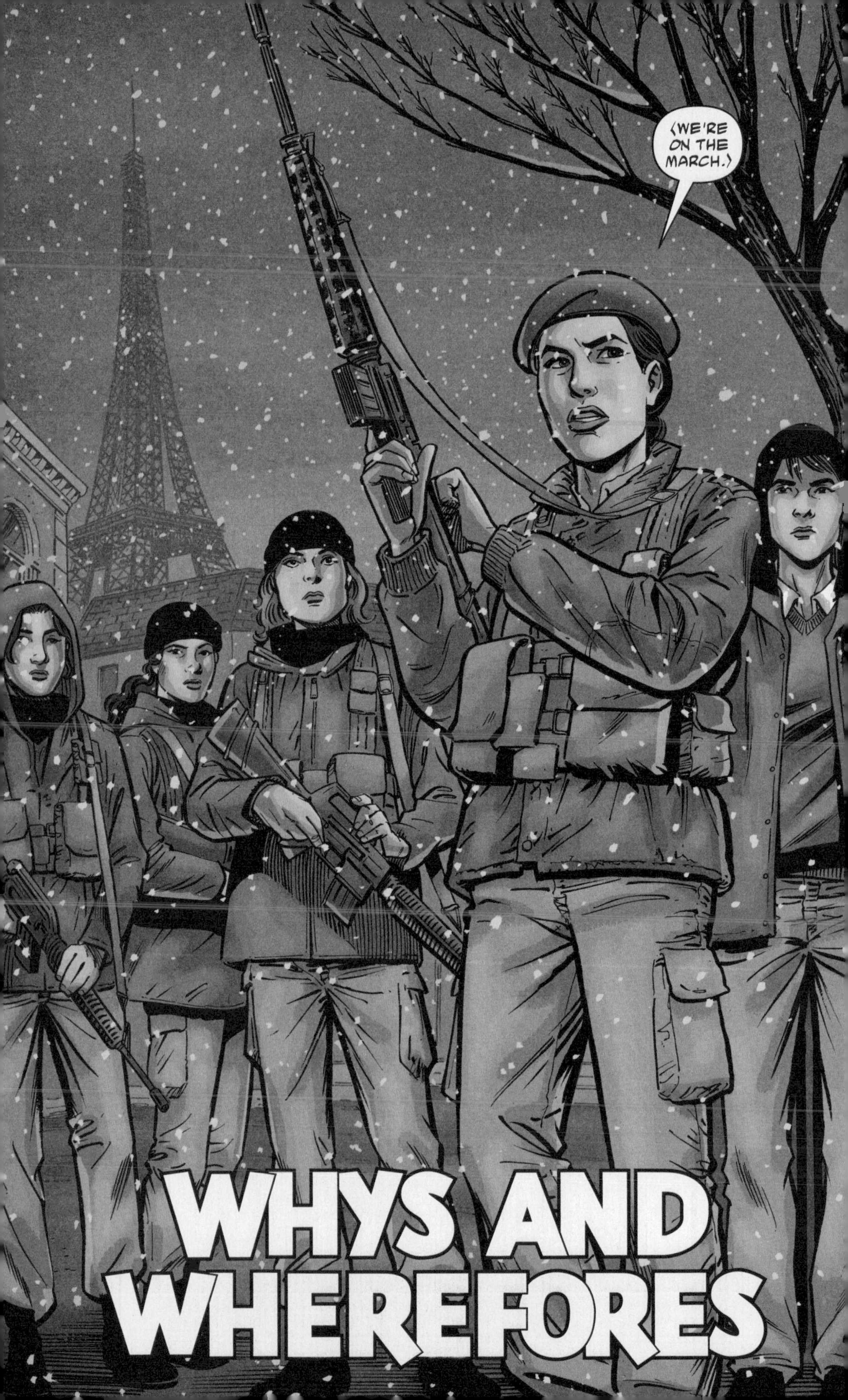
⟨WE'RE ON THE MARCH.⟩
WHYS AND WHEREFORES

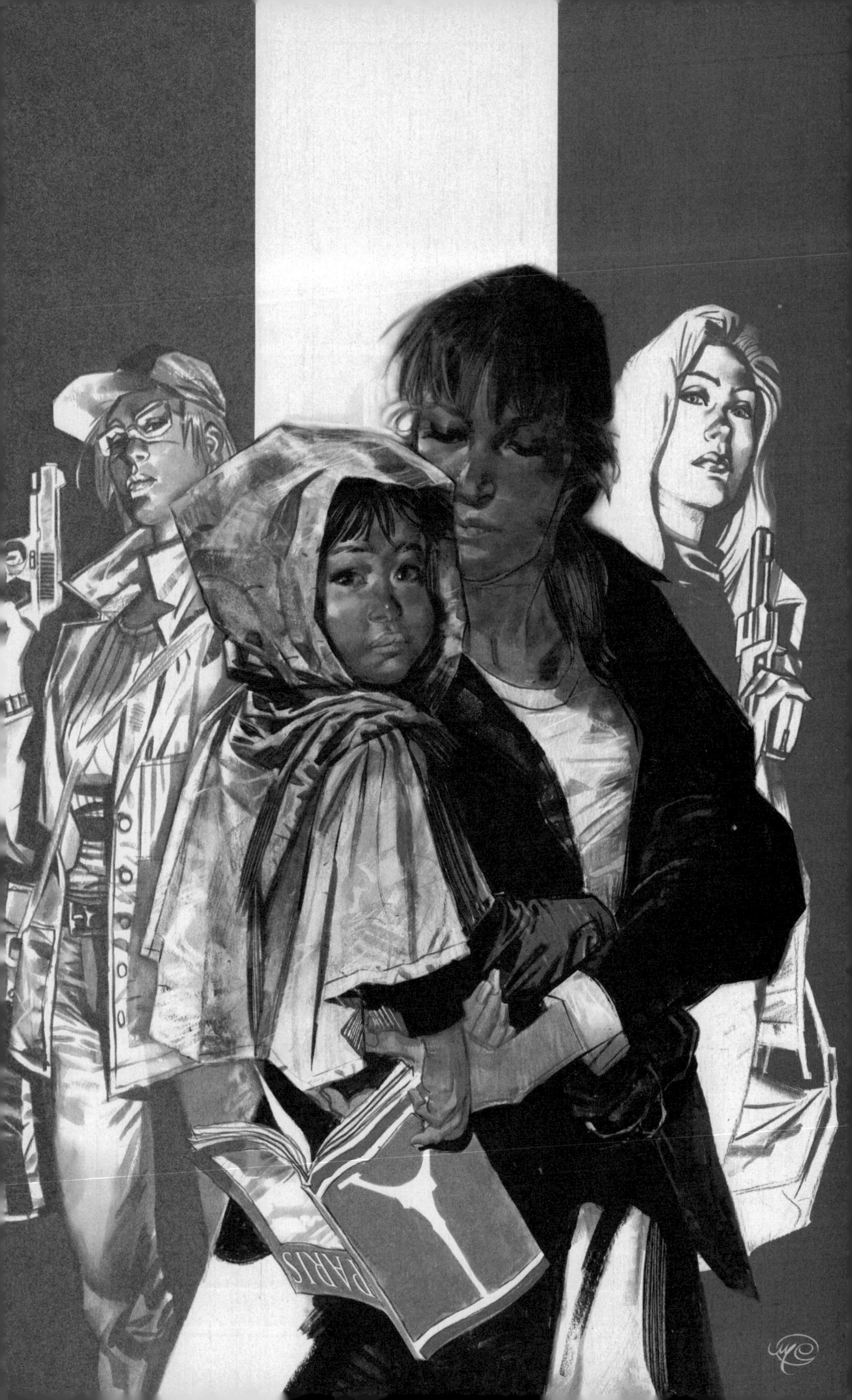
PARIS

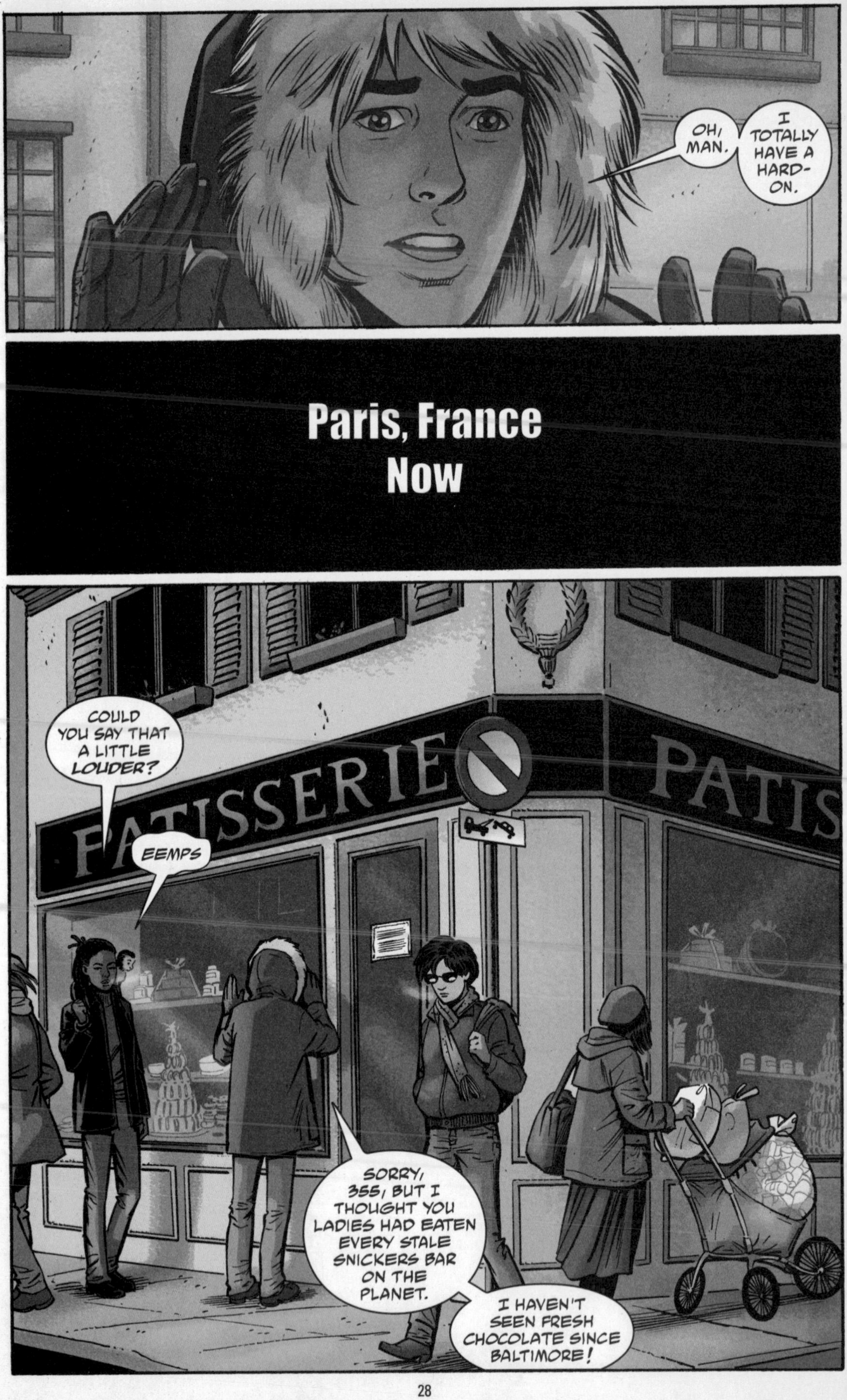
OH, MAN.
I TOTALLY HAVE A HARD-ON.
Paris, France
Now
COULD YOU SAY THAT A LITTLE LOUDER?
EEMPS
PATISSERIE
PATIS
SORRY, 355, BUT I THOUGHT YOU LADIES HAD EATEN EVERY STALE SNICKERS BAR ON THE PLANET.
I HAVEN'T SEEN FRESH CHOCOLATE SINCE BALTIMORE!

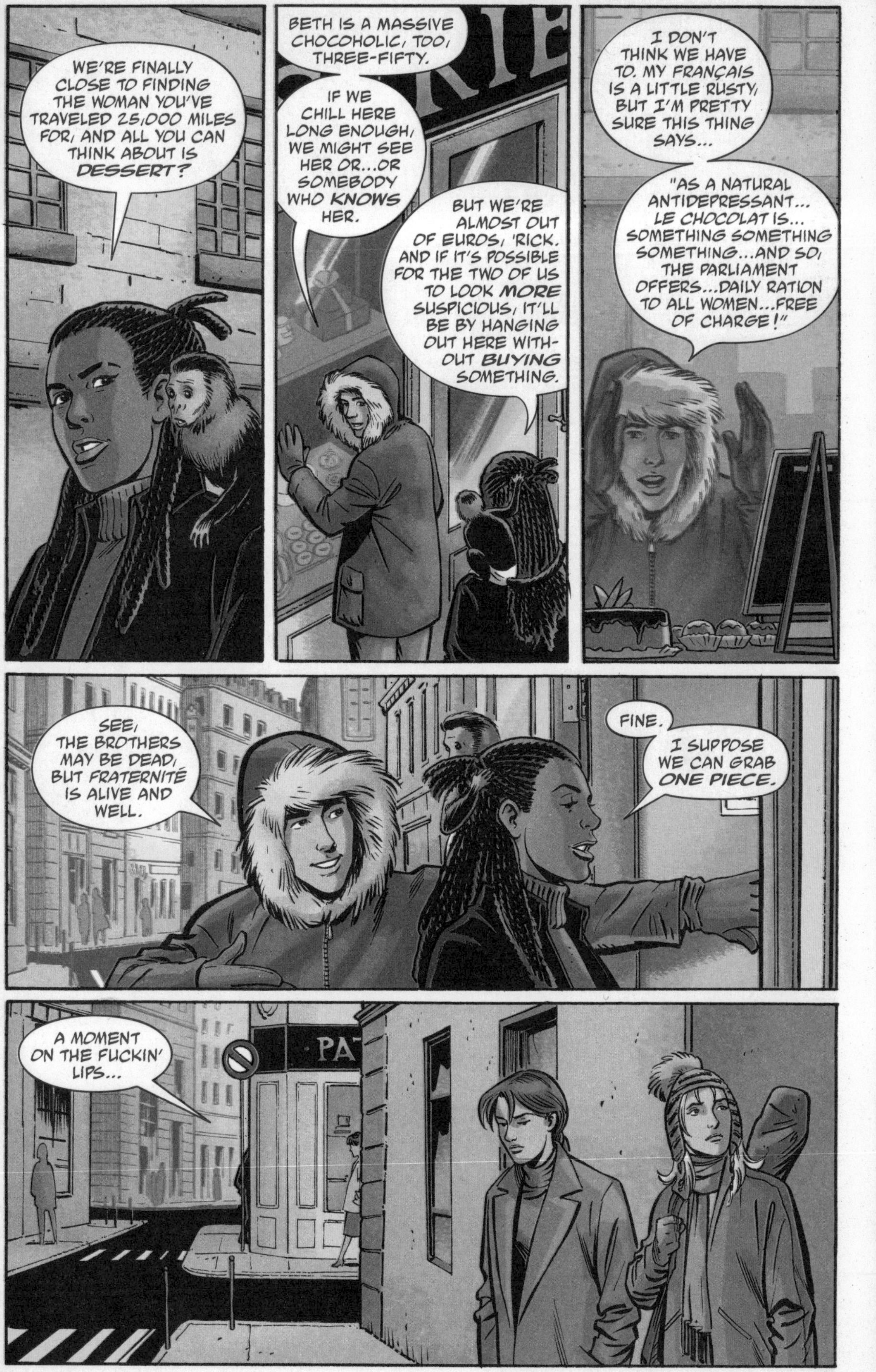
WE'RE FINALLY CLOSE TO FINDING THE WOMAN YOU'VE TRAVELED 25,000 MILES FOR, AND ALL YOU CAN THINK ABOUT IS DESSERT?
BETH IS A MASSIVE CHOCOHOLIC, TOO, THREE-FIFTY.
IF WE CHILL HERE LONG ENOUGH, WE MIGHT SEE HER OR...OR SOMEBODY WHO KNOWS HER.
BUT WE'RE ALMOST OUT OF EUROS, 'RICK. AND IF IT'S POSSIBLE FOR THE TWO OF US TO LOOK MORE SUSPICIOUS, IT'LL BE BY HANGING OUT HERE WITHOUT BUYING SOMETHING.
I DON'T THINK WE HAVE TO. MY FRANÇAIS IS A LITTLE RUSTY, BUT I'M PRETTY SURE THIS THING SAYS...
"AS A NATURAL ANTIDEPRESSANT... LE CHOCOLAT IS... SOMETHING SOMETHING SOMETHING...AND SO, THE PARLIAMENT OFFERS...DAILY RATION TO ALL WOMEN...FREE OF CHARGE!"
SEE, THE BROTHERS MAY BE DEAD, BUT FRATERNITÉ IS ALIVE AND WELL.
FINE.
I SUPPOSE WE CAN GRAB ONE PIECE.
A MOMENT ON THE FUCKIN' LIPS...
PAT

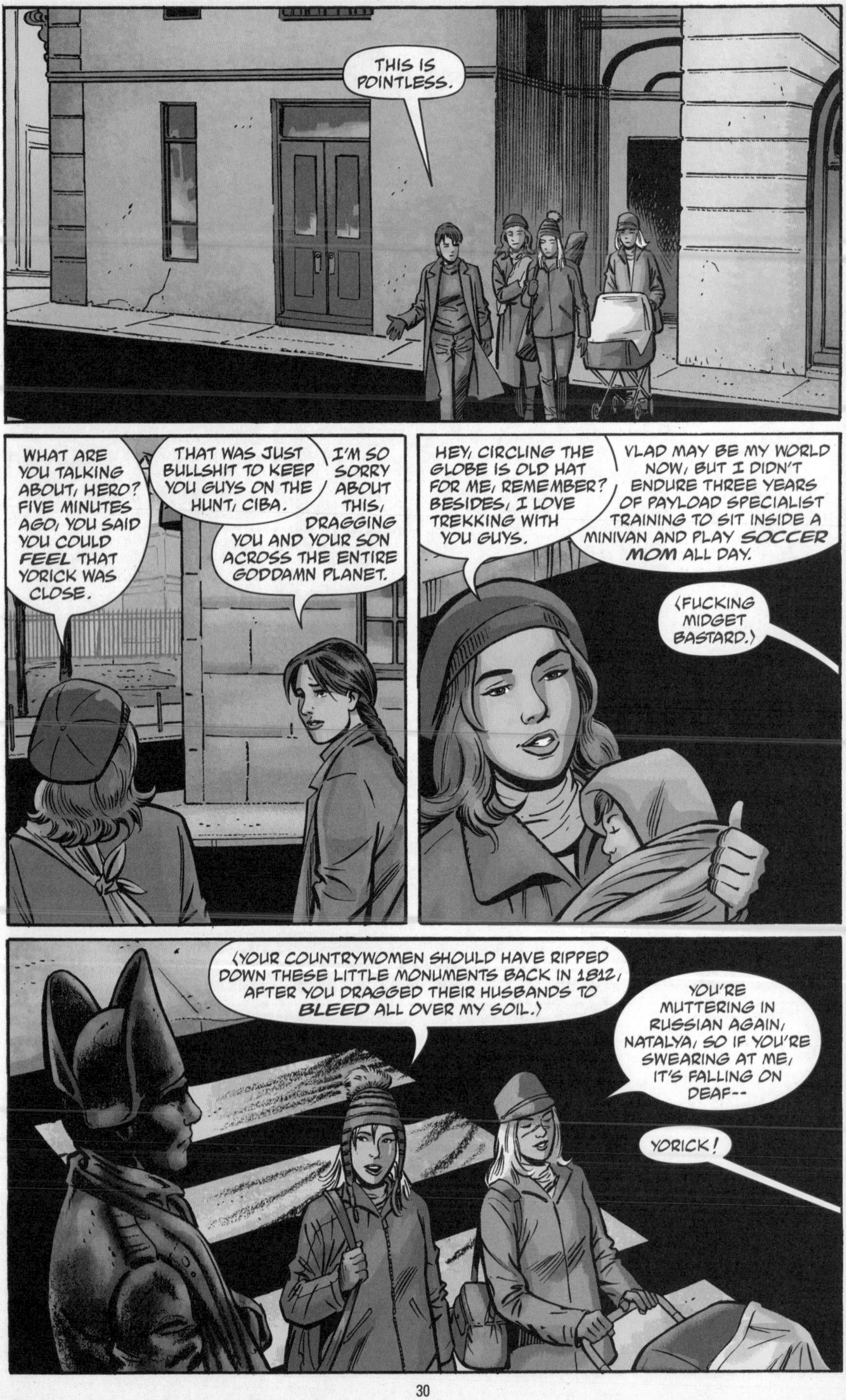
THIS IS POINTLESS.
WHAT ARE YOU TALKING ABOUT, HERO? FIVE MINUTES AGO, YOU SAID YOU COULD FEEL THAT YORICK WAS CLOSE.
THAT WAS JUST BULLSHIT TO KEEP YOU GUYS ON THE HUNT, CIBA.
I'M SO SORRY ABOUT THIS, DRAGGING YOU AND YOUR SON ACROSS THE ENTIRE GODDAMN PLANET.
HEY, CIRCLING THE GLOBE IS OLD HAT FOR ME, REMEMBER? BESIDES, I LOVE TREKKING WITH YOU GUYS.
VLAD MAY BE MY WORLD NOW, BUT I DIDN'T ENDURE THREE YEARS OF PAYLOAD SPECIALIST TRAINING TO SIT INSIDE A MINIVAN AND PLAY SOCCER MOM ALL DAY.
‹FUCKING MIDGET BASTARD.›
‹YOUR COUNTRYWOMEN SHOULD HAVE RIPPED DOWN THESE LITTLE MONUMENTS BACK IN 1812, AFTER YOU DRAGGED THEIR HUSBANDS TO BLEED ALL OVER MY SOIL.›
YOU'RE MUTTERING IN RUSSIAN AGAIN, NATALYA, SO IF YOU'RE SWEARING AT ME, IT'S FALLING ON DEAF--
YORICK!

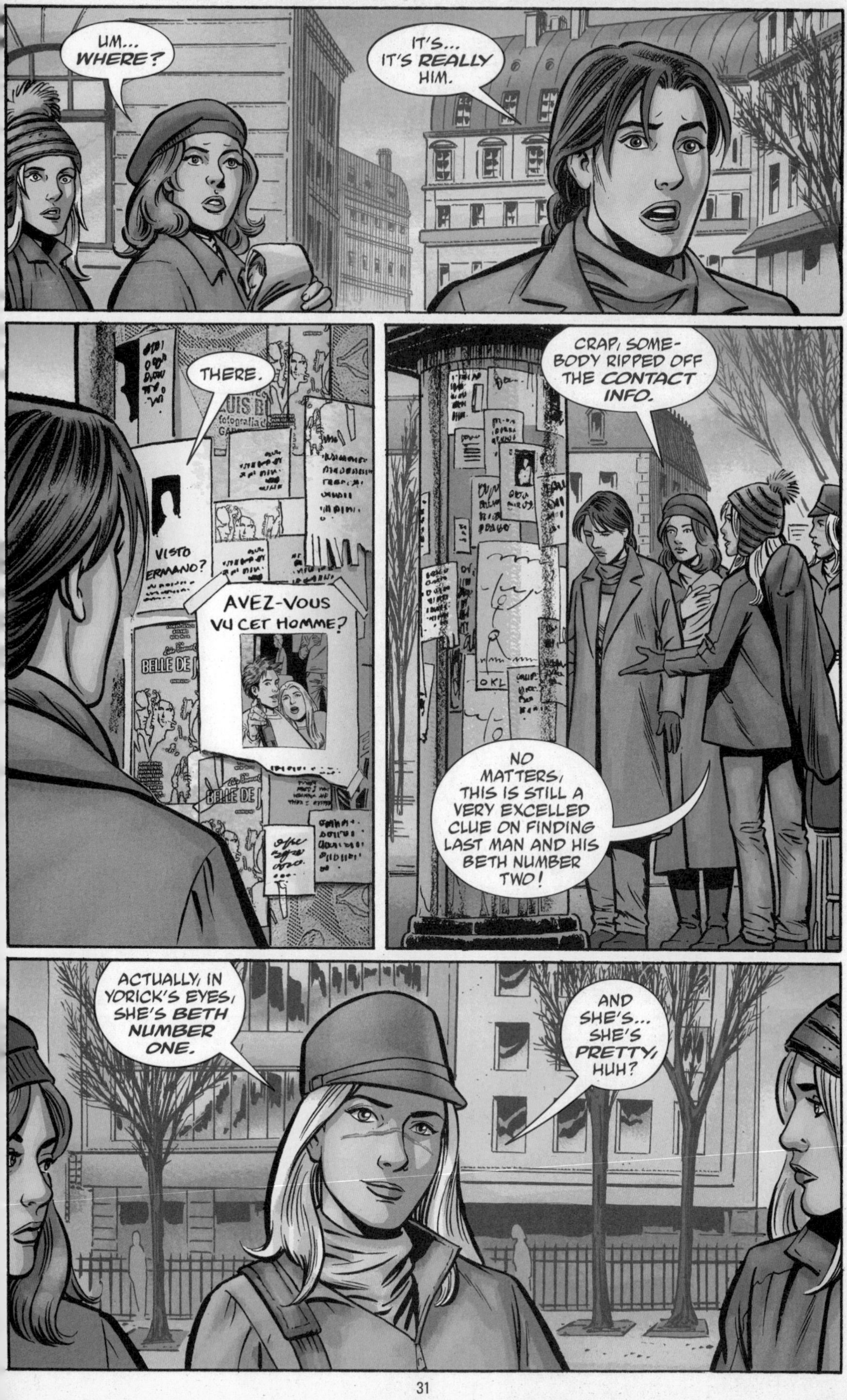
UM... WHERE?
IT'S... IT'S REALLY HIM.
THERE.
AVEZ-VOUS VU CET HOMME?
CRAP, SOMEBODY RIPPED OFF THE CONTACT INFO.
NO MATTERS, THIS IS STILL A VERY EXCELLED CLUE ON FINDING LAST MAN AND HIS BETH NUMBER TWO!
ACTUALLY, IN YORICK'S EYES, SHE'S BETH NUMBER ONE.
AND SHE'S... SHE'S PRETTY, HUH?

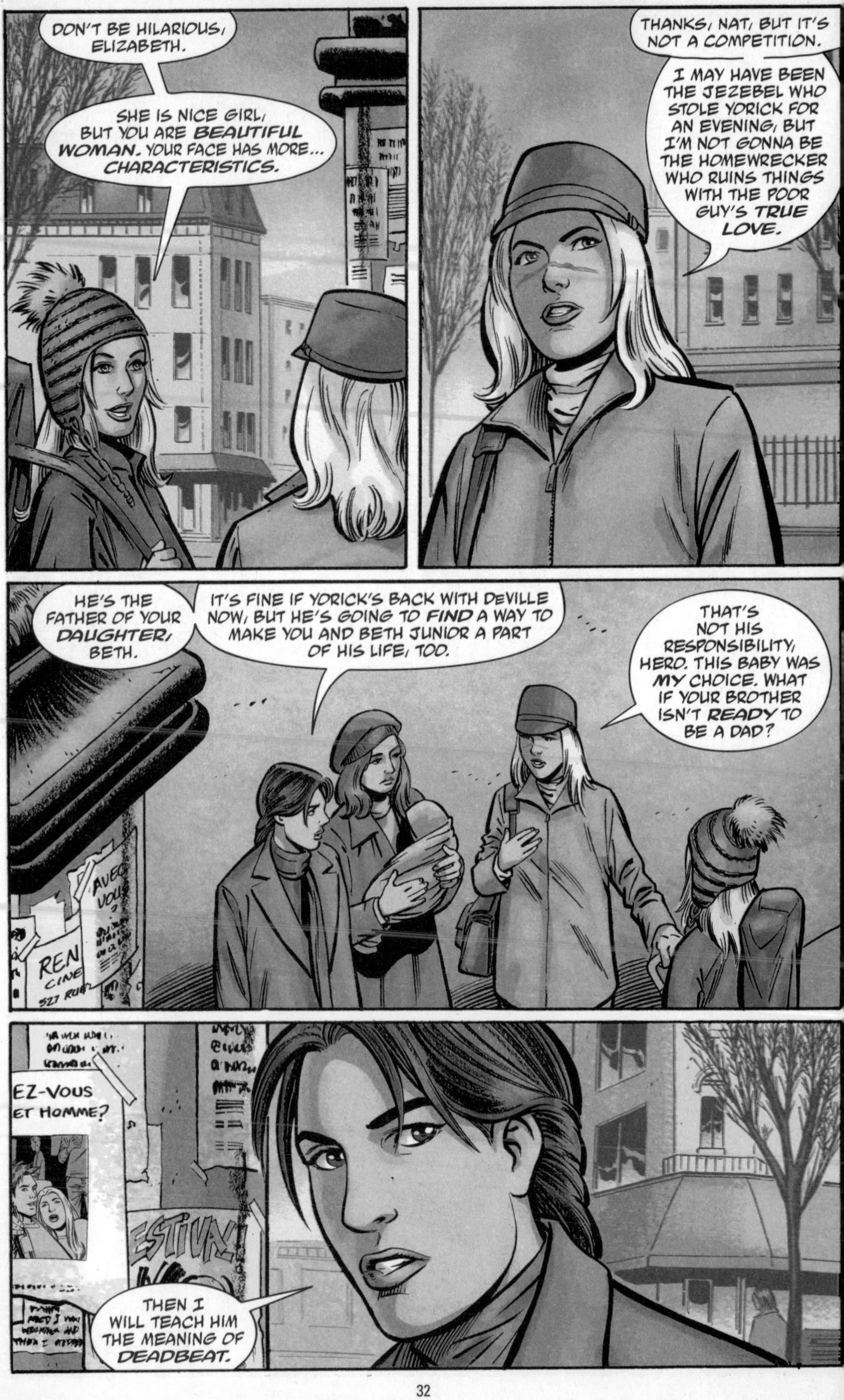

DON'T BE HILARIOUS, ELIZABETH.
SHE IS NICE GIRL, BUT YOU ARE BEAUTIFUL WOMAN. YOUR FACE HAS MORE... CHARACTERISTICS.
THANKS, NAT, BUT IT'S NOT A COMPETITION.
I MAY HAVE BEEN THE JEZEBEL WHO STOLE YORICK FOR AN EVENING, BUT I'M NOT GONNA BE THE HOMEWRECKER WHO RUINS THINGS WITH THE POOR GUY'S TRUE LOVE.
HE'S THE FATHER OF YOUR DAUGHTER, BETH.
IT'S FINE IF YORICK'S BACK WITH DEVILLE NOW, BUT HE'S GOING TO FIND A WAY TO MAKE YOU AND BETH JUNIOR A PART OF HIS LIFE, TOO.
THAT'S NOT HIS RESPONSIBILITY, HERO. THIS BABY WAS MY CHOICE. WHAT IF YOUR BROTHER ISN'T READY TO BE A DAD?
THEN I WILL TEACH HIM THE MEANING OF DEADBEAT.

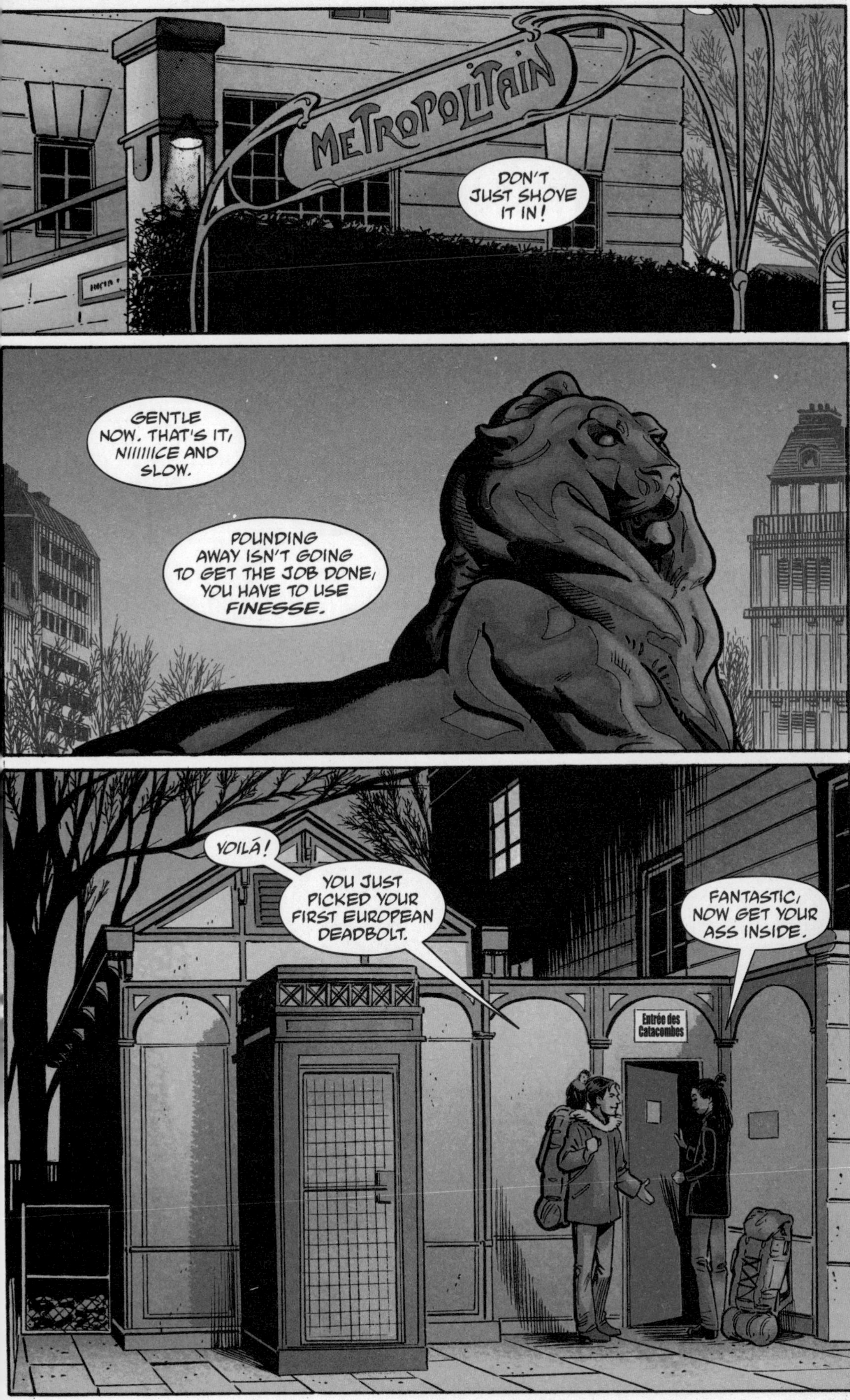
METROPOLITAIN
DON'T JUST SHOVE IT IN!
GENTLE NOW. THAT'S IT, NIIIIIICE AND SLOW.
POUNDING AWAY ISN'T GOING TO GET THE JOB DONE, YOU HAVE TO USE FINESSE.
VOILÁ!
YOU JUST PICKED YOUR FIRST EUROPEAN DEADBOLT.
Entrée des Catacombes
FANTASTIC, NOW GET YOUR ASS INSIDE.

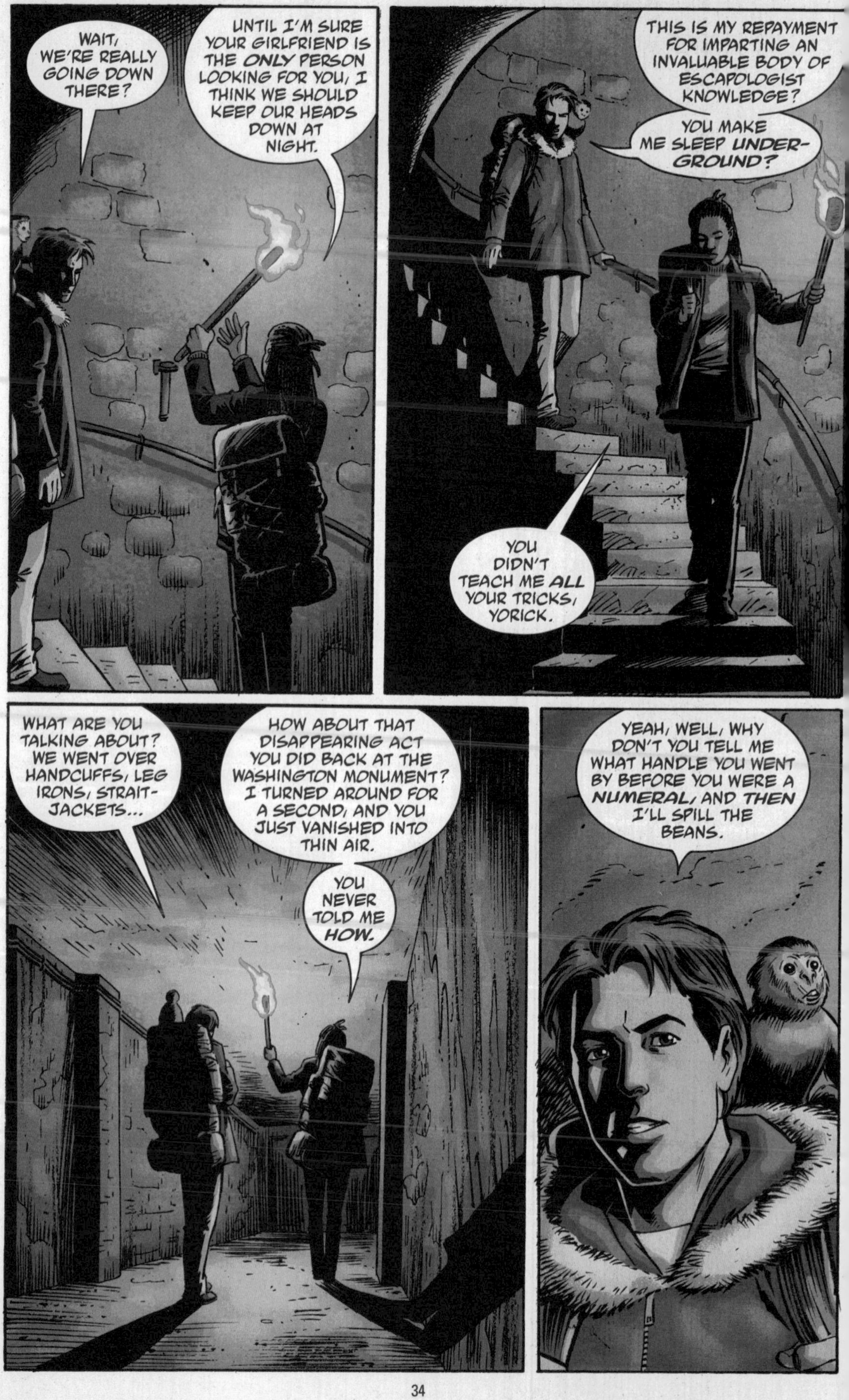
WAIT, WE'RE REALLY GOING DOWN THERE?
UNTIL I'M SURE YOUR GIRLFRIEND IS THE ONLY PERSON LOOKING FOR YOU, I THINK WE SHOULD KEEP OUR HEADS DOWN AT NIGHT.
THIS IS MY REPAYMENT FOR IMPARTING AN INVALUABLE BODY OF ESCAPOLOGIST KNOWLEDGE?
YOU MAKE ME SLEEP UNDER-GROUND?
YOU DIDN'T TEACH ME ALL YOUR TRICKS, YORICK.
WHAT ARE YOU TALKING ABOUT? WE WENT OVER HANDCUFFS, LEG IRONS, STRAIT-JACKETS...
HOW ABOUT THAT DISAPPEARING ACT YOU DID BACK AT THE WASHINGTON MONUMENT? I TURNED AROUND FOR A SECOND, AND YOU JUST VANISHED INTO THIN AIR.
YOU NEVER TOLD ME HOW.
YEAH, WELL, WHY DON'T YOU TELL ME WHAT HANDLE YOU WENT BY BEFORE YOU WERE A NUMERAL, AND THEN I'LL SPILL THE BEANS.

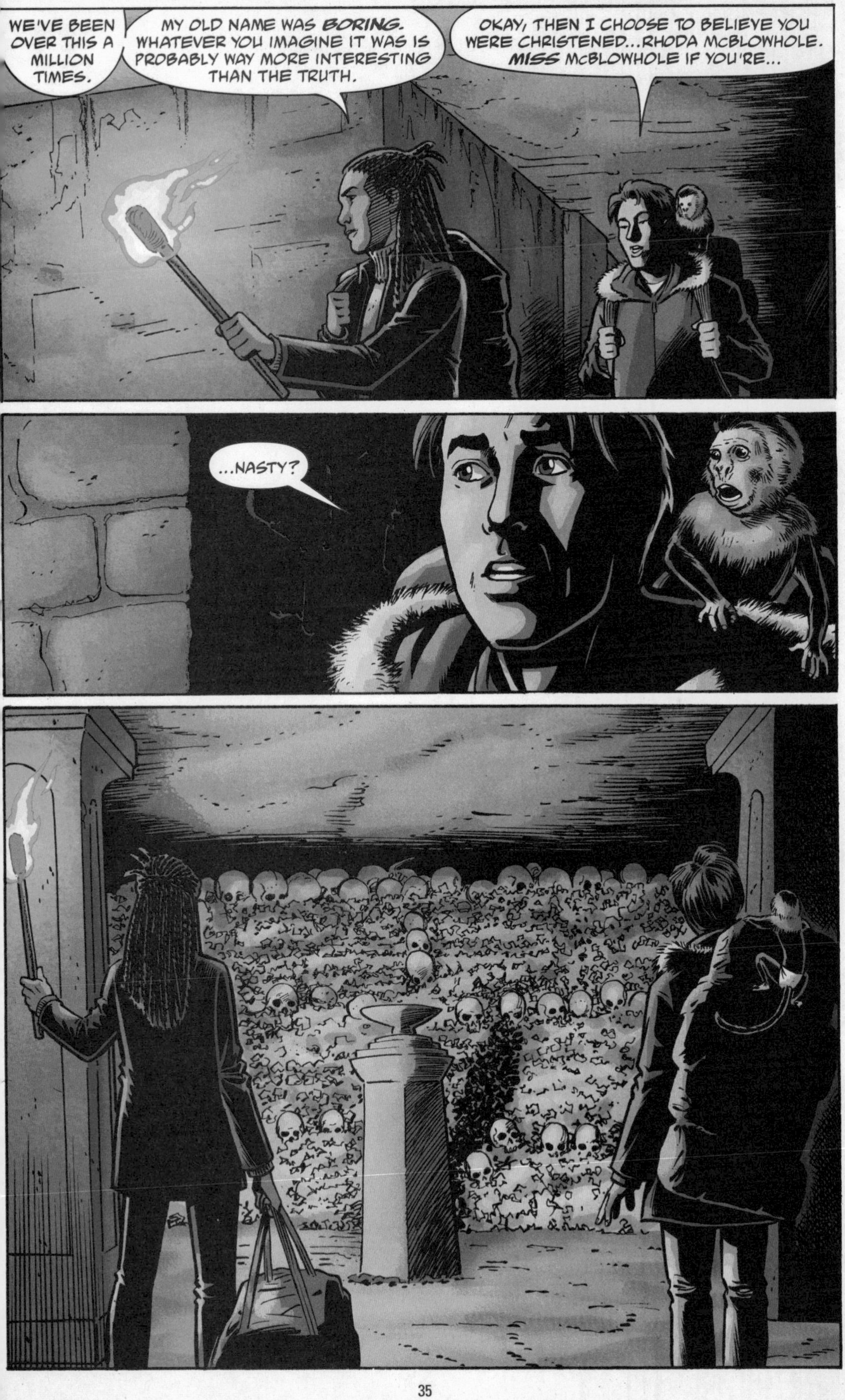

WE'VE BEEN OVER THIS A MILLION TIMES.
MY OLD NAME WAS BORING. WHATEVER YOU IMAGINE IT WAS IS PROBABLY WAY MORE INTERESTING THAN THE TRUTH.
OKAY, THEN I CHOOSE TO BELIEVE YOU WERE CHRISTENED...RHODA McBLOWHOLE. MISS McBLOWHOLE IF YOU'RE...
...NASTY?

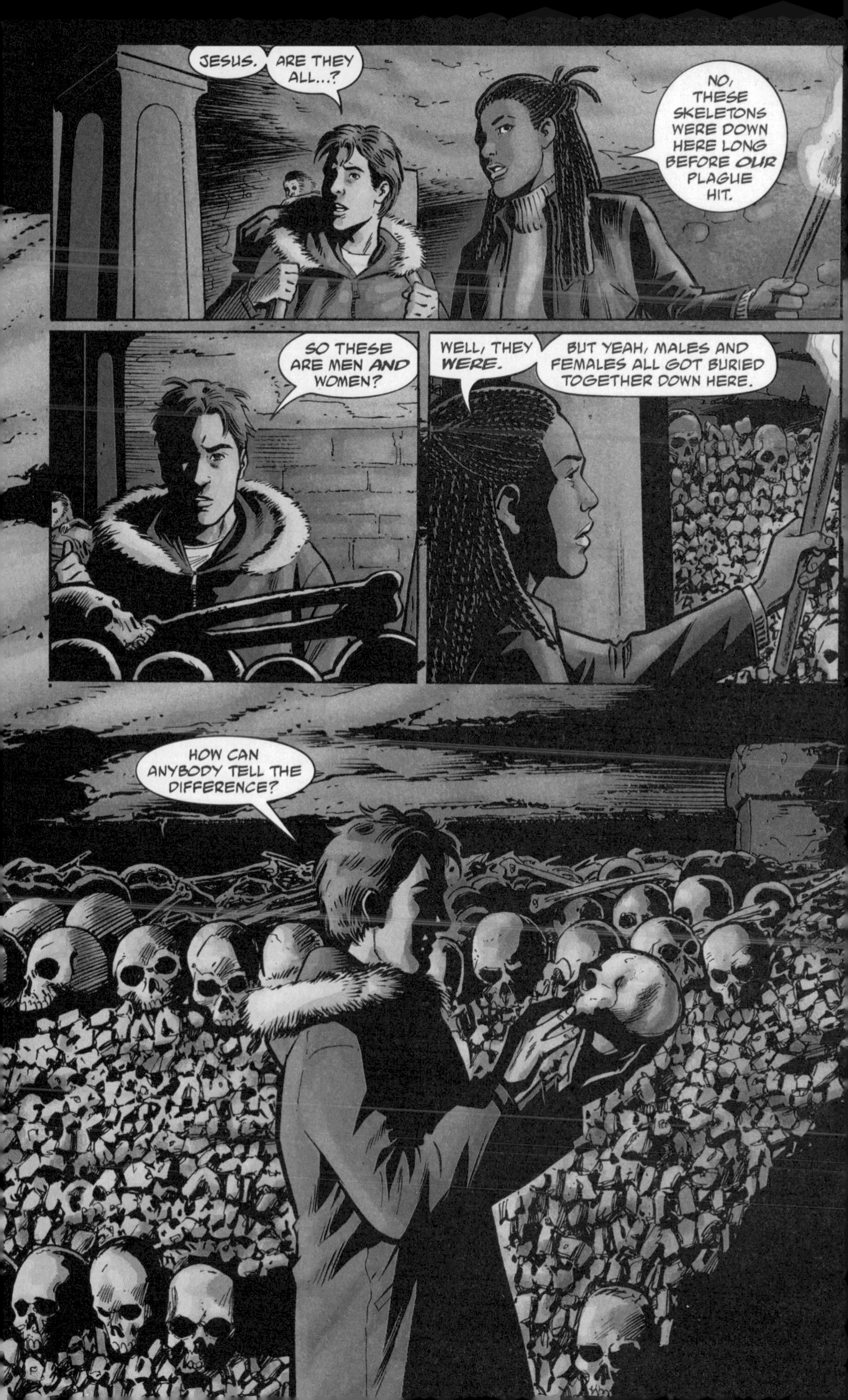

JESUS.
ARE THEY ALL...?
NO, THESE SKELETONS WERE DOWN HERE LONG BEFORE *OUR* PLAGUE HIT.
SO THESE ARE MEN *AND* WOMEN?
WELL, THEY *WERE*.
BUT YEAH, MALES AND FEMALES ALL GOT BURIED TOGETHER DOWN HERE.
HOW CAN ANYBODY TELL THE DIFFERENCE?

I THOUGHT WE WERE LOOKING FOR A MALE, ALTER.

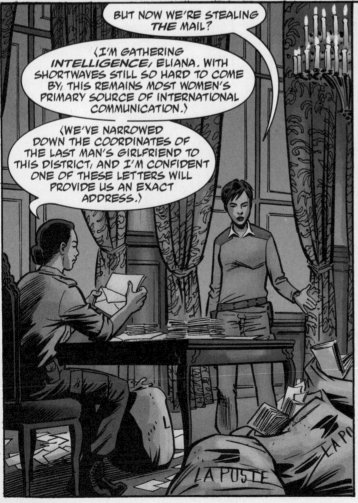

BUT NOW WE'RE STEALING *THE* MAIL?

⟨I'M GATHERING *INTELLIGENCE,* ELIANA. WITH SHORTWAVES STILL SO HARD TO COME BY, THIS REMAINS MOST WOMEN'S PRIMARY SOURCE OF INTERNATIONAL COMMUNICATION.⟩

⟨WE'VE NARROWED DOWN THE COORDINATES OF THE LAST MAN'S GIRLFRIEND TO THIS DISTRICT, AND I'M CONFIDENT ONE OF THESE LETTERS WILL PROVIDE US AN EXACT ADDRESS.⟩

⟨AND IF IT DOESN'T, I SUPPOSE YOU'LL BURN THE *POST OFFICE* TO THE GROUND, AS WELL?⟩

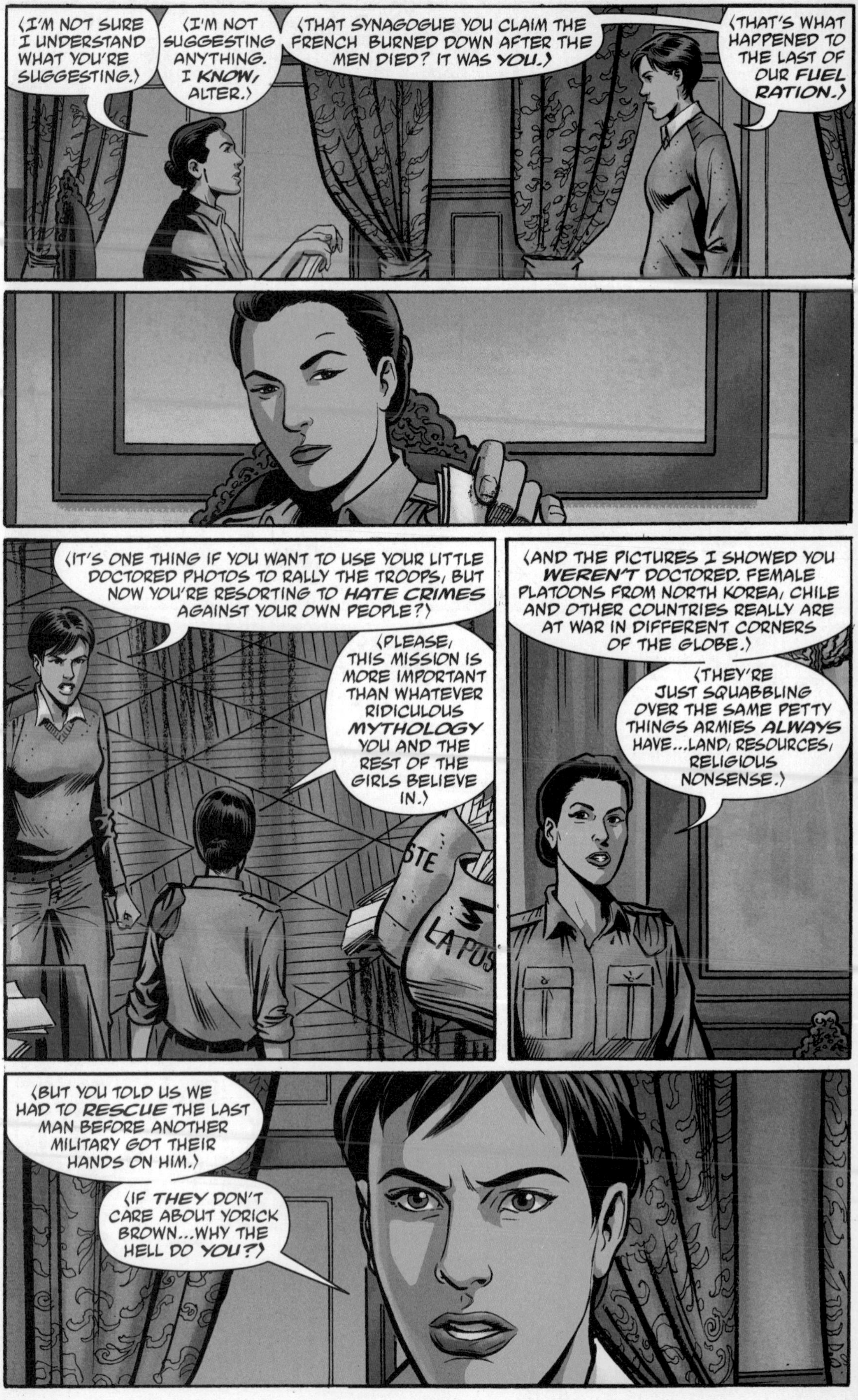
⟨I'M NOT SURE I UNDERSTAND WHAT YOU'RE SUGGESTING.⟩
⟨I'M NOT SUGGESTING ANYTHING. I KNOW, ALTER.⟩
⟨THAT SYNAGOGUE YOU CLAIM THE FRENCH BURNED DOWN AFTER THE MEN DIED? IT WAS YOU.⟩
⟨THAT'S WHAT HAPPENED TO THE LAST OF OUR FUEL RATION.⟩
⟨IT'S ONE THING IF YOU WANT TO USE YOUR LITTLE DOCTORED PHOTOS TO RALLY THE TROOPS, BUT NOW YOU'RE RESORTING TO HATE CRIMES AGAINST YOUR OWN PEOPLE?⟩
⟨PLEASE, THIS MISSION IS MORE IMPORTANT THAN WHATEVER RIDICULOUS MYTHOLOGY YOU AND THE REST OF THE GIRLS BELIEVE IN.⟩
STE
LA POS
⟨AND THE PICTURES I SHOWED YOU WEREN'T DOCTORED. FEMALE PLATOONS FROM NORTH KOREA, CHILE AND OTHER COUNTRIES REALLY ARE AT WAR IN DIFFERENT CORNERS OF THE GLOBE.⟩
⟨THEY'RE JUST SQUABBLING OVER THE SAME PETTY THINGS ARMIES ALWAYS HAVE...LAND, RESOURCES, RELIGIOUS NONSENSE.⟩
⟨BUT YOU TOLD US WE HAD TO RESCUE THE LAST MAN BEFORE ANOTHER MILITARY GOT THEIR HANDS ON HIM.⟩
⟨IF THEY DON'T CARE ABOUT YORICK BROWN...WHY THE HELL DO YOU?⟩

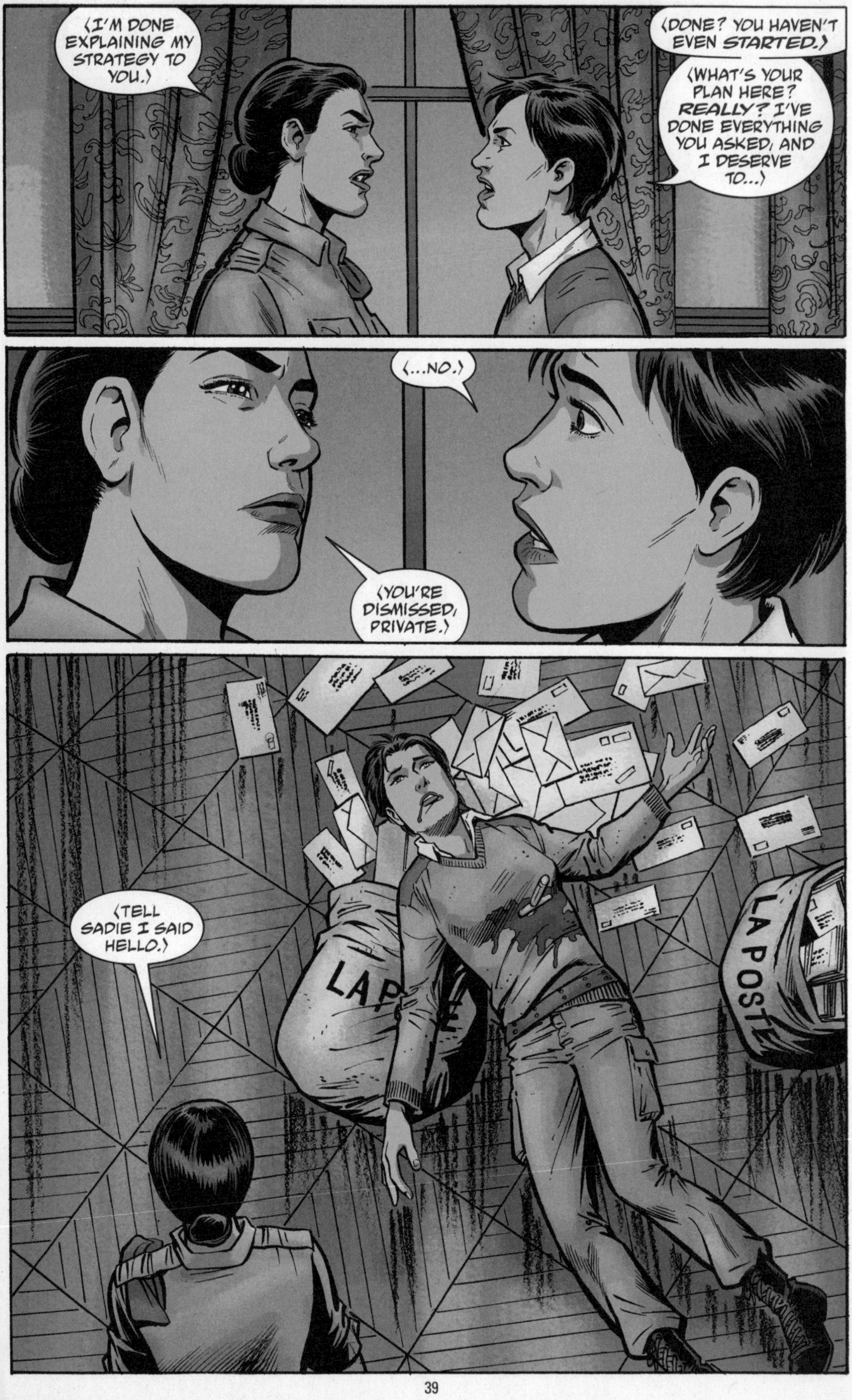
<I'M DONE EXPLAINING MY STRATEGY TO YOU.>
<DONE? YOU HAVEN'T EVEN *STARTED.*>
<WHAT'S YOUR PLAN HERE? *REALLY*? I'VE DONE EVERYTHING YOU ASKED, AND I DESERVE TO...>
<...NO.>
<YOU'RE DISMISSED, PRIVATE.>
<TELL SADIE I SAID HELLO.>
LA POST

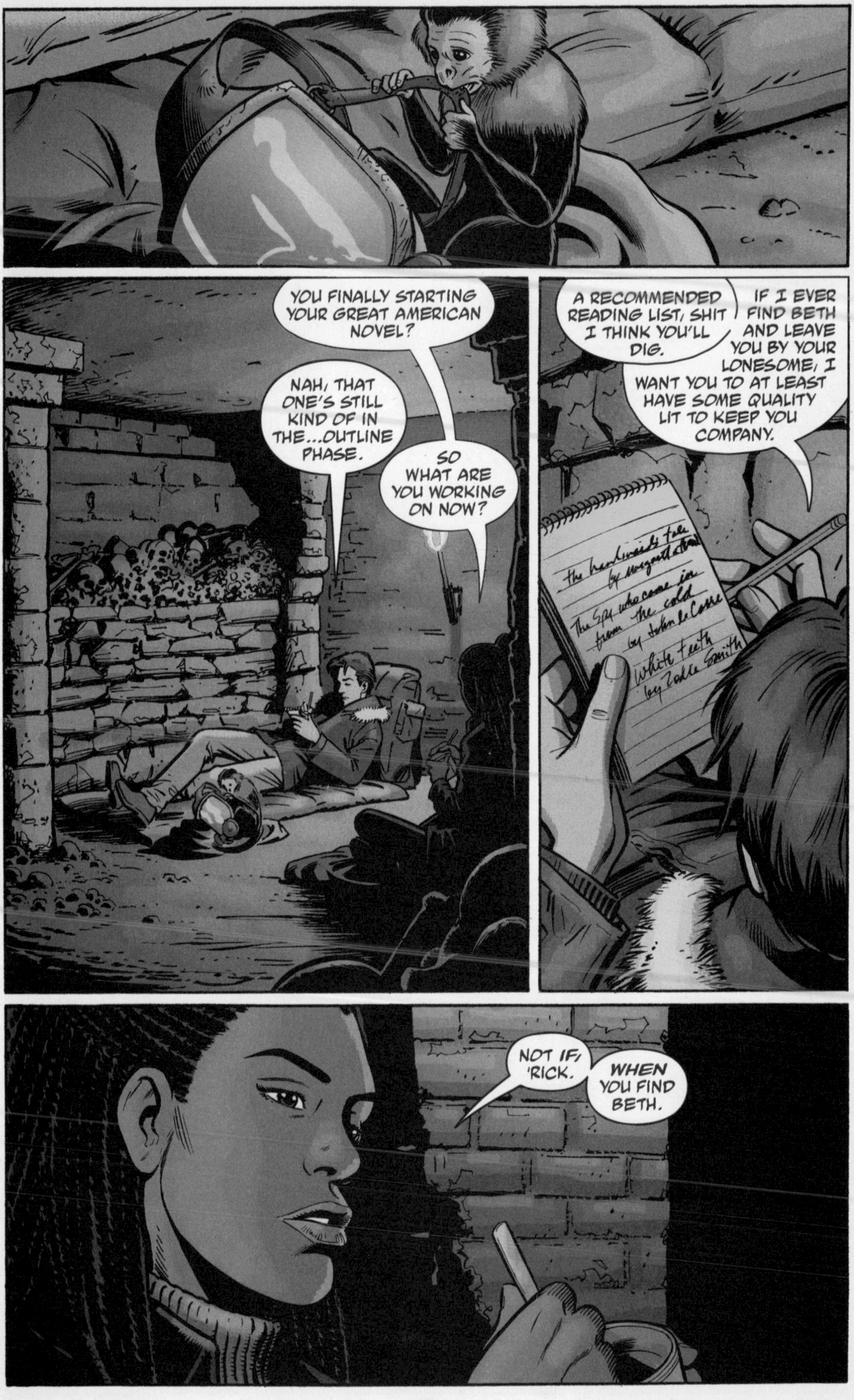
YOU FINALLY STARTING YOUR GREAT AMERICAN NOVEL?
NAH, THAT ONE'S STILL KIND OF IN THE...OUTLINE PHASE.
SO WHAT ARE YOU WORKING ON NOW?
A RECOMMENDED READING LIST, SHIT I THINK YOU'LL DIG.
IF I EVER FIND BETH AND LEAVE YOU BY YOUR LONESOME, I WANT YOU TO AT LEAST HAVE SOME QUALITY LIT TO KEEP YOU COMPANY.
NOT IF, 'RICK.
WHEN YOU FIND BETH.

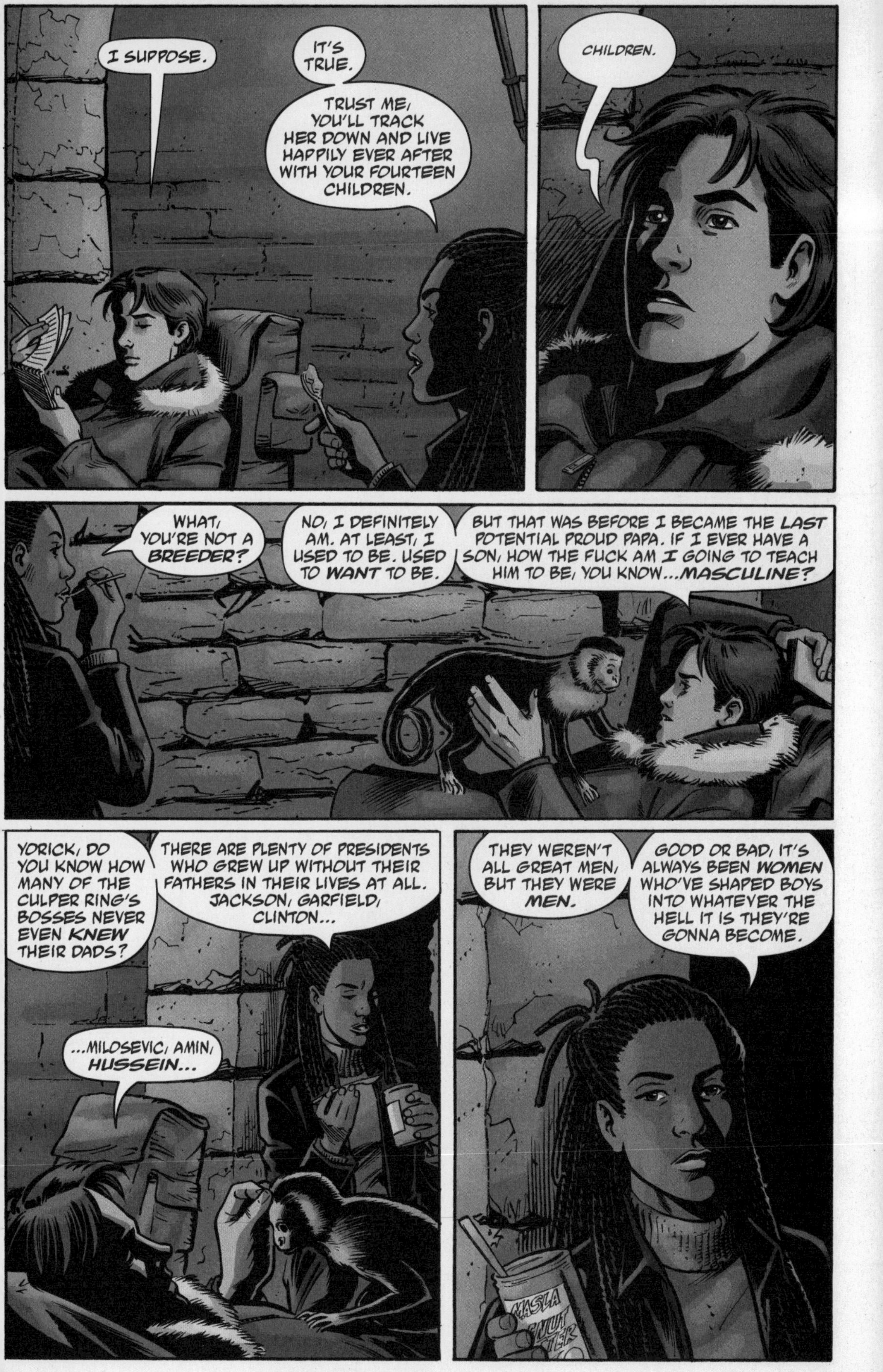
I SUPPOSE.
IT'S TRUE.
TRUST ME, YOU'LL TRACK HER DOWN AND LIVE HAPPILY EVER AFTER WITH YOUR FOURTEEN CHILDREN.
CHILDREN.
WHAT, YOU'RE NOT A BREEDER?
NO, I DEFINITELY AM. AT LEAST, I USED TO BE. USED TO WANT TO BE.
BUT THAT WAS BEFORE I BECAME THE LAST POTENTIAL PROUD PAPA. IF I EVER HAVE A SON, HOW THE FUCK AM I GOING TO TEACH HIM TO BE, YOU KNOW...MASCULINE?
YORICK, DO YOU KNOW HOW MANY OF THE CULPER RING'S BOSSES NEVER EVEN KNEW THEIR DADS?
THERE ARE PLENTY OF PRESIDENTS WHO GREW UP WITHOUT THEIR FATHERS IN THEIR LIVES AT ALL. JACKSON, GARFIELD, CLINTON...
...MILOSEVIC, AMIN, HUSSEIN...
THEY WEREN'T ALL GREAT MEN, BUT THEY WERE MEN.
GOOD OR BAD, IT'S ALWAYS BEEN WOMEN WHO'VE SHAPED BOYS INTO WHATEVER THE HELL IT IS THEY'RE GONNA BECOME.

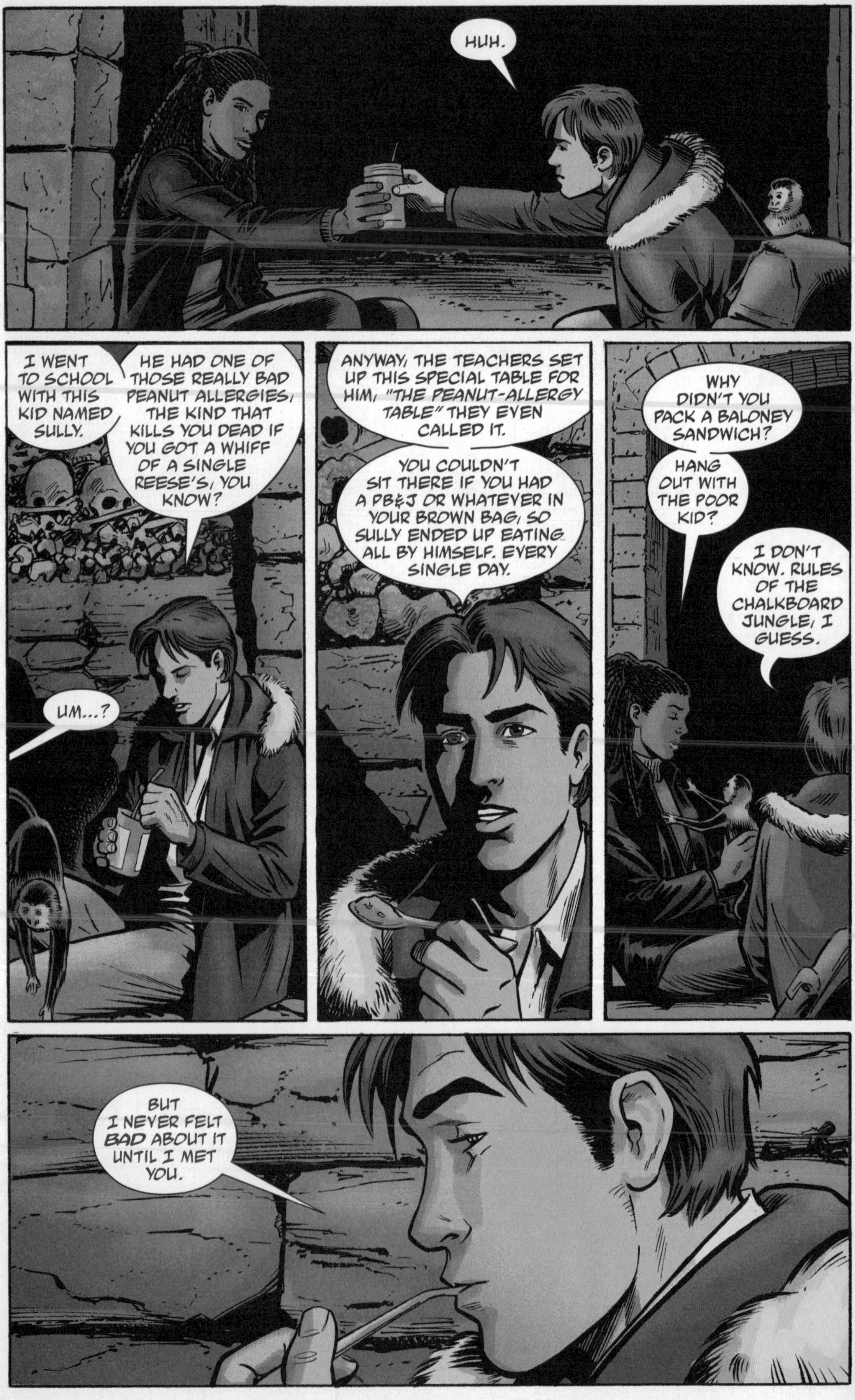
HUH.
I WENT TO SCHOOL WITH THIS KID NAMED SULLY.
HE HAD ONE OF THOSE REALLY BAD PEANUT ALLERGIES, THE KIND THAT KILLS YOU DEAD IF YOU GOT A WHIFF OF A SINGLE REESE'S, YOU KNOW?
UM...?
ANYWAY, THE TEACHERS SET UP THIS SPECIAL TABLE FOR HIM, "THE PEANUT-ALLERGY TABLE" THEY EVEN CALLED IT.
YOU COULDN'T SIT THERE IF YOU HAD A PB&J OR WHATEVER IN YOUR BROWN BAG, SO SULLY ENDED UP EATING ALL BY HIMSELF. EVERY SINGLE DAY.
WHY DIDN'T YOU PACK A BALONEY SANDWICH?
HANG OUT WITH THE POOR KID?
I DON'T KNOW. RULES OF THE CHALKBOARD JUNGLE, I GUESS.
BUT I NEVER FELT *BAD* ABOUT IT UNTIL I MET YOU.

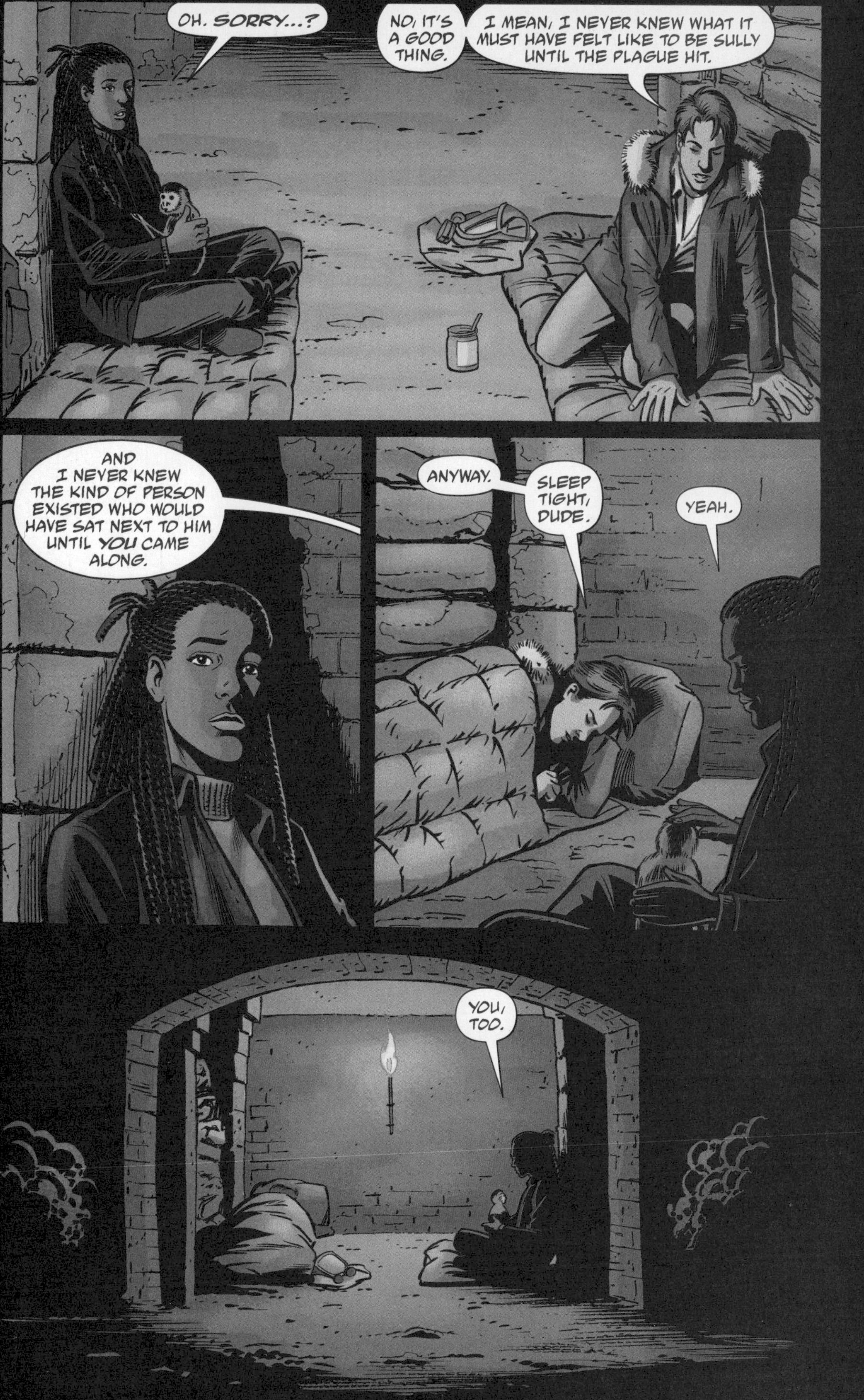
OH. SORRY...?
NO, IT'S A GOOD THING.
I MEAN, I NEVER KNEW WHAT IT MUST HAVE FELT LIKE TO BE SULLY UNTIL THE PLAGUE HIT.
AND I NEVER KNEW THE KIND OF PERSON EXISTED WHO WOULD HAVE SAT NEXT TO HIM UNTIL YOU CAME ALONG.
ANYWAY.
SLEEP TIGHT, DUDE.
YEAH.
YOU, TOO.

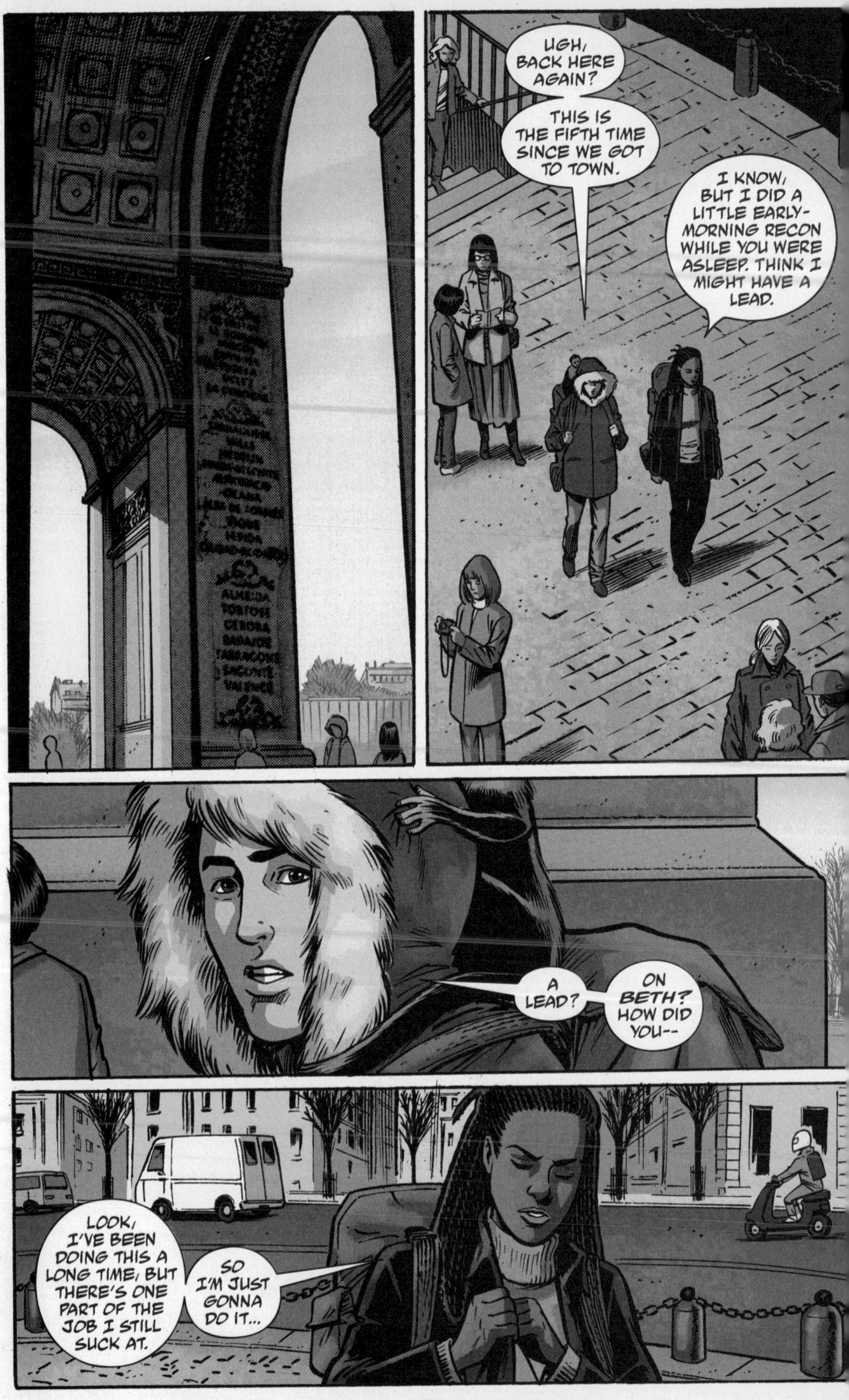
UGH, BACK HERE AGAIN?
THIS IS THE FIFTH TIME SINCE WE GOT TO TOWN.
I KNOW, BUT I DID A LITTLE EARLY-MORNING RECON WHILE YOU WERE ASLEEP. THINK I MIGHT HAVE A LEAD.
A LEAD?
ON BETH? HOW DID YOU--
LOOK, I'VE BEEN DOING THIS A LONG TIME, BUT THERE'S ONE PART OF THE JOB I STILL SUCK AT.
SO I'M JUST GONNA DO IT...

WHAT ARE YOU--

THIS IS FOR YOU.

SORRY I DIDN'T HAVE TIME TO WRAP IT.

THIS...THIS IS YOUR *SCARF.*

YOU'VE BEEN KNITTING THIS THING FOR ALMOST, LIKE, *FIVE YEARS.*

WELL, I FUCKED UP A LOT, SO I HAD TO START OVER A BUNCH OF TIMES.

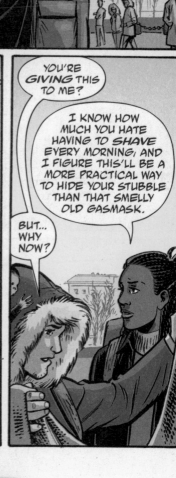

YOU'RE *GIVING* THIS TO ME?

I KNOW HOW MUCH YOU HATE HAVING TO *SHAVE* EVERY MORNING, AND I FIGURE THIS'LL BE A MORE PRACTICAL WAY TO HIDE YOUR STUBBLE THAN THAT SMELLY OLD GASMASK.

BUT... WHY NOW?

JUST AS A THANK-YOU, 'RICK.

FOR...YOU KNOW.

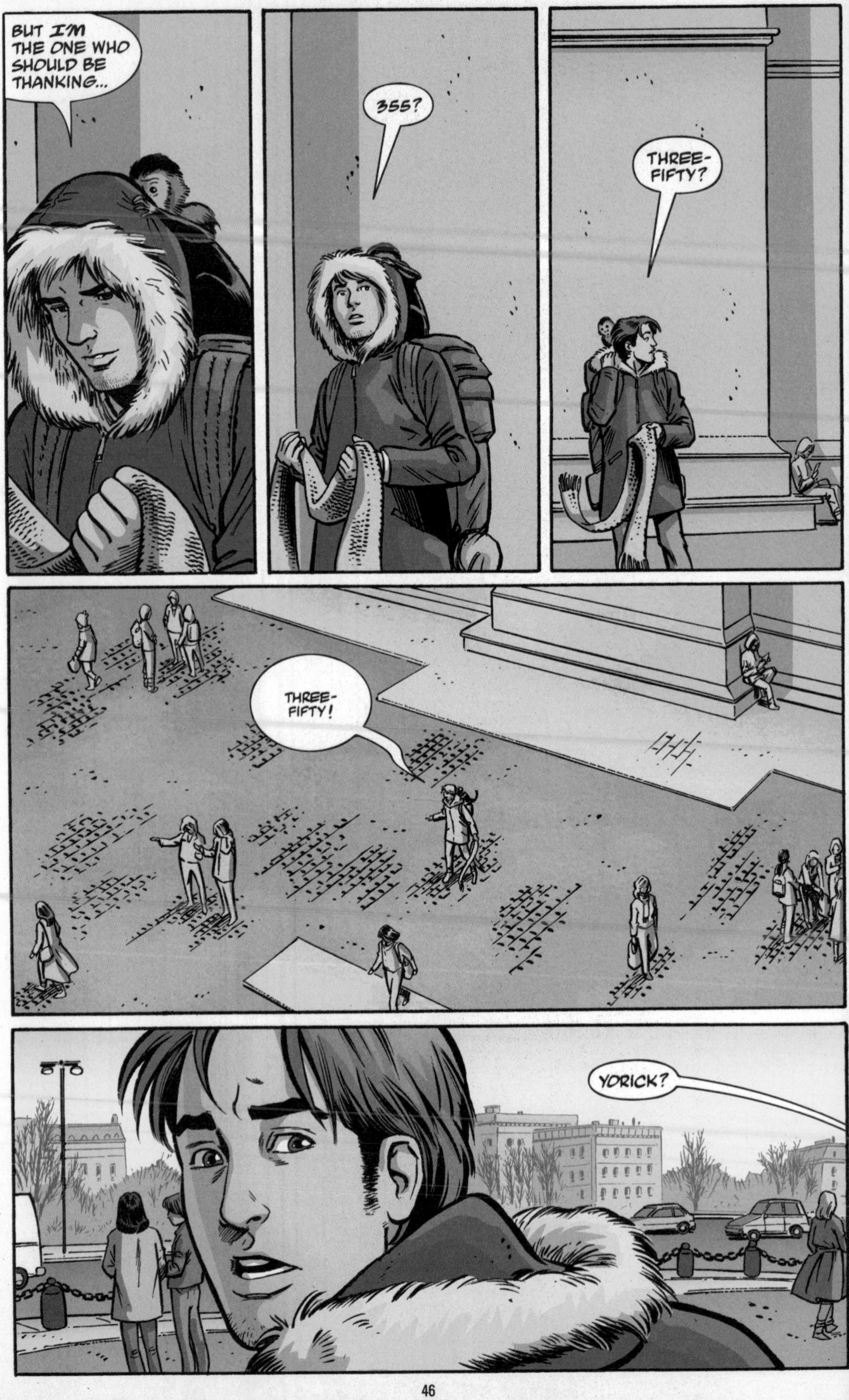
BUT I'M THE ONE WHO SHOULD BE THANKING...
355?
THREE-FIFTY?
THREE-FIFTY!
YORICK?

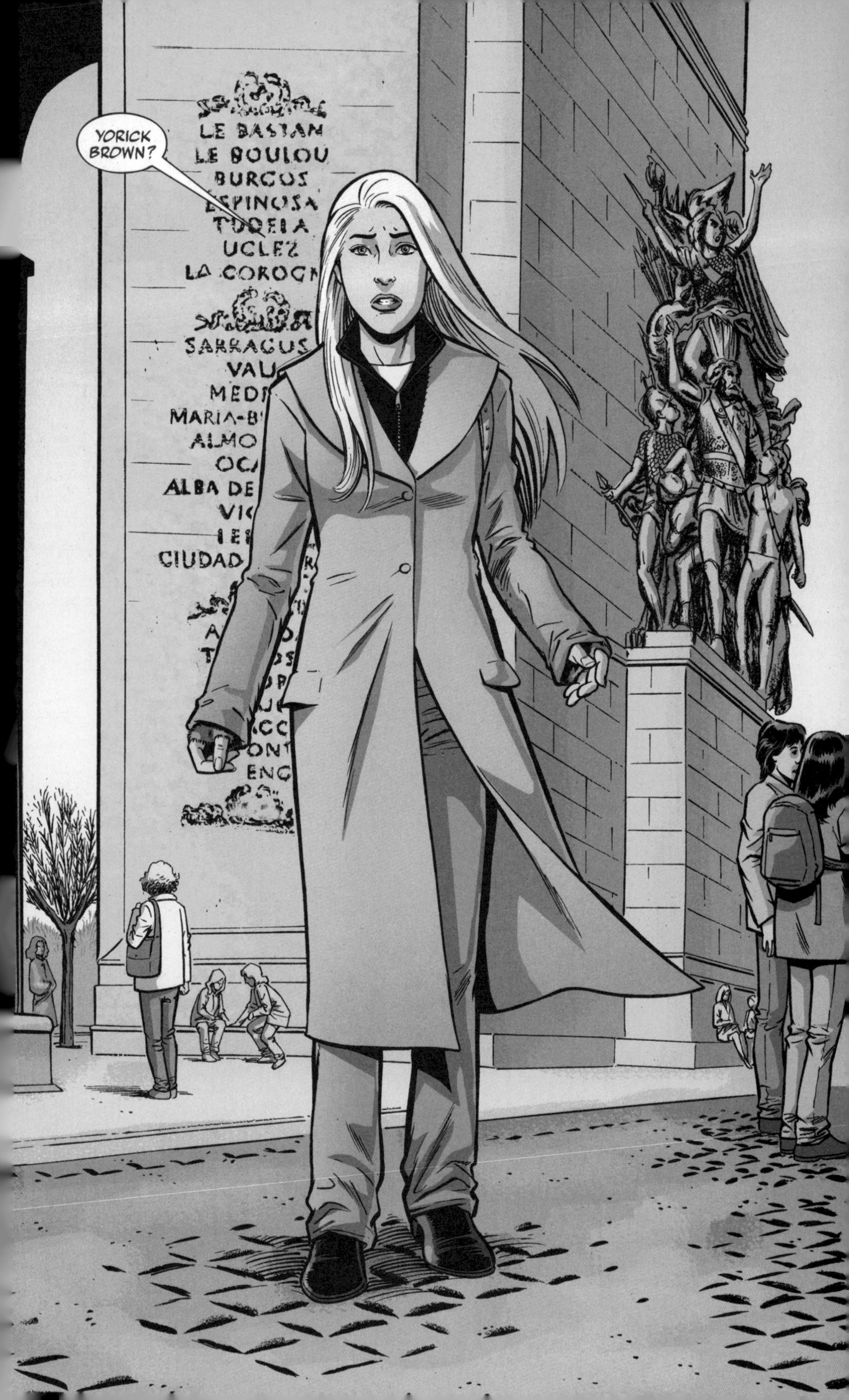
YORICK BROWN?
LE BASTAN
LE BOULOU
BURGOS
ESPINOSA
UCLEZ
SARRAGUS

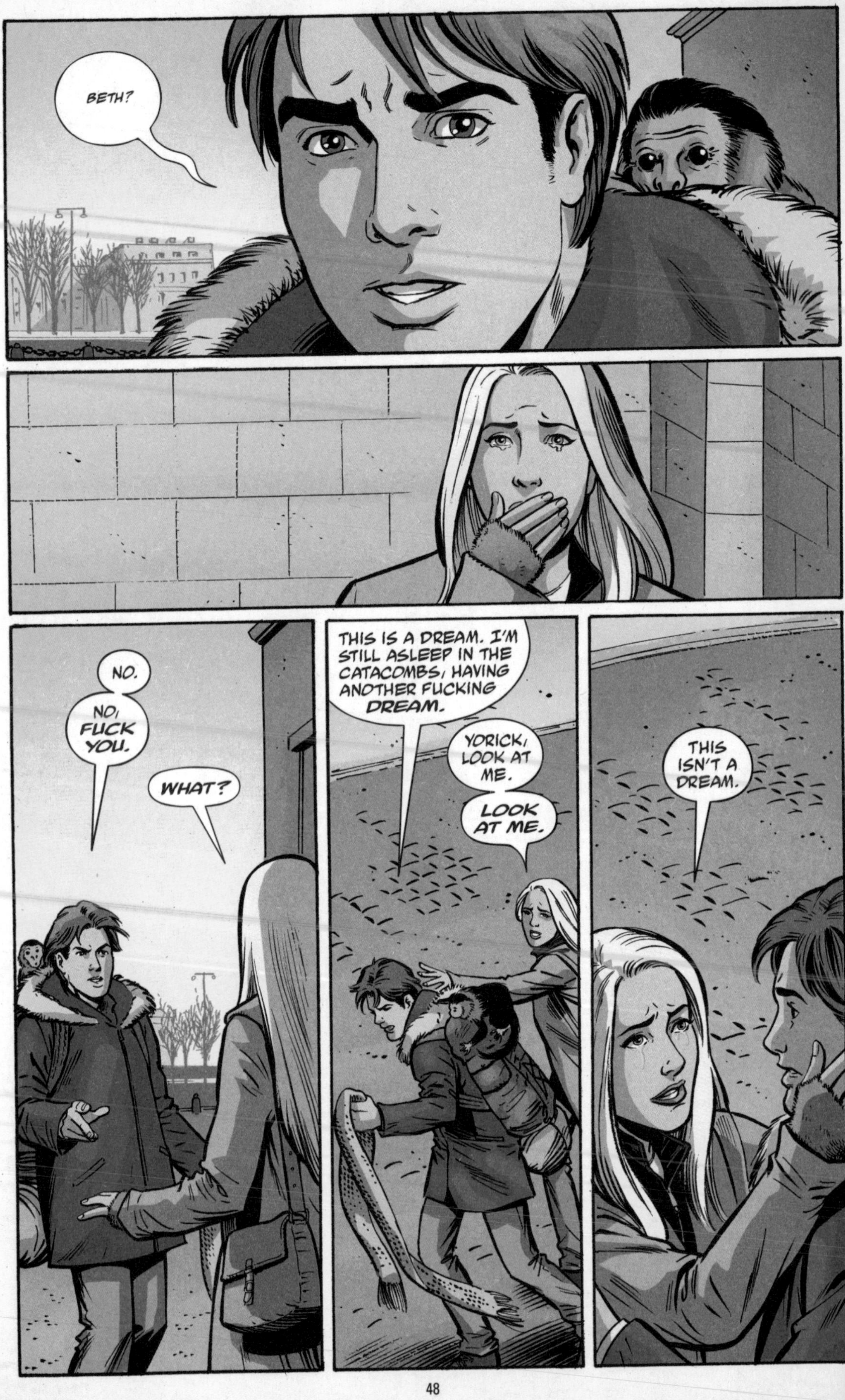
BETH?
NO.
NO, FUCK YOU.
WHAT?
THIS IS A DREAM. I'M STILL ASLEEP IN THE CATACOMBS, HAVING ANOTHER FUCKING DREAM.
YORICK, LOOK AT ME.
LOOK AT ME.
THIS ISN'T A DREAM.

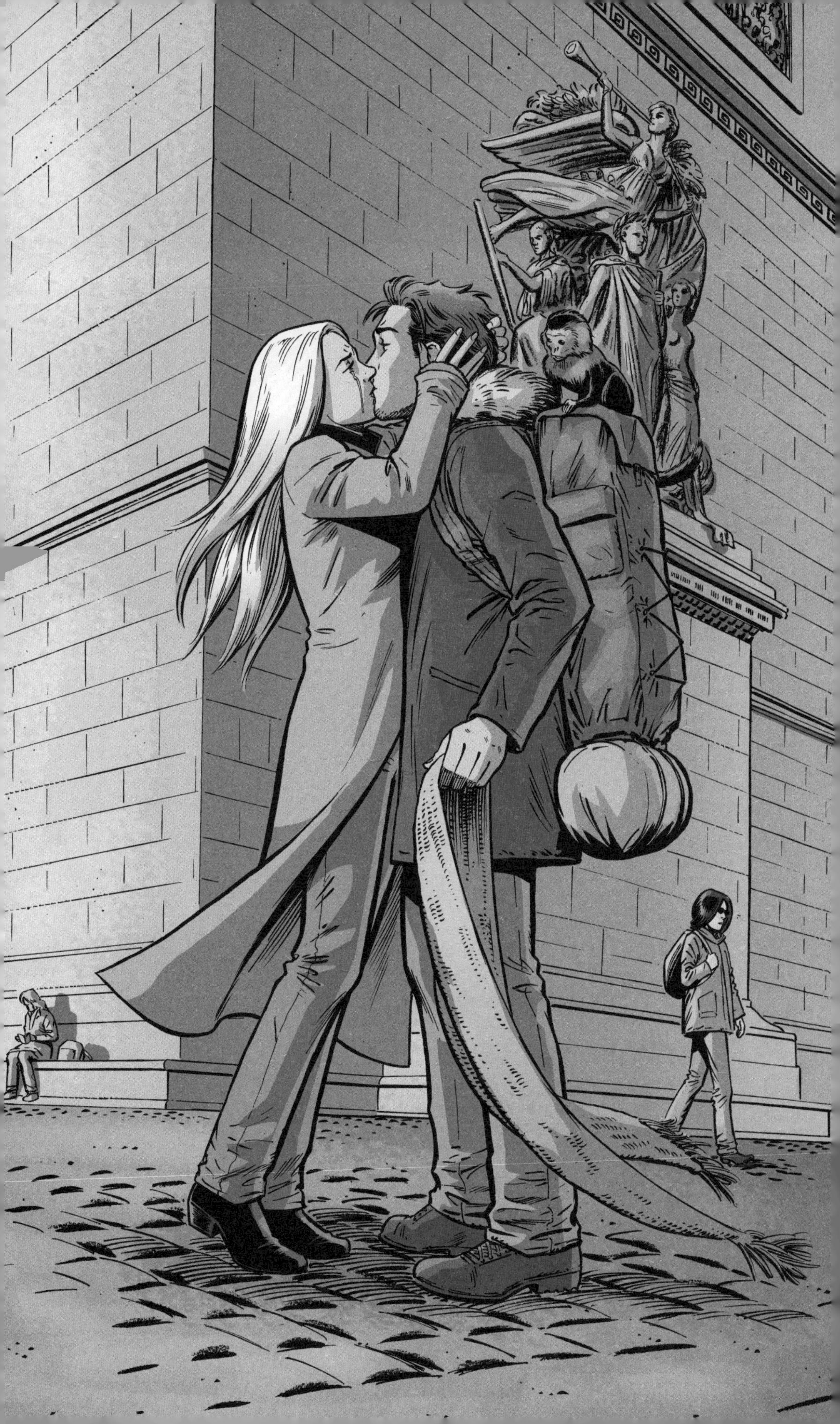

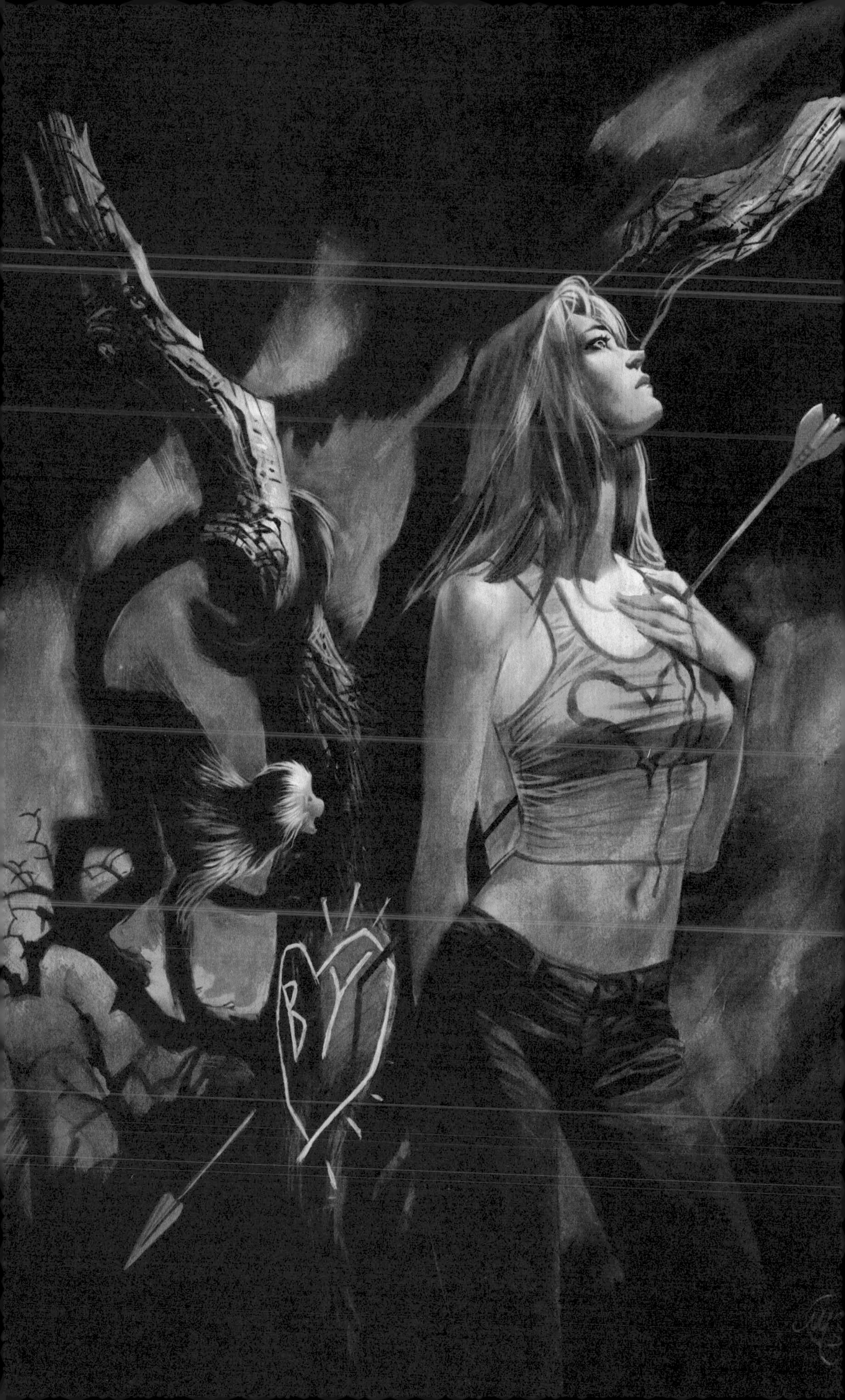

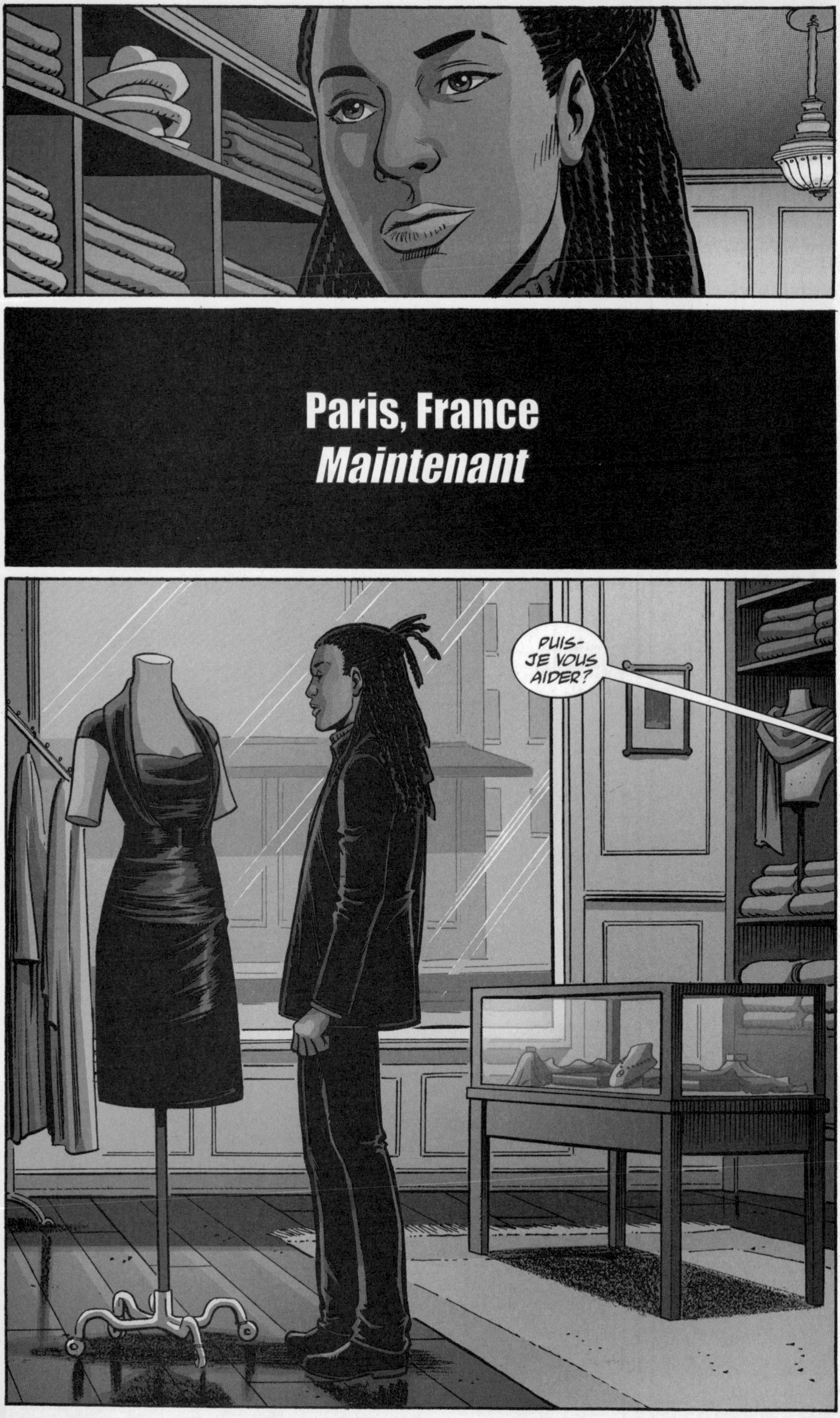
Paris, France
Maintenant
PUIS-JE VOUS AIDER?

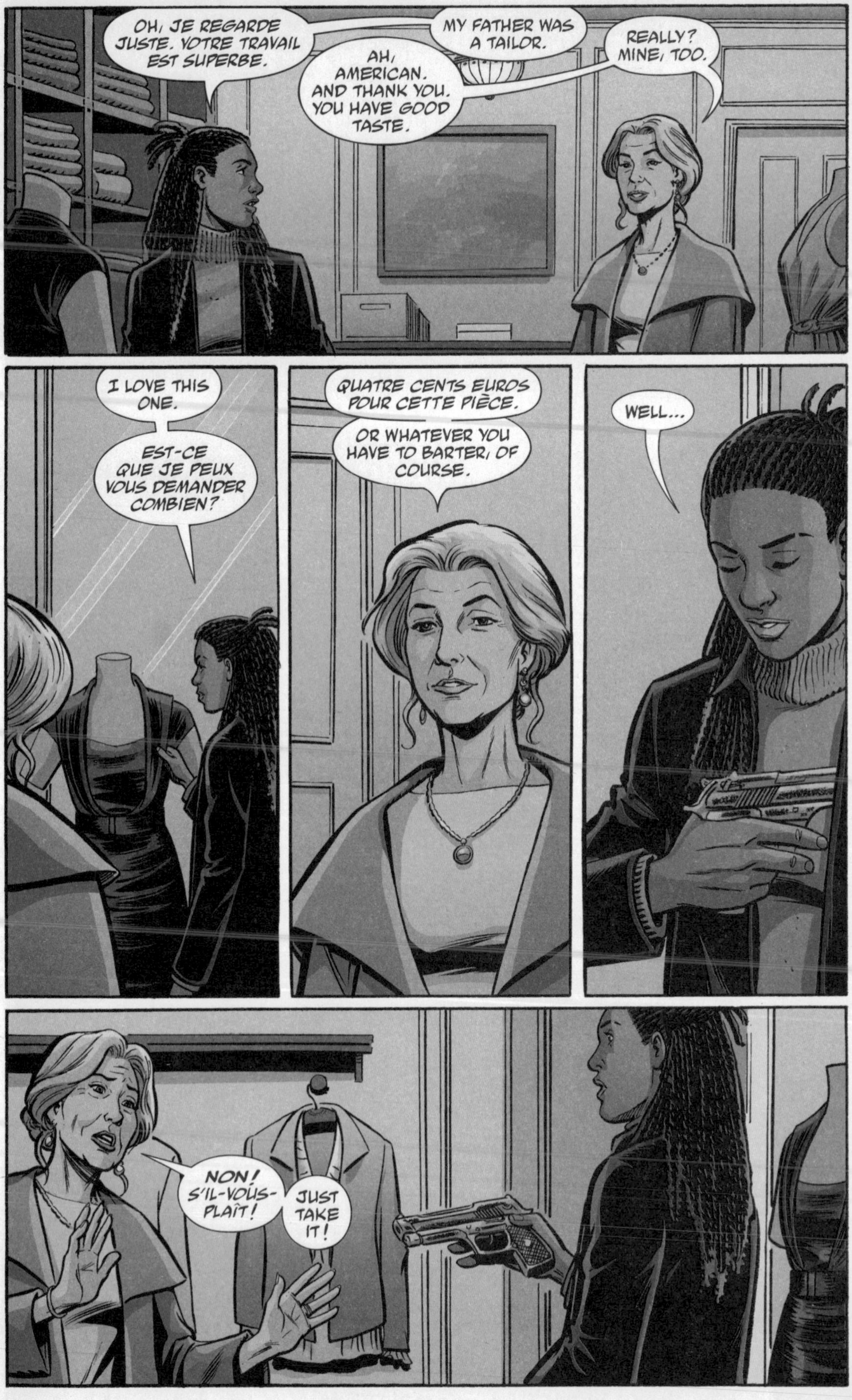
OH, JE REGARDE JUSTE. VOTRE TRAVAIL EST SUPERBE.
AH, AMERICAN. AND THANK YOU. YOU HAVE GOOD TASTE.
MY FATHER WAS A TAILOR.
REALLY? MINE, TOO.
I LOVE THIS ONE.
EST-CE QUE JE PEUX VOUS DEMANDER COMBIEN?
QUATRE CENTS EUROS POUR CETTE PIÈCE.
OR WHATEVER YOU HAVE TO BARTER, OF COURSE.
WELL...
NON! S'IL-VOUS-PLAÎT!
JUST TAKE IT!

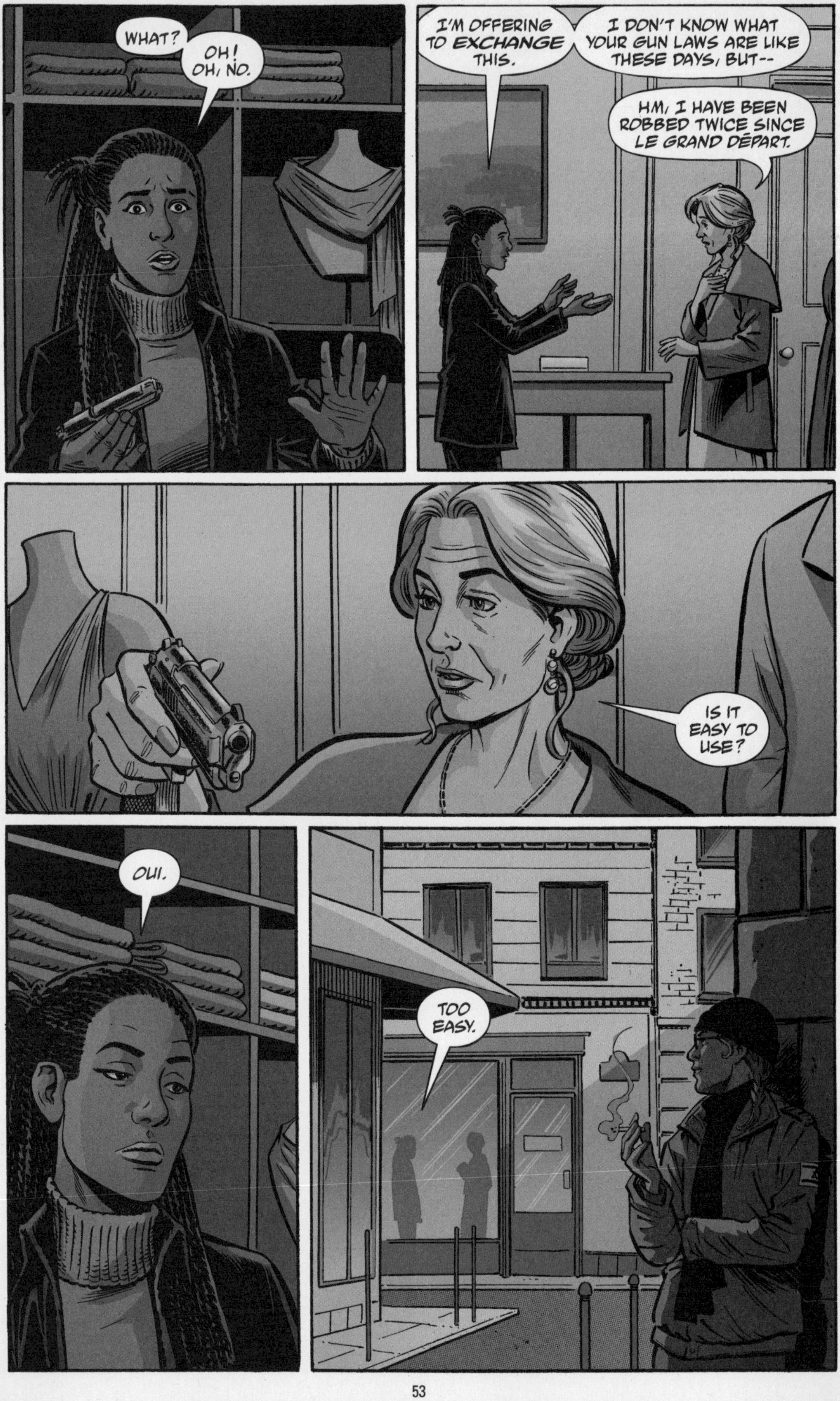
WHAT?
OH! OH, NO.
I'M OFFERING TO EXCHANGE THIS.
I DON'T KNOW WHAT YOUR GUN LAWS ARE LIKE THESE DAYS, BUT--
HM, I HAVE BEEN ROBBED TWICE SINCE LE GRAND DÉPART.
IS IT EASY TO USE?
OUI.
TOO EASY.

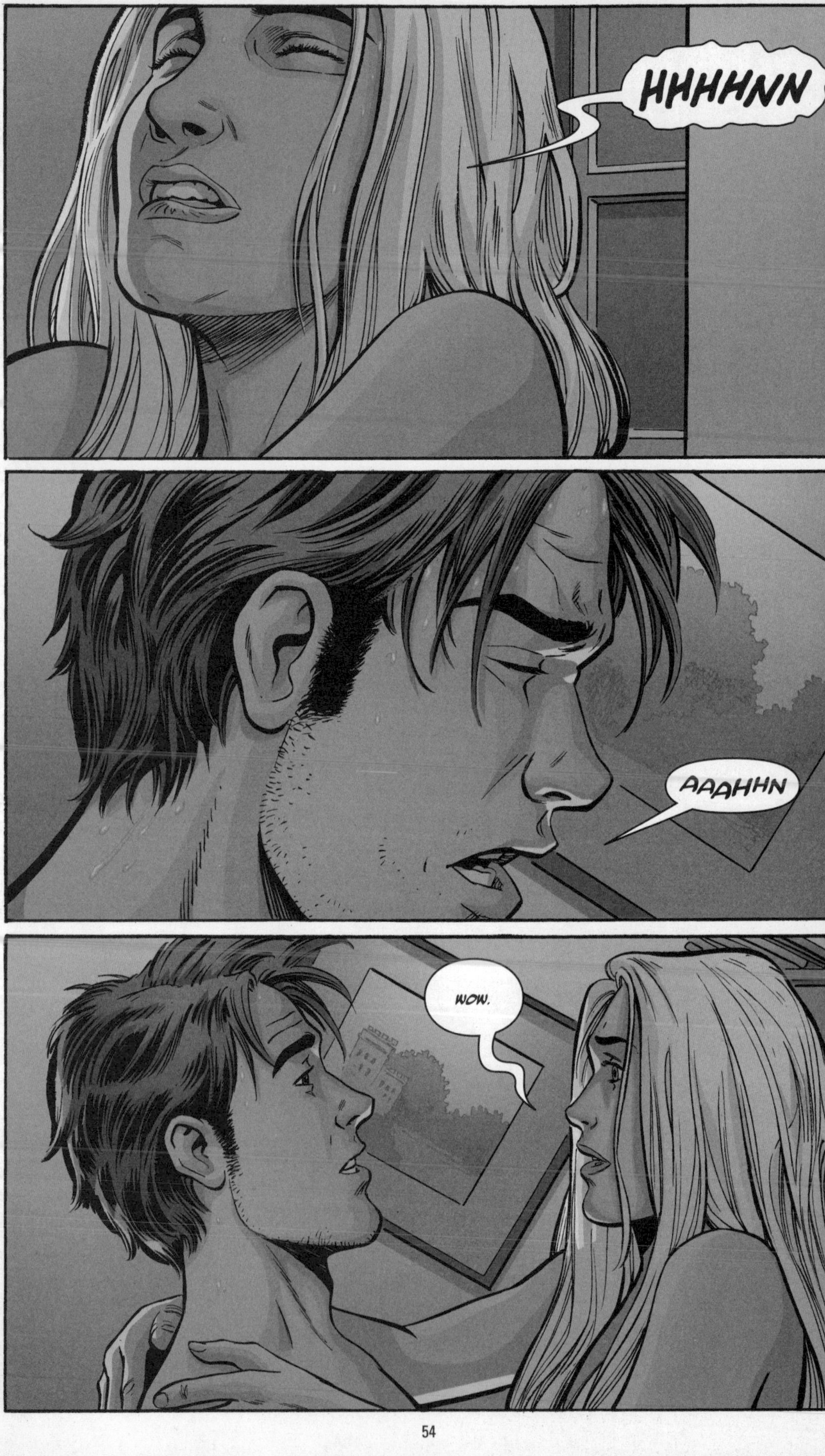
HHHHNN
AAAHHN
WOW.

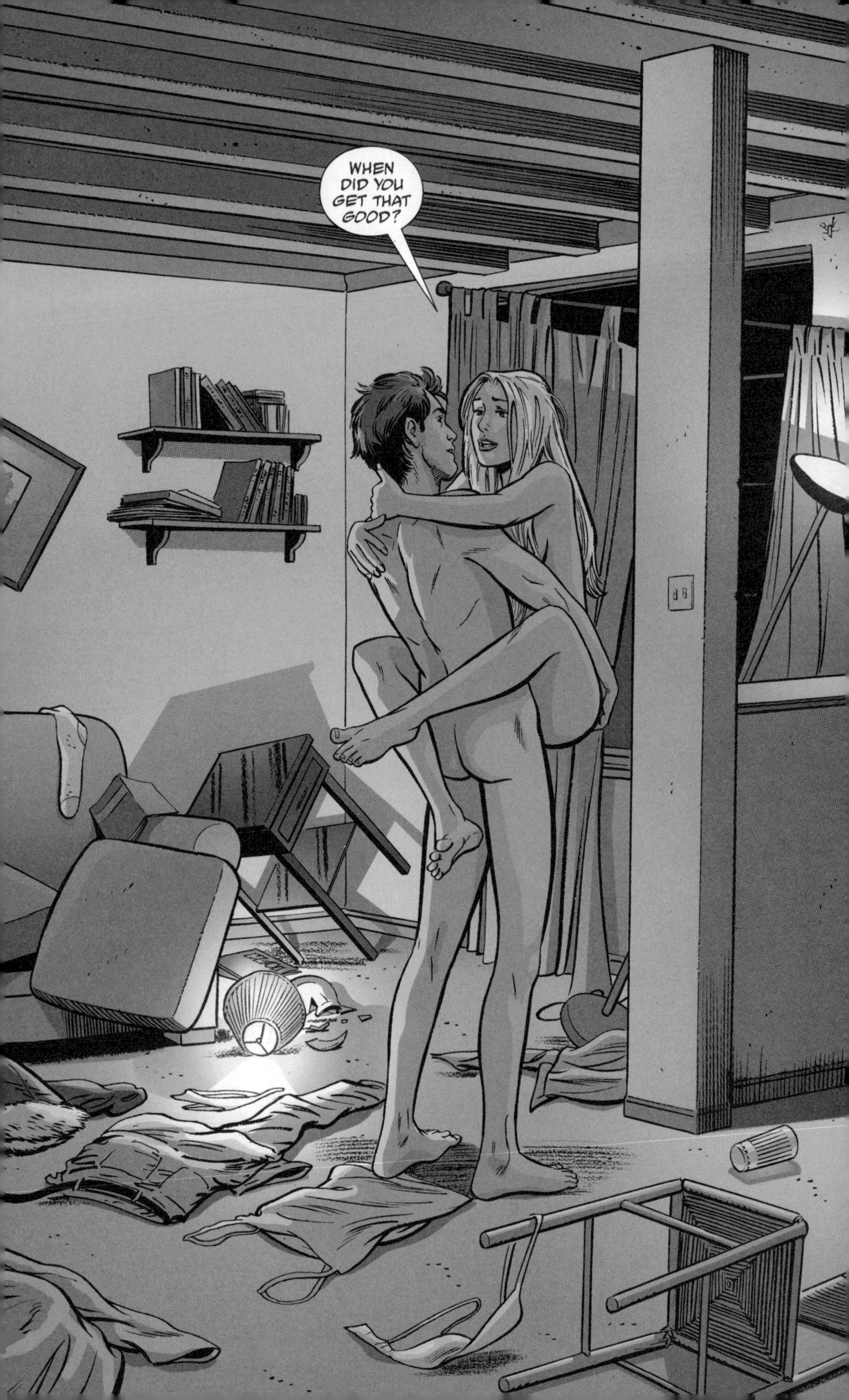
WHEN DID YOU GET THAT GOOD?

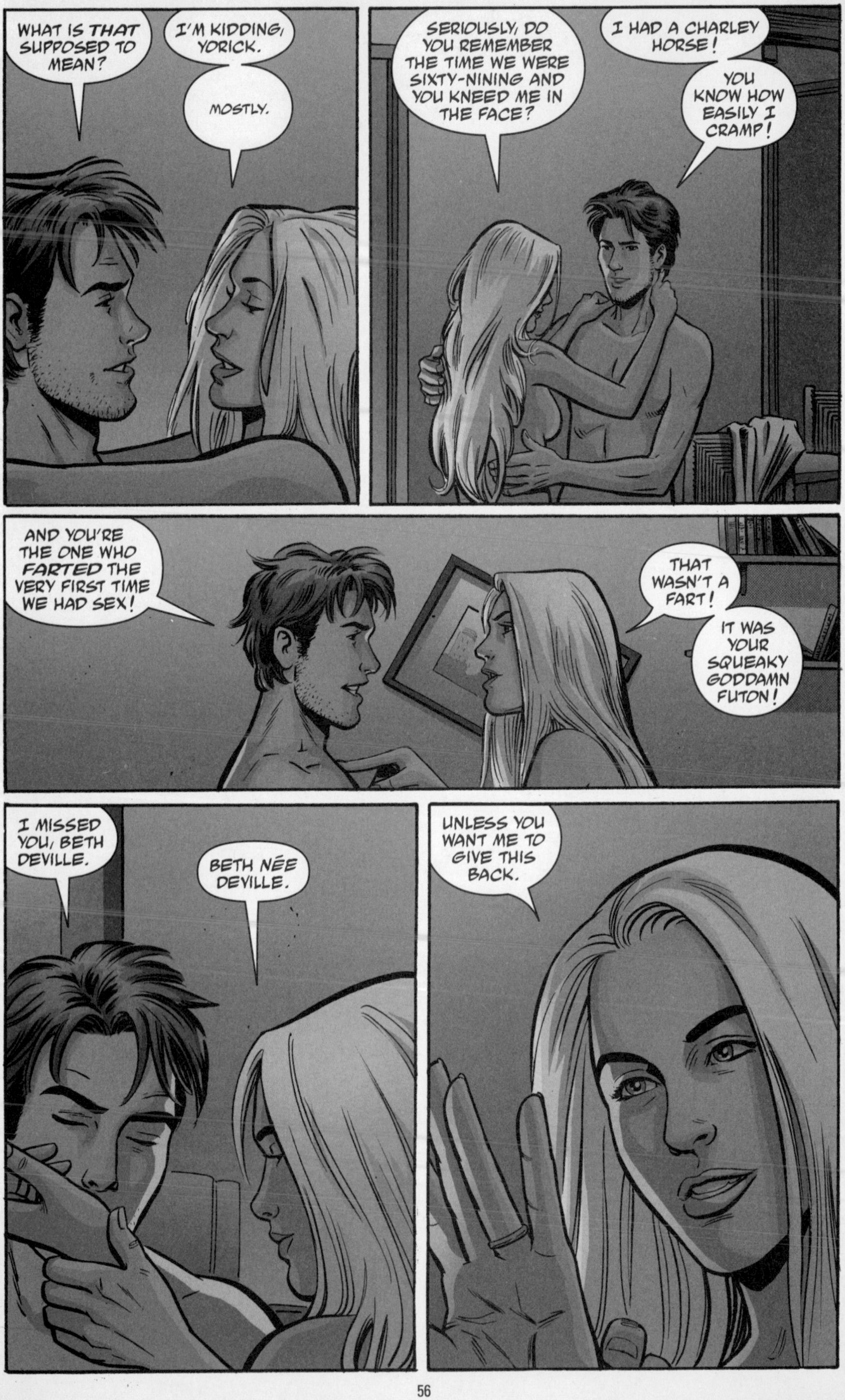

WHAT IS *THAT* SUPPOSED TO MEAN?
I'M KIDDING, YORICK.
MOSTLY.
SERIOUSLY, DO YOU REMEMBER THE TIME WE WERE SIXTY-NINING AND YOU KNEED ME IN THE FACE?
I HAD A CHARLEY HORSE!
YOU KNOW HOW EASILY I CRAMP!
AND YOU'RE THE ONE WHO *FARTED* THE VERY FIRST TIME WE HAD SEX!
THAT WASN'T A FART!
IT WAS YOUR SQUEAKY GODDAMN FUTON!
I MISSED YOU, BETH DEVILLE.
BETH NÉE DEVILLE.
UNLESS YOU WANT ME TO GIVE THIS BACK.

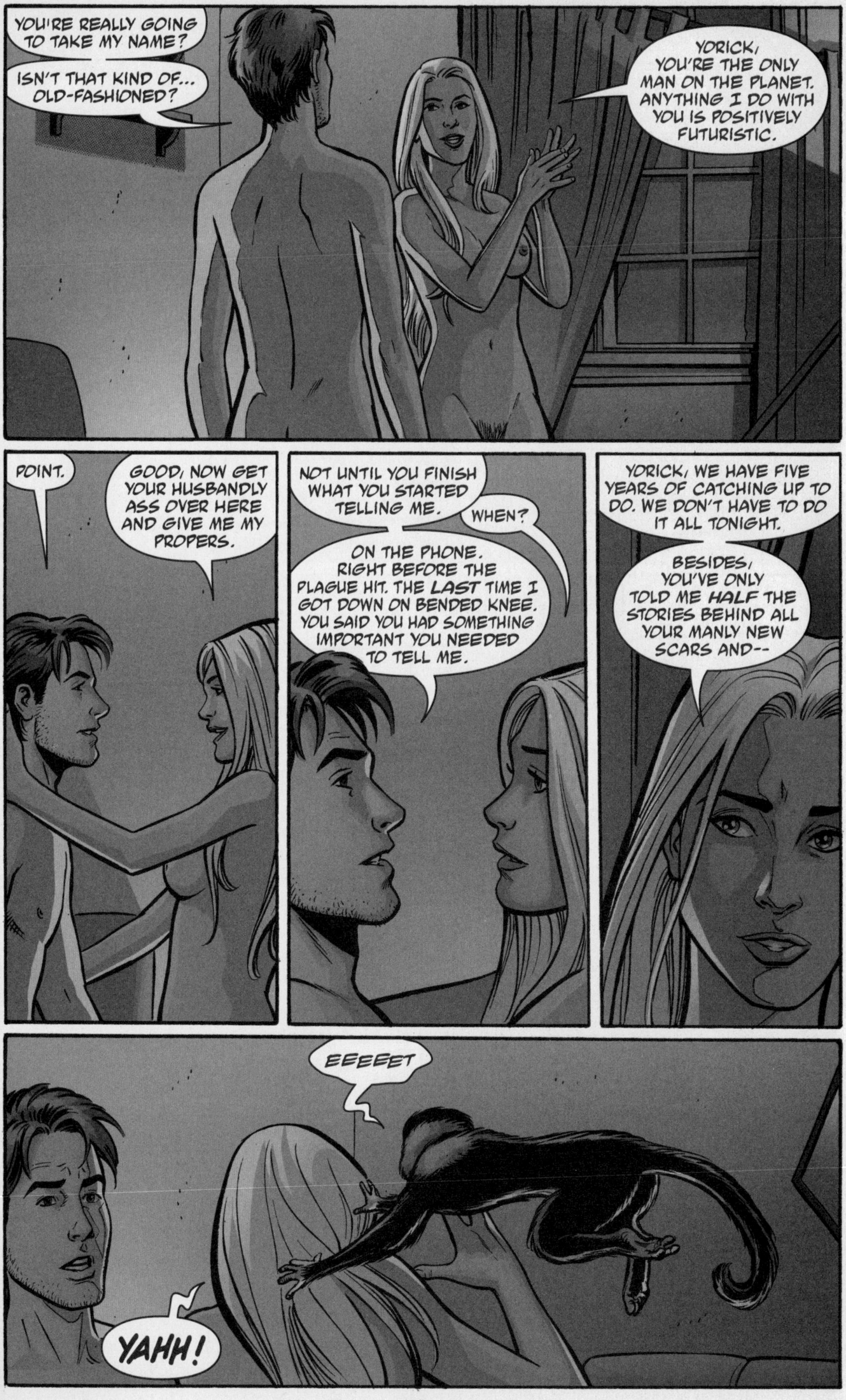
YOU'RE REALLY GOING TO TAKE MY NAME?
ISN'T THAT KIND OF... OLD-FASHIONED?
YORICK, YOU'RE THE ONLY MAN ON THE PLANET. ANYTHING I DO WITH YOU IS POSITIVELY FUTURISTIC.
POINT.
GOOD, NOW GET YOUR HUSBANDLY ASS OVER HERE AND GIVE ME MY PROPERS.
NOT UNTIL YOU FINISH WHAT YOU STARTED TELLING ME.
WHEN?
ON THE PHONE. RIGHT BEFORE THE PLAGUE HIT. THE LAST TIME I GOT DOWN ON BENDED KNEE. YOU SAID YOU HAD SOMETHING IMPORTANT YOU NEEDED TO TELL ME.
YORICK, WE HAVE FIVE YEARS OF CATCHING UP TO DO. WE DON'T HAVE TO DO IT ALL TONIGHT.
BESIDES, YOU'VE ONLY TOLD ME HALF THE STORIES BEHIND ALL YOUR MANLY NEW SCARS AND--
EEEEET
YAHH!

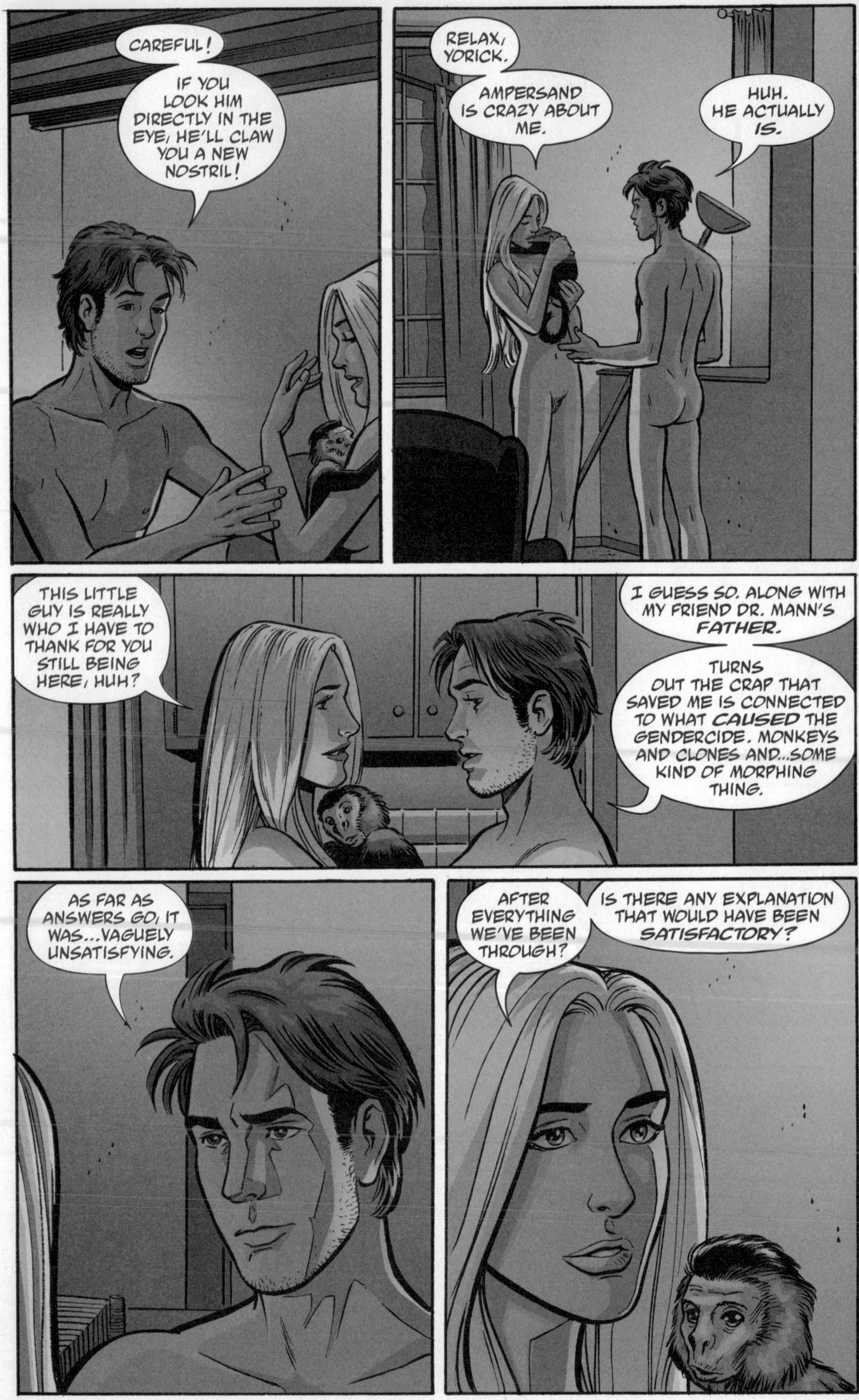

CAREFUL!
IF YOU LOOK HIM DIRECTLY IN THE EYE, HE'LL CLAW YOU A NEW NOSTRIL!
RELAX, YORICK.
AMPERSAND IS CRAZY ABOUT ME.
HUH. HE ACTUALLY *IS.*
THIS LITTLE GUY IS REALLY WHO I HAVE TO THANK FOR YOU STILL BEING HERE, HUH?
I GUESS SO. ALONG WITH MY FRIEND DR. MANN'S ***FATHER.***
TURNS OUT THE CRAP THAT SAVED ME IS CONNECTED TO WHAT ***CAUSED*** THE GENDERCIDE. MONKEYS AND CLONES AND...SOME KIND OF MORPHING THING.
AS FAR AS ANSWERS GO, IT WAS...VAGUELY UNSATISFYING.
AFTER EVERYTHING WE'VE BEEN THROUGH?
IS THERE ANY EXPLANATION THAT WOULD HAVE BEEN ***SATISFACTORY?***

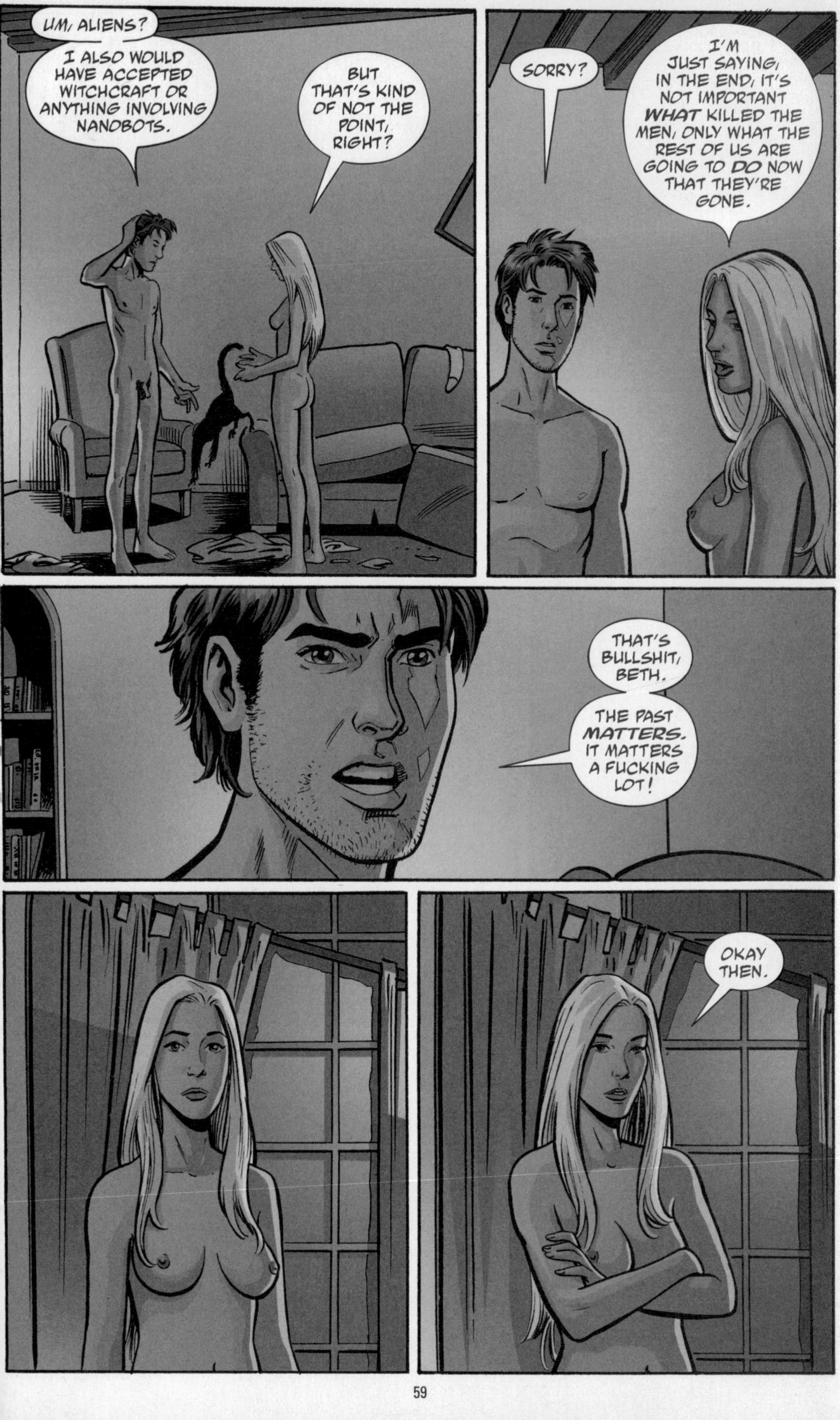
UM, ALIENS?
I ALSO WOULD HAVE ACCEPTED WITCHCRAFT OR ANYTHING INVOLVING NANOBOTS.
BUT THAT'S KIND OF NOT THE POINT, RIGHT?
SORRY?
I'M JUST SAYING, IN THE END, IT'S NOT IMPORTANT WHAT KILLED THE MEN, ONLY WHAT THE REST OF US ARE GOING TO DO NOW THAT THEY'RE GONE.
THAT'S BULLSHIT, BETH.
THE PAST MATTERS. IT MATTERS A FUCKING LOT!
OKAY THEN.

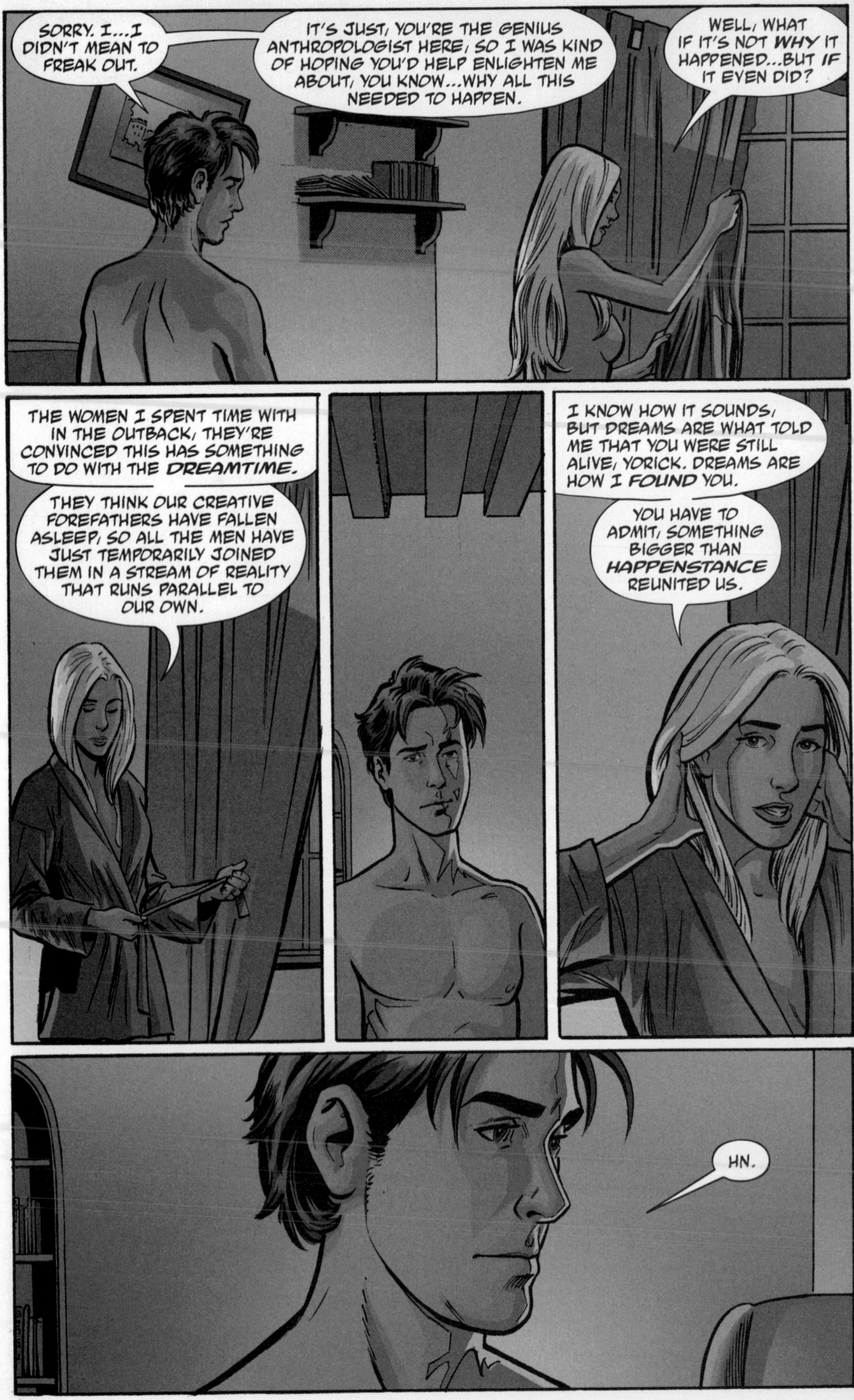
SORRY. I...I DIDN'T MEAN TO FREAK OUT.
IT'S JUST, YOU'RE THE GENIUS ANTHROPOLOGIST HERE, SO I WAS KIND OF HOPING YOU'D HELP ENLIGHTEN ME ABOUT, YOU KNOW...WHY ALL THIS NEEDED TO HAPPEN.
WELL, WHAT IF IT'S NOT *WHY* IT HAPPENED...BUT *IF* IT EVEN DID?
THE WOMEN I SPENT TIME WITH IN THE OUTBACK, THEY'RE CONVINCED THIS HAS SOMETHING TO DO WITH THE *DREAMTIME.*
THEY THINK OUR CREATIVE FOREFATHERS HAVE FALLEN ASLEEP, SO ALL THE MEN HAVE JUST TEMPORARILY JOINED THEM IN A STREAM OF REALITY THAT RUNS PARALLEL TO OUR OWN.
I KNOW HOW IT SOUNDS, BUT DREAMS ARE WHAT TOLD ME THAT YOU WERE STILL ALIVE, YORICK. DREAMS ARE HOW I *FOUND* YOU.
YOU HAVE TO ADMIT, SOMETHING BIGGER THAN *HAPPENSTANCE* REUNITED US.
HN.

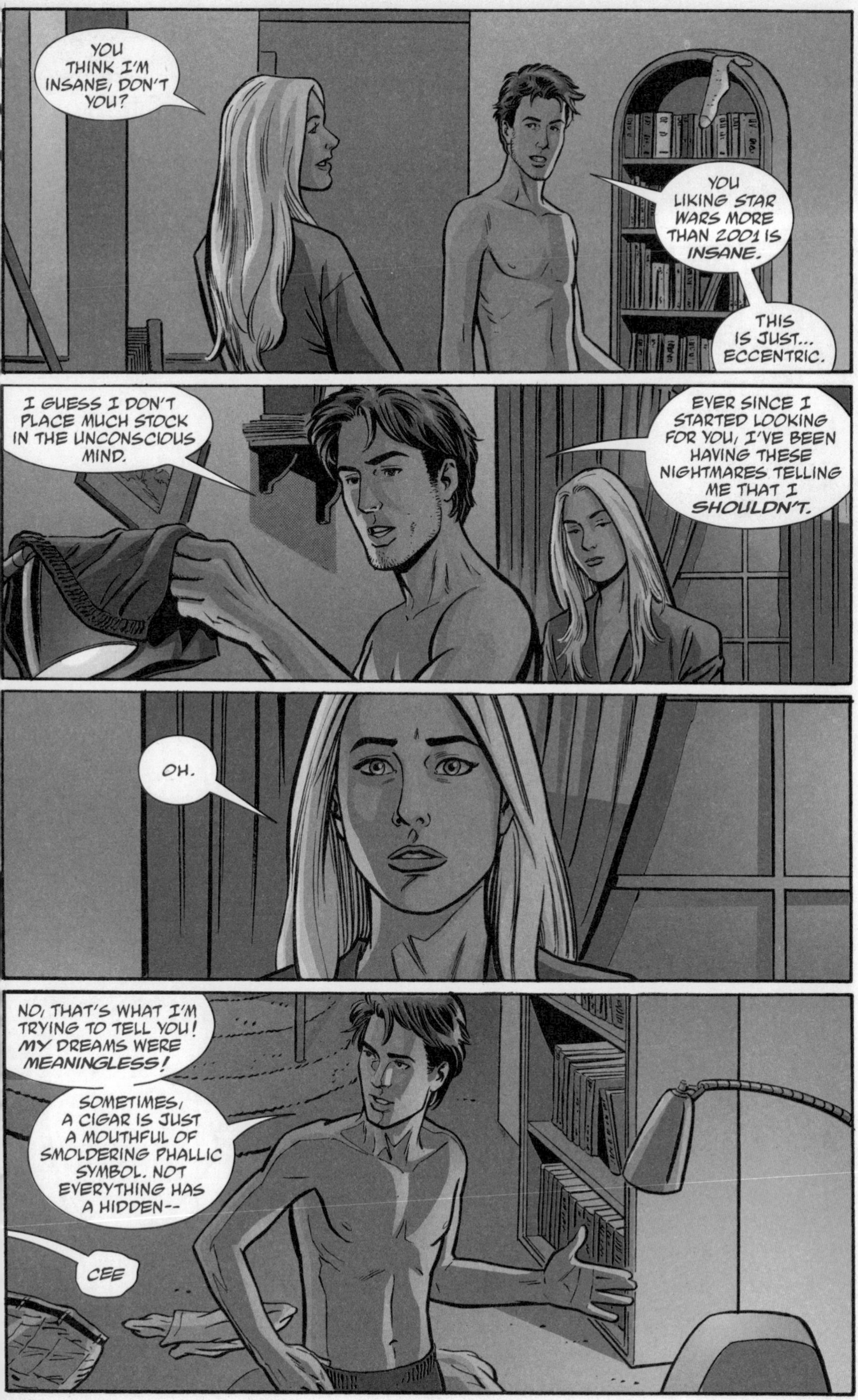
YOU THINK I'M INSANE, DON'T YOU?
YOU LIKING STAR WARS MORE THAN 2001 IS INSANE.
THIS IS JUST... ECCENTRIC.
I GUESS I DON'T PLACE MUCH STOCK IN THE UNCONSCIOUS MIND.
EVER SINCE I STARTED LOOKING FOR YOU, I'VE BEEN HAVING THESE NIGHTMARES TELLING ME THAT I SHOULDN'T.
OH.
NO, THAT'S WHAT I'M TRYING TO TELL YOU! MY DREAMS WERE MEANINGLESS!
SOMETIMES, A CIGAR IS JUST A MOUTHFUL OF SMOLDERING PHALLIC SYMBOL. NOT EVERYTHING HAS A HIDDEN--
CEE

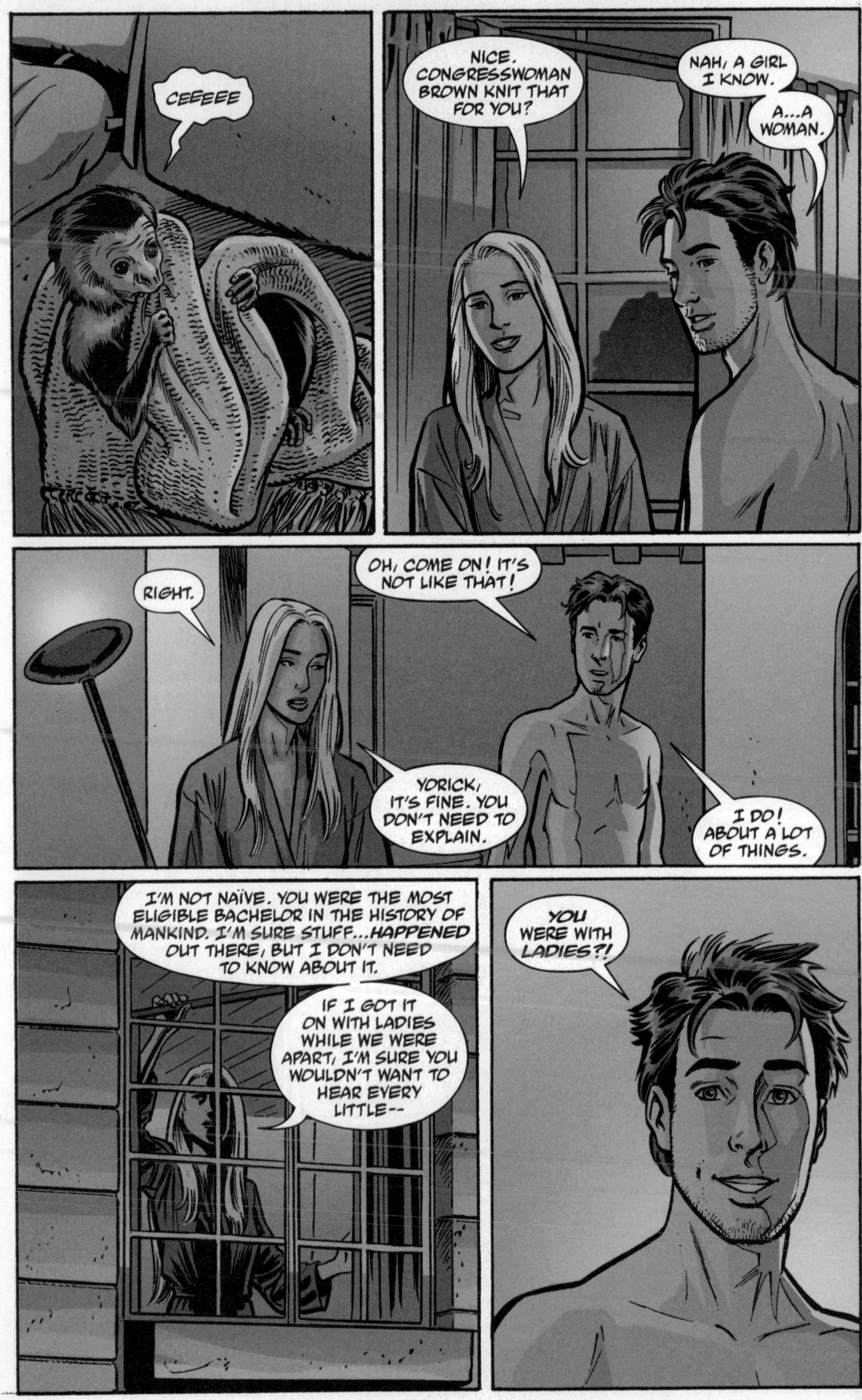

CEEEEE
NICE. CONGRESSWOMAN BROWN KNIT THAT FOR YOU?
NAH, A GIRL I KNOW.
A...A WOMAN.
RIGHT.
OH, COME ON! IT'S NOT LIKE THAT!
YORICK, IT'S FINE. YOU DON'T NEED TO EXPLAIN.
I DO! ABOUT A LOT OF THINGS.
I'M NOT NAÏVE. YOU WERE THE MOST ELIGIBLE BACHELOR IN THE HISTORY OF MANKIND. I'M SURE STUFF...HAPPENED OUT THERE, BUT I DON'T NEED TO KNOW ABOUT IT.
IF I GOT IT ON WITH LADIES WHILE WE WERE APART, I'M SURE YOU WOULDN'T WANT TO HEAR EVERY LITTLE--
YOU WERE WITH LADIES?!

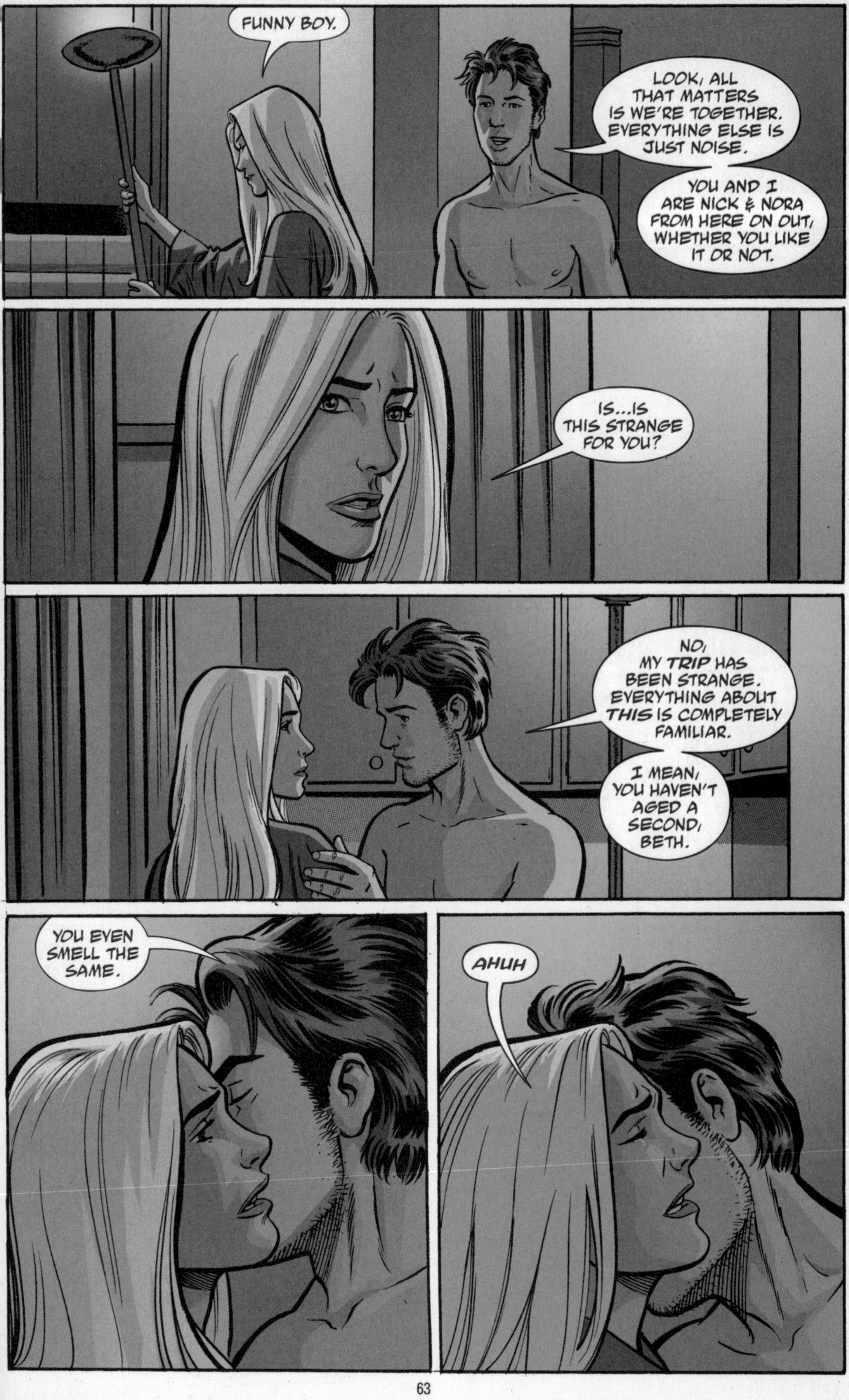
FUNNY BOY.
LOOK, ALL THAT MATTERS IS WE'RE TOGETHER. EVERYTHING ELSE IS JUST NOISE.
YOU AND I ARE NICK & NORA FROM HERE ON OUT, WHETHER YOU LIKE IT OR NOT.
IS...IS THIS STRANGE FOR YOU?
NO, MY *TRIP* HAS BEEN STRANGE. EVERYTHING ABOUT *THIS* IS COMPLETELY FAMILIAR.
I MEAN, YOU HAVEN'T AGED A SECOND, BETH.
YOU EVEN SMELL THE SAME.
AHUH

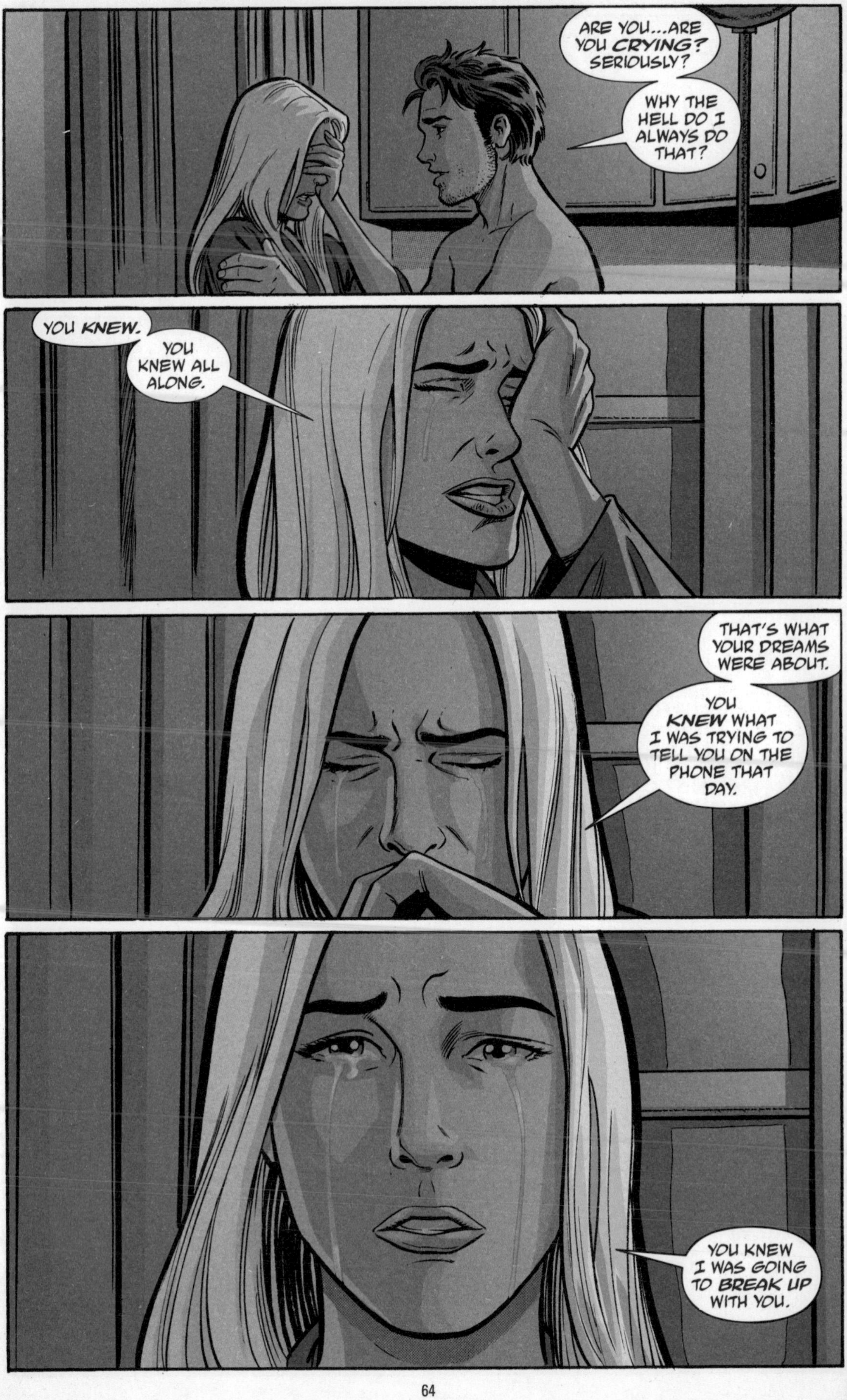
ARE YOU...ARE YOU CRYING? SERIOUSLY?
WHY THE HELL DO I ALWAYS DO THAT?
YOU KNEW.
YOU KNEW ALL ALONG.
THAT'S WHAT YOUR DREAMS WERE ABOUT.
YOU KNEW WHAT I WAS TRYING TO TELL YOU ON THE PHONE THAT DAY.
YOU KNEW I WAS GOING TO BREAK UP WITH YOU.

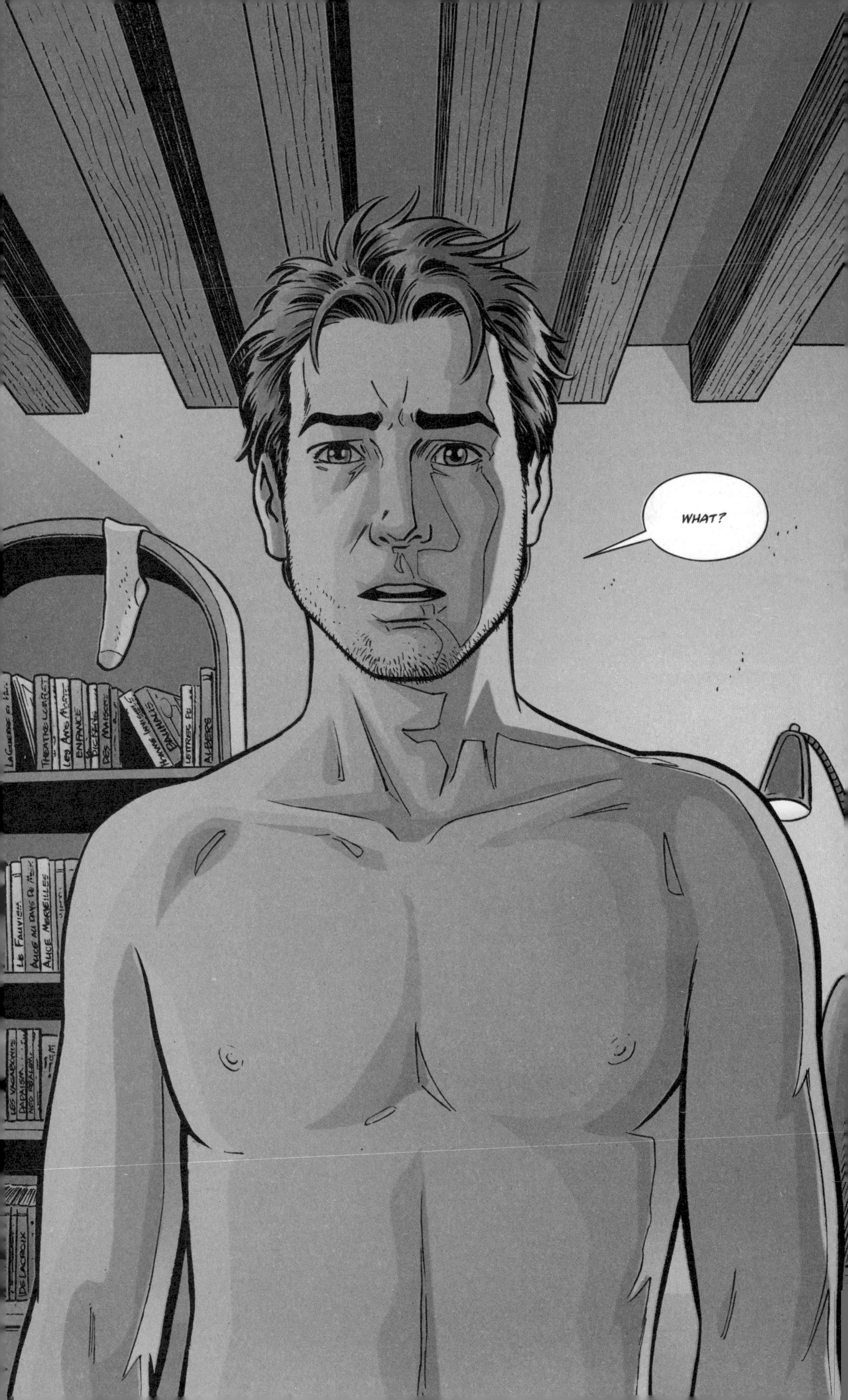
WHAT?

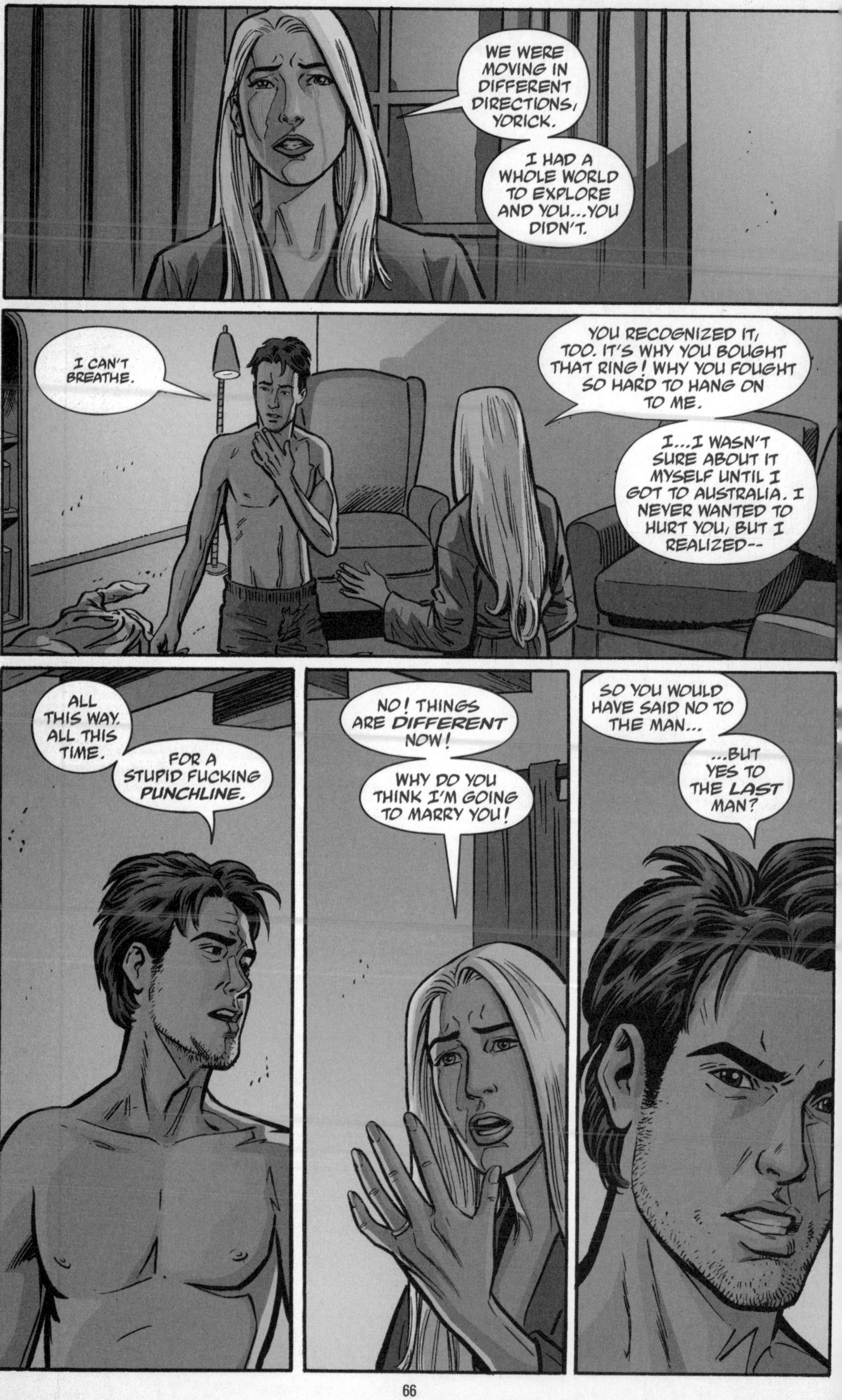
WE WERE MOVING IN DIFFERENT DIRECTIONS, YORICK.
I HAD A WHOLE WORLD TO EXPLORE AND YOU...YOU DIDN'T.
I CAN'T BREATHE.
YOU RECOGNIZED IT, TOO. IT'S WHY YOU BOUGHT THAT RING! WHY YOU FOUGHT SO HARD TO HANG ON TO ME.
I...I WASN'T SURE ABOUT IT MYSELF UNTIL I GOT TO AUSTRALIA. I NEVER WANTED TO HURT YOU, BUT I REALIZED--
ALL THIS WAY. ALL THIS TIME.
FOR A STUPID FUCKING PUNCHLINE.
NO! THINGS ARE DIFFERENT NOW!
WHY DO YOU THINK I'M GOING TO MARRY YOU!
SO YOU WOULD HAVE SAID NO TO THE MAN...
...BUT YES TO THE LAST MAN?

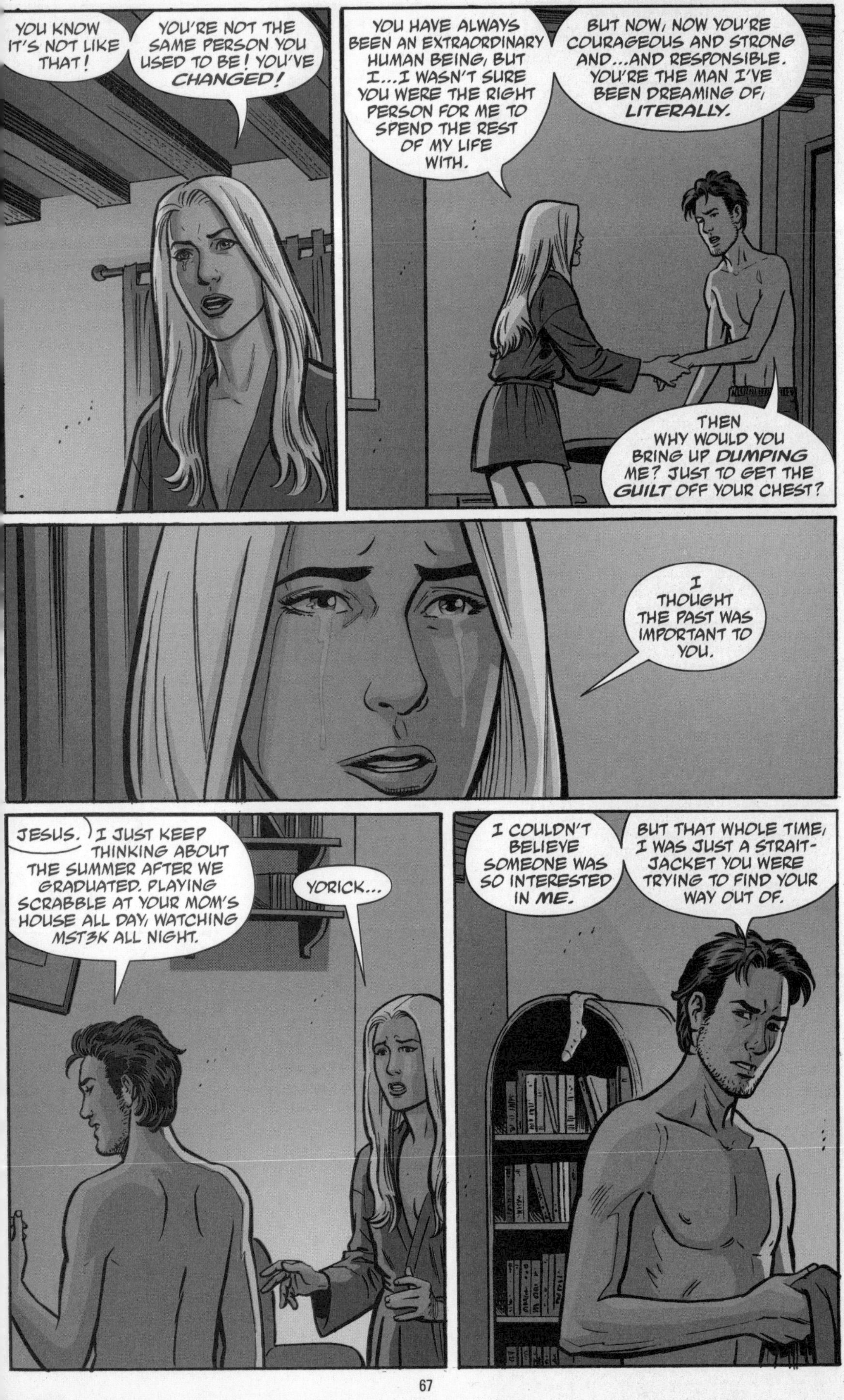
YOU KNOW IT'S NOT LIKE THAT!
YOU'RE NOT THE SAME PERSON YOU USED TO BE! YOU'VE *CHANGED!*
YOU HAVE ALWAYS BEEN AN EXTRAORDINARY HUMAN BEING, BUT I...I WASN'T SURE YOU WERE THE RIGHT PERSON FOR ME TO SPEND THE REST OF MY LIFE WITH.
BUT NOW, NOW YOU'RE COURAGEOUS AND STRONG AND...AND RESPONSIBLE. YOU'RE THE MAN I'VE BEEN DREAMING OF, *LITERALLY.*
THEN WHY WOULD YOU BRING UP *DUMPING* ME? JUST TO GET THE *GUILT* OFF YOUR CHEST?
I THOUGHT THE PAST WAS IMPORTANT TO YOU.
JESUS.
I JUST KEEP THINKING ABOUT THE SUMMER AFTER WE GRADUATED. PLAYING SCRABBLE AT YOUR MOM'S HOUSE ALL DAY, WATCHING MST3K ALL NIGHT.
YORICK...
I COULDN'T BELIEVE SOMEONE WAS SO INTERESTED IN *ME.*
BUT THAT WHOLE TIME, I WAS JUST A STRAIT-JACKET YOU WERE TRYING TO FIND YOUR WAY OUT OF.

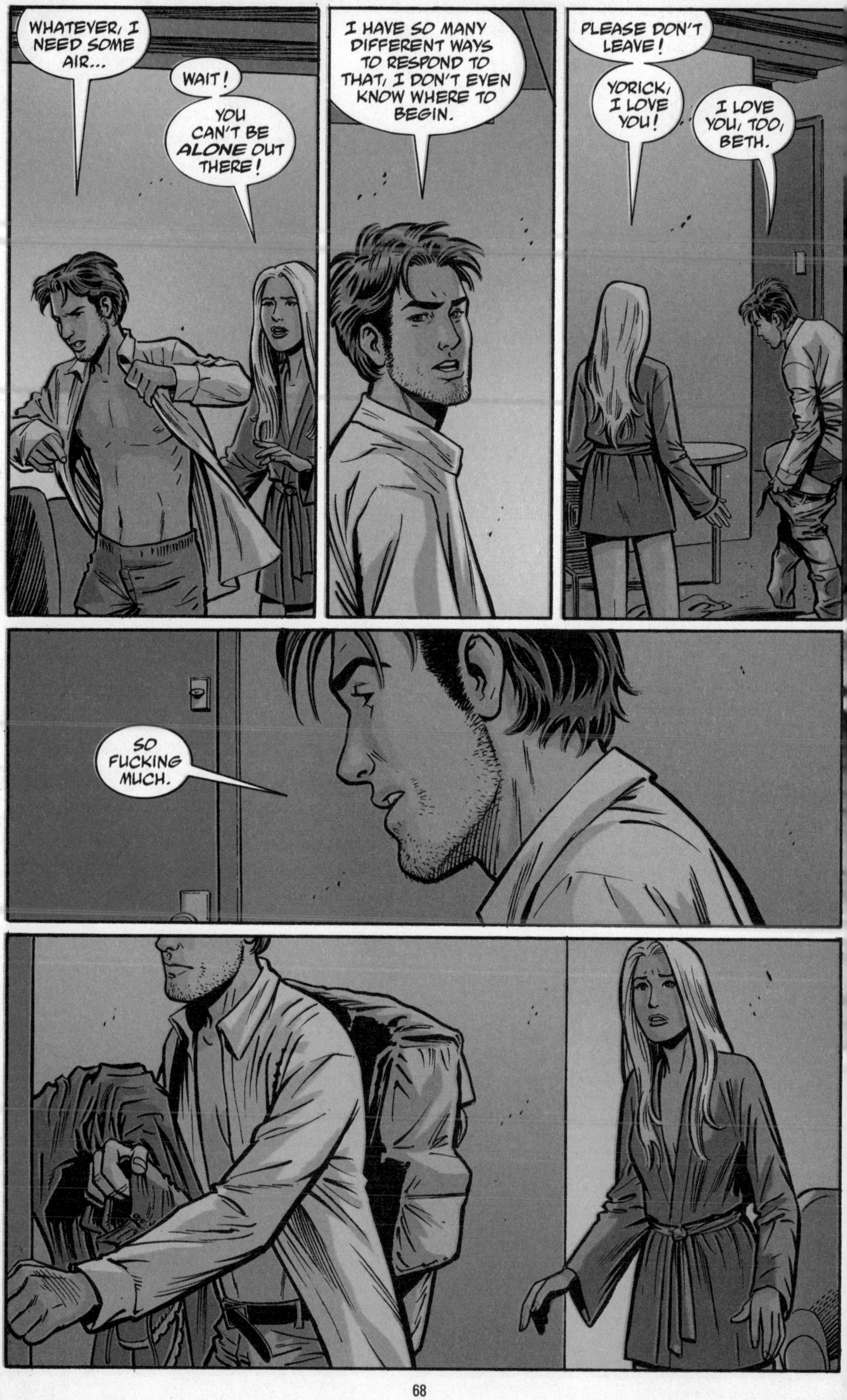
WHATEVER, I NEED SOME AIR...
WAIT!
YOU CAN'T BE ALONE OUT THERE!
I HAVE SO MANY DIFFERENT WAYS TO RESPOND TO THAT, I DON'T EVEN KNOW WHERE TO BEGIN.
PLEASE DON'T LEAVE!
YORICK, I LOVE YOU!
I LOVE YOU, TOO, BETH.
SO FUCKING MUCH.

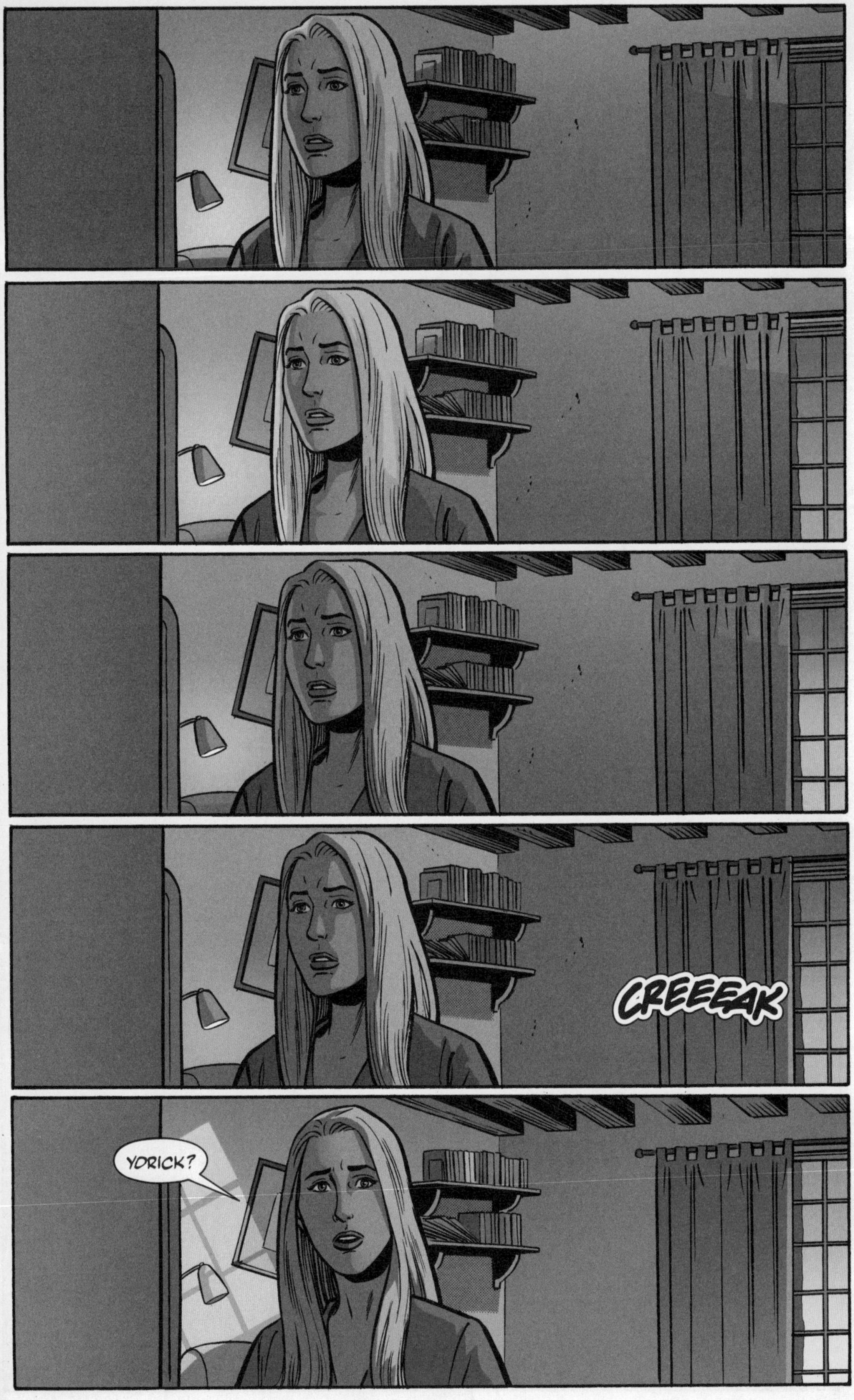
CREEEAK
YORICK?

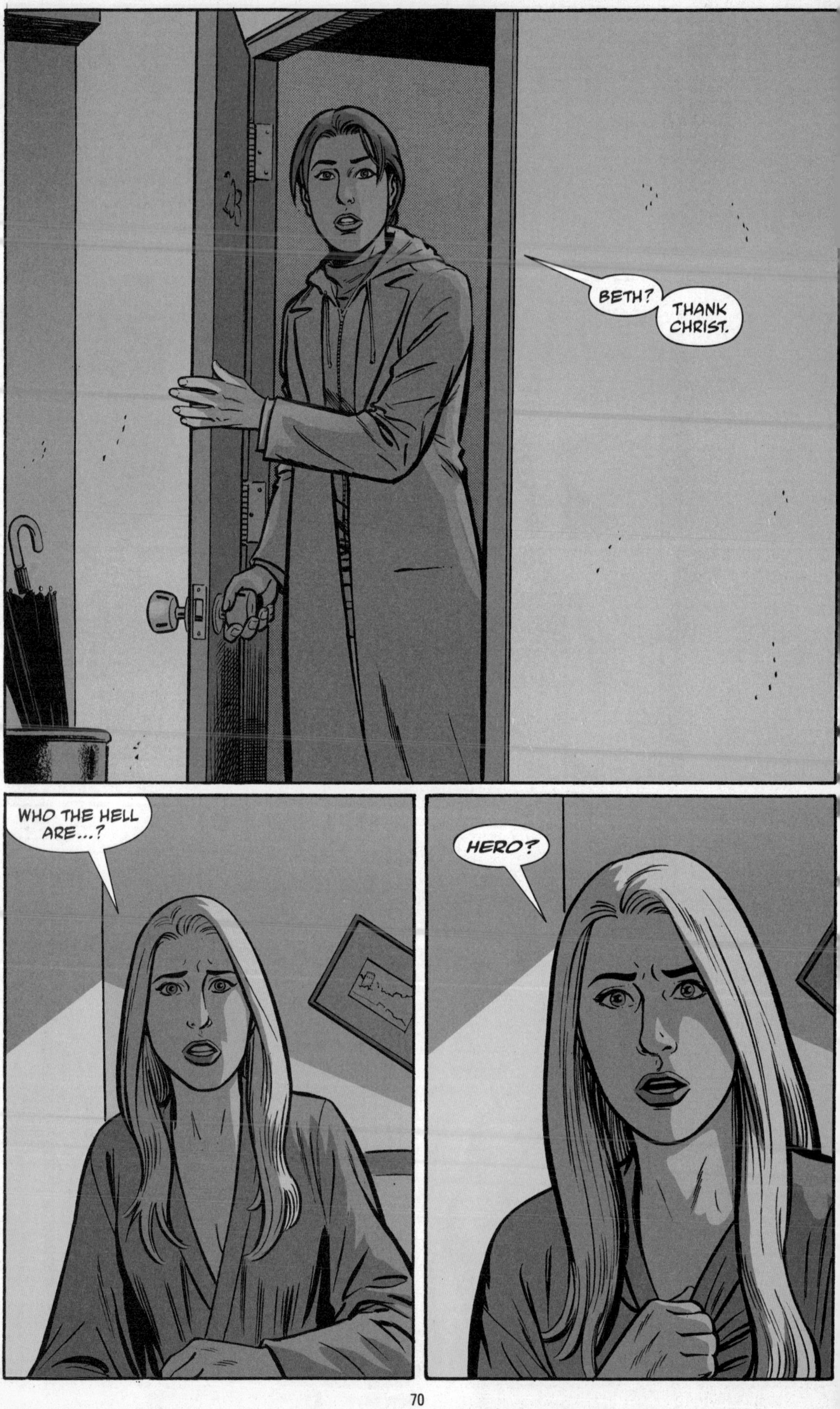
BETH?
THANK CHRIST.
WHO THE HELL ARE...?
HERO?

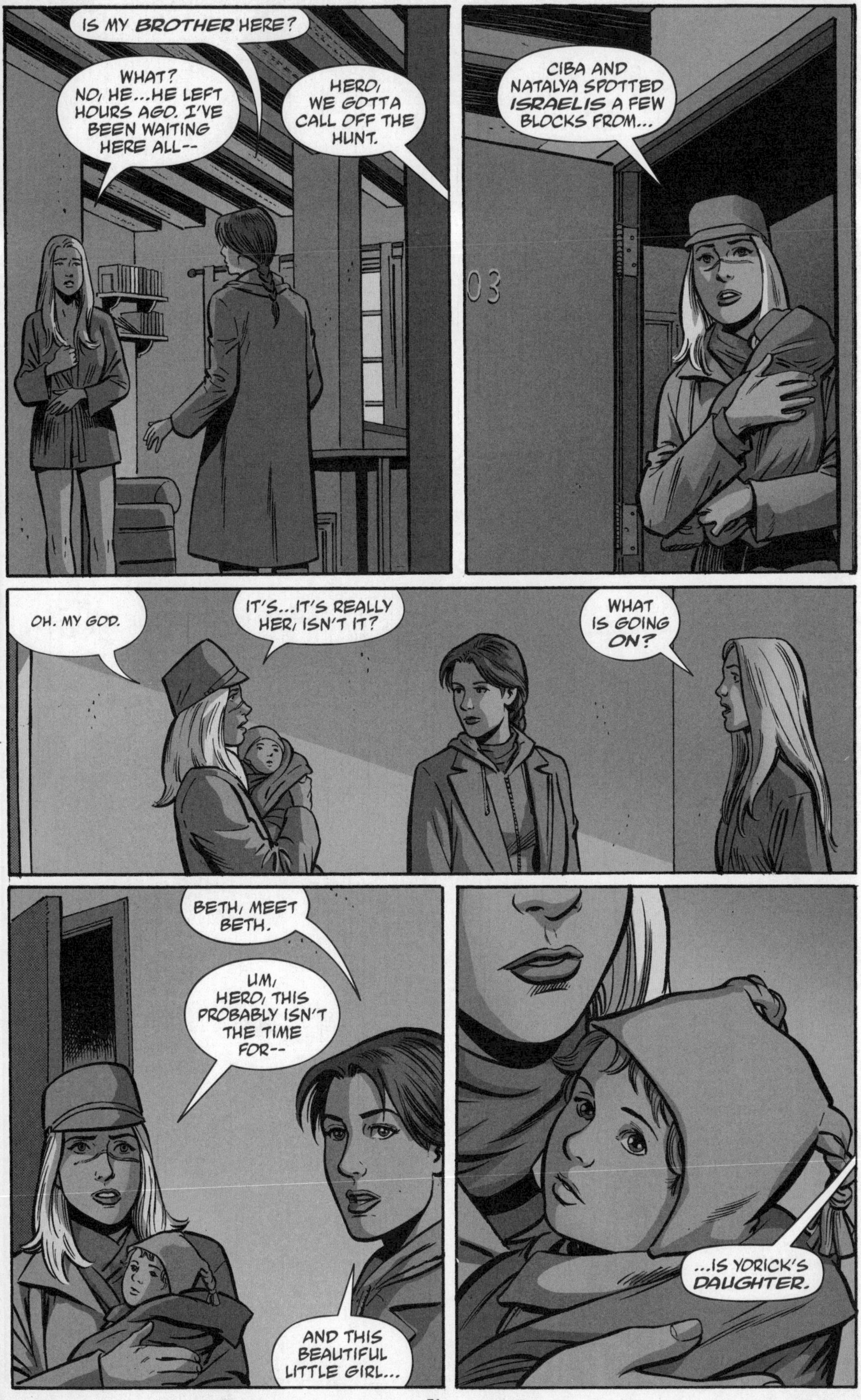
IS MY BROTHER HERE?
WHAT? NO, HE...HE LEFT HOURS AGO. I'VE BEEN WAITING HERE ALL--
HERO, WE GOTTA CALL OFF THE HUNT.
CIBA AND NATALYA SPOTTED ISRAELIS A FEW BLOCKS FROM...
03
OH. MY GOD.
IT'S...IT'S REALLY HER, ISN'T IT?
WHAT IS GOING ON?
BETH, MEET BETH.
UM, HERO, THIS PROBABLY ISN'T THE TIME FOR--
AND THIS BEAUTIFUL LITTLE GIRL...
...IS YORICK'S DAUGHTER.

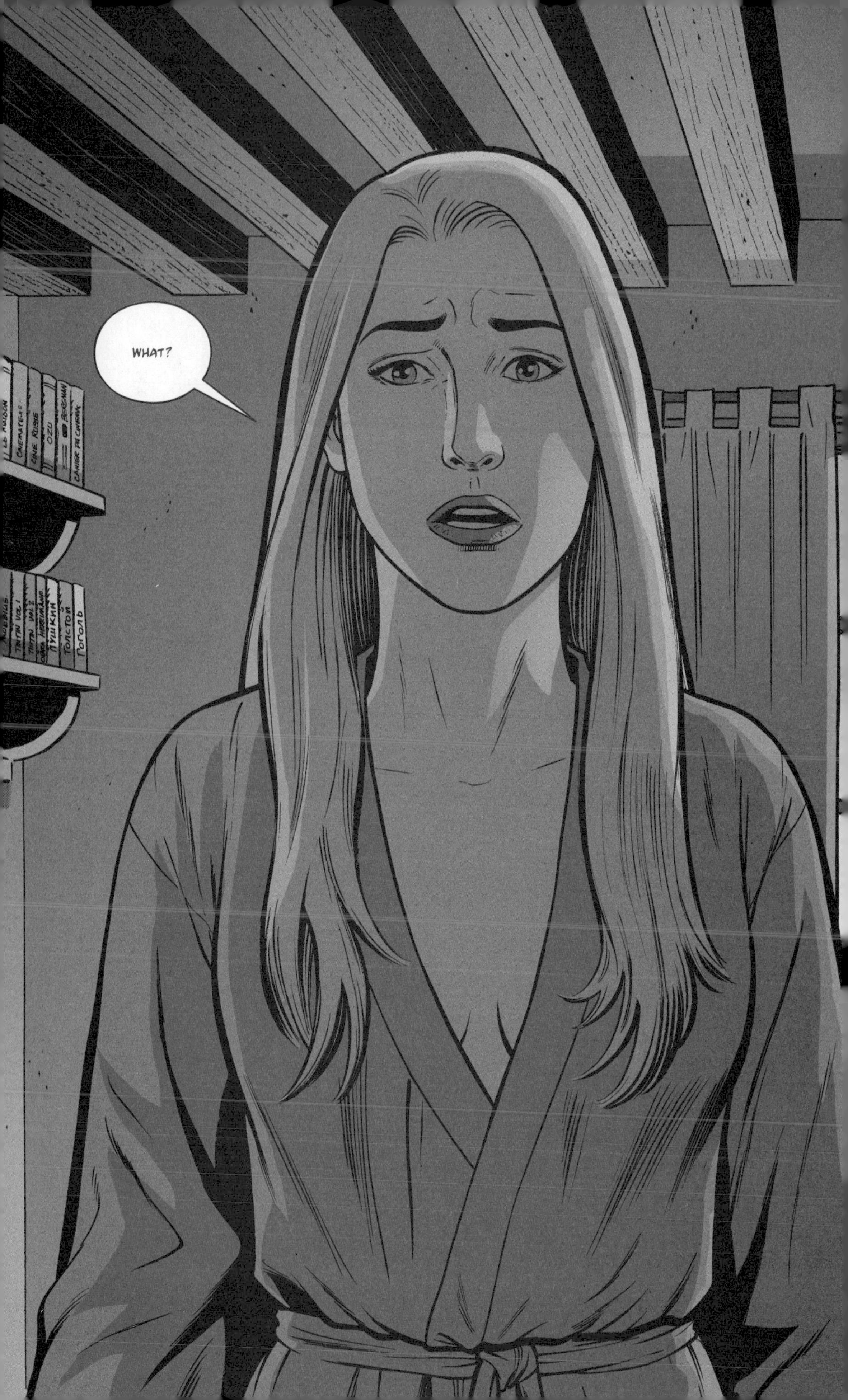
WHAT?

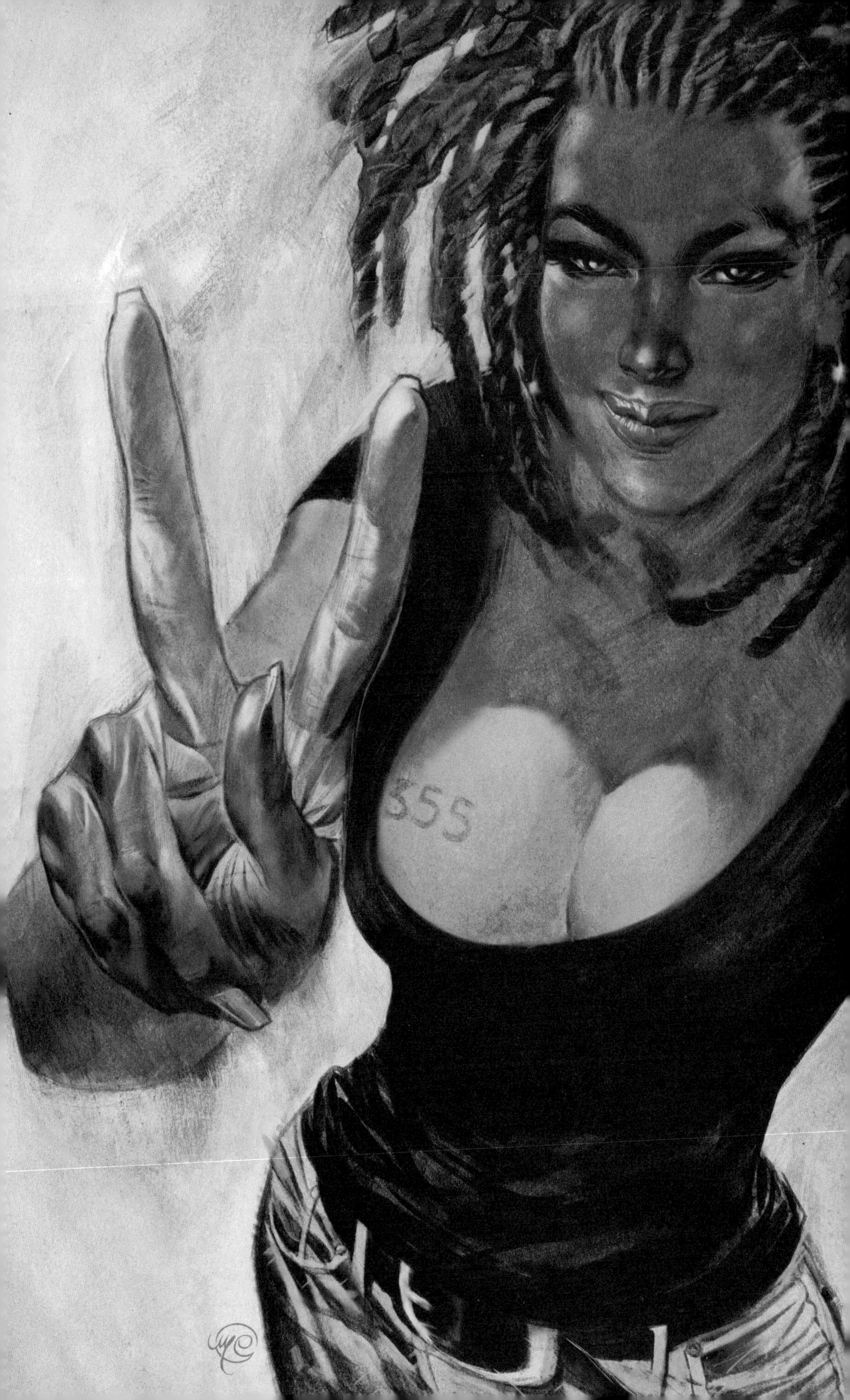

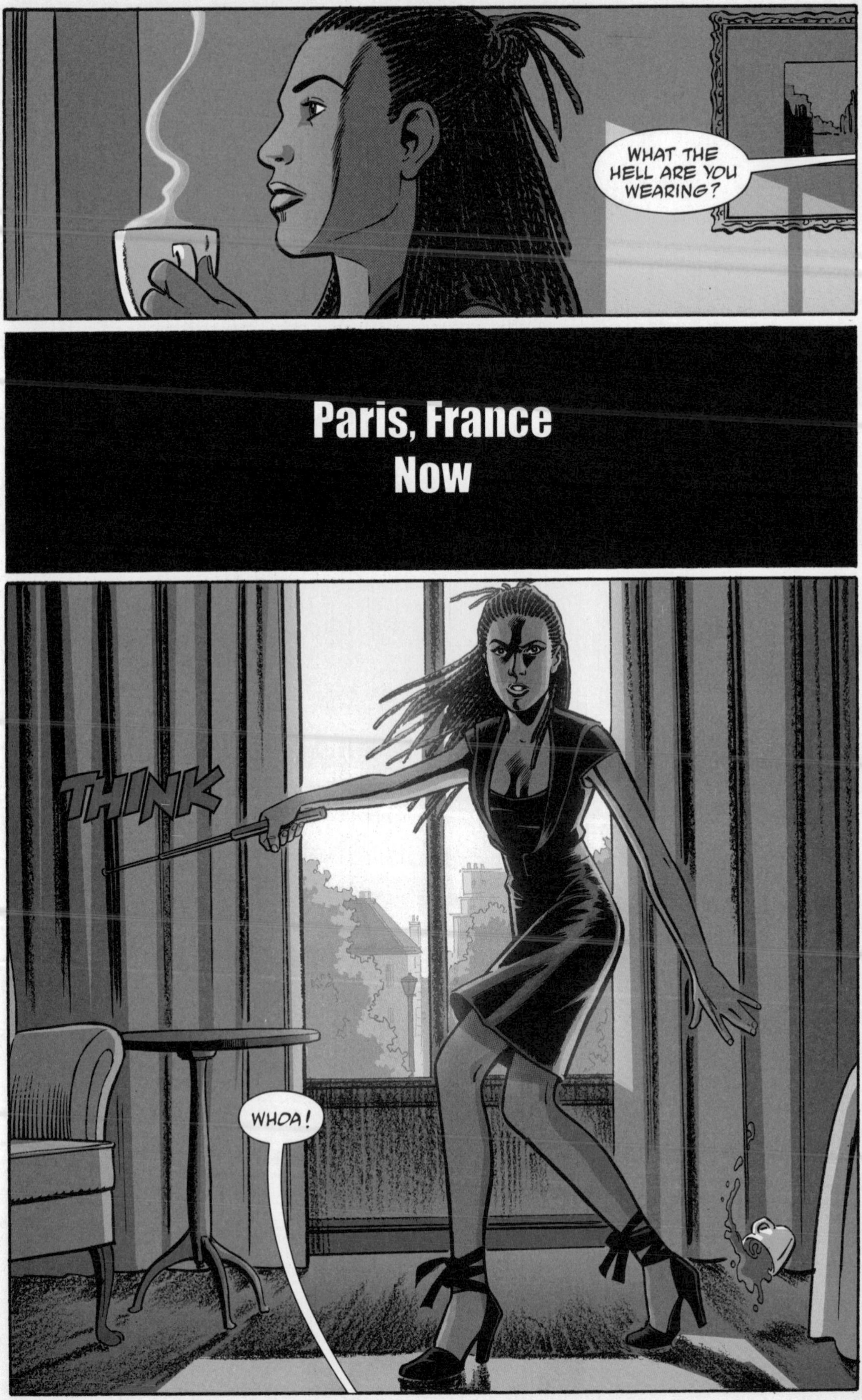
WHAT THE HELL ARE YOU WEARING?
Paris, France
Now
THINK
WHOA!

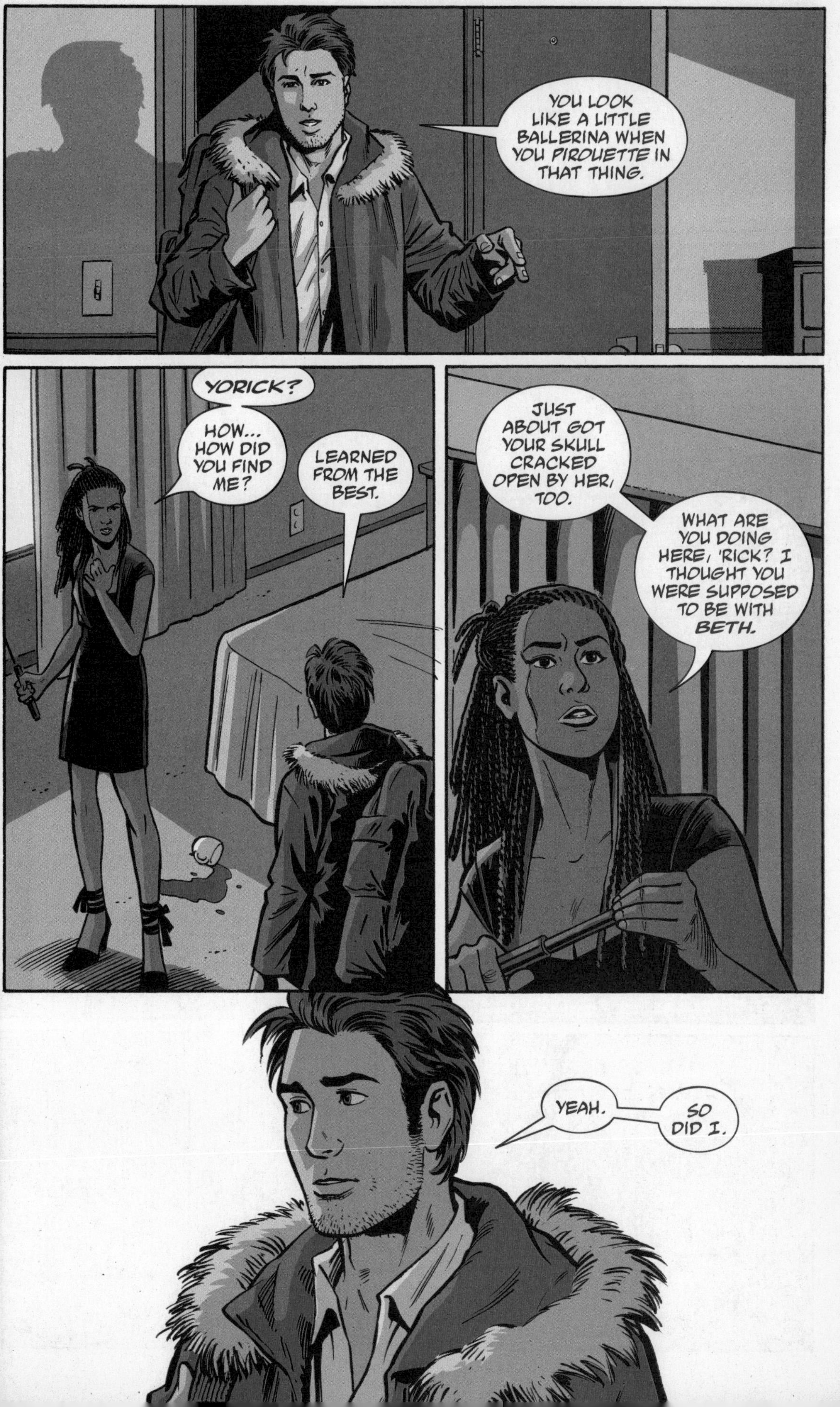
YOU LOOK LIKE A LITTLE BALLERINA WHEN YOU PIROUETTE IN THAT THING.
YORICK?
HOW... HOW DID YOU FIND ME?
LEARNED FROM THE BEST.
JUST ABOUT GOT YOUR SKULL CRACKED OPEN BY HER, TOO.
WHAT ARE YOU DOING HERE, 'RICK? I THOUGHT YOU WERE SUPPOSED TO BE WITH BETH.
YEAH.
SO DID I.

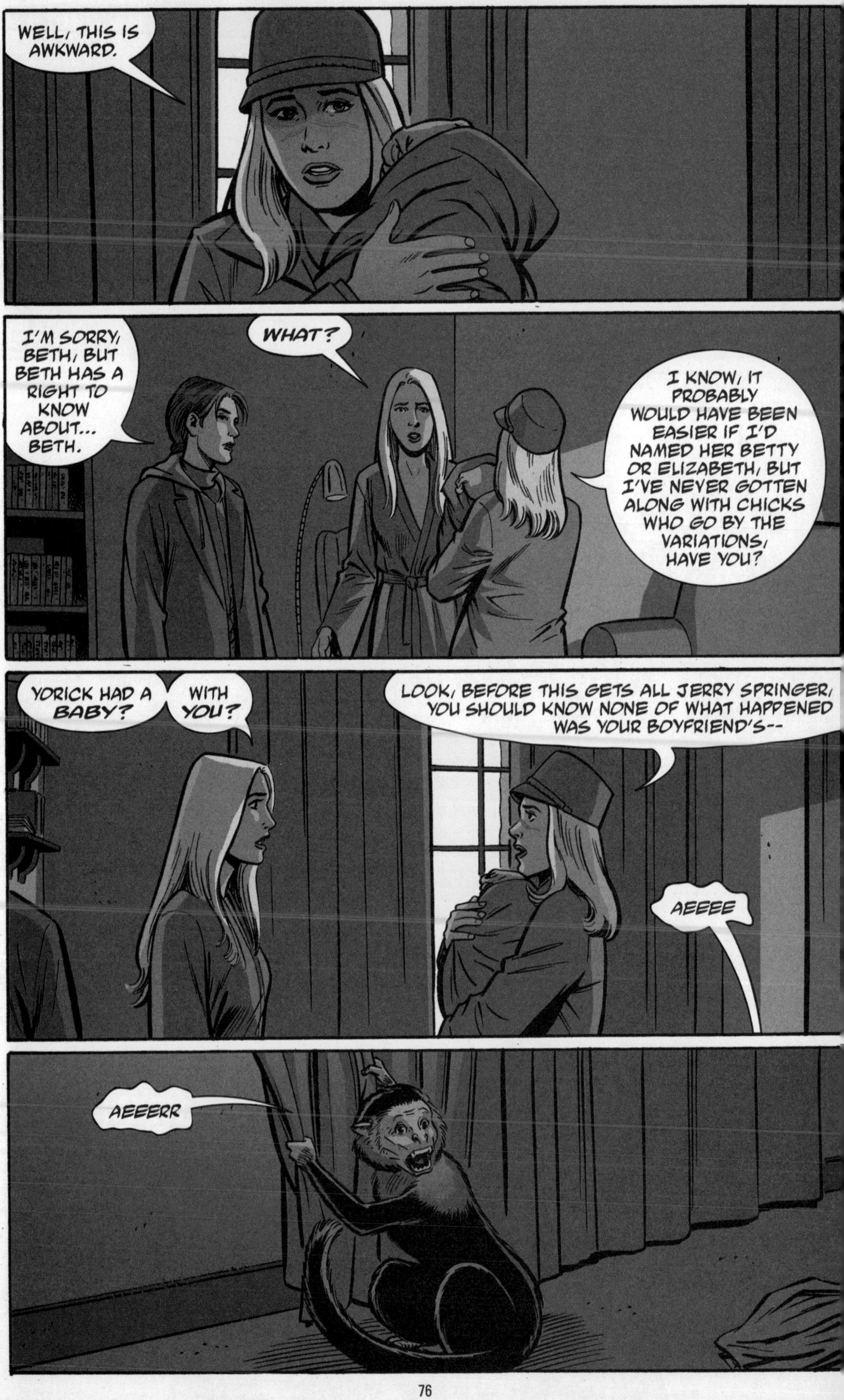
WELL, THIS IS AWKWARD.
I'M SORRY, BETH, BUT BETH HAS A RIGHT TO KNOW ABOUT... BETH.
WHAT?
I KNOW, IT PROBABLY WOULD HAVE BEEN EASIER IF I'D NAMED HER BETTY OR ELIZABETH, BUT I'VE NEVER GOTTEN ALONG WITH CHICKS WHO GO BY THE VARIATIONS, HAVE YOU?
YORICK HAD A BABY?
WITH YOU?
LOOK, BEFORE THIS GETS ALL JERRY SPRINGER, YOU SHOULD KNOW NONE OF WHAT HAPPENED WAS YOUR BOYFRIEND'S--
AEEEE
AEEERR

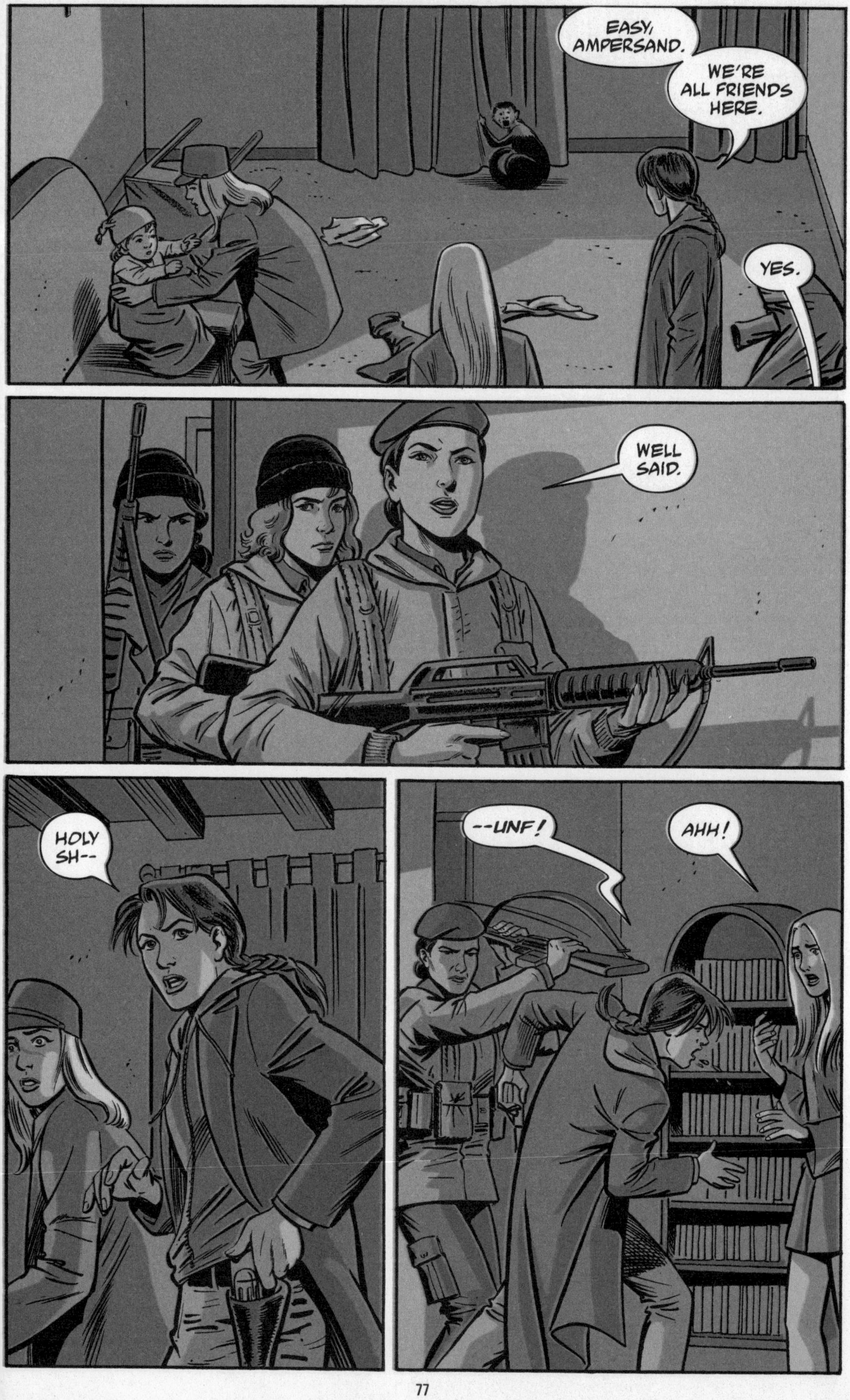
EASY, AMPERSAND.
WE'RE ALL FRIENDS HERE.
YES.
WELL SAID.
HOLY SH--
--UNF!
AHH!

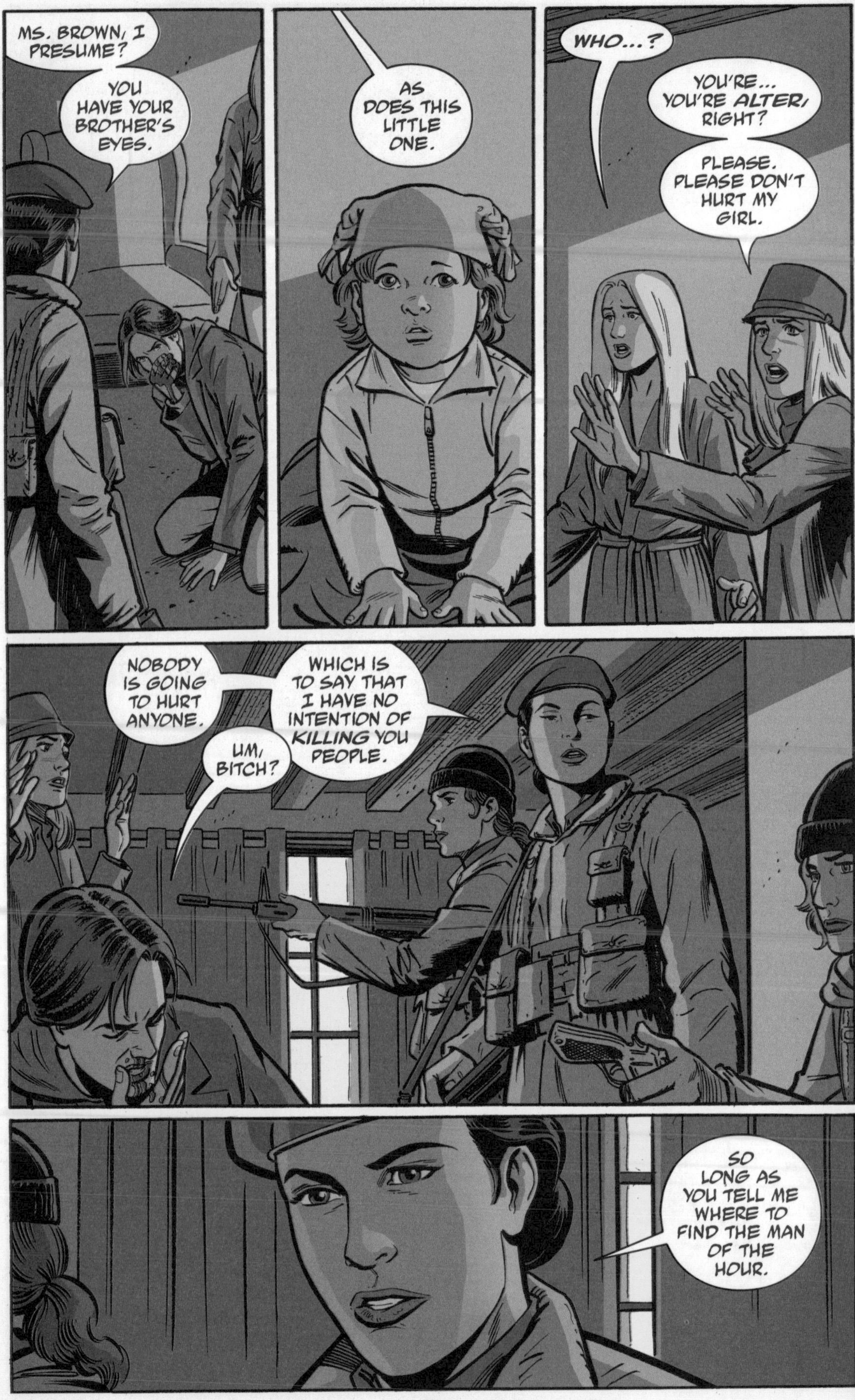
MS. BROWN, I PRESUME?
YOU HAVE YOUR BROTHER'S EYES.
AS DOES THIS LITTLE ONE.
WHO...?
YOU'RE... YOU'RE ALTER, RIGHT?
PLEASE. PLEASE DON'T HURT MY GIRL.
NOBODY IS GOING TO HURT ANYONE.
WHICH IS TO SAY THAT I HAVE NO INTENTION OF KILLING YOU PEOPLE.
UM, BITCH?
SO LONG AS YOU TELL ME WHERE TO FIND THE MAN OF THE HOUR.

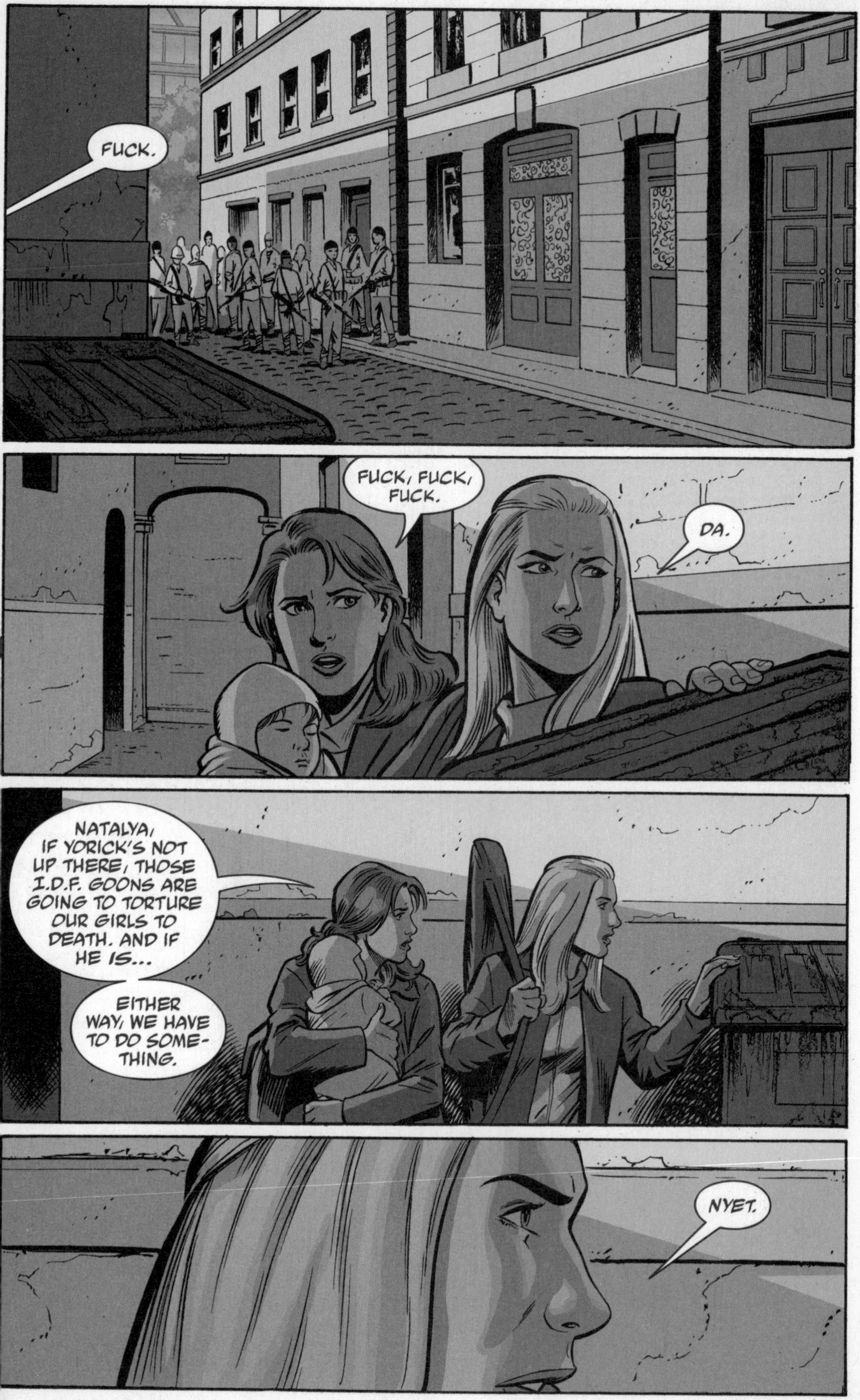
FUCK.
FUCK, FUCK, FUCK.
DA.
NATALYA, IF YORICK'S NOT UP THERE, THOSE I.D.F. GOONS ARE GOING TO TORTURE OUR GIRLS TO DEATH. AND IF HE IS...
EITHER WAY, WE HAVE TO DO SOME-THING.
NYET.

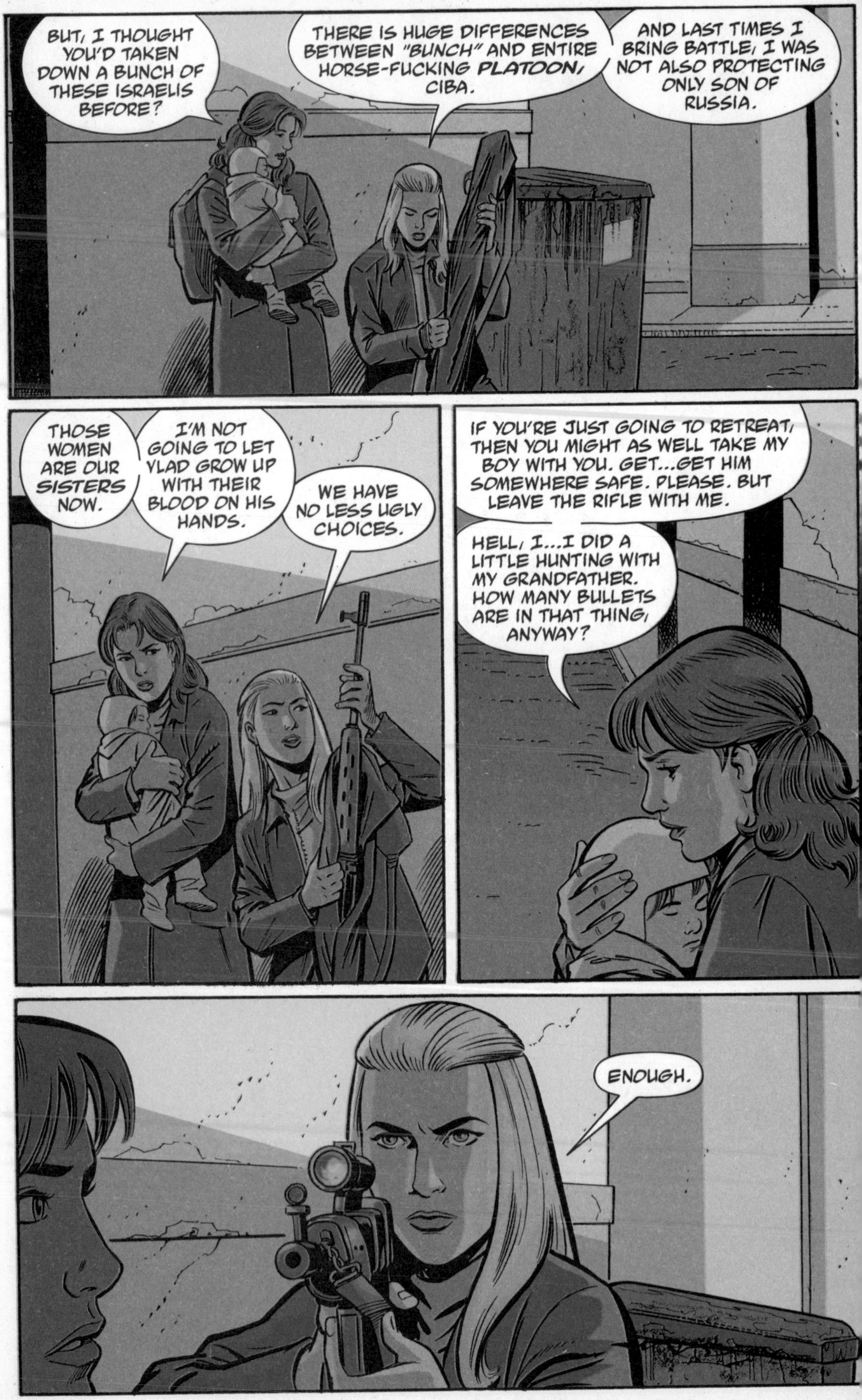
BUT, I THOUGHT YOU'D TAKEN DOWN A BUNCH OF THESE ISRAELIS BEFORE?
THERE IS HUGE DIFFERENCES BETWEEN "BUNCH" AND ENTIRE HORSE-FUCKING PLATOON, CIBA.
AND LAST TIMES I BRING BATTLE, I WAS NOT ALSO PROTECTING ONLY SON OF RUSSIA.
THOSE WOMEN ARE OUR SISTERS NOW.
I'M NOT GOING TO LET VLAD GROW UP WITH THEIR BLOOD ON HIS HANDS.
WE HAVE NO LESS UGLY CHOICES.
IF YOU'RE JUST GOING TO RETREAT, THEN YOU MIGHT AS WELL TAKE MY BOY WITH YOU. GET...GET HIM SOMEWHERE SAFE. PLEASE. BUT LEAVE THE RIFLE WITH ME.
HELL, I...I DID A LITTLE HUNTING WITH MY GRANDFATHER. HOW MANY BULLETS ARE IN THAT THING, ANYWAY?
ENOUGH.

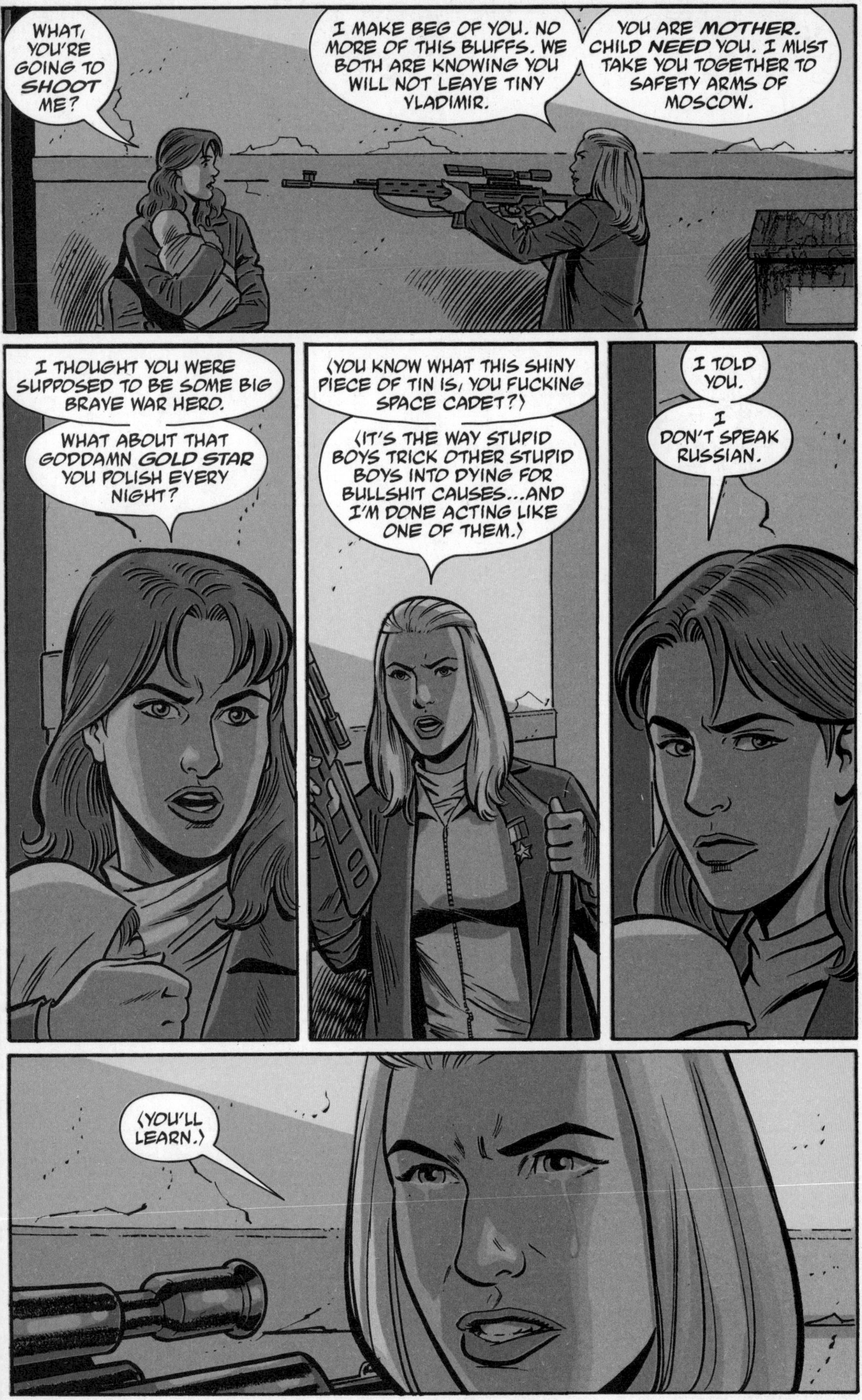
WHAT, YOU'RE GOING TO SHOOT ME?
I MAKE BEG OF YOU. NO MORE OF THIS BLUFFS. WE BOTH ARE KNOWING YOU WILL NOT LEAVE TINY VLADIMIR.
YOU ARE MOTHER. CHILD NEED YOU. I MUST TAKE YOU TOGETHER TO SAFETY ARMS OF MOSCOW.
I THOUGHT YOU WERE SUPPOSED TO BE SOME BIG BRAVE WAR HERO.
WHAT ABOUT THAT GODDAMN GOLD STAR YOU POLISH EVERY NIGHT?
<YOU KNOW WHAT THIS SHINY PIECE OF TIN IS, YOU FUCKING SPACE CADET?>
<IT'S THE WAY STUPID BOYS TRICK OTHER STUPID BOYS INTO DYING FOR BULLSHIT CAUSES...AND I'M DONE ACTING LIKE ONE OF THEM.>
I TOLD YOU.
I DON'T SPEAK RUSSIAN.
<YOU'LL LEARN.>

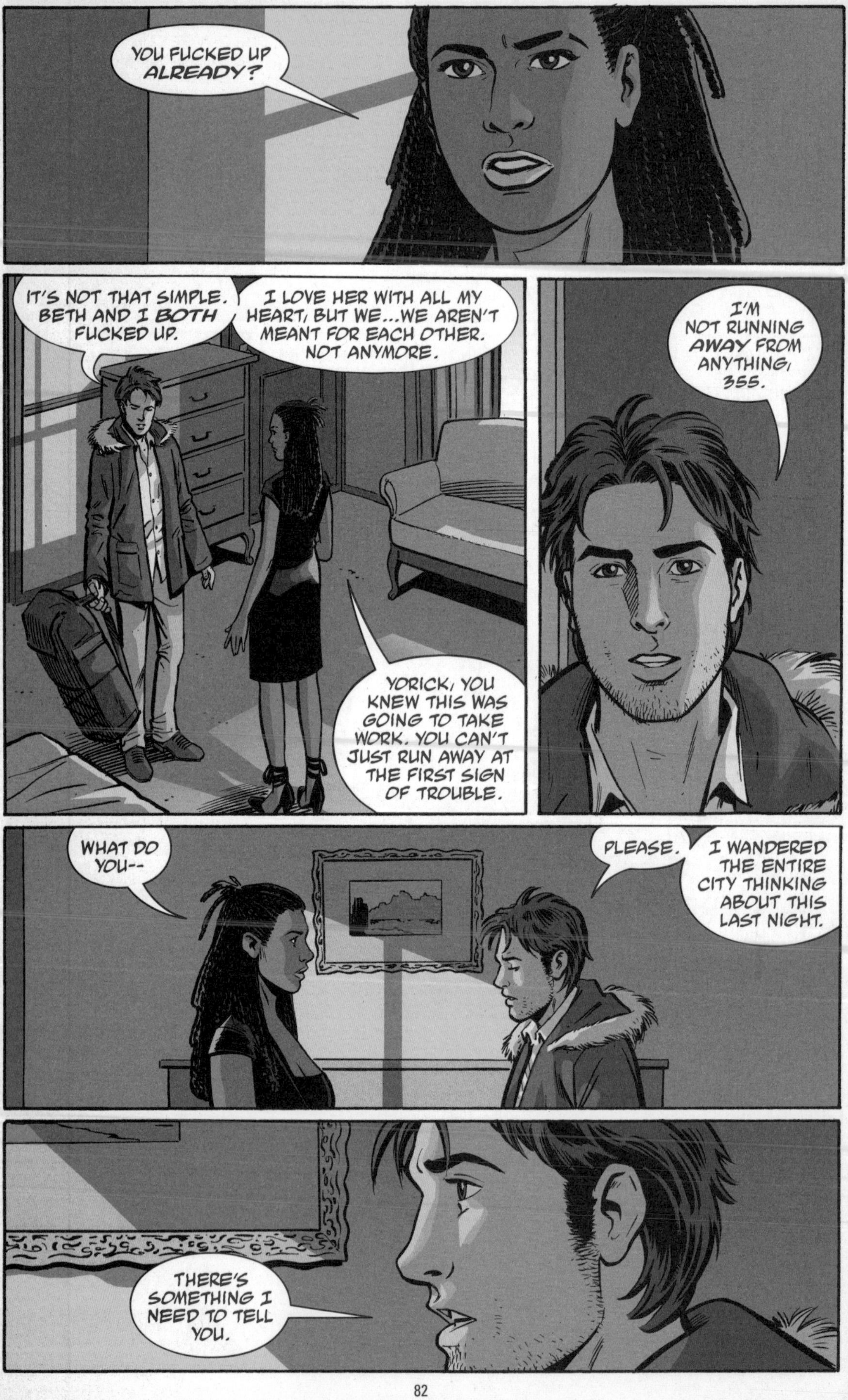

YOU FUCKED UP *ALREADY?*
IT'S NOT THAT SIMPLE. BETH AND I *BOTH* FUCKED UP.
I LOVE HER WITH ALL MY HEART, BUT WE...WE AREN'T MEANT FOR EACH OTHER. NOT ANYMORE.
YORICK, YOU KNEW THIS WAS GOING TO TAKE WORK. YOU CAN'T JUST RUN AWAY AT THE FIRST SIGN OF TROUBLE.
I'M NOT RUNNING *AWAY* FROM ANYTHING, 355.
WHAT DO YOU--
PLEASE.
I WANDERED THE ENTIRE CITY THINKING ABOUT THIS LAST NIGHT.
THERE'S SOMETHING I NEED TO TELL YOU.

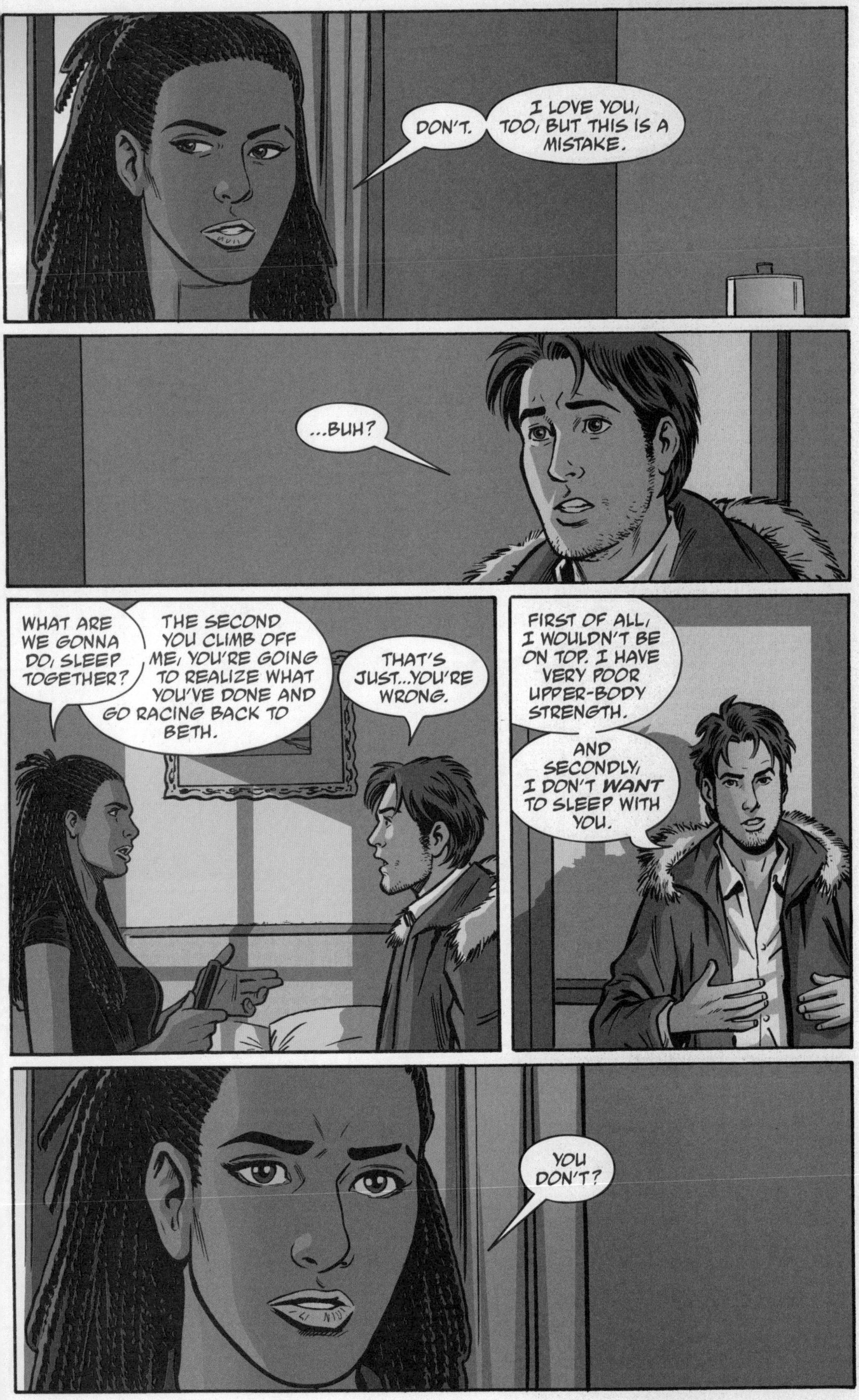
DON'T.
I LOVE YOU, TOO, BUT THIS IS A MISTAKE.
...BUH?
WHAT ARE WE GONNA DO, SLEEP TOGETHER?
THE SECOND YOU CLIMB OFF ME, YOU'RE GOING TO REALIZE WHAT YOU'VE DONE AND GO RACING BACK TO BETH.
THAT'S JUST...YOU'RE WRONG.
FIRST OF ALL, I WOULDN'T BE ON TOP. I HAVE VERY POOR UPPER-BODY STRENGTH.
AND SECONDLY, I DON'T *WANT* TO SLEEP WITH YOU.
YOU DON'T?

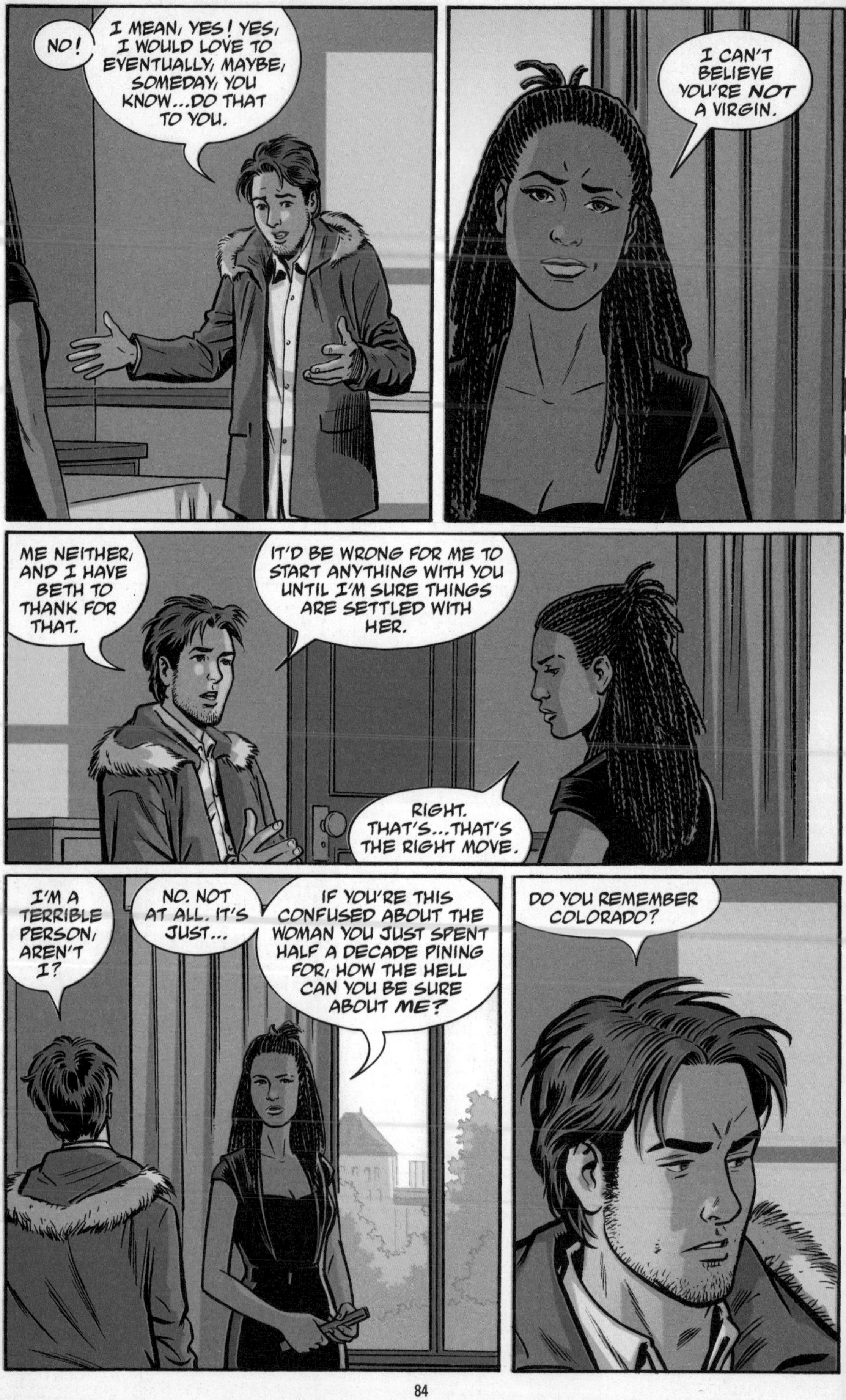
NO!
I MEAN, YES! YES, I WOULD LOVE TO EVENTUALLY, MAYBE, SOMEDAY, YOU KNOW...DO THAT TO YOU.
I CAN'T BELIEVE YOU'RE NOT A VIRGIN.
ME NEITHER, AND I HAVE BETH TO THANK FOR THAT.
IT'D BE WRONG FOR ME TO START ANYTHING WITH YOU UNTIL I'M SURE THINGS ARE SETTLED WITH HER.
RIGHT. THAT'S...THAT'S THE RIGHT MOVE.
I'M A TERRIBLE PERSON, AREN'T I?
NO. NOT AT ALL. IT'S JUST...
IF YOU'RE THIS CONFUSED ABOUT THE WOMAN YOU JUST SPENT HALF A DECADE PINING FOR, HOW THE HELL CAN YOU BE SURE ABOUT ME?
DO YOU REMEMBER COLORADO?

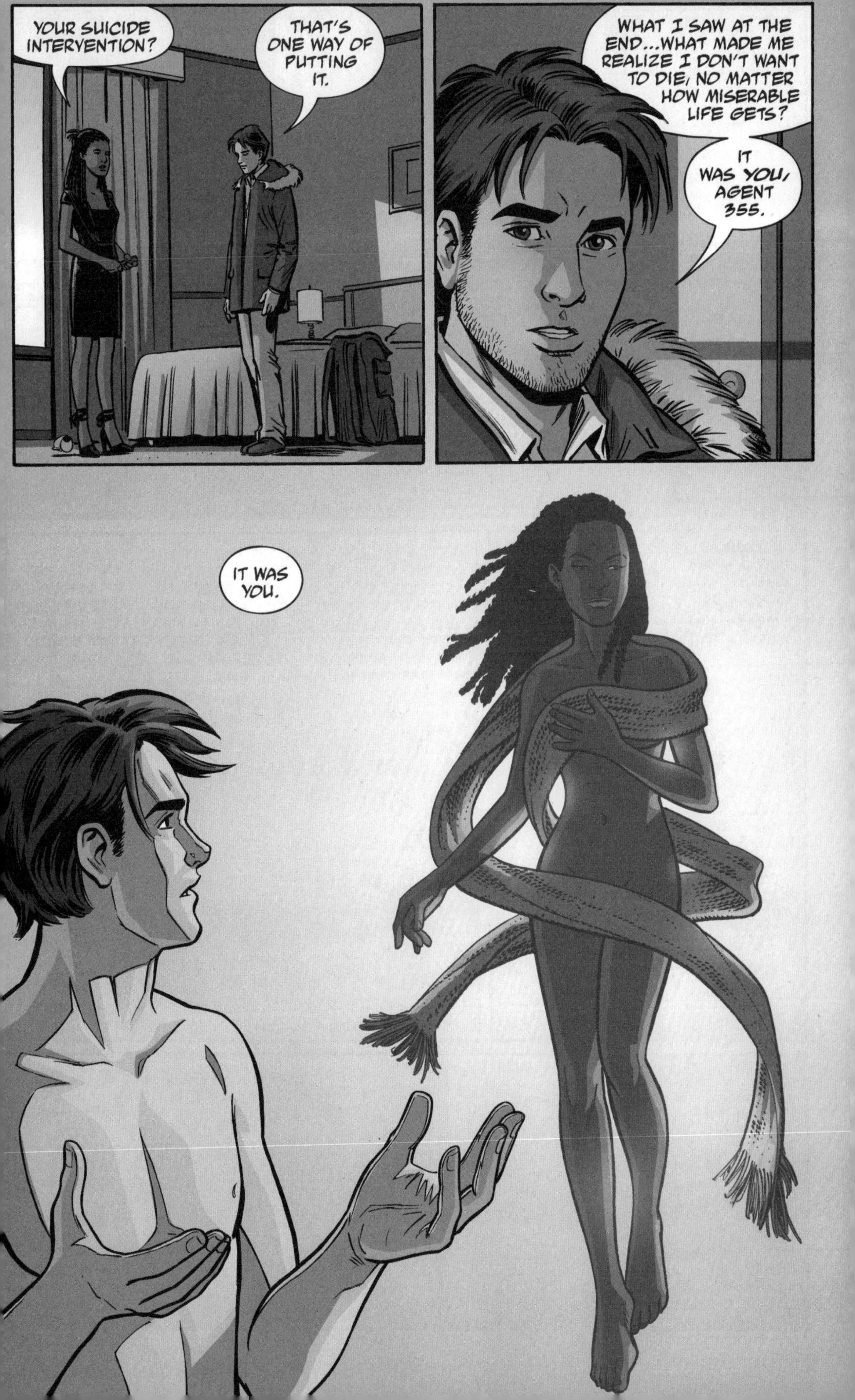
YOUR SUICIDE INTERVENTION?
THAT'S ONE WAY OF PUTTING IT.
WHAT I SAW AT THE END...WHAT MADE ME REALIZE I DON'T WANT TO DIE, NO MATTER HOW MISERABLE LIFE GETS?
IT WAS YOU, AGENT 355.
IT WAS YOU.

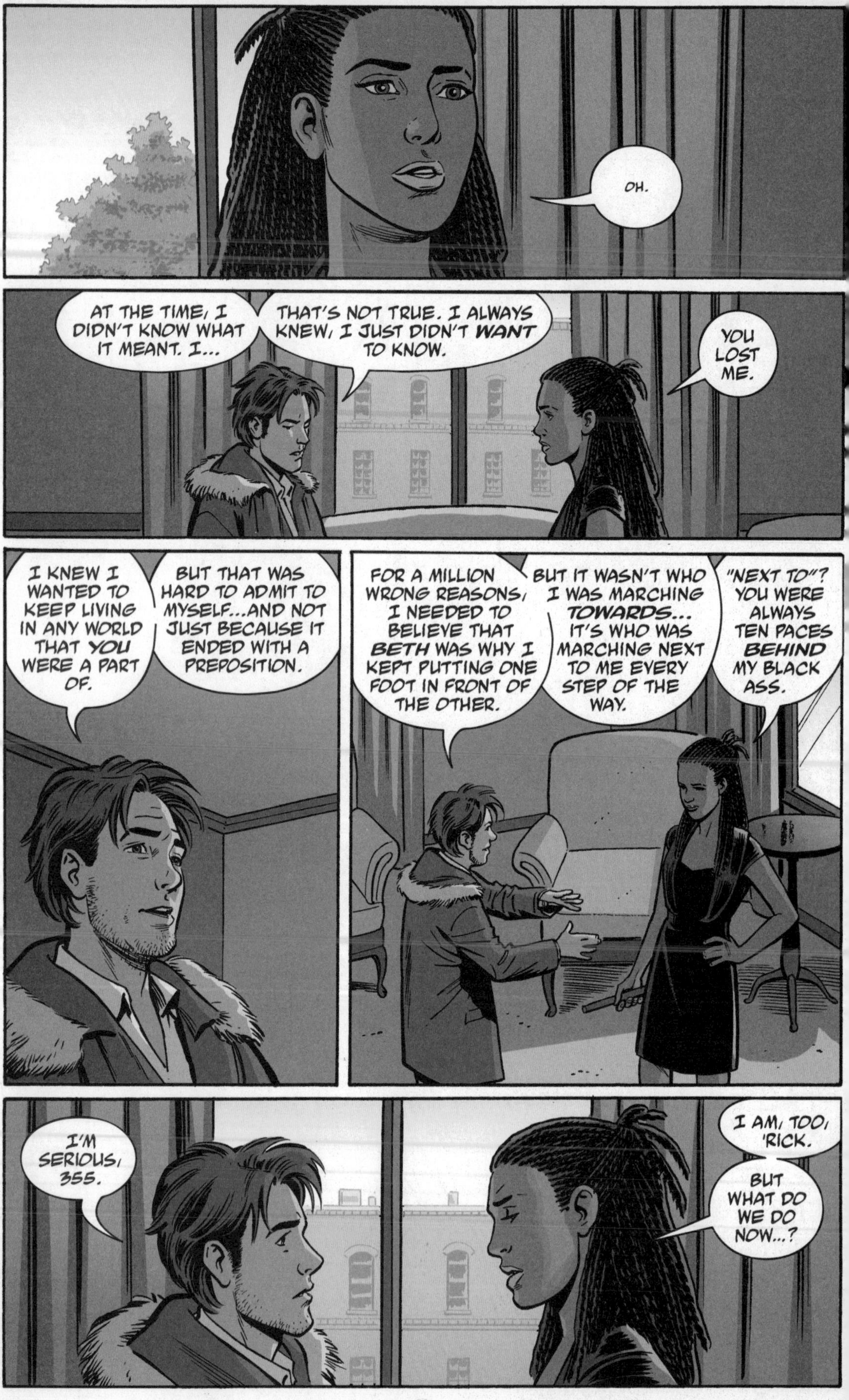
OH.
AT THE TIME, I DIDN'T KNOW WHAT IT MEANT. I...
THAT'S NOT TRUE. I ALWAYS KNEW, I JUST DIDN'T WANT TO KNOW.
YOU LOST ME.
I KNEW I WANTED TO KEEP LIVING IN ANY WORLD THAT YOU WERE A PART OF.
BUT THAT WAS HARD TO ADMIT TO MYSELF...AND NOT JUST BECAUSE IT ENDED WITH A PREPOSITION.
FOR A MILLION WRONG REASONS, I NEEDED TO BELIEVE THAT BETH WAS WHY I KEPT PUTTING ONE FOOT IN FRONT OF THE OTHER.
BUT IT WASN'T WHO I WAS MARCHING TOWARDS... IT'S WHO WAS MARCHING NEXT TO ME EVERY STEP OF THE WAY.
"NEXT TO"? YOU WERE ALWAYS TEN PACES BEHIND MY BLACK ASS.
I'M SERIOUS, 355.
I AM, TOO, 'RICK.
BUT WHAT DO WE DO NOW...?

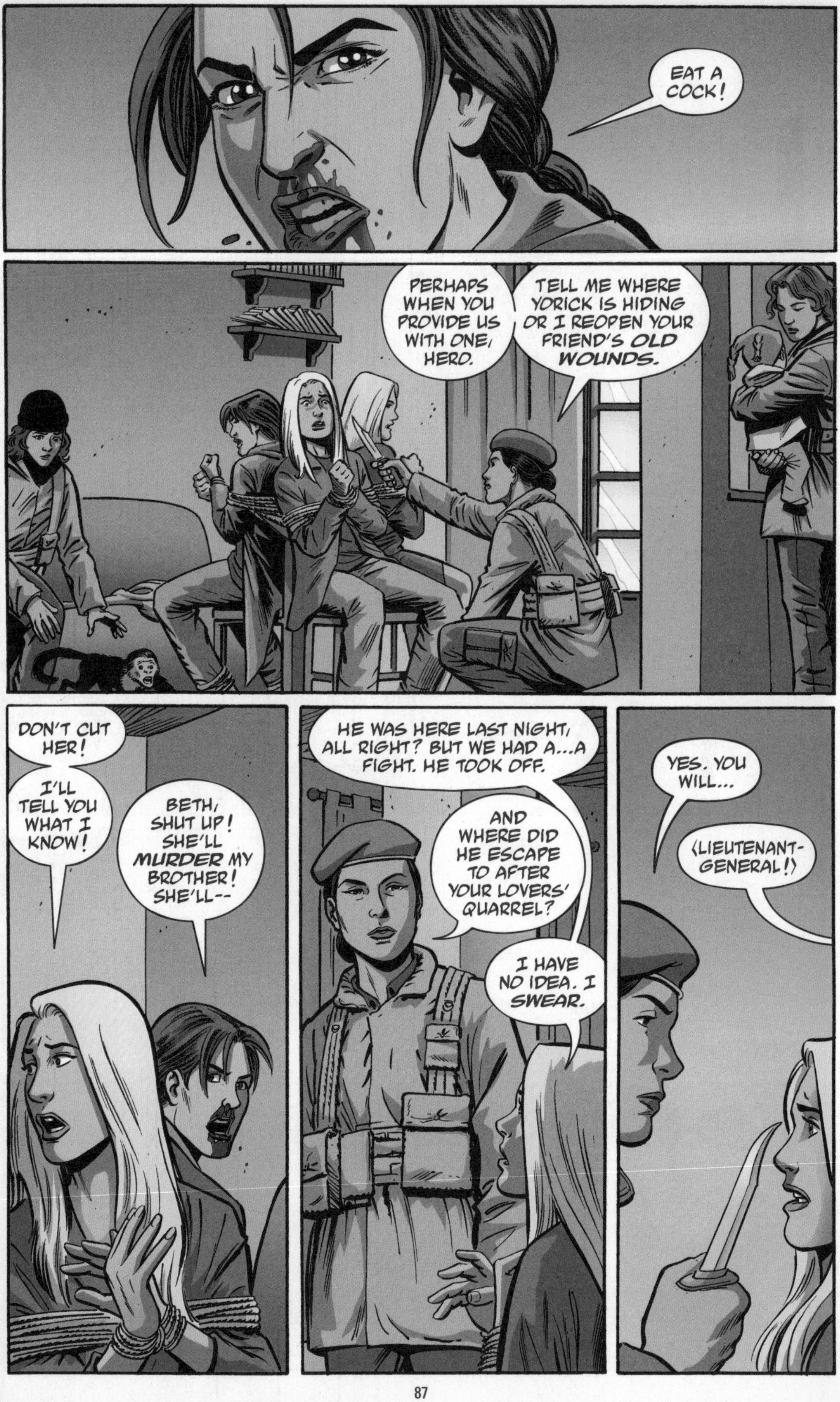
EAT A COCK!
PERHAPS WHEN YOU PROVIDE US WITH ONE, HERO.
TELL ME WHERE YORICK IS HIDING OR I REOPEN YOUR FRIEND'S OLD WOUNDS.
DON'T CUT HER!
I'LL TELL YOU WHAT I KNOW!
BETH, SHUT UP! SHE'LL MURDER MY BROTHER! SHE'LL--
HE WAS HERE LAST NIGHT, ALL RIGHT? BUT WE HAD A...A FIGHT. HE TOOK OFF.
AND WHERE DID HE ESCAPE TO AFTER YOUR LOVERS' QUARREL?
I HAVE NO IDEA. I SWEAR.
YES. YOU WILL...
⟨LIEUTENANT-GENERAL!⟩

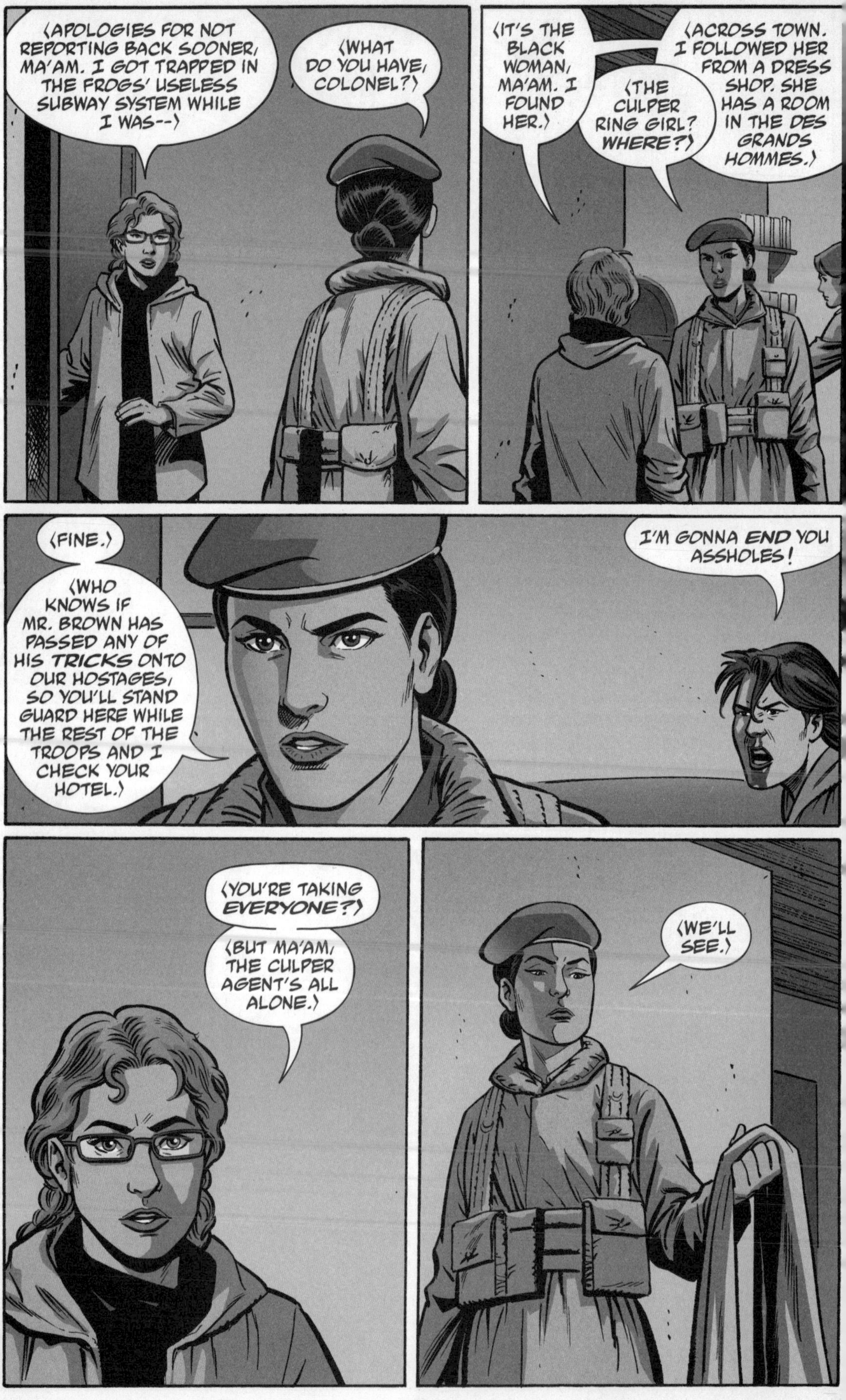
⟨APOLOGIES FOR NOT REPORTING BACK SOONER, MA'AM. I GOT TRAPPED IN THE FROGS' USELESS SUBWAY SYSTEM WHILE I WAS--⟩
⟨WHAT DO YOU HAVE, COLONEL?⟩
⟨IT'S THE BLACK WOMAN, MA'AM. I FOUND HER.⟩
⟨THE CULPER RING GIRL? WHERE?⟩
⟨ACROSS TOWN. I FOLLOWED HER FROM A DRESS SHOP. SHE HAS A ROOM IN THE DES GRANDS HOMMES.⟩
⟨FINE.⟩
⟨WHO KNOWS IF MR. BROWN HAS PASSED ANY OF HIS TRICKS ONTO OUR HOSTAGES, SO YOU'LL STAND GUARD HERE WHILE THE REST OF THE TROOPS AND I CHECK YOUR HOTEL.⟩
I'M GONNA END YOU ASSHOLES!
⟨YOU'RE TAKING EVERYONE?⟩
⟨BUT MA'AM, THE CULPER AGENT'S ALL ALONE.⟩
⟨WE'LL SEE.⟩

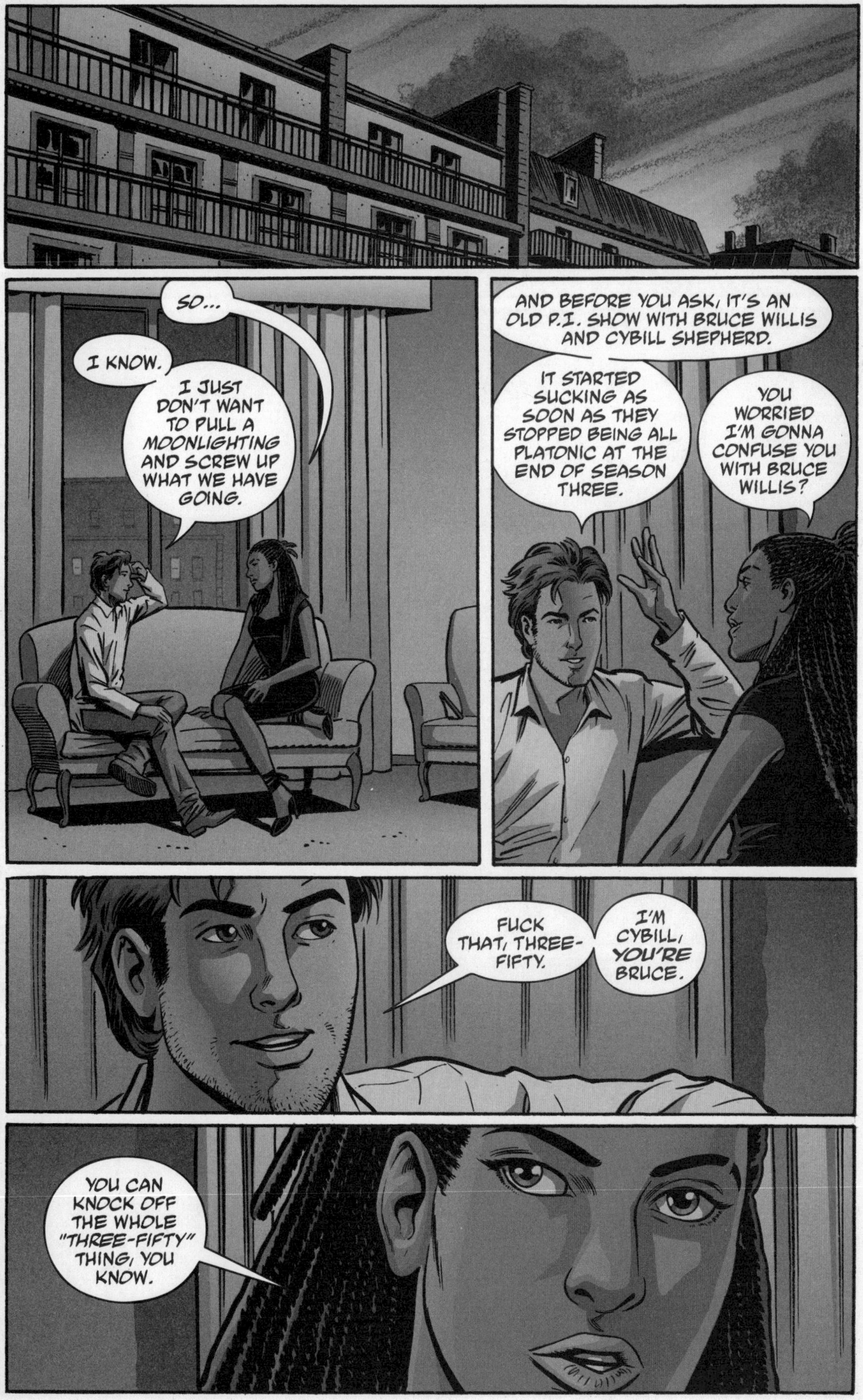
SO...
I KNOW.
I JUST DON'T WANT TO PULL A MOONLIGHTING AND SCREW UP WHAT WE HAVE GOING.
AND BEFORE YOU ASK, IT'S AN OLD P.I. SHOW WITH BRUCE WILLIS AND CYBILL SHEPHERD.
IT STARTED SUCKING AS SOON AS THEY STOPPED BEING ALL PLATONIC AT THE END OF SEASON THREE.
YOU WORRIED I'M GONNA CONFUSE YOU WITH BRUCE WILLIS?
FUCK THAT, THREE-FIFTY.
I'M CYBILL, YOU'RE BRUCE.
YOU CAN KNOCK OFF THE WHOLE "THREE-FIFTY" THING, YOU KNOW.

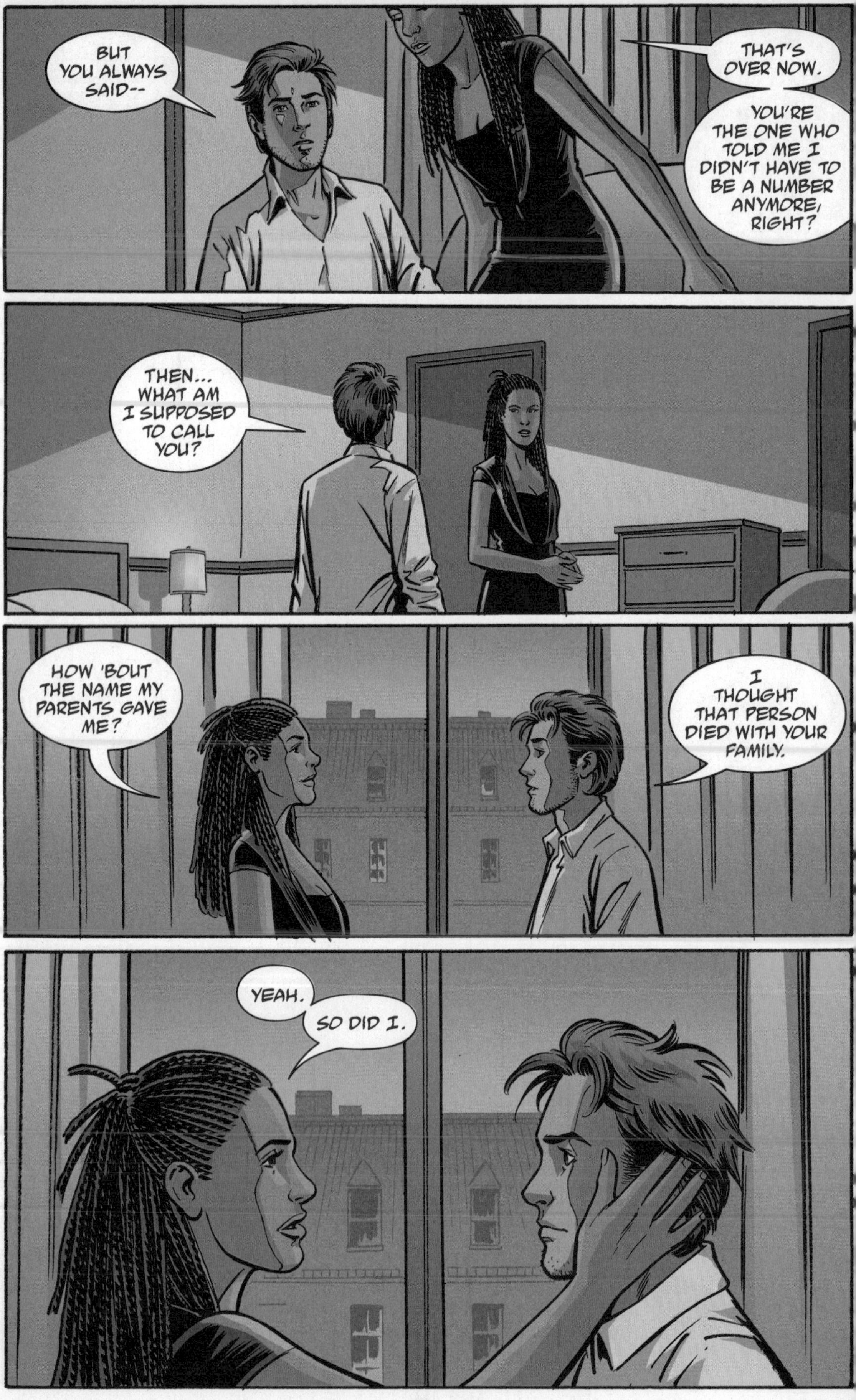
BUT YOU ALWAYS SAID--
THAT'S OVER NOW.
YOU'RE THE ONE WHO TOLD ME I DIDN'T HAVE TO BE A NUMBER ANYMORE, RIGHT?
THEN... WHAT AM I SUPPOSED TO CALL YOU?
HOW 'BOUT THE NAME MY PARENTS GAVE ME?
I THOUGHT THAT PERSON DIED WITH YOUR FAMILY.
YEAH.
SO DID I.

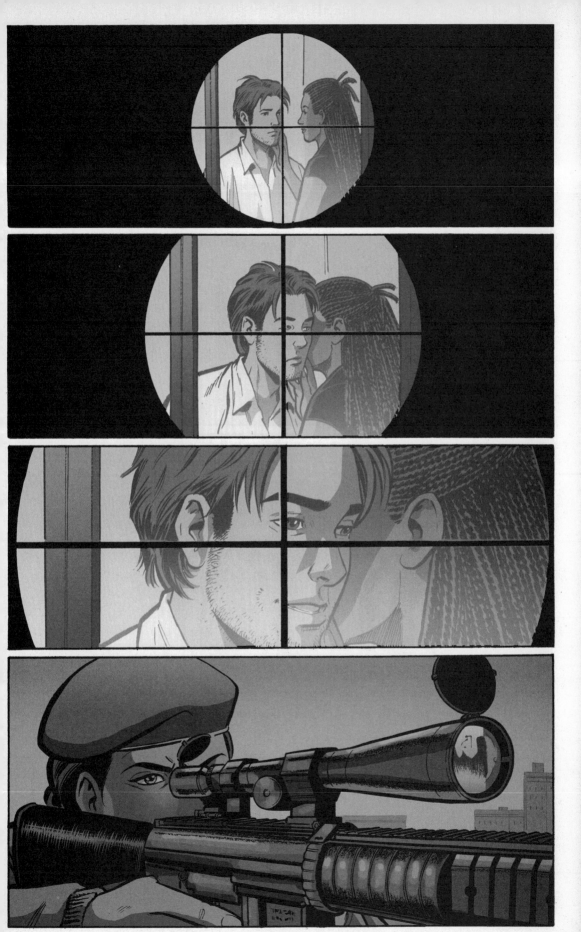

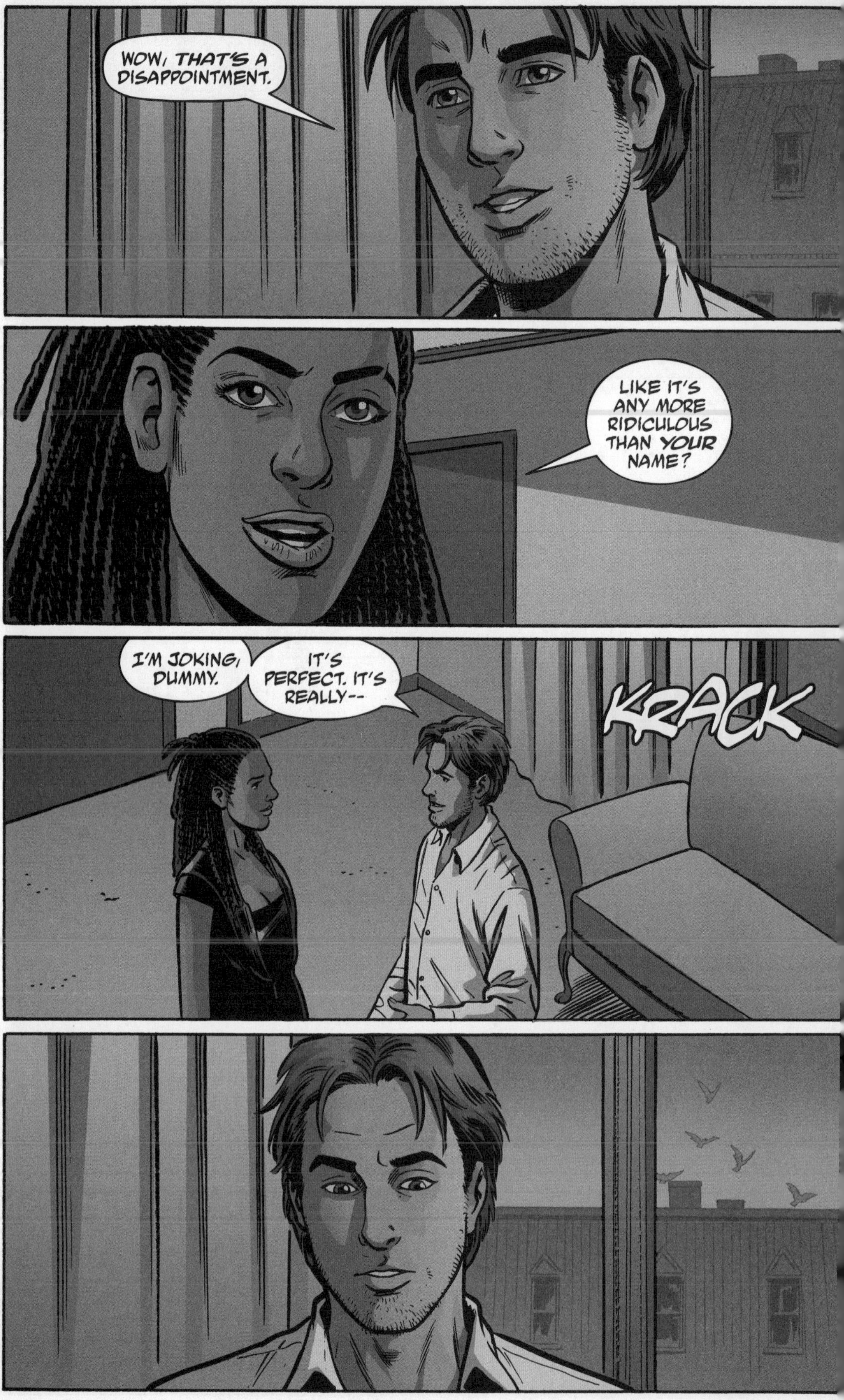
WOW, THAT'S A DISAPPOINTMENT.
LIKE IT'S ANY MORE RIDICULOUS THAN YOUR NAME?
I'M JOKING, DUMMY.
IT'S PERFECT. IT'S REALLY--
KRACK

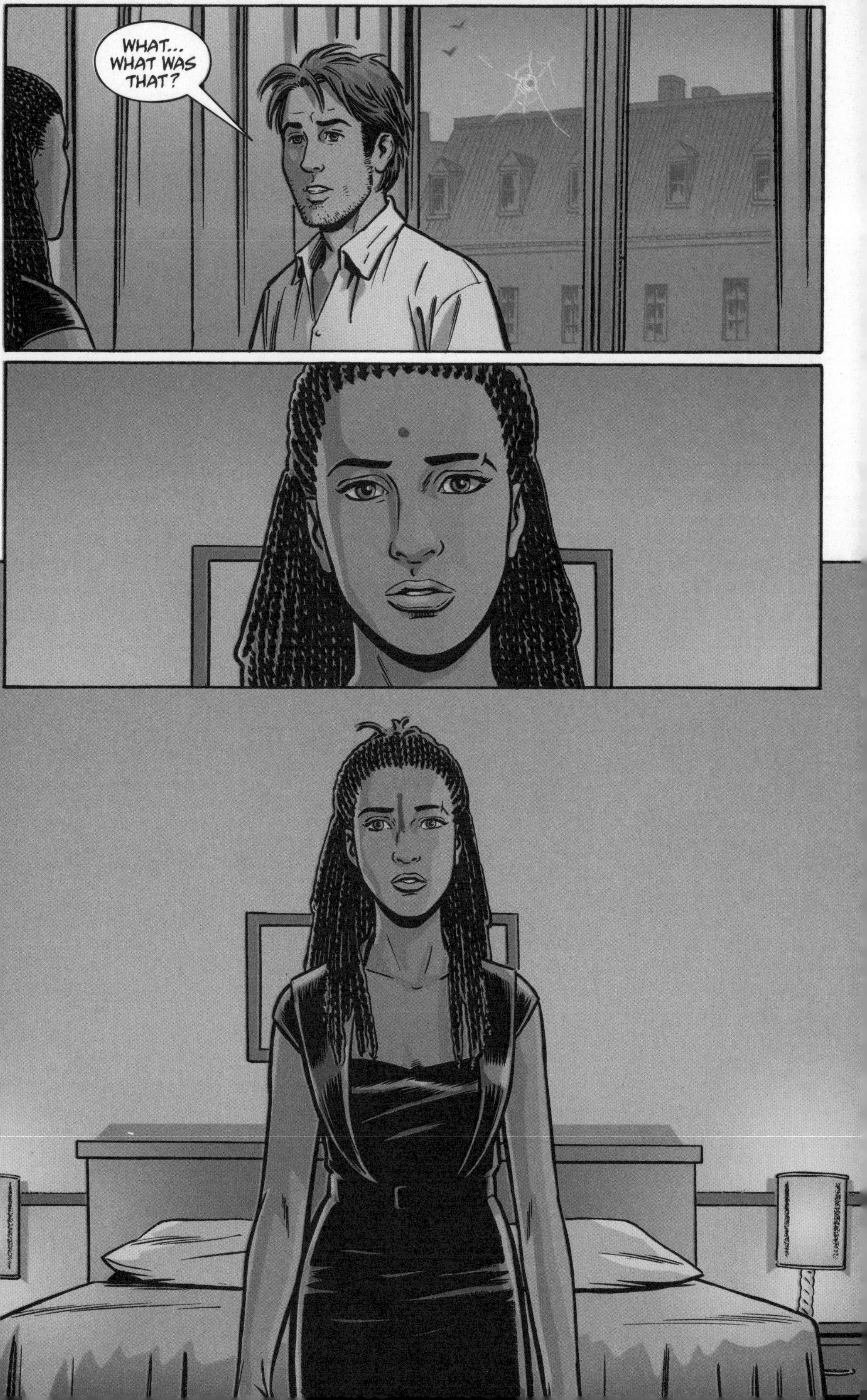
WHAT... WHAT WAS THAT?

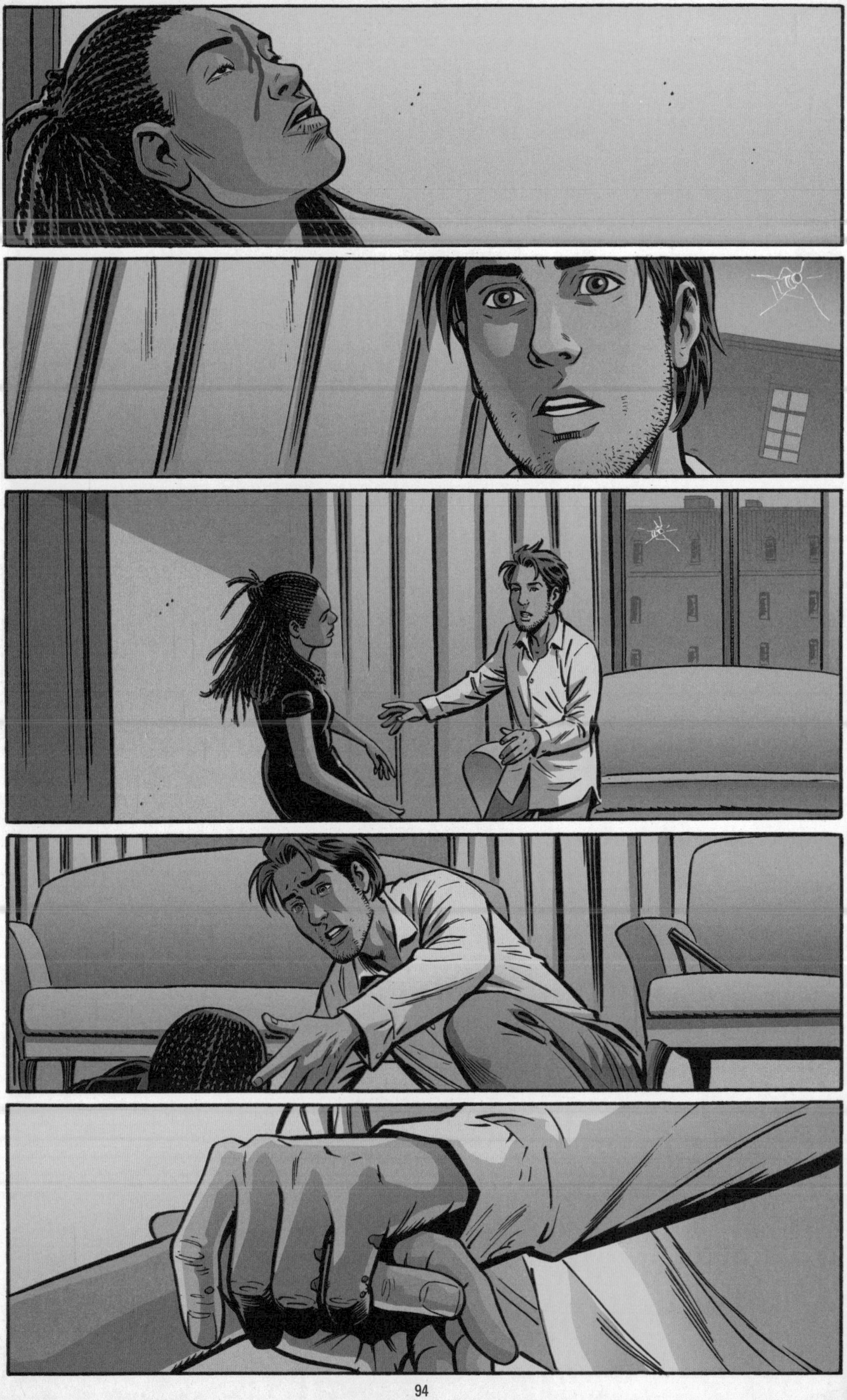

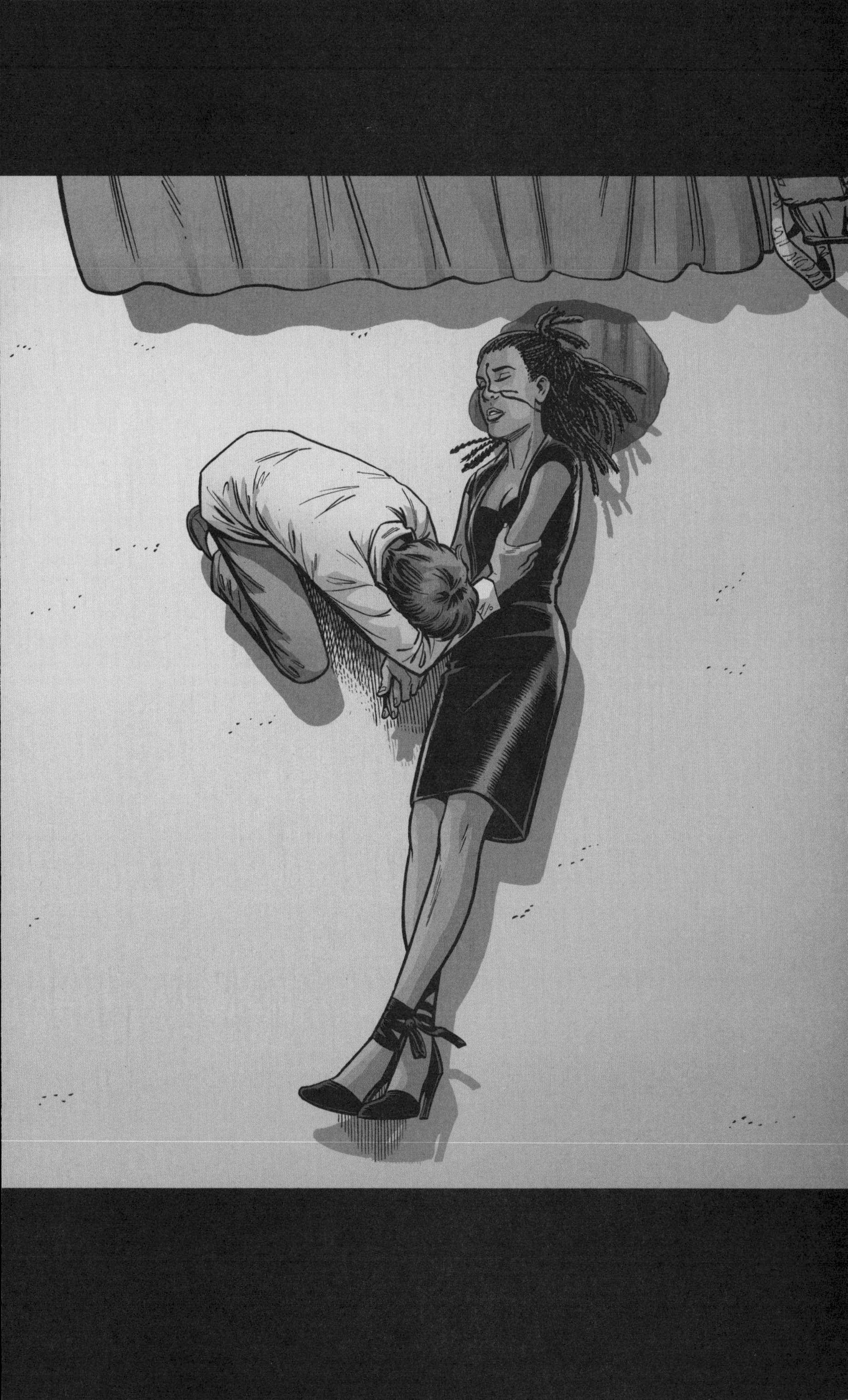

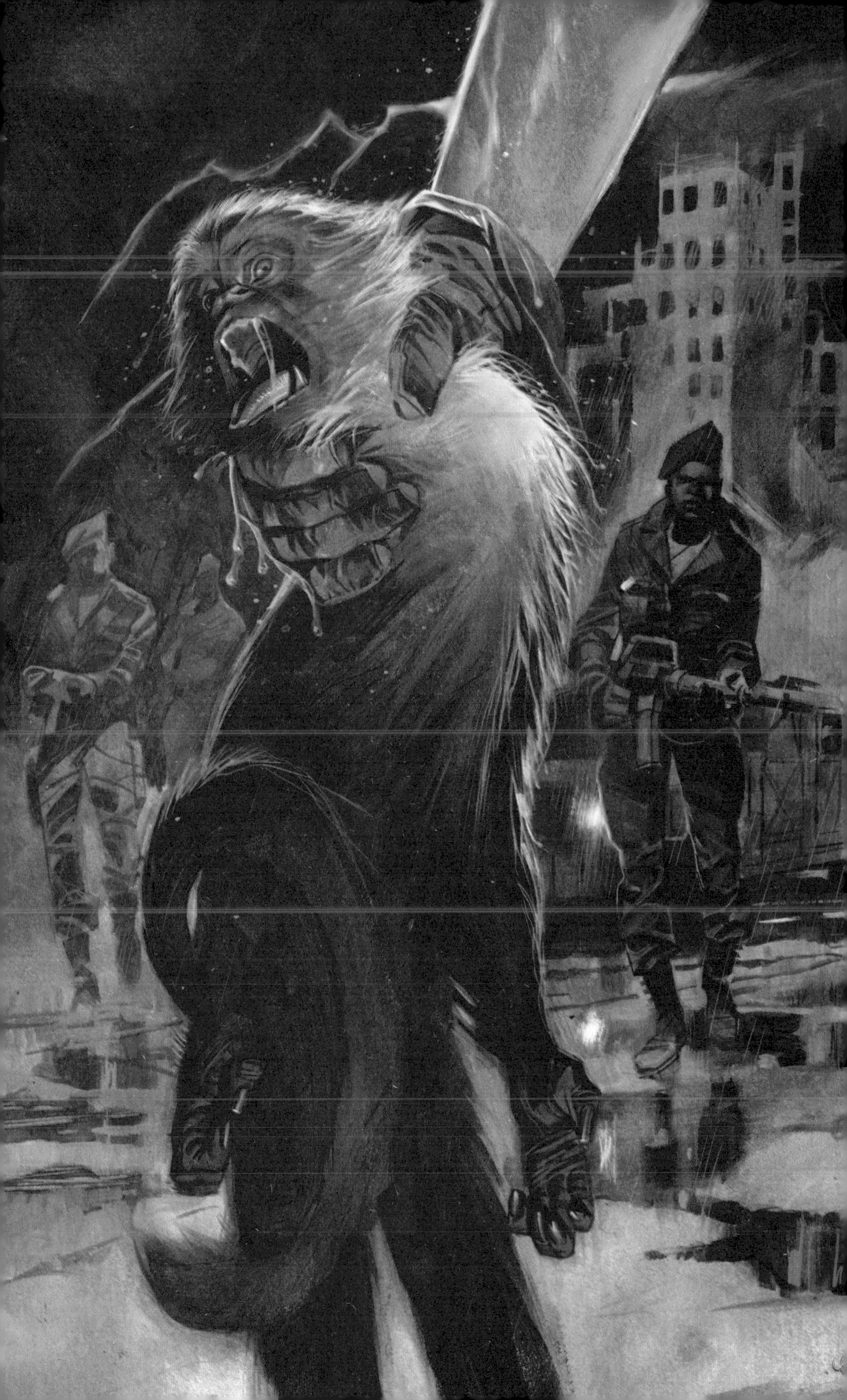

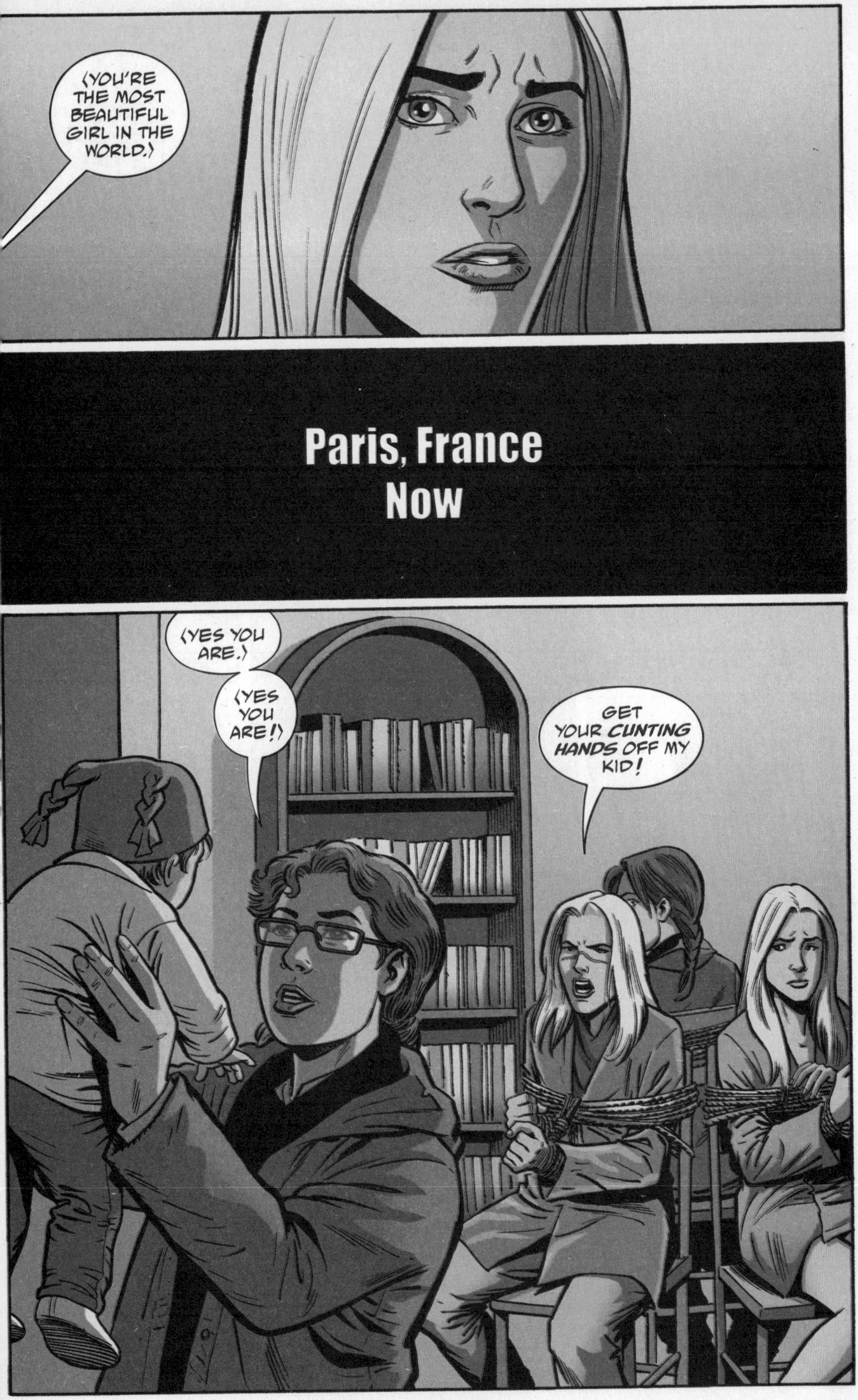
⟨YOU'RE THE MOST BEAUTIFUL GIRL IN THE WORLD.⟩
Paris, France
Now
⟨YES YOU ARE.⟩
⟨YES YOU ARE!⟩
GET YOUR *CUNTING HANDS* OFF MY KID!

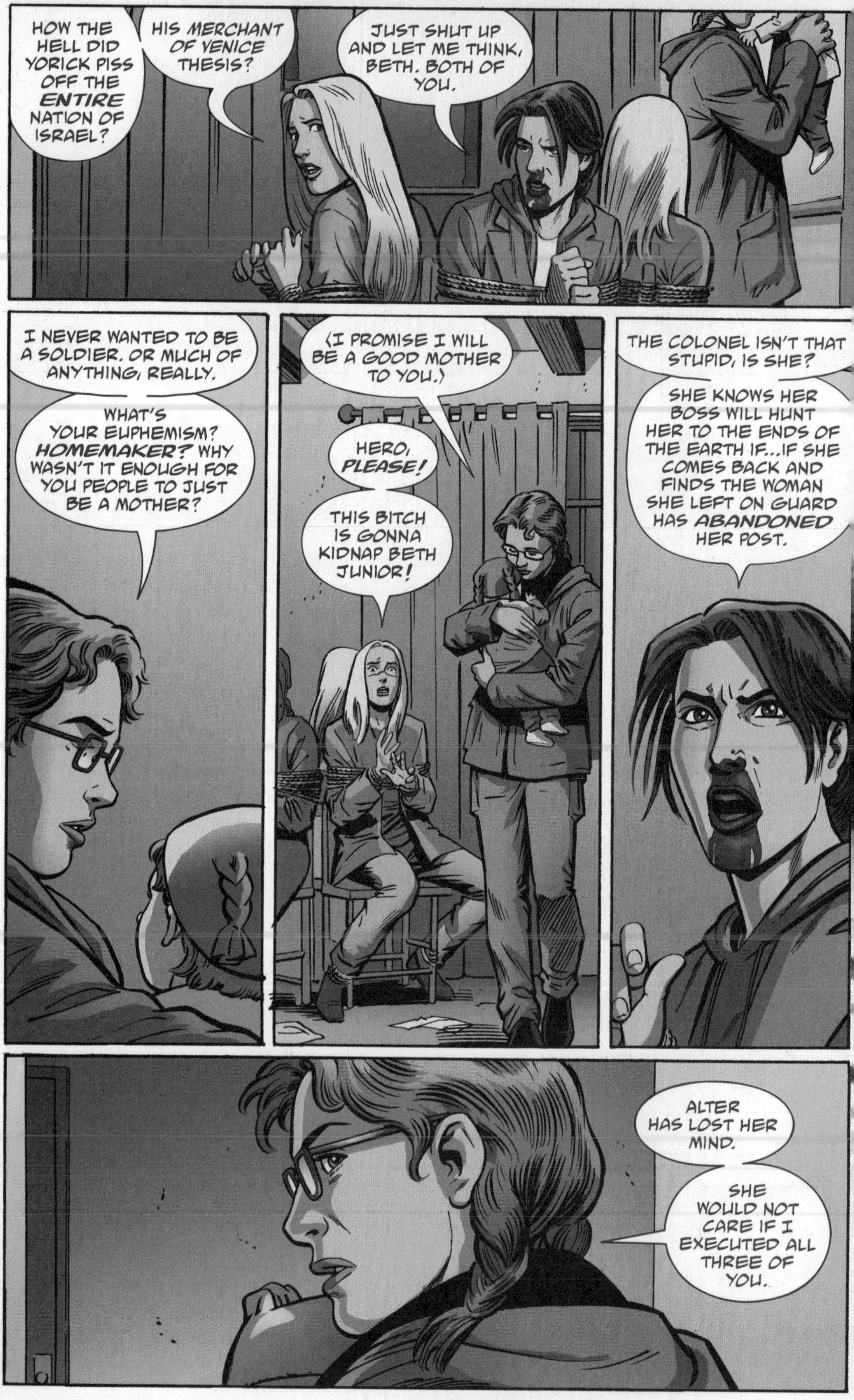
HOW THE HELL DID YORICK PISS OFF THE ENTIRE NATION OF ISRAEL?
HIS MERCHANT OF VENICE THESIS?
JUST SHUT UP AND LET ME THINK, BETH. BOTH OF YOU.
I NEVER WANTED TO BE A SOLDIER. OR MUCH OF ANYTHING, REALLY.
WHAT'S YOUR EUPHEMISM? HOMEMAKER? WHY WASN'T IT ENOUGH FOR YOU PEOPLE TO JUST BE A MOTHER?
⟨I PROMISE I WILL BE A GOOD MOTHER TO YOU.⟩
HERO, PLEASE!
THIS BITCH IS GONNA KIDNAP BETH JUNIOR!
THE COLONEL ISN'T THAT STUPID, IS SHE?
SHE KNOWS HER BOSS WILL HUNT HER TO THE ENDS OF THE EARTH IF...IF SHE COMES BACK AND FINDS THE WOMAN SHE LEFT ON GUARD HAS ABANDONED HER POST.
ALTER HAS LOST HER MIND.
SHE WOULD NOT CARE IF I EXECUTED ALL THREE OF YOU.

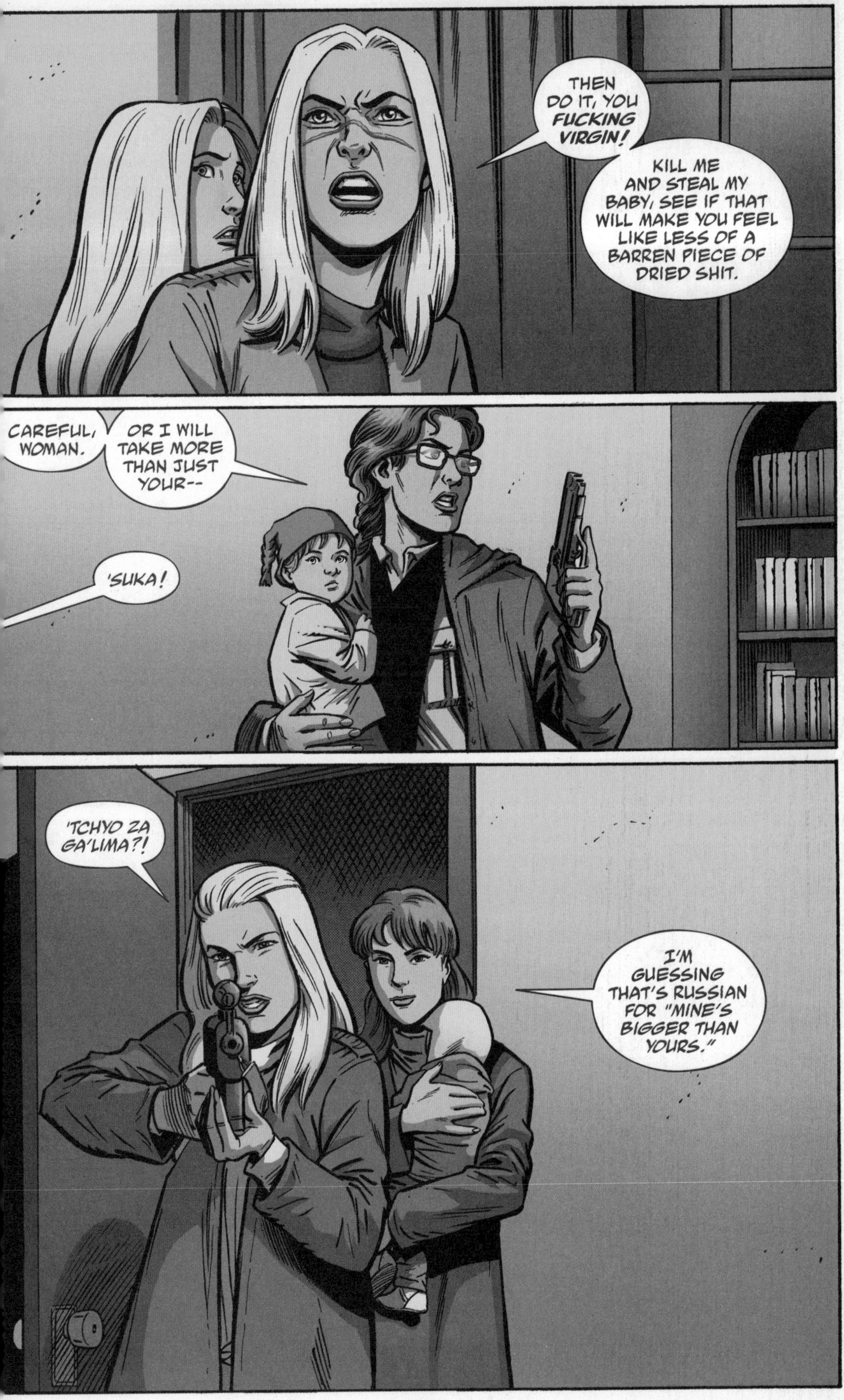
THEN DO IT, YOU FUCKING VIRGIN!
KILL ME AND STEAL MY BABY, SEE IF THAT WILL MAKE YOU FEEL LIKE LESS OF A BARREN PIECE OF DRIED SHIT.
CAREFUL, WOMAN.
OR I WILL TAKE MORE THAN JUST YOUR--
'SUKA!
'TCHYO ZA GA'LIMA?!
I'M GUESSING THAT'S RUSSIAN FOR "MINE'S BIGGER THAN YOURS."

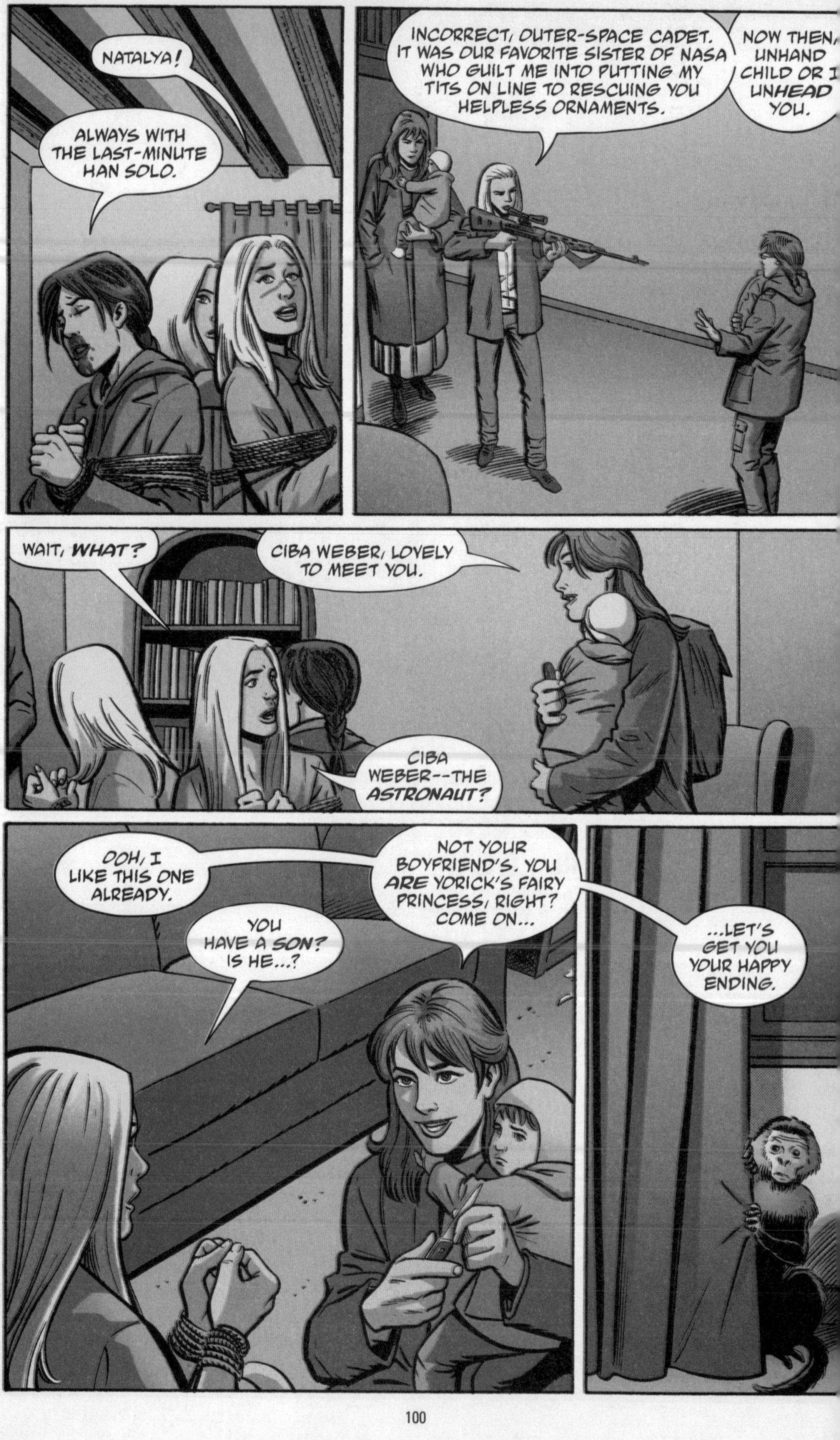
NATALYA!
ALWAYS WITH THE LAST-MINUTE HAN SOLO.
INCORRECT, OUTER-SPACE CADET. IT WAS OUR FAVORITE SISTER OF NASA WHO GUILT ME INTO PUTTING MY TITS ON LINE TO RESCUING YOU HELPLESS ORNAMENTS.
NOW THEN, UNHAND CHILD OR I UNHEAD YOU.
WAIT, WHAT?
CIBA WEBER, LOVELY TO MEET YOU.
CIBA WEBER--THE ASTRONAUT?
OOH, I LIKE THIS ONE ALREADY.
YOU HAVE A SON? IS HE...?
NOT YOUR BOYFRIEND'S. YOU ARE YORICK'S FAIRY PRINCESS, RIGHT? COME ON...
...LET'S GET YOU YOUR HAPPY ENDING.

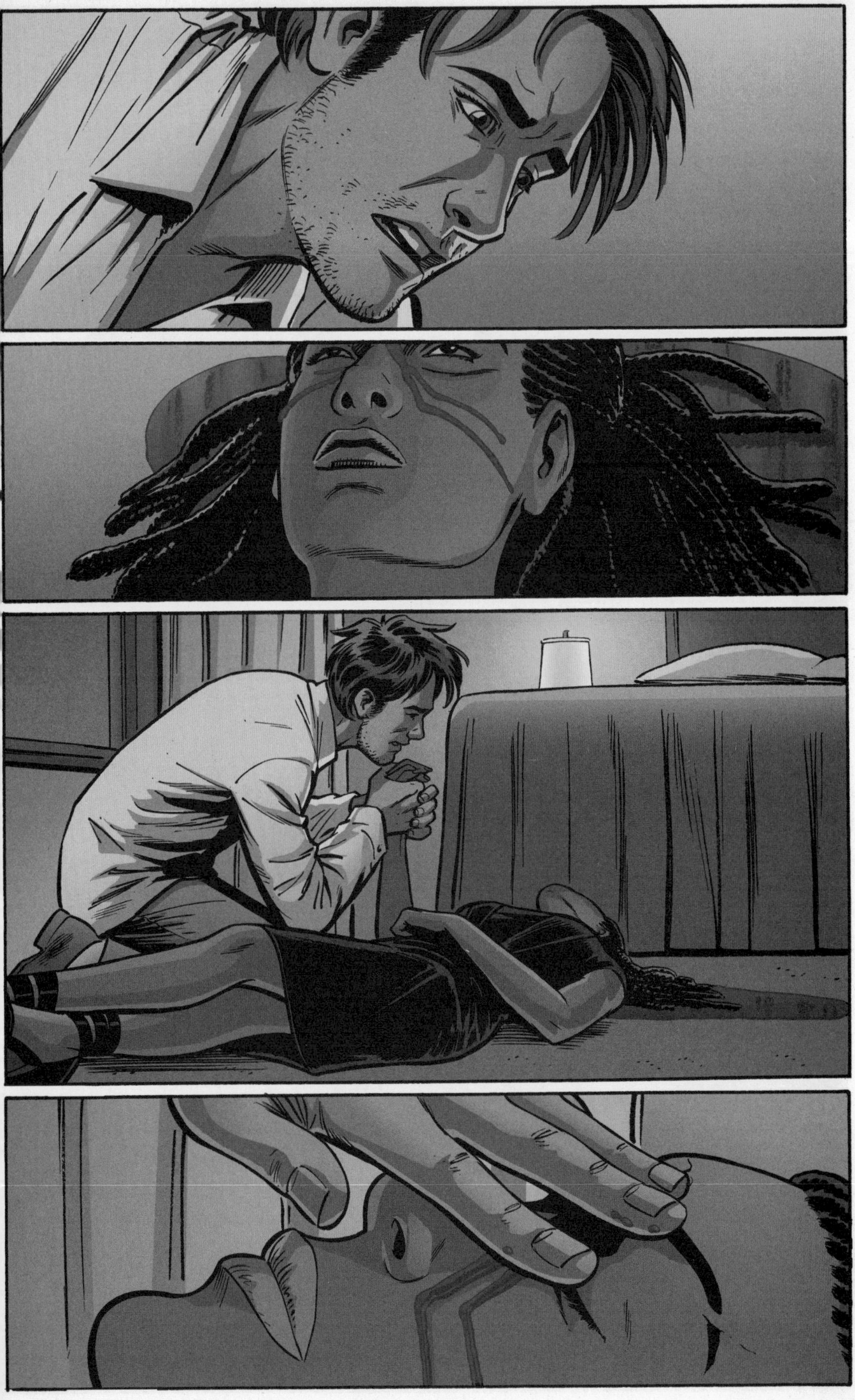

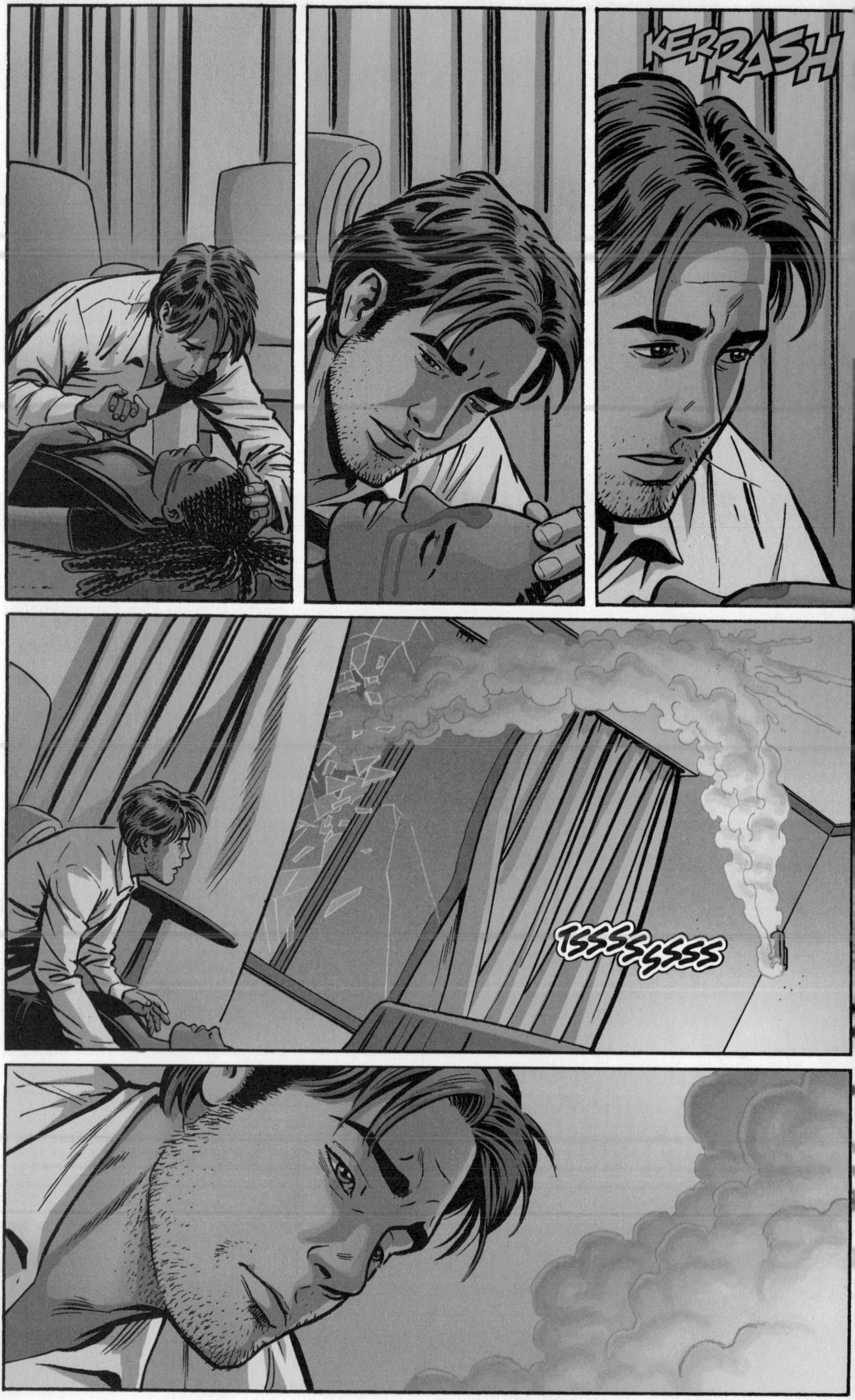
KERRASH
TSSSSSSSS

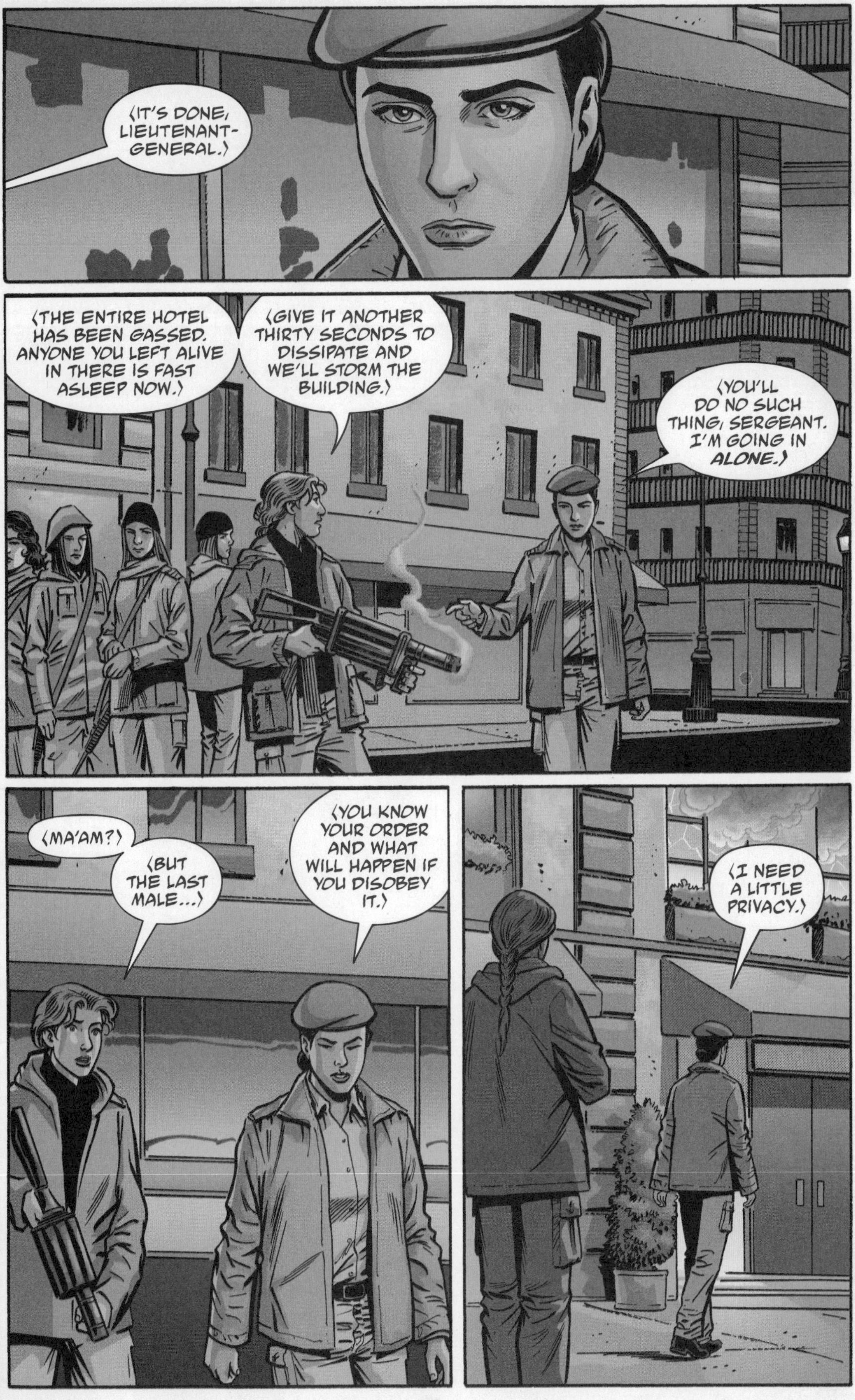

⟨IT'S DONE, LIEUTENANT-GENERAL.⟩
⟨THE ENTIRE HOTEL HAS BEEN GASSED. ANYONE YOU LEFT ALIVE IN THERE IS FAST ASLEEP NOW.⟩
⟨GIVE IT ANOTHER THIRTY SECONDS TO DISSIPATE AND WE'LL STORM THE BUILDING.⟩
⟨YOU'LL DO NO SUCH THING, SERGEANT. I'M GOING IN ALONE.⟩
⟨MA'AM?⟩
⟨BUT THE LAST MALE...⟩
⟨YOU KNOW YOUR ORDER AND WHAT WILL HAPPEN IF YOU DISOBEY IT.⟩
⟨I NEED A LITTLE PRIVACY.⟩

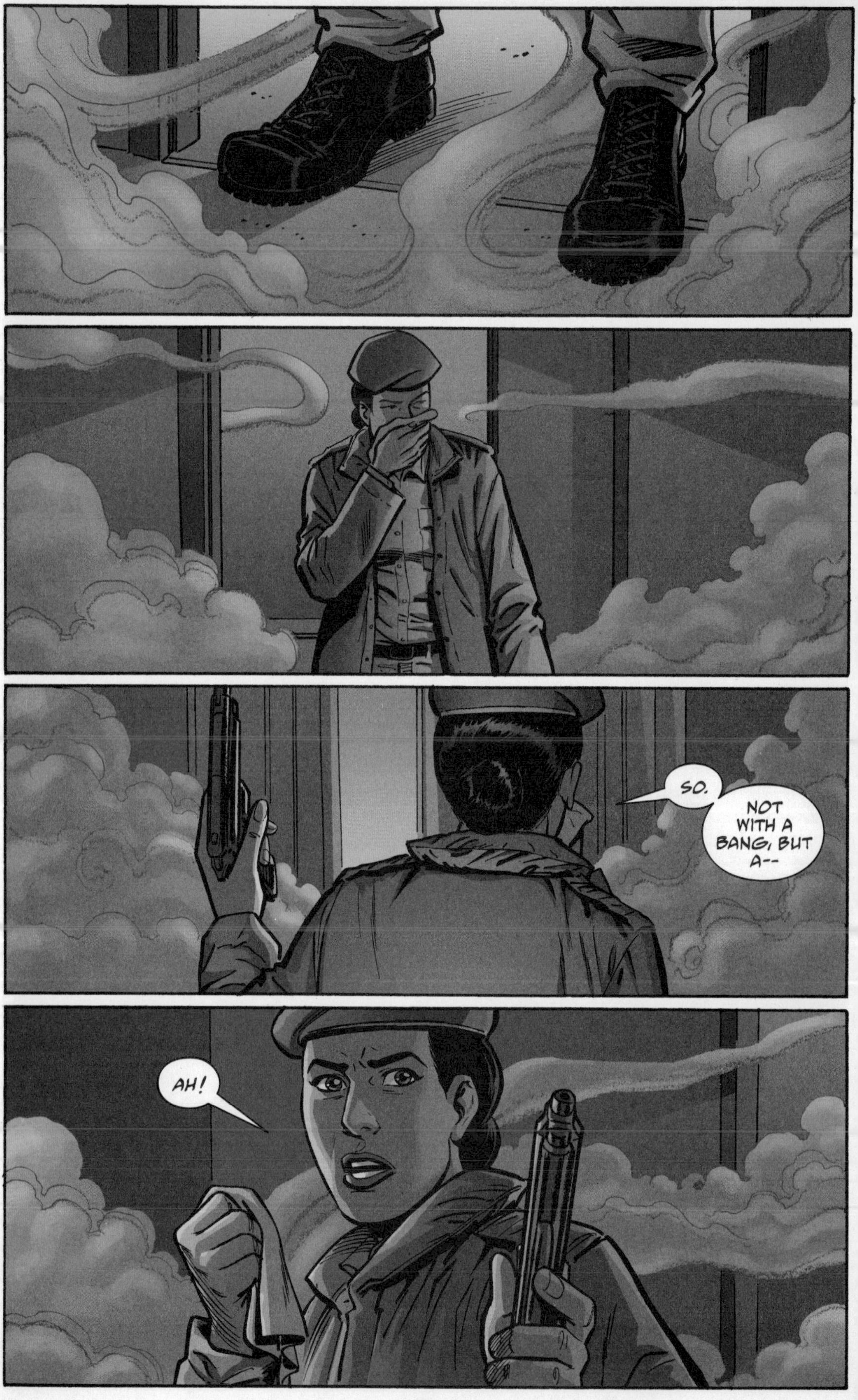
SO.
NOT WITH A BANG, BUT A--
AH!

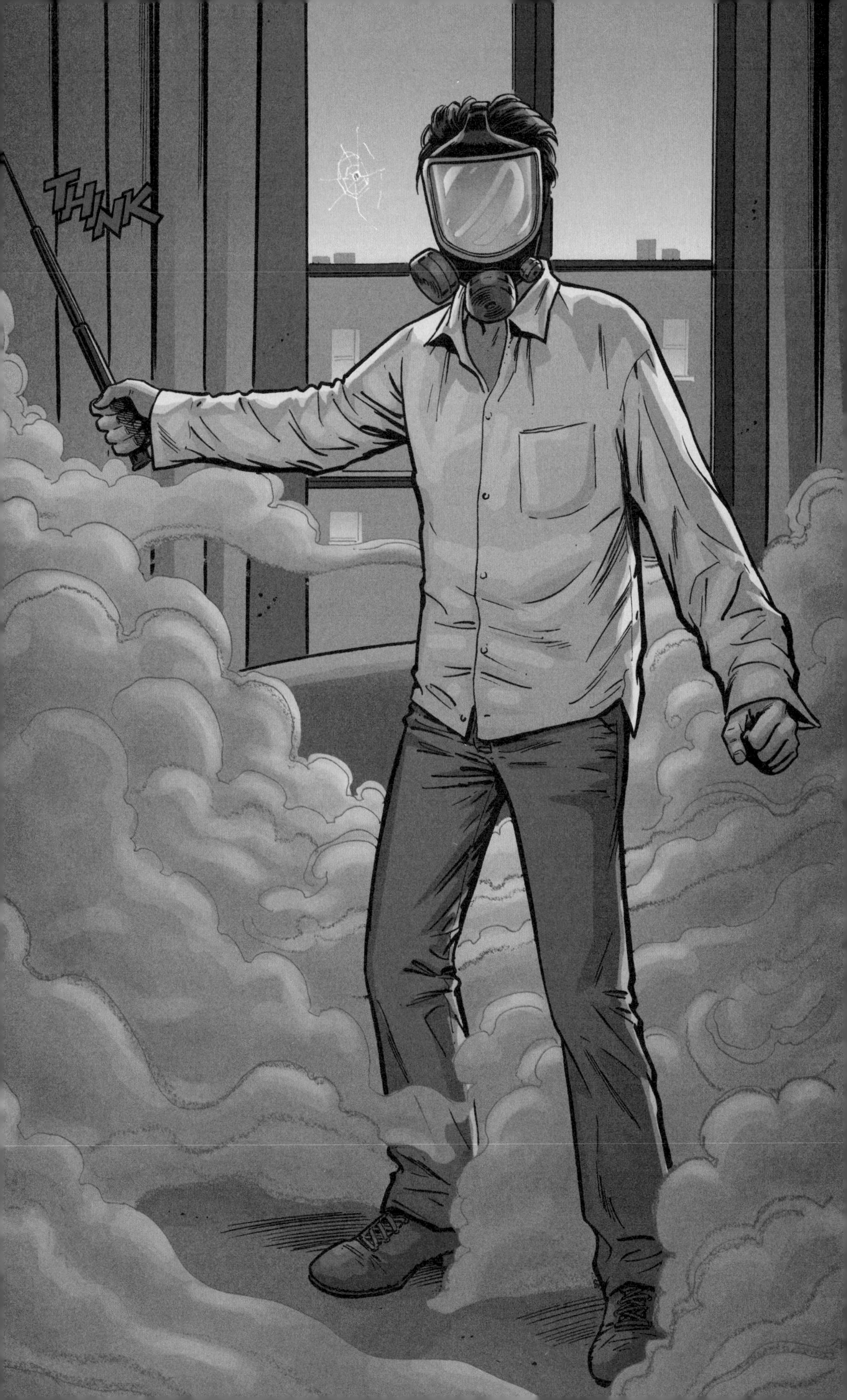
THINK

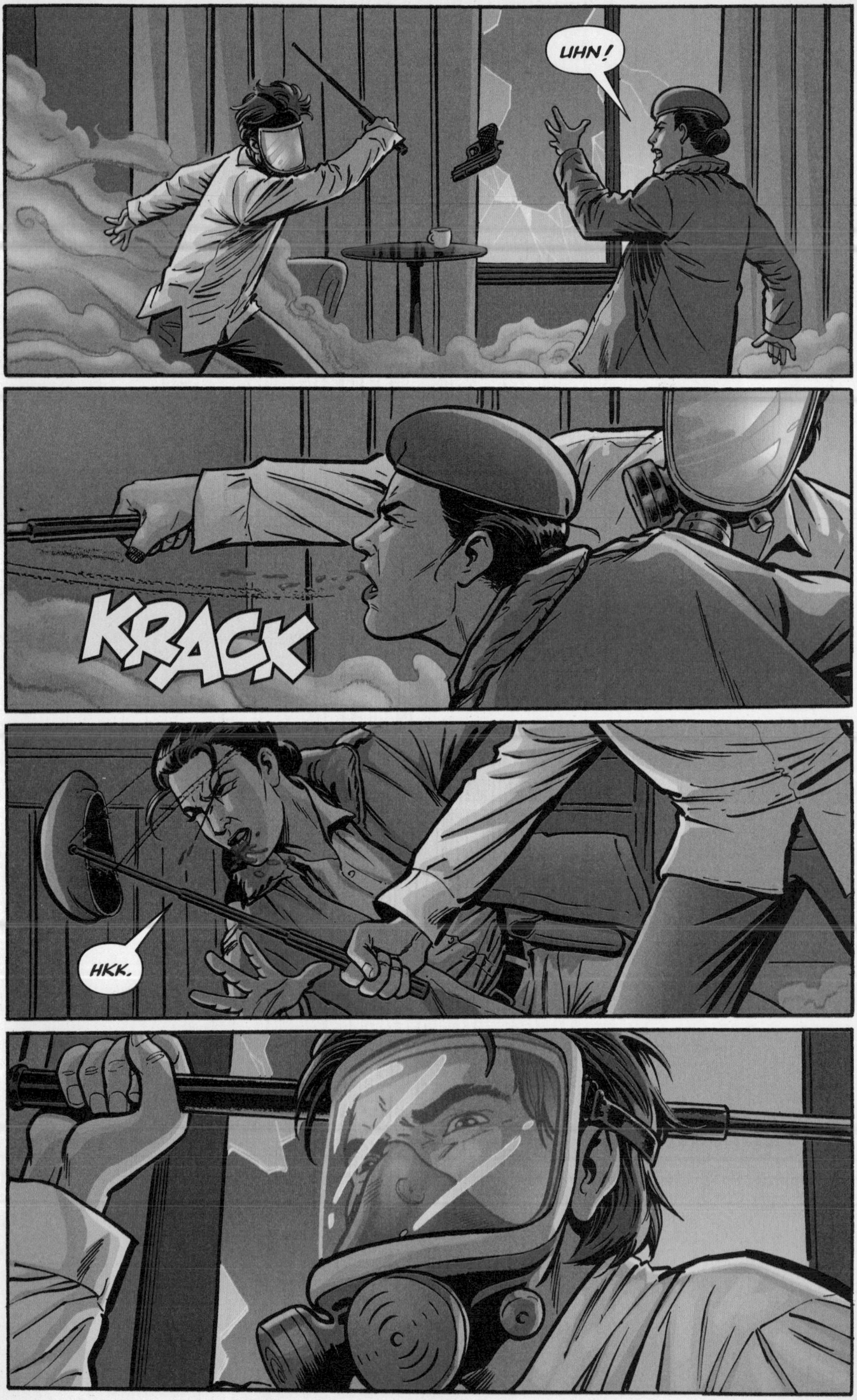
UHN!
KRACK
HKK.

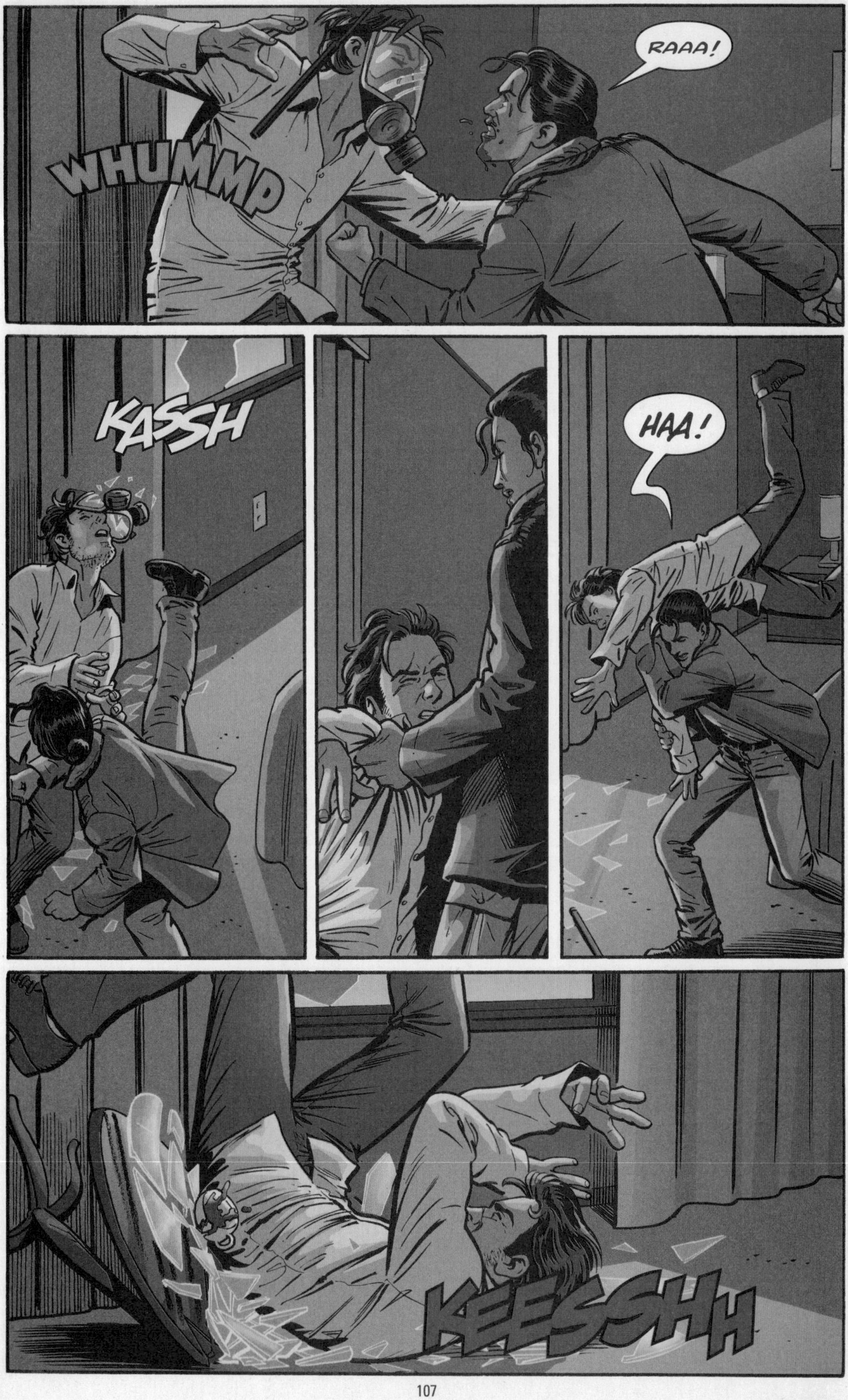
WHUMMP
RAAA!
KASSH
HAA!
KEESHH

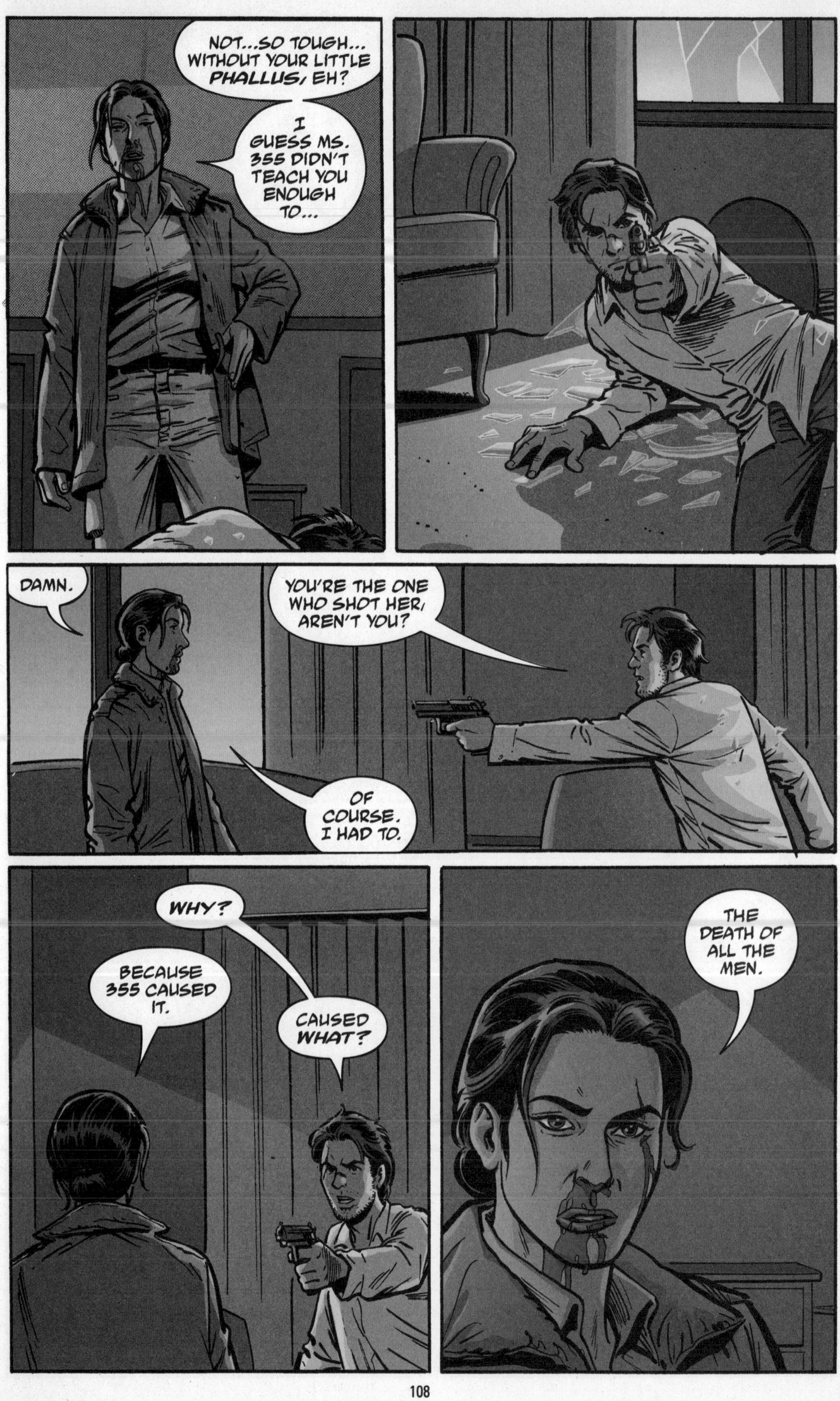
NOT...SO TOUGH... WITHOUT YOUR LITTLE PHALLUS, EH?
I GUESS MS. 355 DIDN'T TEACH YOU ENOUGH TO...
DAMN.
YOU'RE THE ONE WHO SHOT HER, AREN'T YOU?
OF COURSE. I HAD TO.
WHY?
BECAUSE 355 CAUSED IT.
CAUSED WHAT?
THE DEATH OF ALL THE MEN.

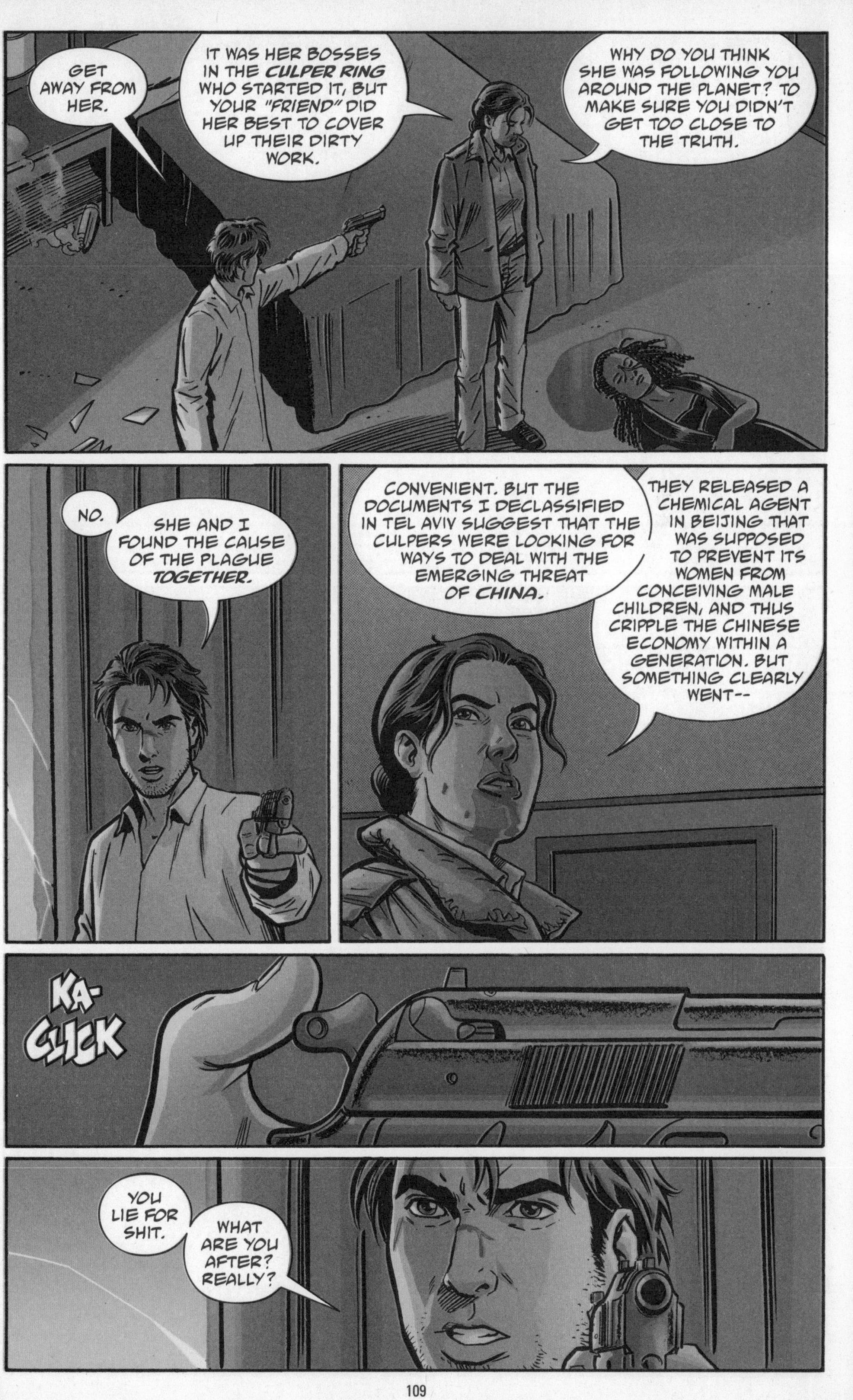
GET AWAY FROM HER.
IT WAS HER BOSSES IN THE CULPER RING WHO STARTED IT, BUT YOUR "FRIEND" DID HER BEST TO COVER UP THEIR DIRTY WORK.
WHY DO YOU THINK SHE WAS FOLLOWING YOU AROUND THE PLANET? TO MAKE SURE YOU DIDN'T GET TOO CLOSE TO THE TRUTH.
NO.
SHE AND I FOUND THE CAUSE OF THE PLAGUE TOGETHER.
CONVENIENT. BUT THE DOCUMENTS I DECLASSIFIED IN TEL AVIV SUGGEST THAT THE CULPERS WERE LOOKING FOR WAYS TO DEAL WITH THE EMERGING THREAT OF CHINA.
THEY RELEASED A CHEMICAL AGENT IN BEIJING THAT WAS SUPPOSED TO PREVENT ITS WOMEN FROM CONCEIVING MALE CHILDREN, AND THUS CRIPPLE THE CHINESE ECONOMY WITHIN A GENERATION. BUT SOMETHING CLEARLY WENT--
KA-CLICK
YOU LIE FOR SHIT.
WHAT ARE YOU AFTER? REALLY?

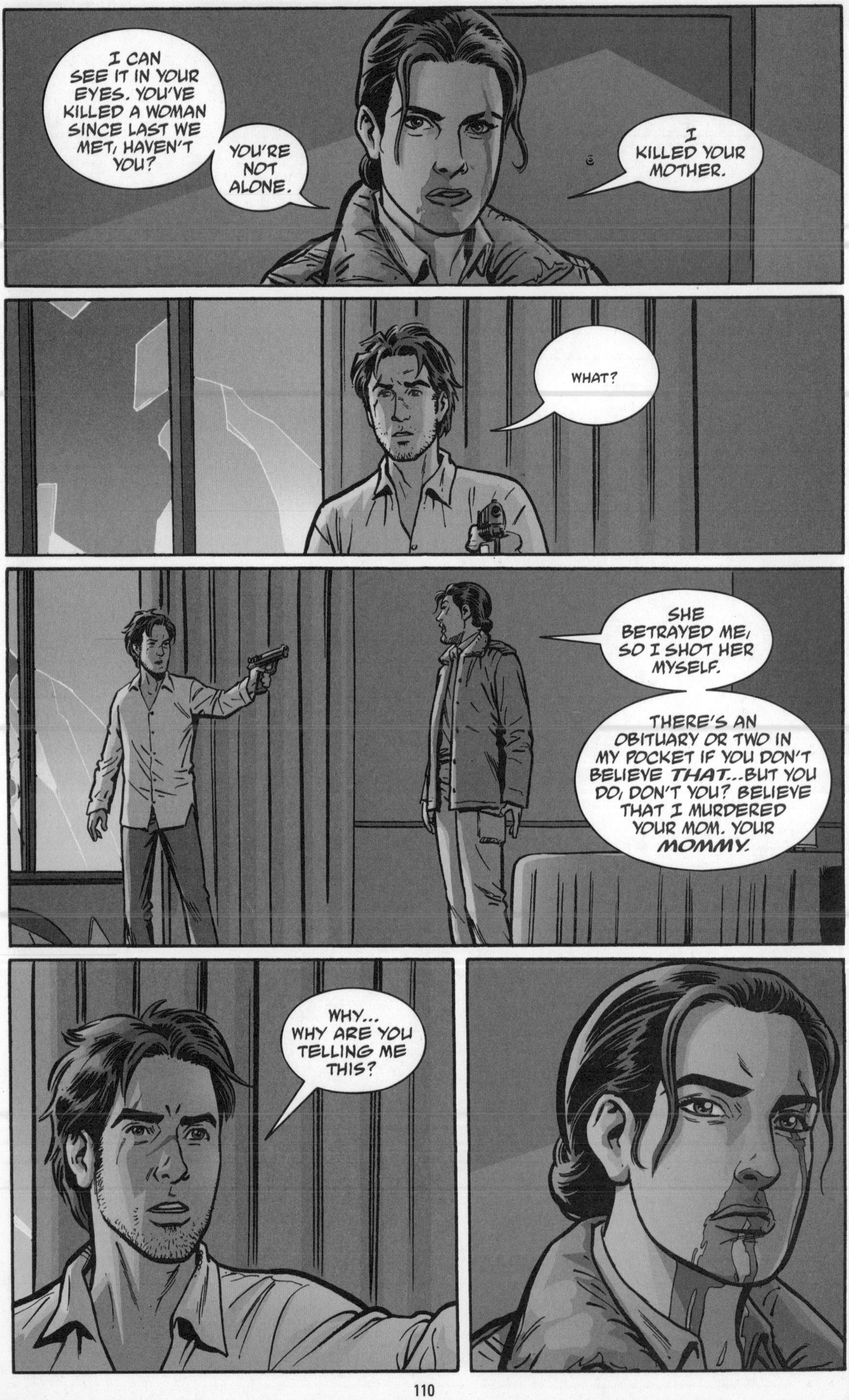
I CAN SEE IT IN YOUR EYES. YOU'VE KILLED A WOMAN SINCE LAST WE MET, HAVEN'T YOU?
YOU'RE NOT ALONE.
I KILLED YOUR MOTHER.
WHAT?
SHE BETRAYED ME, SO I SHOT HER MYSELF.
THERE'S AN OBITUARY OR TWO IN MY POCKET IF YOU DON'T BELIEVE *THAT*...BUT YOU DO, DON'T YOU? BELIEVE THAT I MURDERED YOUR MOM. YOUR **MOMMY.**
WHY... WHY ARE YOU TELLING ME THIS?

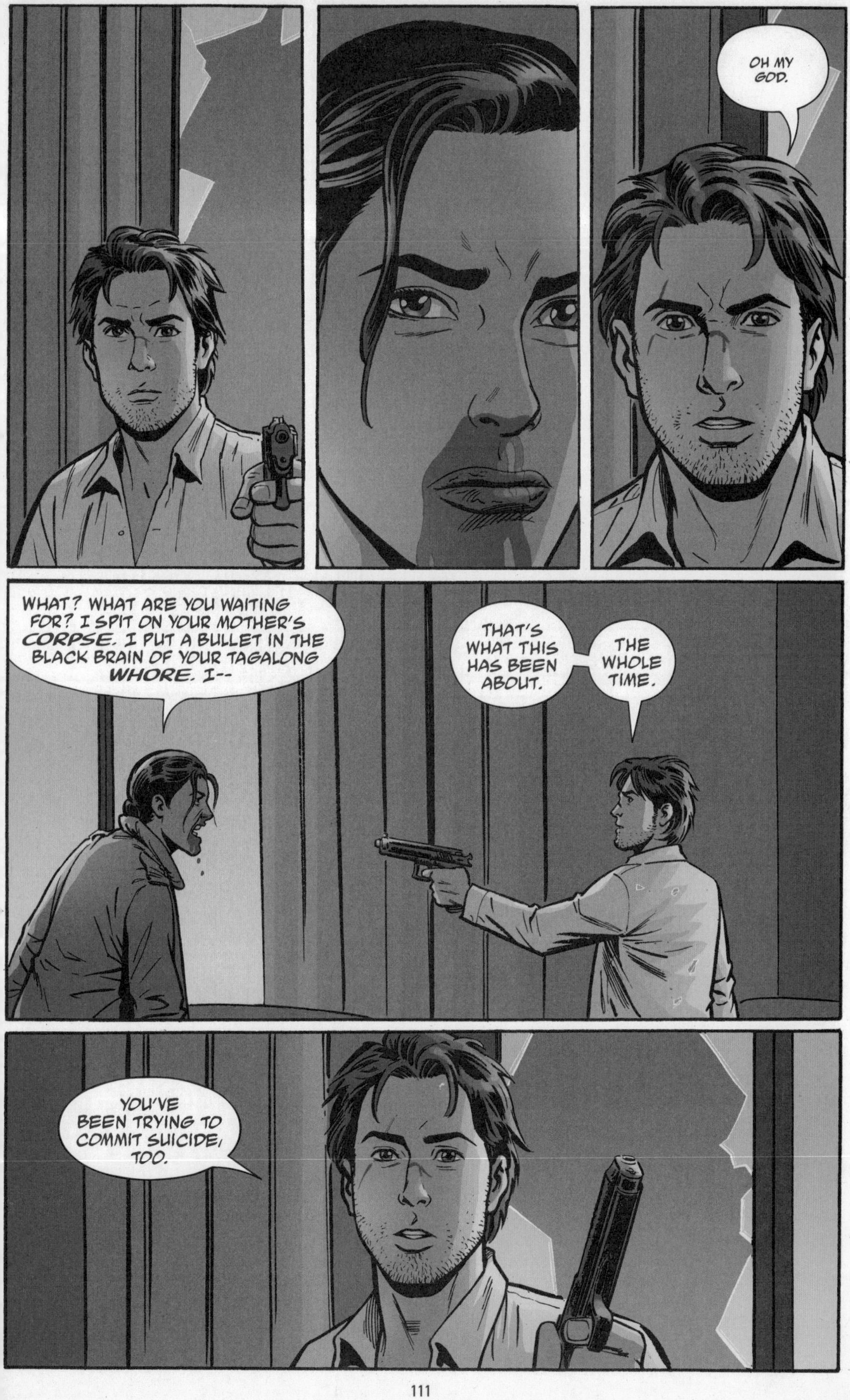
OH MY GOD.
WHAT? WHAT ARE YOU WAITING FOR? I SPIT ON YOUR MOTHER'S CORPSE. I PUT A BULLET IN THE BLACK BRAIN OF YOUR TAGALONG WHORE. I--
THAT'S WHAT THIS HAS BEEN ABOUT.
THE WHOLE TIME.
YOU'VE BEEN TRYING TO COMMIT SUICIDE, TOO.

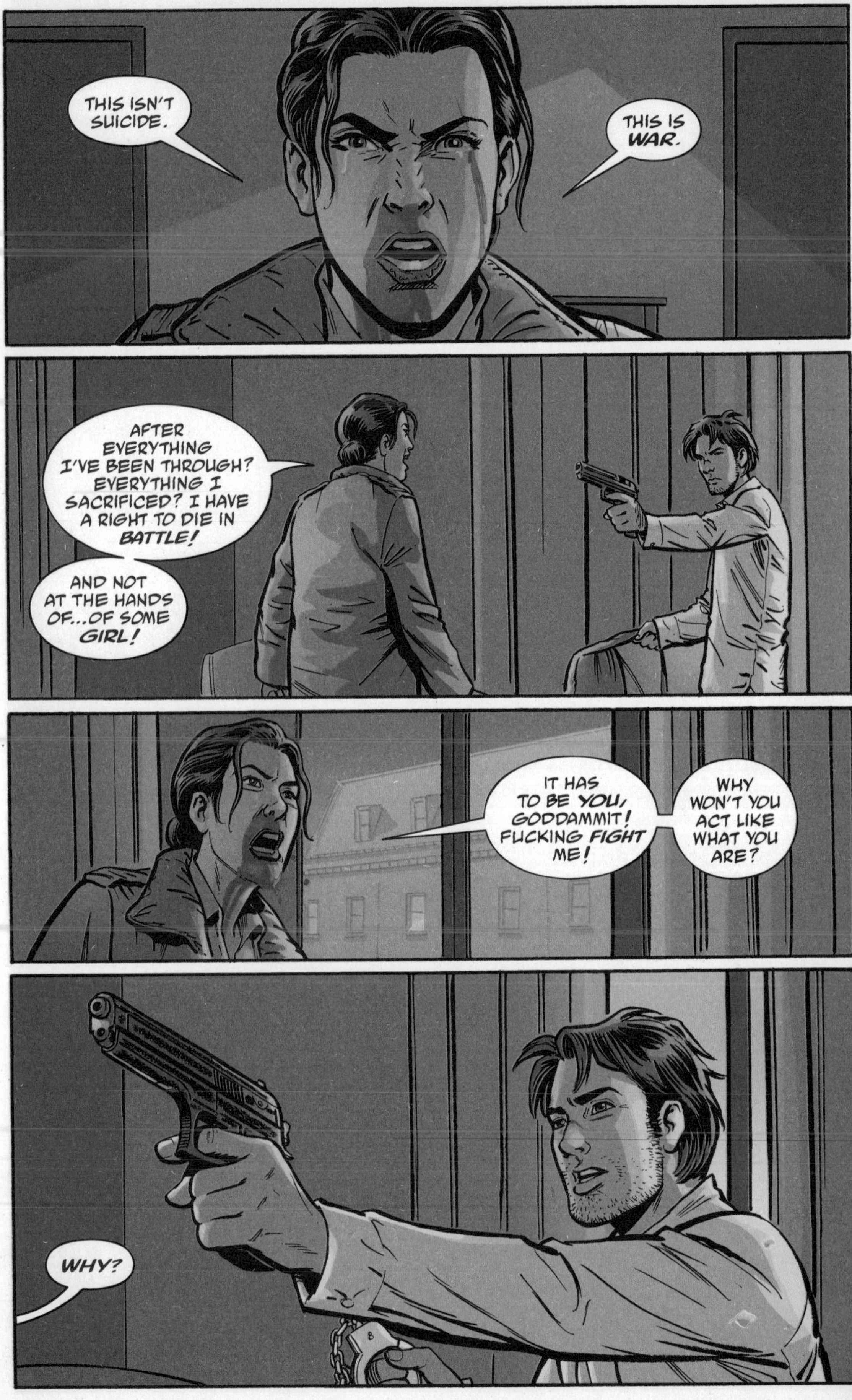
THIS ISN'T SUICIDE.
THIS IS WAR.
AFTER EVERYTHING I'VE BEEN THROUGH? EVERYTHING I SACRIFICED? I HAVE A RIGHT TO DIE IN BATTLE!
AND NOT AT THE HANDS OF...OF SOME GIRL!
IT HAS TO BE YOU, GODDAMMIT! FUCKING FIGHT ME!
WHY WON'T YOU ACT LIKE WHAT YOU ARE?
WHY?

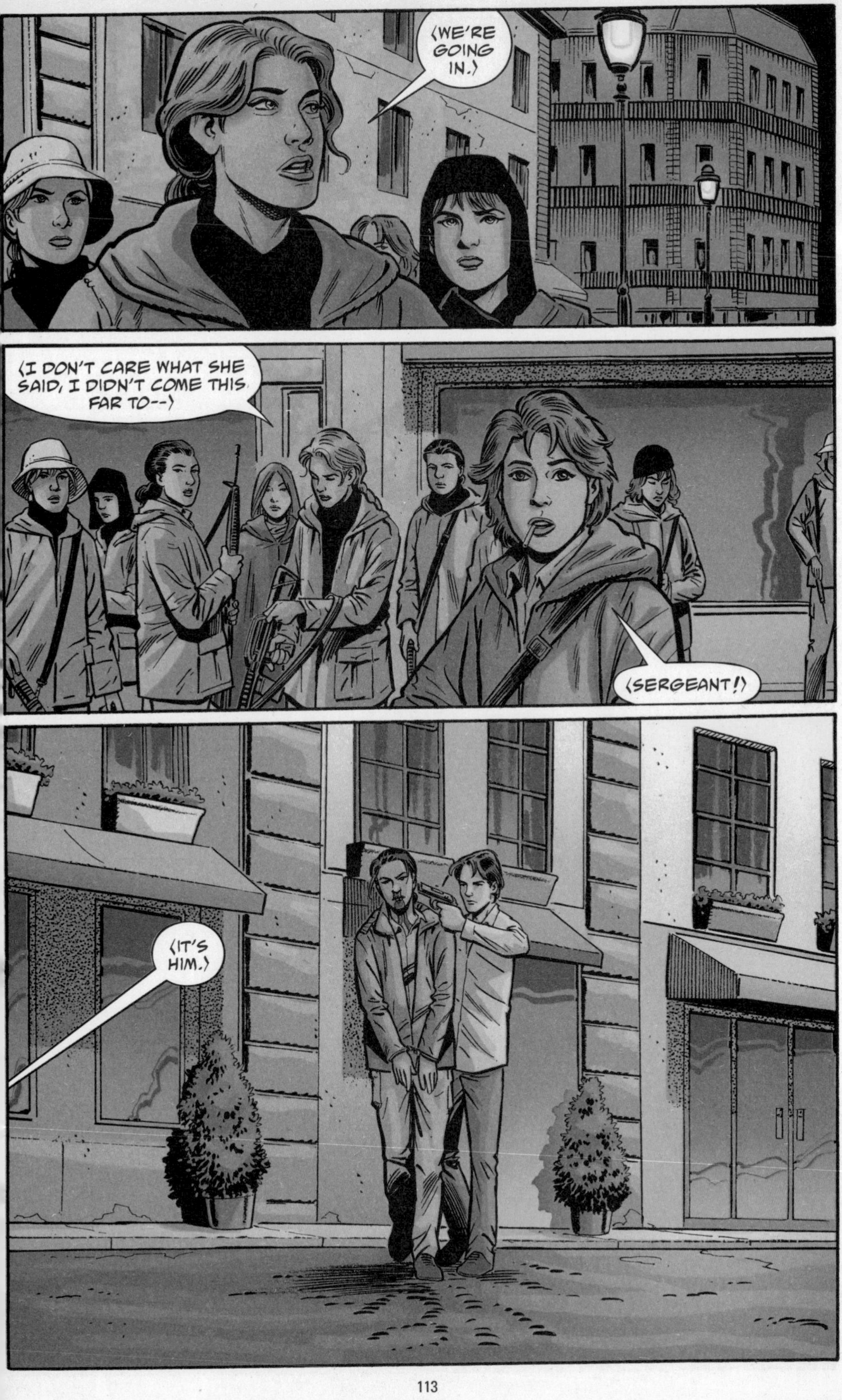
‹WE'RE GOING IN.›
‹I DON'T CARE WHAT SHE SAID, I DIDN'T COME THIS FAR TO--›
‹SERGEANT!›
‹IT'S HIM.›

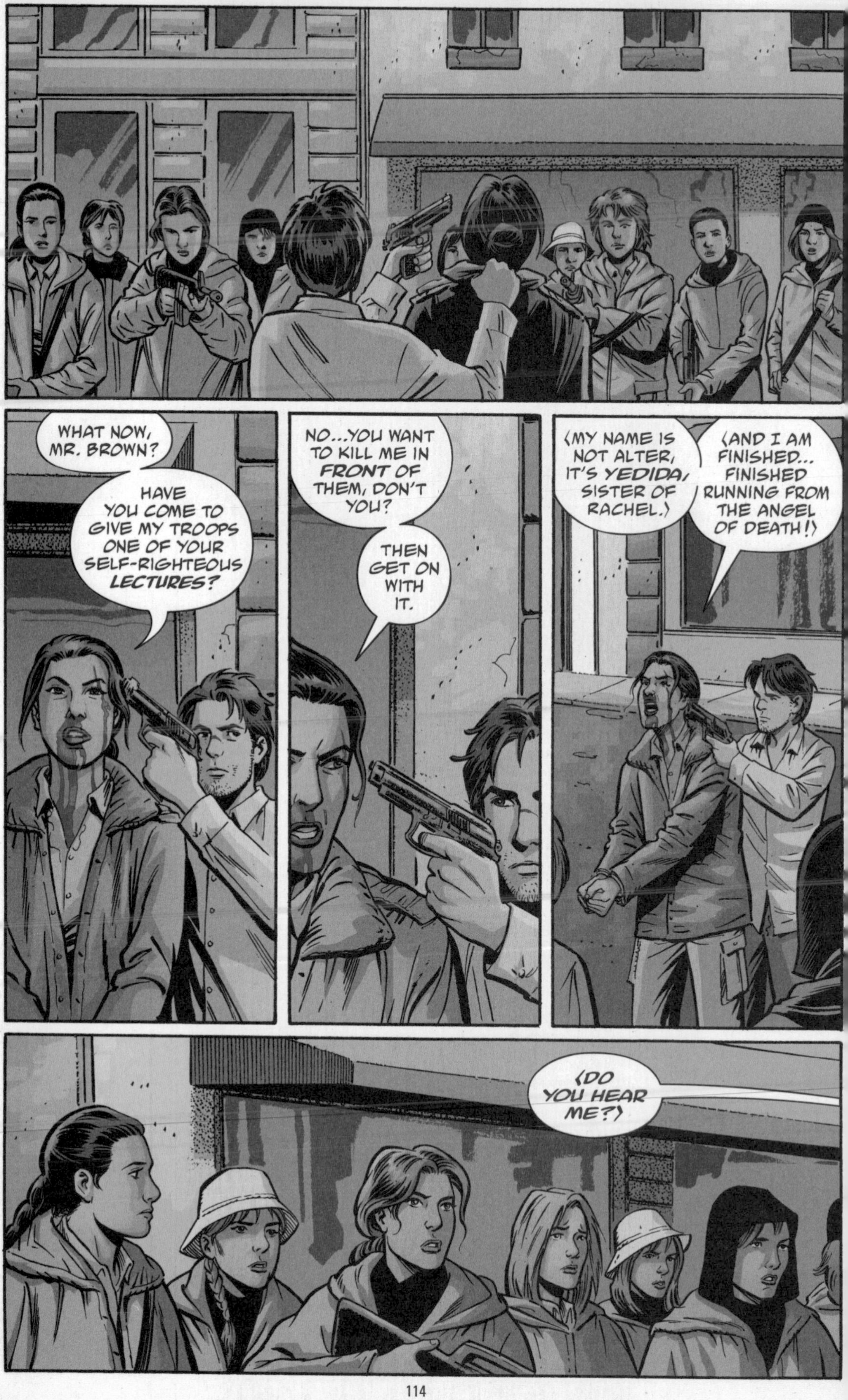
WHAT NOW, MR. BROWN?
HAVE YOU COME TO GIVE MY TROOPS ONE OF YOUR SELF-RIGHTEOUS *LECTURES?*
NO...YOU WANT TO KILL ME IN *FRONT* OF THEM, DON'T YOU?
THEN GET ON WITH IT.
‹MY NAME IS NOT ALTER, IT'S *YEDIDA,* SISTER OF RACHEL.›
‹AND I AM FINISHED... FINISHED RUNNING FROM THE ANGEL OF DEATH!›
‹*DO YOU HEAR ME?*›

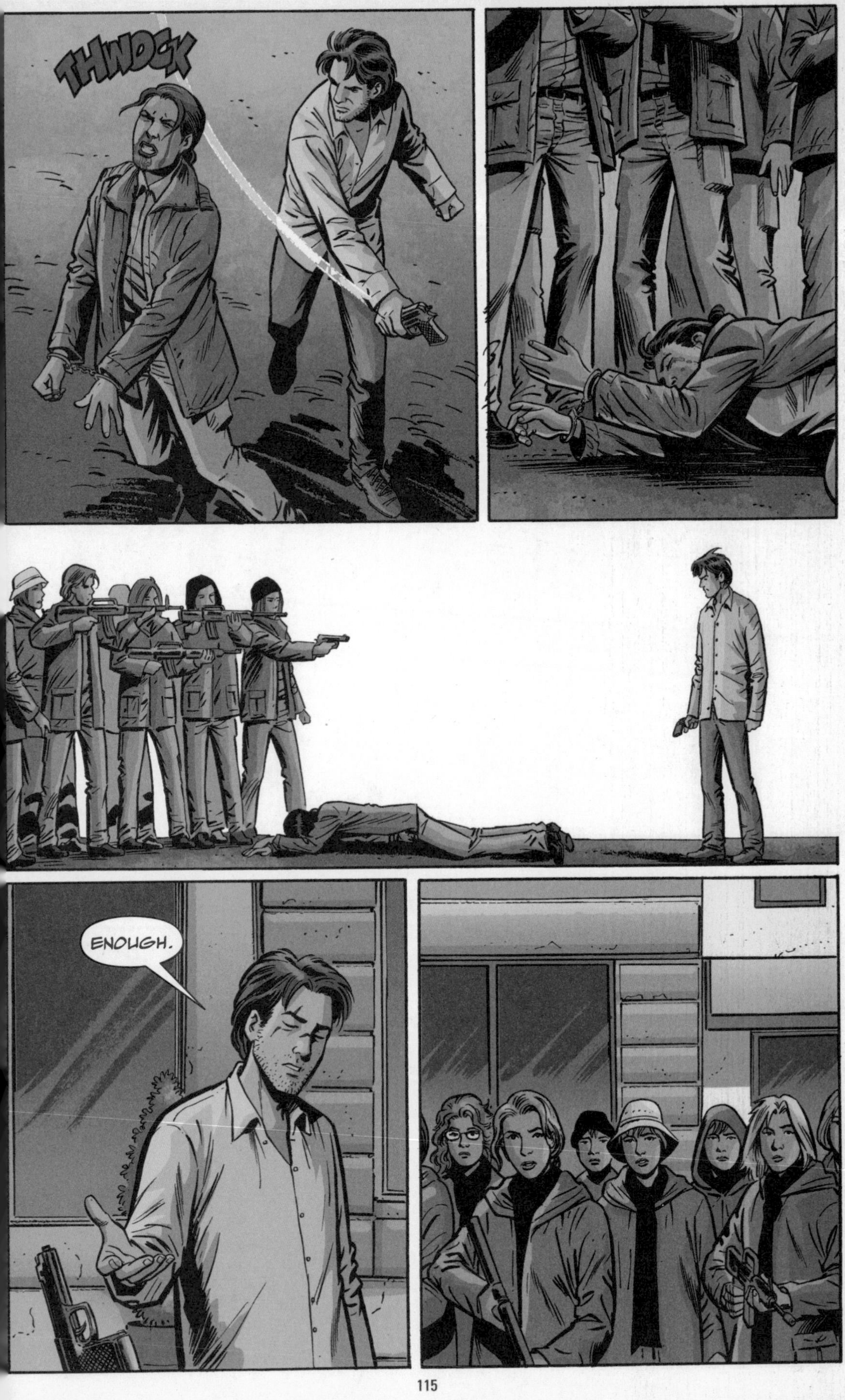
THWOCK
ENOUGH.

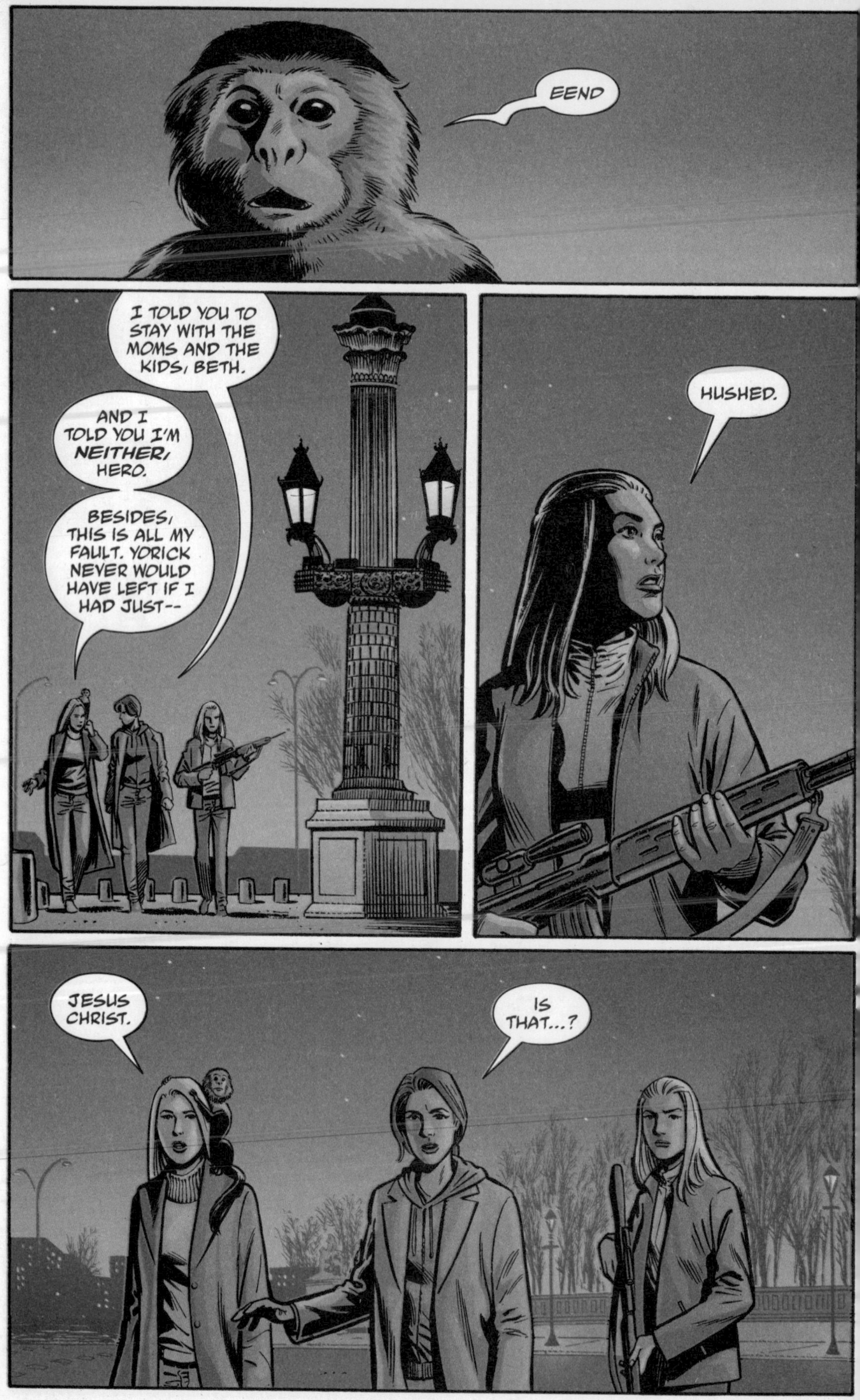
EEND
I TOLD YOU TO STAY WITH THE MOMS AND THE KIDS, BETH.
AND I TOLD YOU I'M NEITHER, HERO.
BESIDES, THIS IS ALL MY FAULT. YORICK NEVER WOULD HAVE LEFT IF I HAD JUST--
HUSHED.
JESUS CHRIST.
IS THAT...?

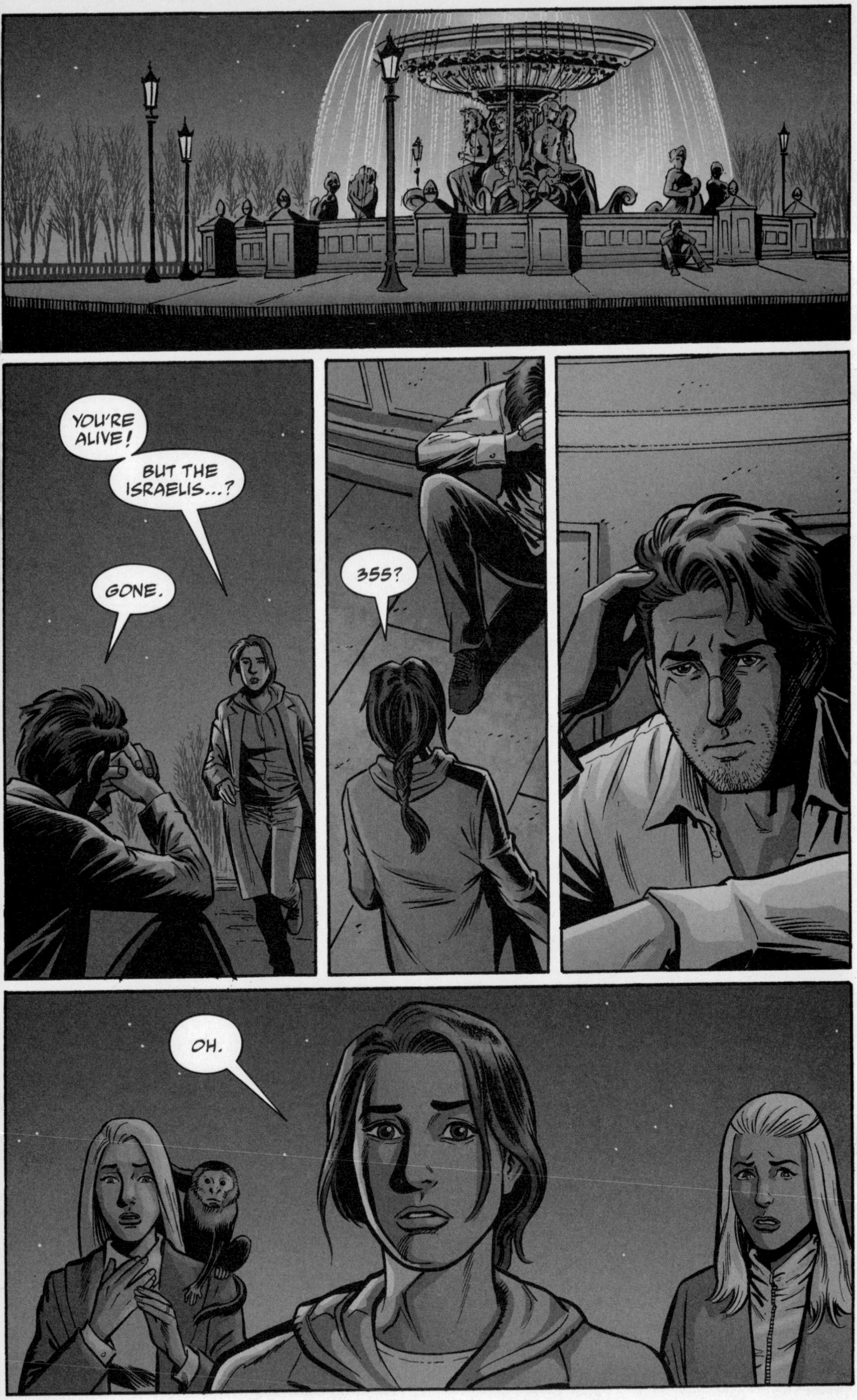
YOU'RE ALIVE!
BUT THE ISRAELIS...?
GONE.
355?
OH.

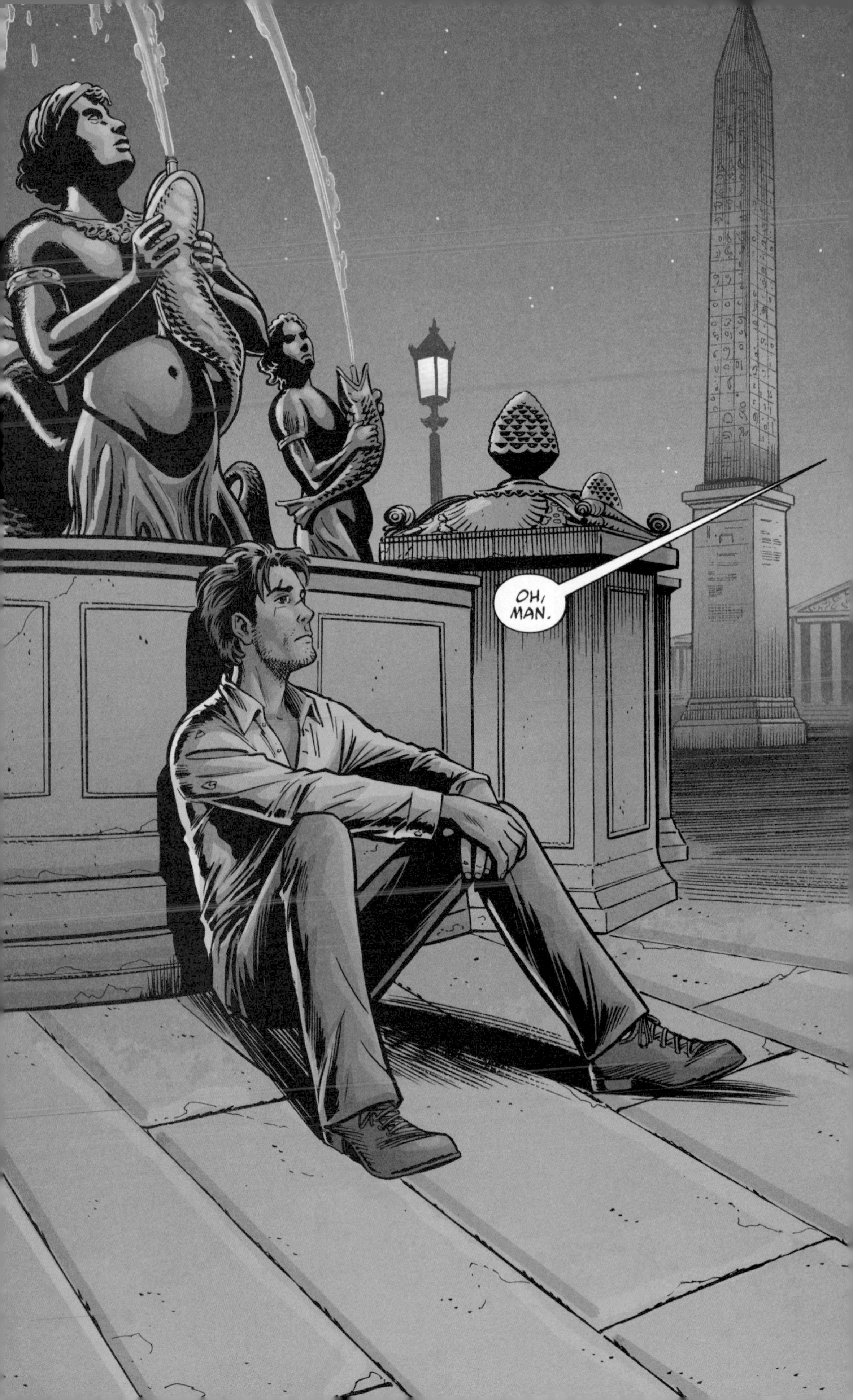
OH, MAN.

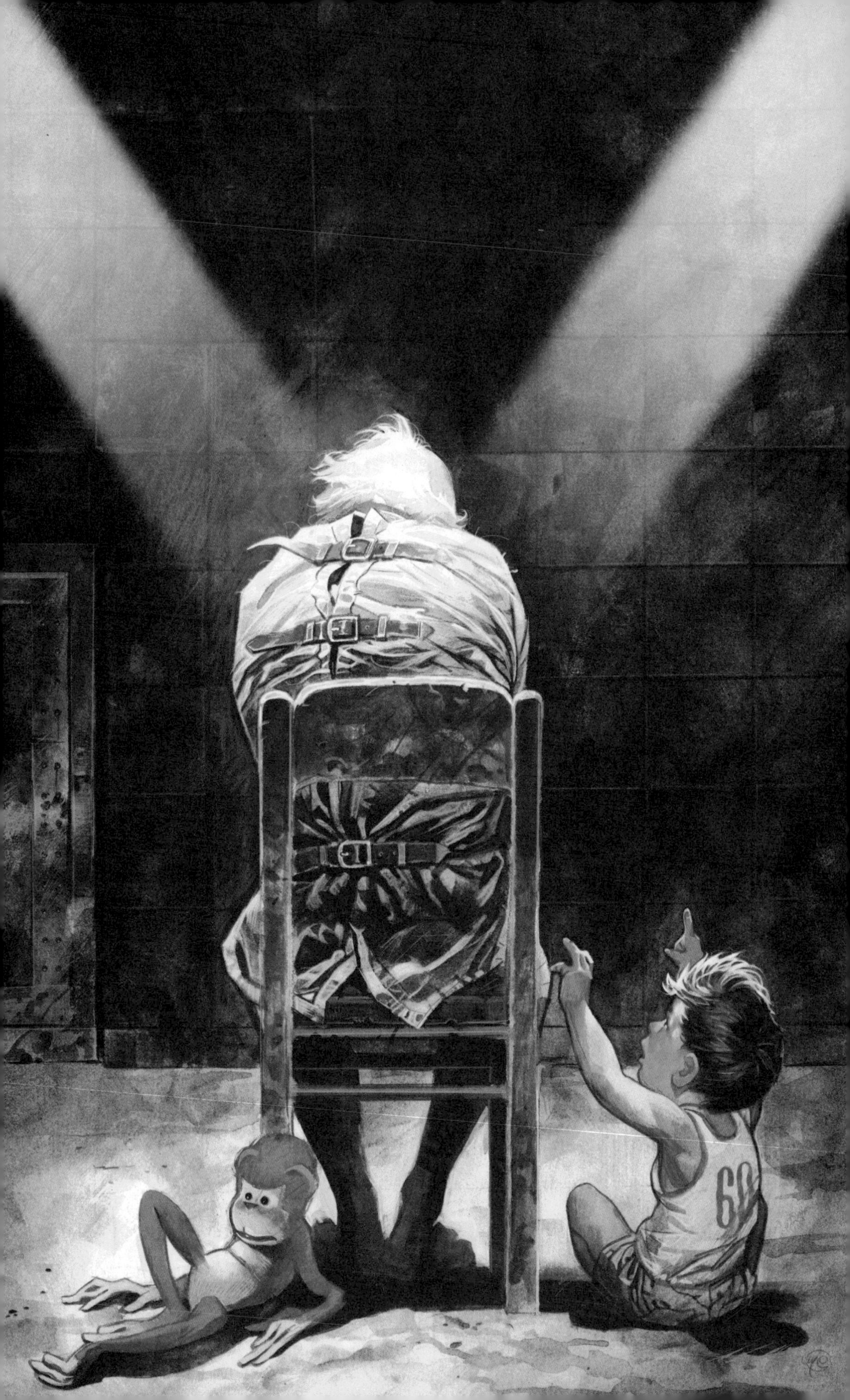
60

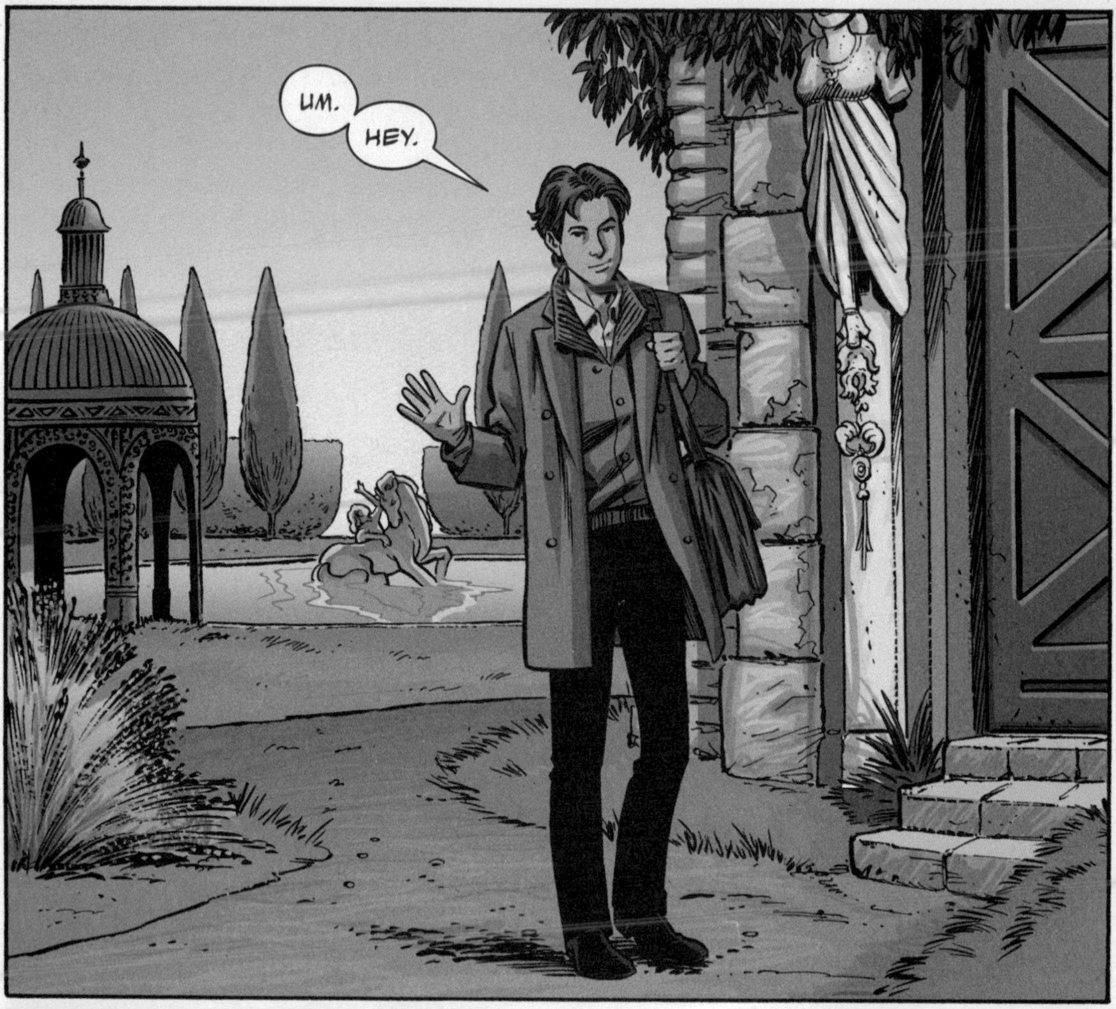
UM.
HEY.

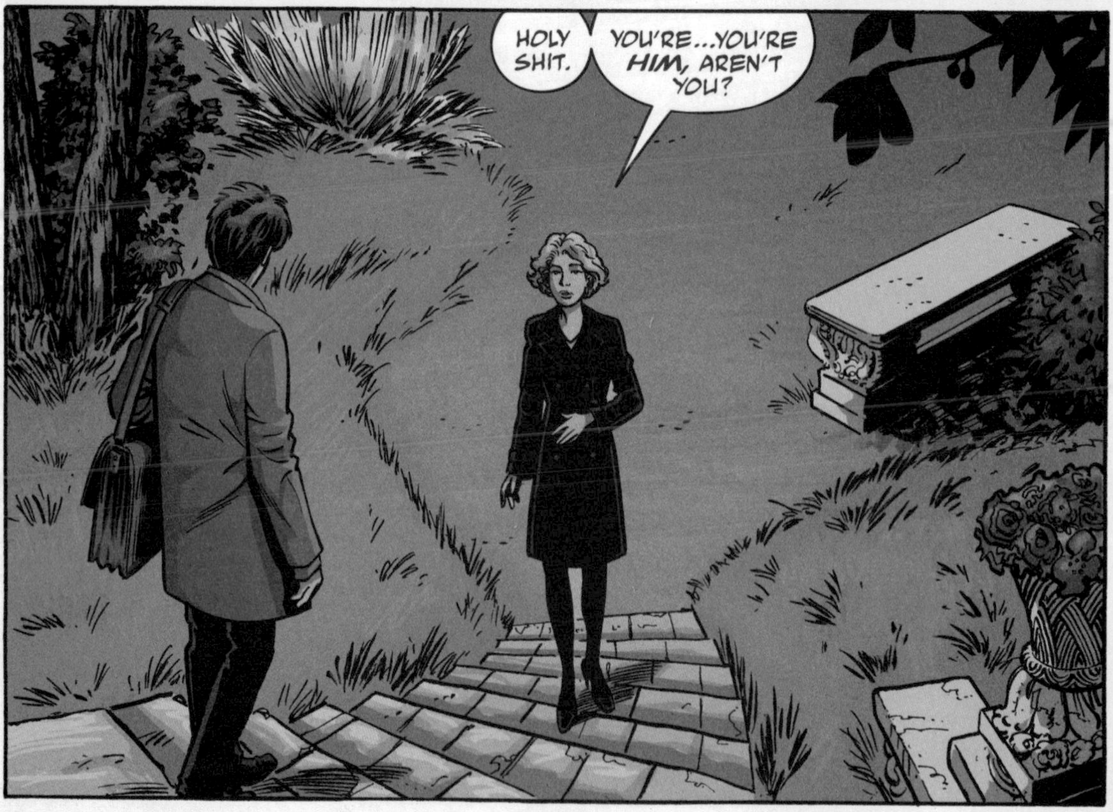
HOLY SHIT.
YOU'RE...YOU'RE *HIM*, AREN'T YOU?

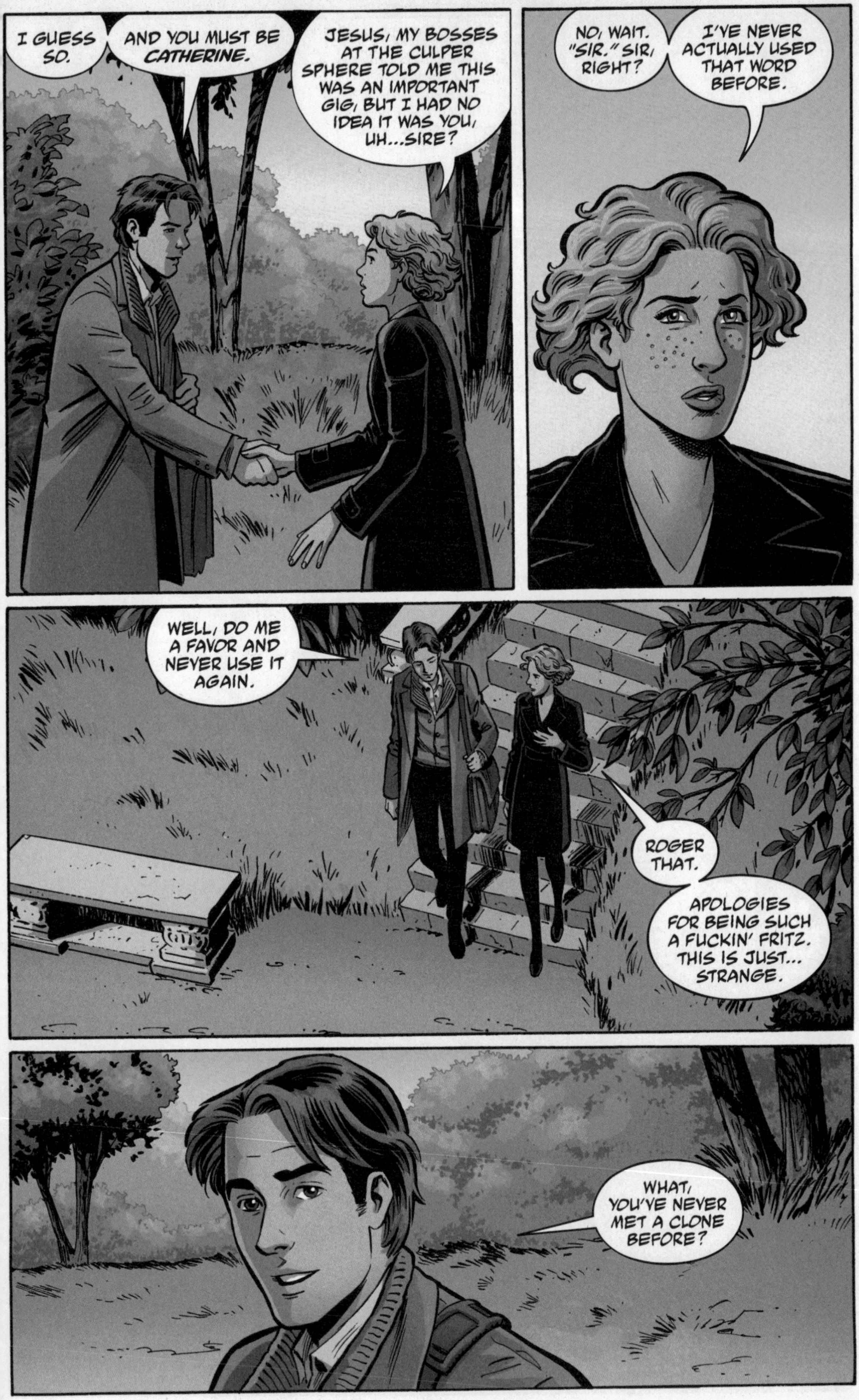
I GUESS SO.
AND YOU MUST BE CATHERINE.
JESUS, MY BOSSES AT THE CULPER SPHERE TOLD ME THIS WAS AN IMPORTANT GIG, BUT I HAD NO IDEA IT WAS YOU, UH...SIRE?
NO, WAIT. "SIR." SIR, RIGHT?
I'VE NEVER ACTUALLY USED THAT WORD BEFORE.
WELL, DO ME A FAVOR AND NEVER USE IT AGAIN.
ROGER THAT.
APOLOGIES FOR BEING SUCH A FUCKIN' FRITZ. THIS IS JUST... STRANGE.
WHAT, YOU'VE NEVER MET A CLONE BEFORE?

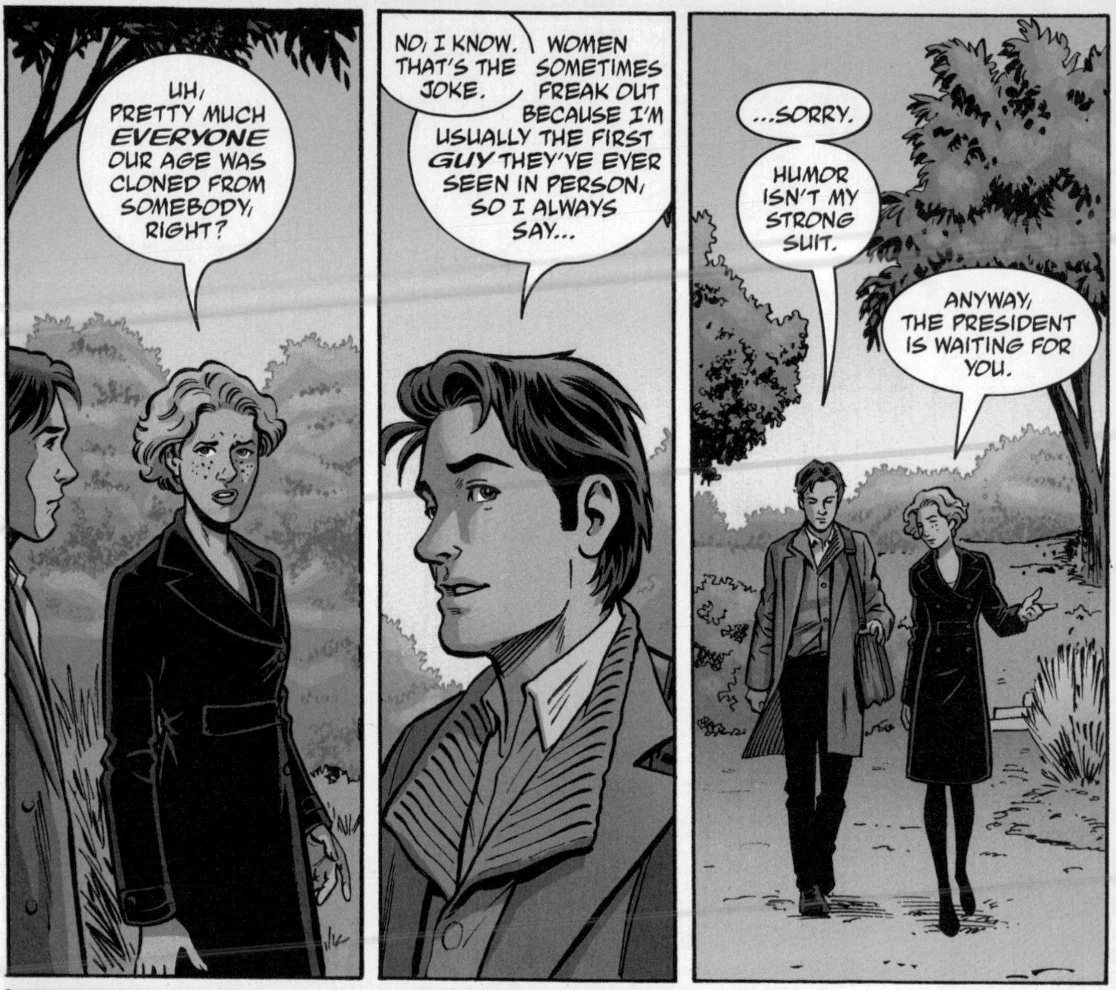
UH, PRETTY MUCH EVERYONE OUR AGE WAS CLONED FROM SOMEBODY, RIGHT?
NO, I KNOW. THAT'S THE JOKE.
WOMEN SOMETIMES FREAK OUT BECAUSE I'M USUALLY THE FIRST GUY THEY'VE EVER SEEN IN PERSON, SO I ALWAYS SAY...
...SORRY.
HUMOR ISN'T MY STRONG SUIT.
ANYWAY, THE PRESIDENT IS WAITING FOR YOU.

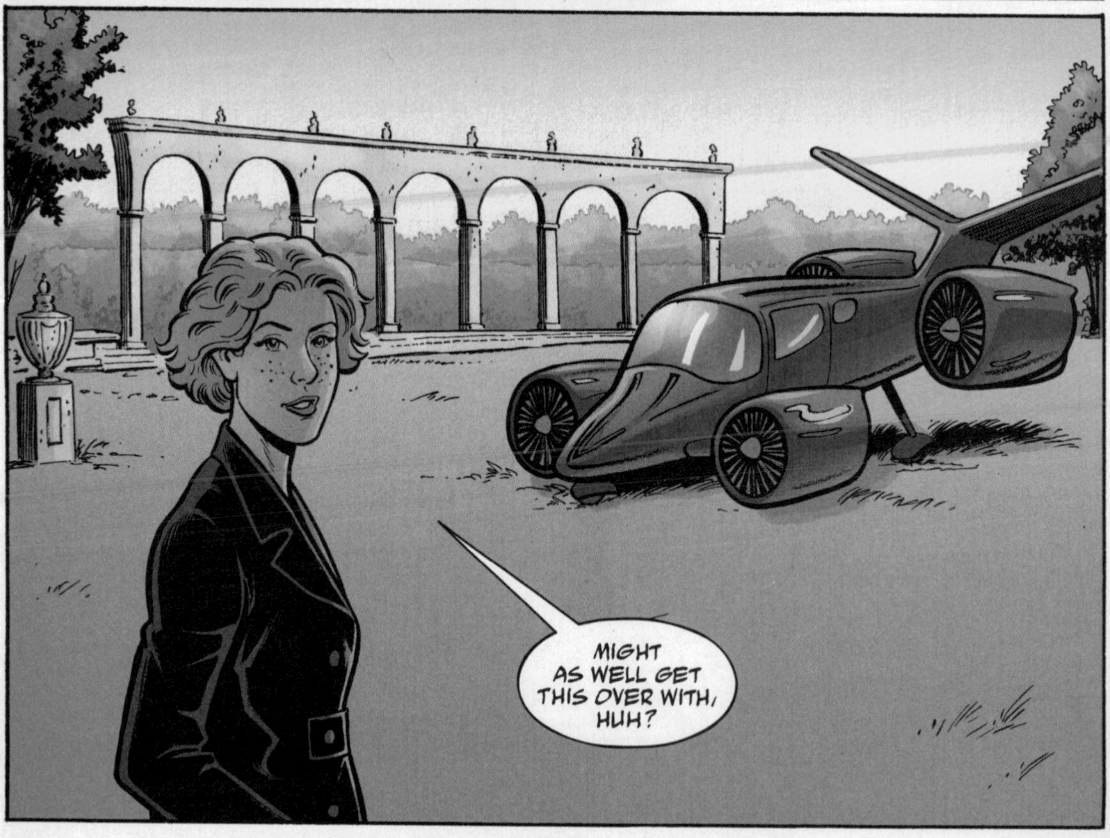
MIGHT AS WELL GET THIS OVER WITH, HUH?

Paris, France
Sixty Years from Now

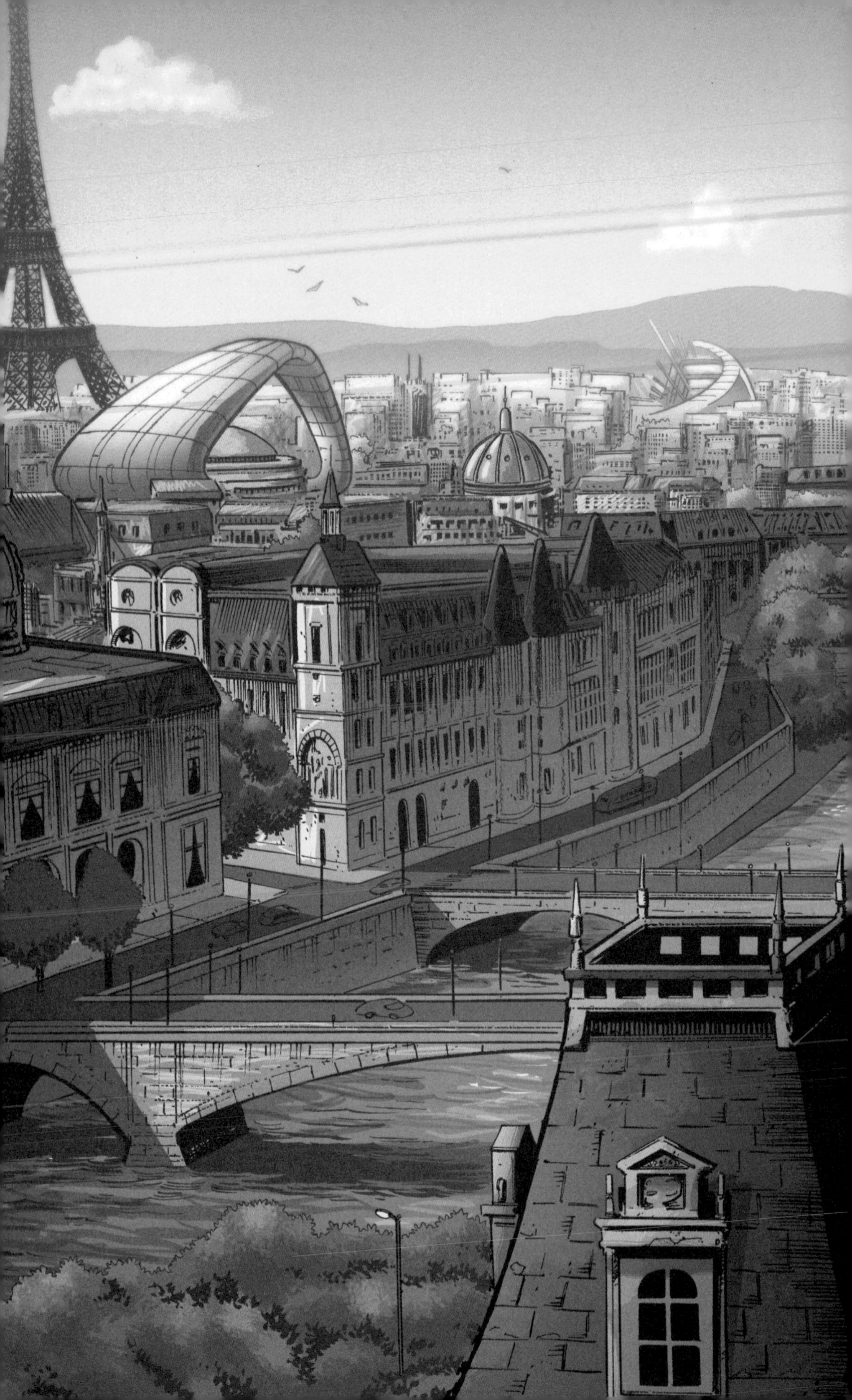

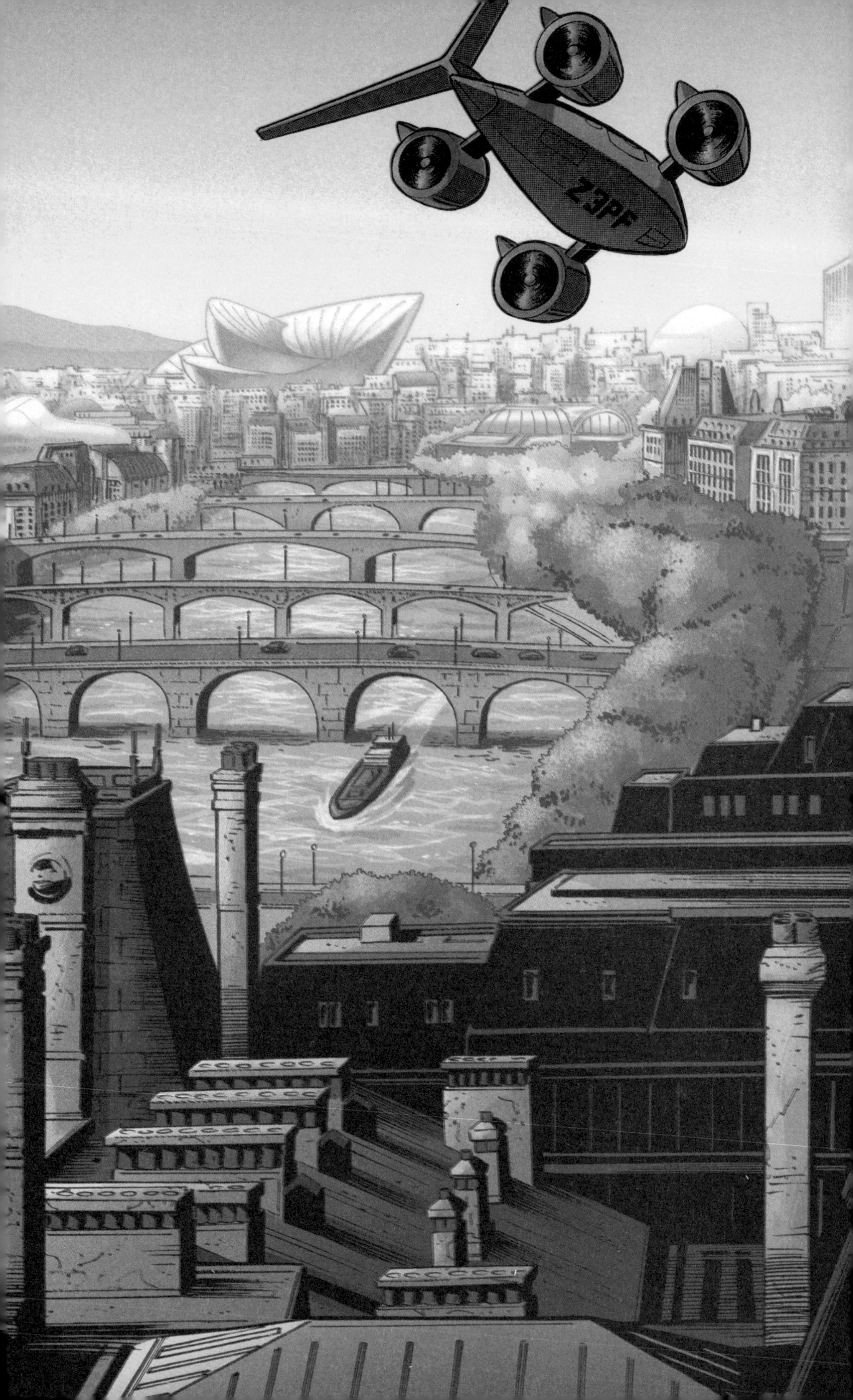
Z3PF

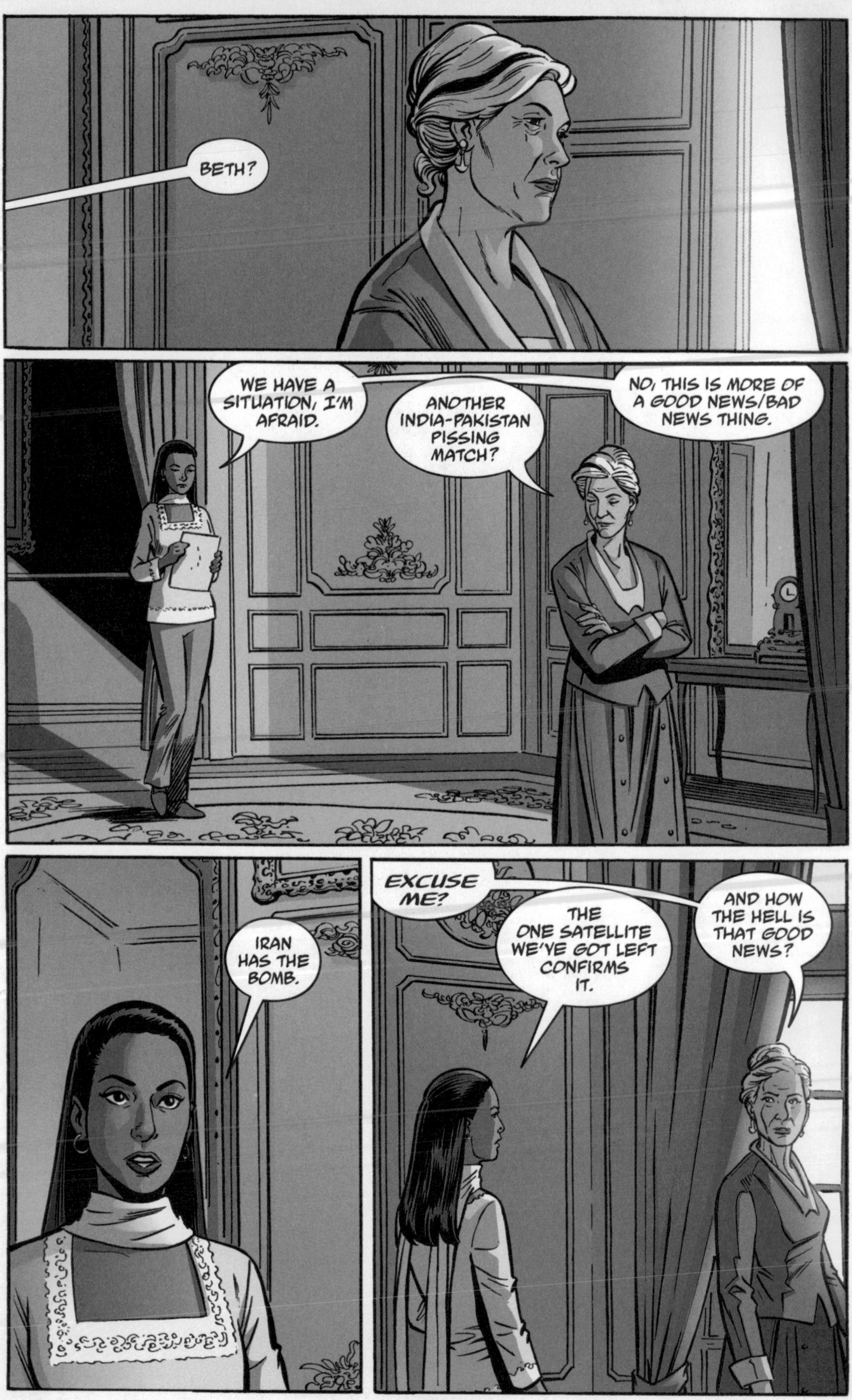
BETH?
WE HAVE A SITUATION, I'M AFRAID.
ANOTHER INDIA-PAKISTAN PISSING MATCH?
NO, THIS IS MORE OF A GOOD NEWS/BAD NEWS THING.
IRAN HAS THE BOMB.
EXCUSE ME?
THE ONE SATELLITE WE'VE GOT LEFT CONFIRMS IT.
AND HOW THE HELL IS THAT GOOD NEWS?

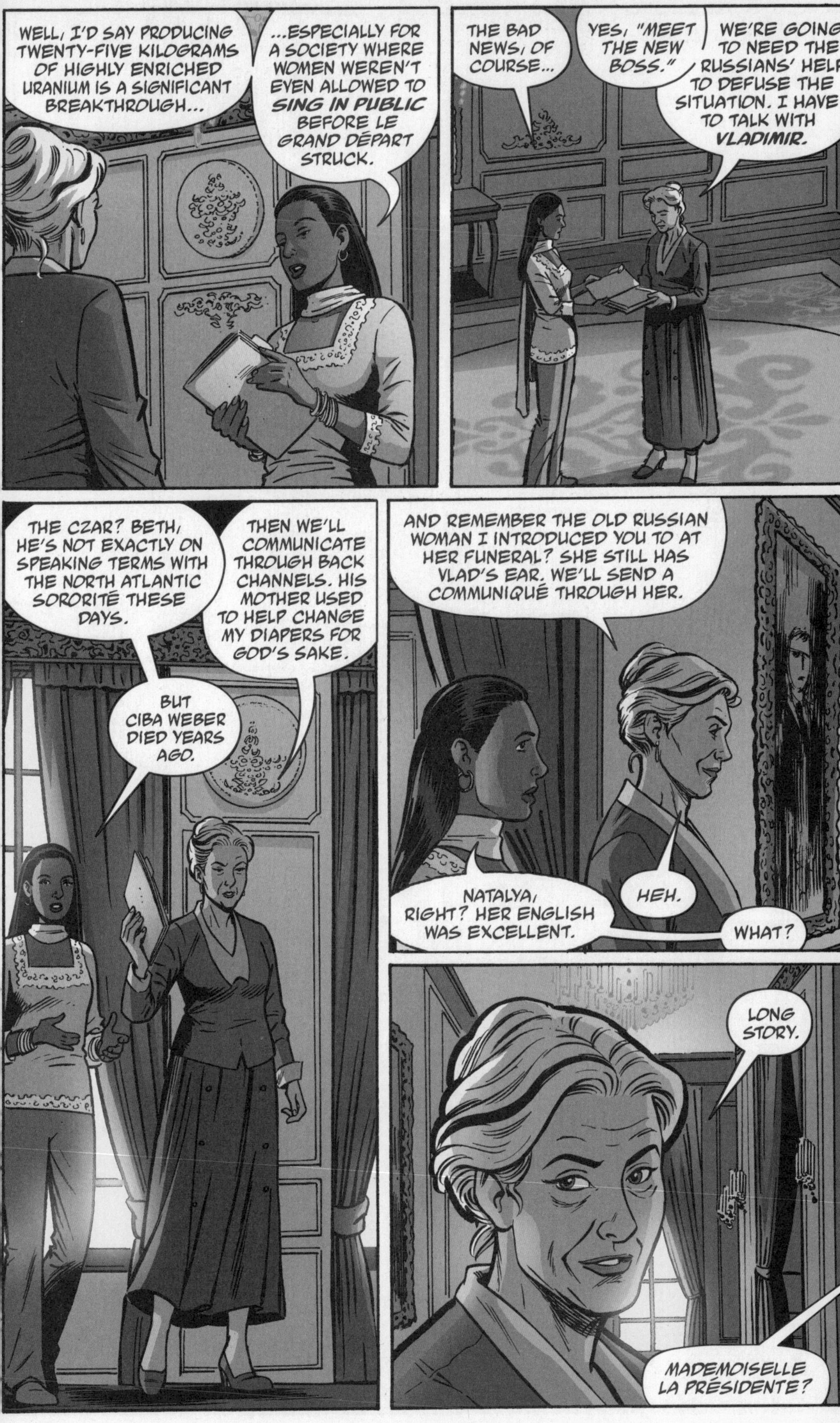

WELL, I'D SAY PRODUCING TWENTY-FIVE KILOGRAMS OF HIGHLY ENRICHED URANIUM IS A SIGNIFICANT BREAKTHROUGH...
...ESPECIALLY FOR A SOCIETY WHERE WOMEN WEREN'T EVEN ALLOWED TO SING IN PUBLIC BEFORE LE GRAND DÉPART STRUCK.
THE BAD NEWS, OF COURSE...
YES, "MEET THE NEW BOSS."
WE'RE GOING TO NEED THE RUSSIANS' HELP TO DEFUSE THE SITUATION. I HAVE TO TALK WITH VLADIMIR.
THE CZAR? BETH, HE'S NOT EXACTLY ON SPEAKING TERMS WITH THE NORTH ATLANTIC SORORITÉ THESE DAYS.
THEN WE'LL COMMUNICATE THROUGH BACK CHANNELS. HIS MOTHER USED TO HELP CHANGE MY DIAPERS FOR GOD'S SAKE.
BUT CIBA WEBER DIED YEARS AGO.
AND REMEMBER THE OLD RUSSIAN WOMAN I INTRODUCED YOU TO AT HER FUNERAL? SHE STILL HAS VLAD'S EAR. WE'LL SEND A COMMUNIQUÉ THROUGH HER.
NATALYA, RIGHT? HER ENGLISH WAS EXCELLENT.
HEH.
WHAT?
LONG STORY.
MADEMOISELLE LA PRÉSIDENTE?

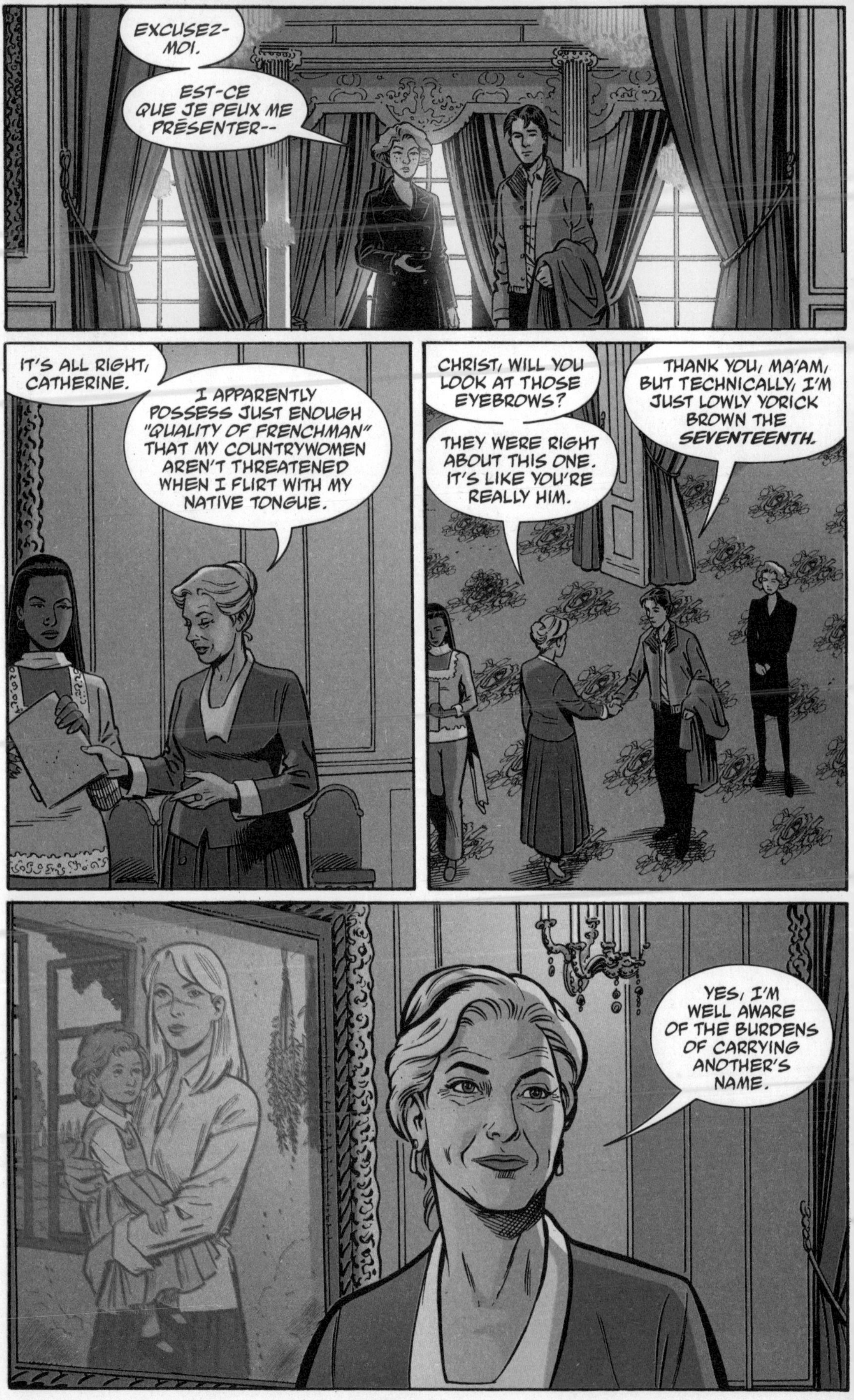

EXCUSEZ-MOI.
EST-CE QUE JE PEUX ME PRÉSENTER--
IT'S ALL RIGHT, CATHERINE.
I APPARENTLY POSSESS JUST ENOUGH "QUALITY OF FRENCHMAN" THAT MY COUNTRYWOMEN AREN'T THREATENED WHEN I FLIRT WITH MY NATIVE TONGUE.
CHRIST, WILL YOU LOOK AT THOSE EYEBROWS?
THEY WERE RIGHT ABOUT THIS ONE. IT'S LIKE YOU'RE REALLY HIM.
THANK YOU, MA'AM, BUT TECHNICALLY, I'M JUST LOWLY YORICK BROWN THE SEVENTEENTH.
YES, I'M WELL AWARE OF THE BURDENS OF CARRYING ANOTHER'S NAME.

MY SURROGATE GAVE ME ONE OF YOUR MOM'S BOOKS ON SECULAR HUMANISM.

IT WAS REALLY... INTERESTING.

NICE OF YOU TO SAY, BUT BETH SENIOR CONVERTED BACK TO POST-VATICAN III CATHOLICISM LATE IN LIFE.

ATHEISM APPARENTLY LOSES ITS LUSTER WHEN THE FINISH LINE APPROACHES.

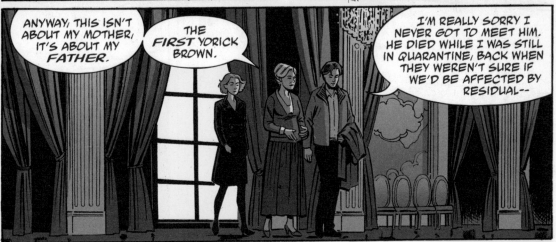

ANYWAY, THIS ISN'T ABOUT MY MOTHER, IT'S ABOUT MY FATHER.

THE FIRST YORICK BROWN.

I'M REALLY SORRY I NEVER GOT TO MEET HIM. HE DIED WHILE I WAS STILL IN QUARANTINE, BACK WHEN THEY WEREN'T SURE IF WE'D BE AFFECTED BY RESIDUAL--

THAT'S THE THING, YORICK.

MY DAD IS STILL ALIVE.

HUH?

129

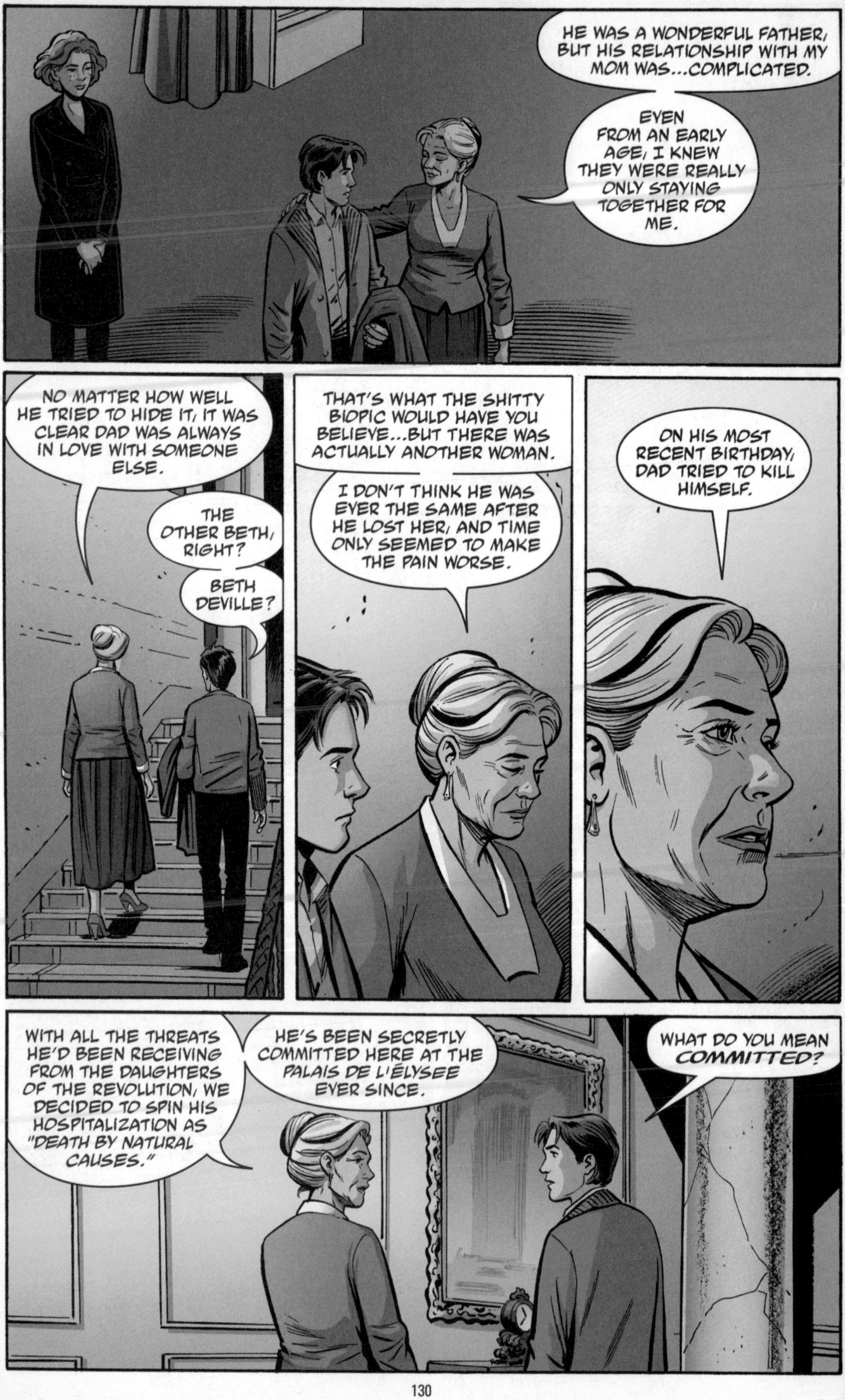
HE WAS A WONDERFUL FATHER, BUT HIS RELATIONSHIP WITH MY MOM WAS...COMPLICATED.
EVEN FROM AN EARLY AGE, I KNEW THEY WERE REALLY ONLY STAYING TOGETHER FOR ME.
NO MATTER HOW WELL HE TRIED TO HIDE IT, IT WAS CLEAR DAD WAS ALWAYS IN LOVE WITH SOMEONE ELSE.
THE OTHER BETH, RIGHT?
BETH DEVILLE?
THAT'S WHAT THE SHITTY BIOPIC WOULD HAVE YOU BELIEVE...BUT THERE WAS ACTUALLY ANOTHER WOMAN.
I DON'T THINK HE WAS EVER THE SAME AFTER HE LOST HER, AND TIME ONLY SEEMED TO MAKE THE PAIN WORSE.
ON HIS MOST RECENT BIRTHDAY, DAD TRIED TO KILL HIMSELF.
WITH ALL THE THREATS HE'D BEEN RECEIVING FROM THE DAUGHTERS OF THE REVOLUTION, WE DECIDED TO SPIN HIS HOSPITALIZATION AS "DEATH BY NATURAL CAUSES."
HE'S BEEN SECRETLY COMMITTED HERE AT THE PALAIS DE L'ÉLYSEE EVER SINCE.
WHAT DO YOU MEAN *COMMITTED?*

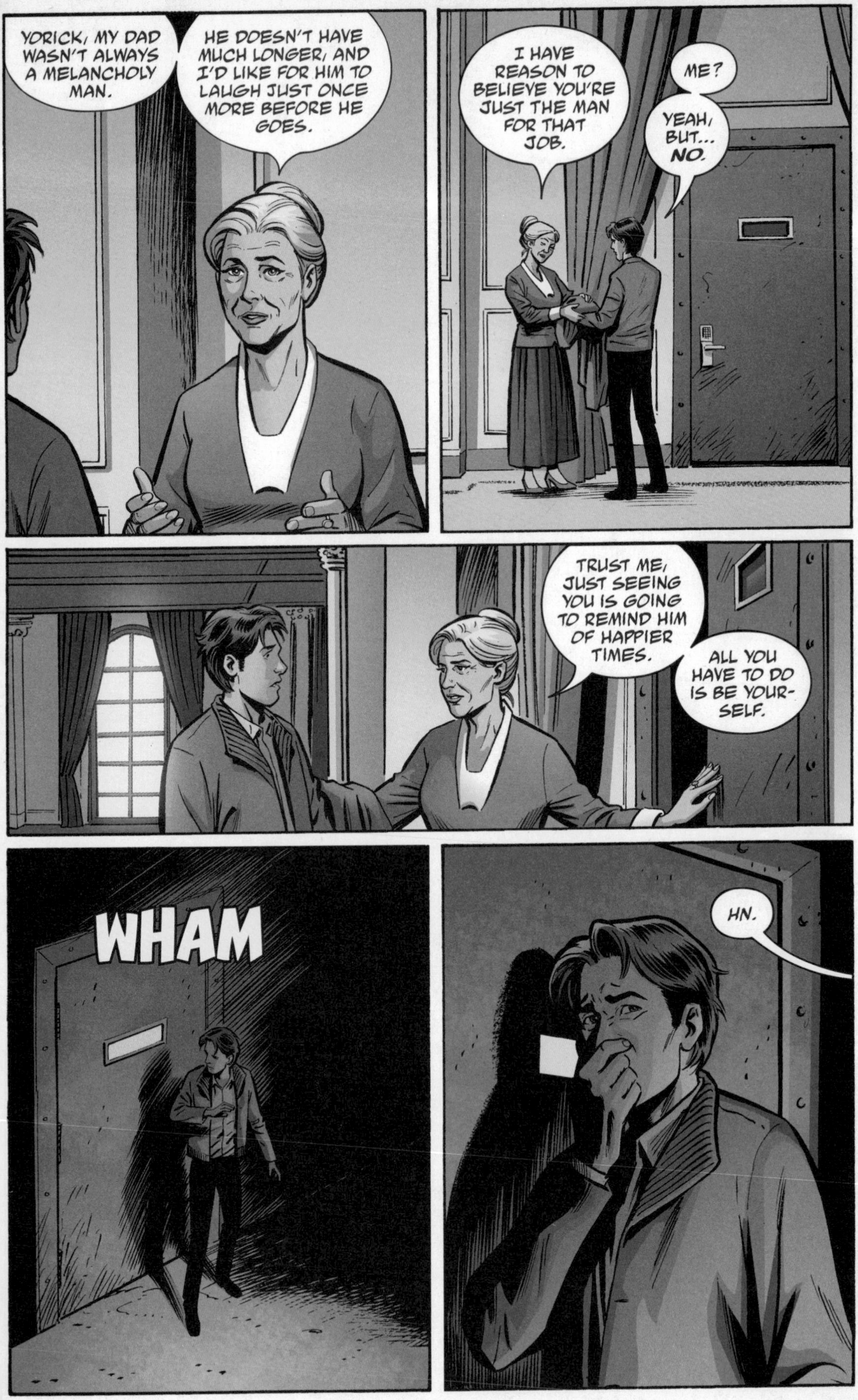
YORICK, MY DAD WASN'T ALWAYS A MELANCHOLY MAN.
HE DOESN'T HAVE MUCH LONGER, AND I'D LIKE FOR HIM TO LAUGH JUST ONCE MORE BEFORE HE GOES.
I HAVE REASON TO BELIEVE YOU'RE JUST THE MAN FOR THAT JOB.
ME?
YEAH, BUT... NO.
TRUST ME, JUST SEEING YOU IS GOING TO REMIND HIM OF HAPPIER TIMES.
ALL YOU HAVE TO DO IS BE YOUR-SELF.
WHAM
HN.

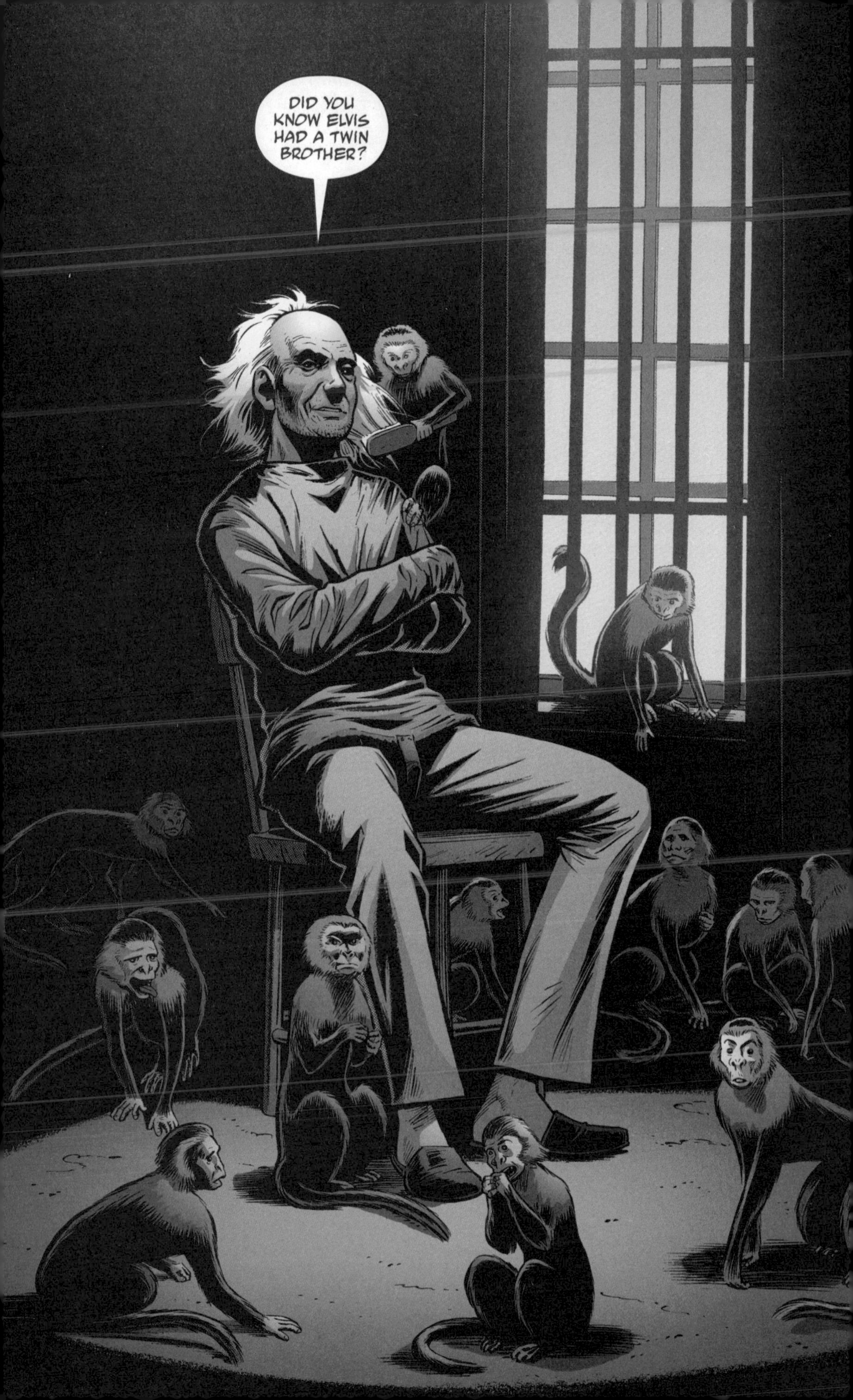
DID YOU KNOW ELVIS HAD A TWIN BROTHER?

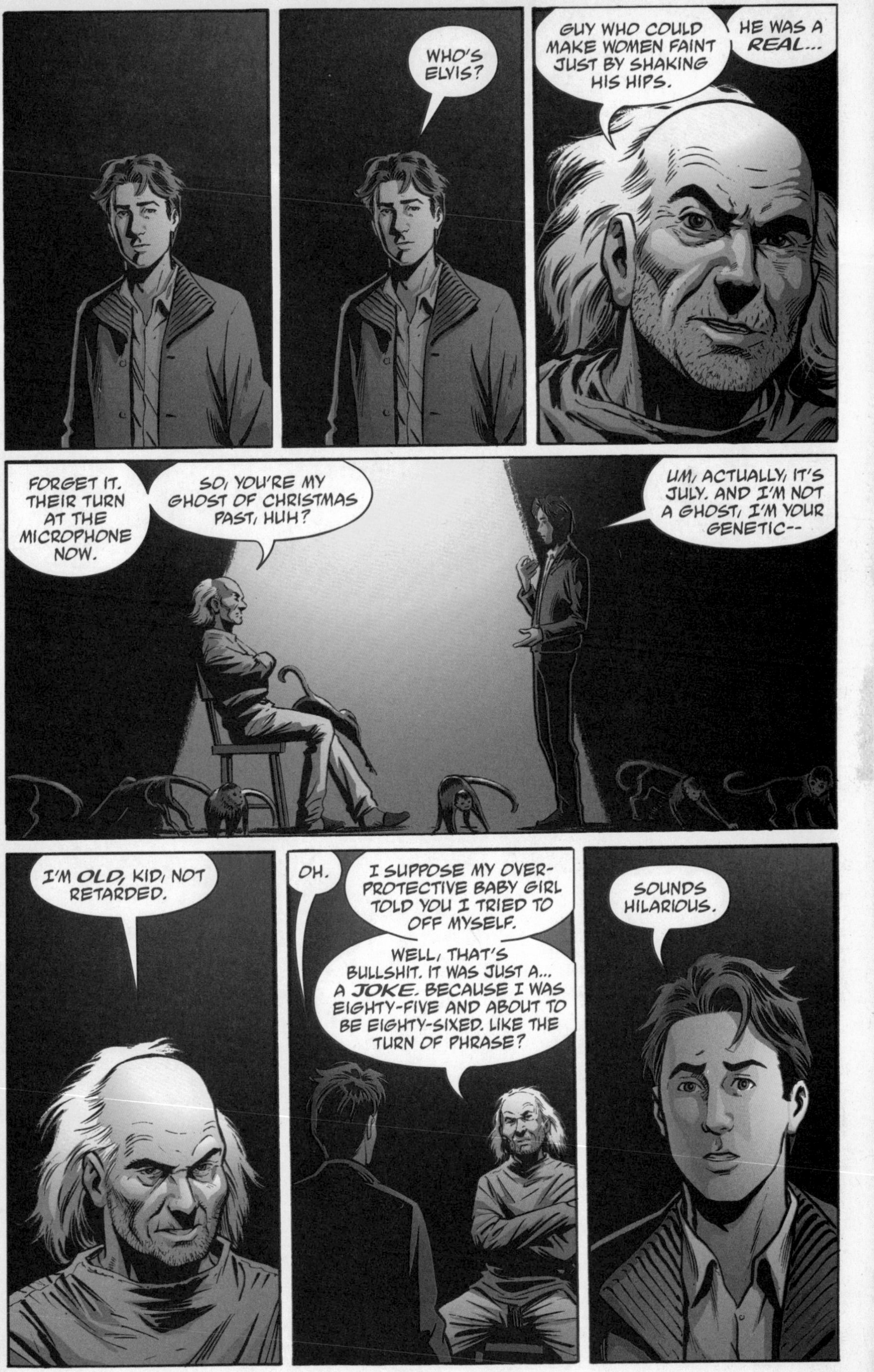
WHO'S ELVIS?
GUY WHO COULD MAKE WOMEN FAINT JUST BY SHAKING HIS HIPS.
HE WAS A *REAL*...
FORGET IT. THEIR TURN AT THE MICROPHONE NOW.
SO, YOU'RE MY GHOST OF CHRISTMAS PAST, HUH?
UM, ACTUALLY, IT'S JULY. AND I'M NOT A GHOST, I'M YOUR GENETIC--
I'M *OLD*, KID, NOT RETARDED.
OH.
I SUPPOSE MY OVER-PROTECTIVE BABY GIRL TOLD YOU I TRIED TO OFF MYSELF.
WELL, THAT'S BULLSHIT. IT WAS JUST A... A *JOKE*. BECAUSE I WAS EIGHTY-FIVE AND ABOUT TO BE EIGHTY-SIXED. LIKE THE TURN OF PHRASE?
SOUNDS HILARIOUS.

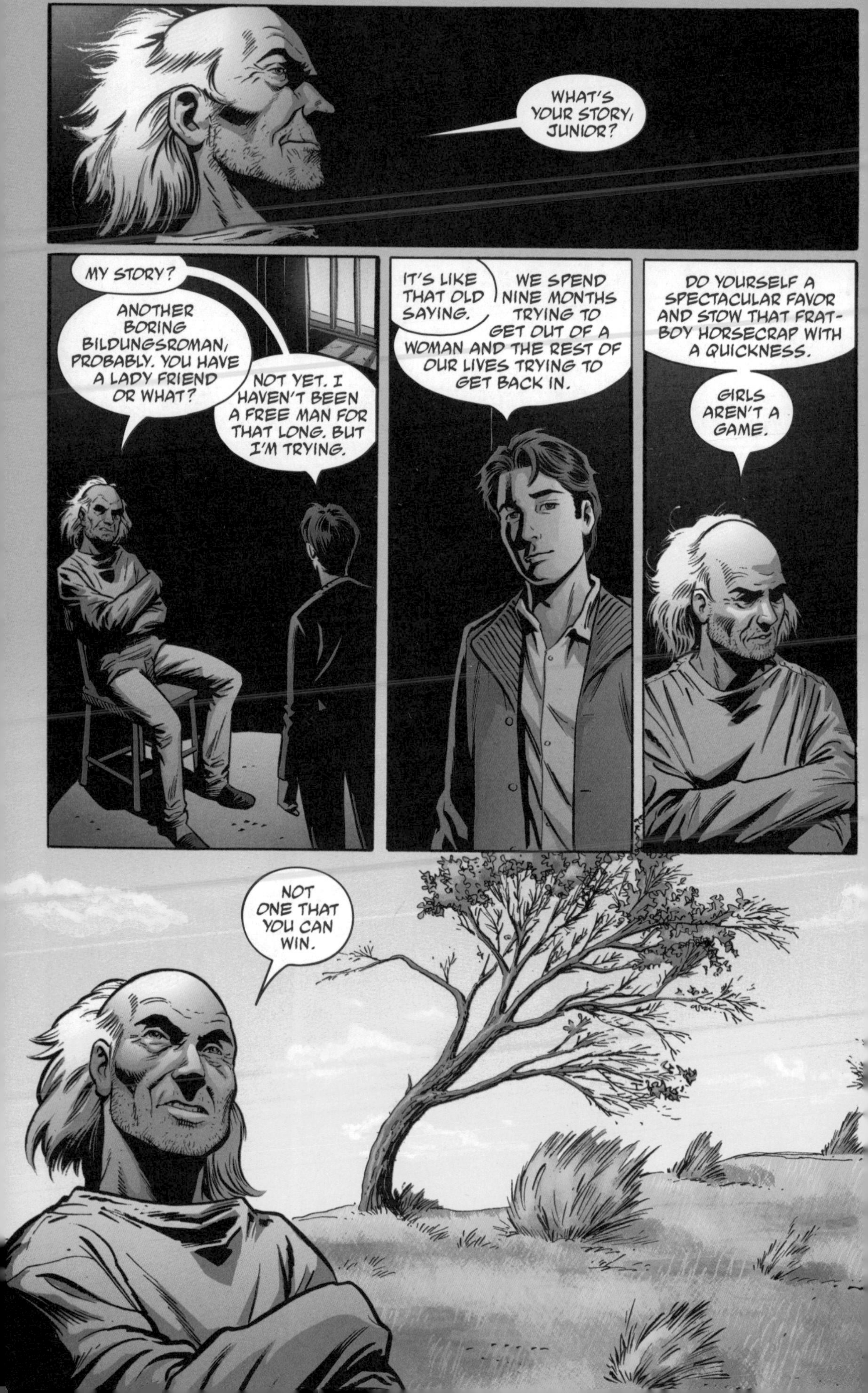
WHAT'S YOUR STORY, JUNIOR?
MY STORY?
ANOTHER BORING BILDUNGSROMAN, PROBABLY. YOU HAVE A LADY FRIEND OR WHAT?
NOT YET. I HAVEN'T BEEN A FREE MAN FOR THAT LONG. BUT I'M TRYING.
IT'S LIKE THAT OLD SAYING.
WE SPEND NINE MONTHS TRYING TO GET OUT OF A WOMAN AND THE REST OF OUR LIVES TRYING TO GET BACK IN.
DO YOURSELF A SPECTACULAR FAVOR AND STOW THAT FRAT-BOY HORSECRAP WITH A QUICKNESS.
GIRLS AREN'T A GAME.
NOT ONE THAT YOU CAN WIN.

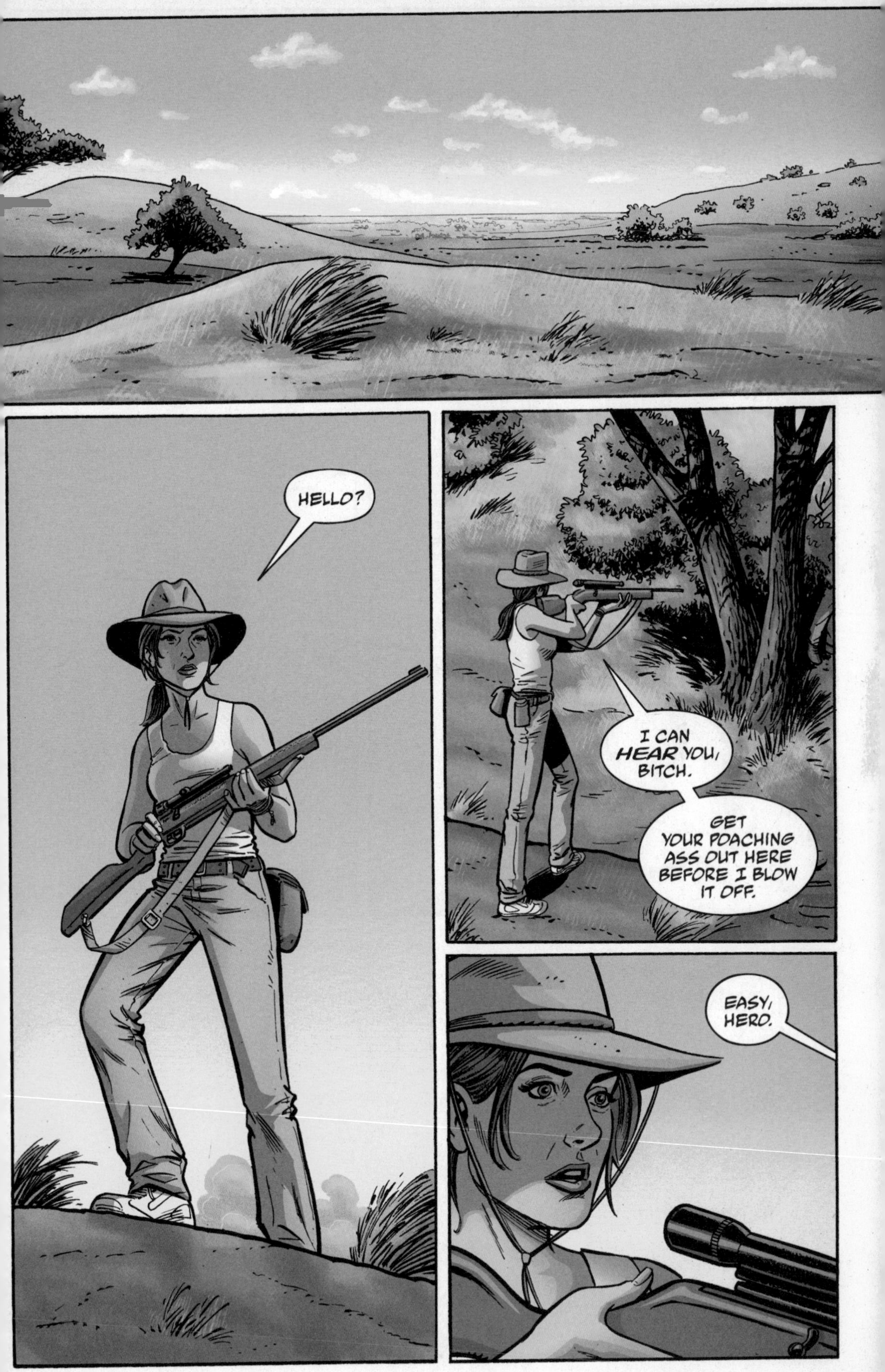
HELLO?
I CAN HEAR YOU, BITCH.
GET YOUR POACHING ASS OUT HERE BEFORE I BLOW IT OFF.
EASY, HERO.

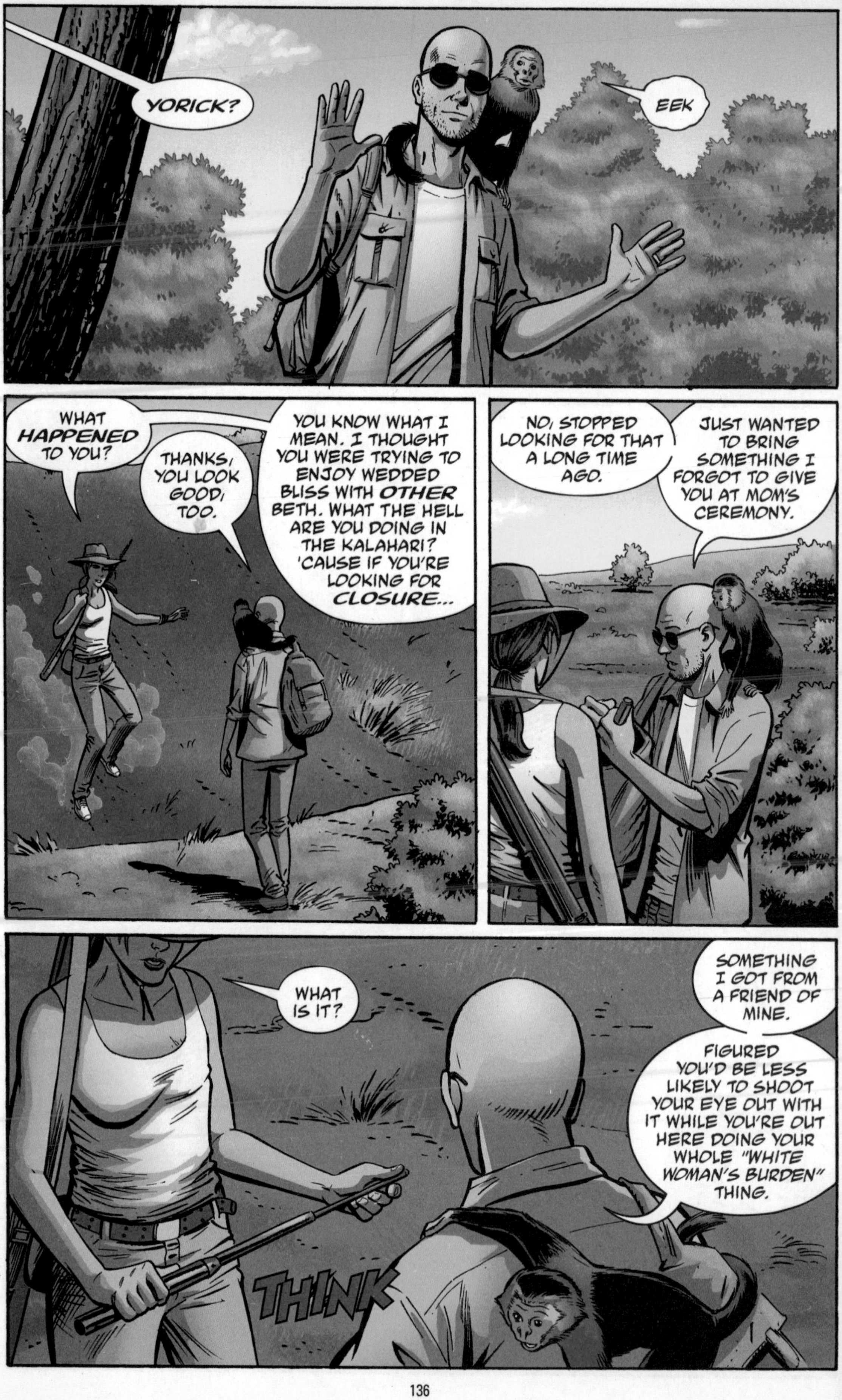
YORICK?
EEK
WHAT HAPPENED TO YOU?
THANKS, YOU LOOK GOOD, TOO.
YOU KNOW WHAT I MEAN. I THOUGHT YOU WERE TRYING TO ENJOY WEDDED BLISS WITH OTHER BETH. WHAT THE HELL ARE YOU DOING IN THE KALAHARI? 'CAUSE IF YOU'RE LOOKING FOR CLOSURE...
NO, STOPPED LOOKING FOR THAT A LONG TIME AGO.
JUST WANTED TO BRING SOMETHING I FORGOT TO GIVE YOU AT MOM'S CEREMONY.
WHAT IS IT?
SOMETHING I GOT FROM A FRIEND OF MINE.
FIGURED YOU'D BE LESS LIKELY TO SHOOT YOUR EYE OUT WITH IT WHILE YOU'RE OUT HERE DOING YOUR WHOLE "WHITE WOMAN'S BURDEN" THING.
THINK

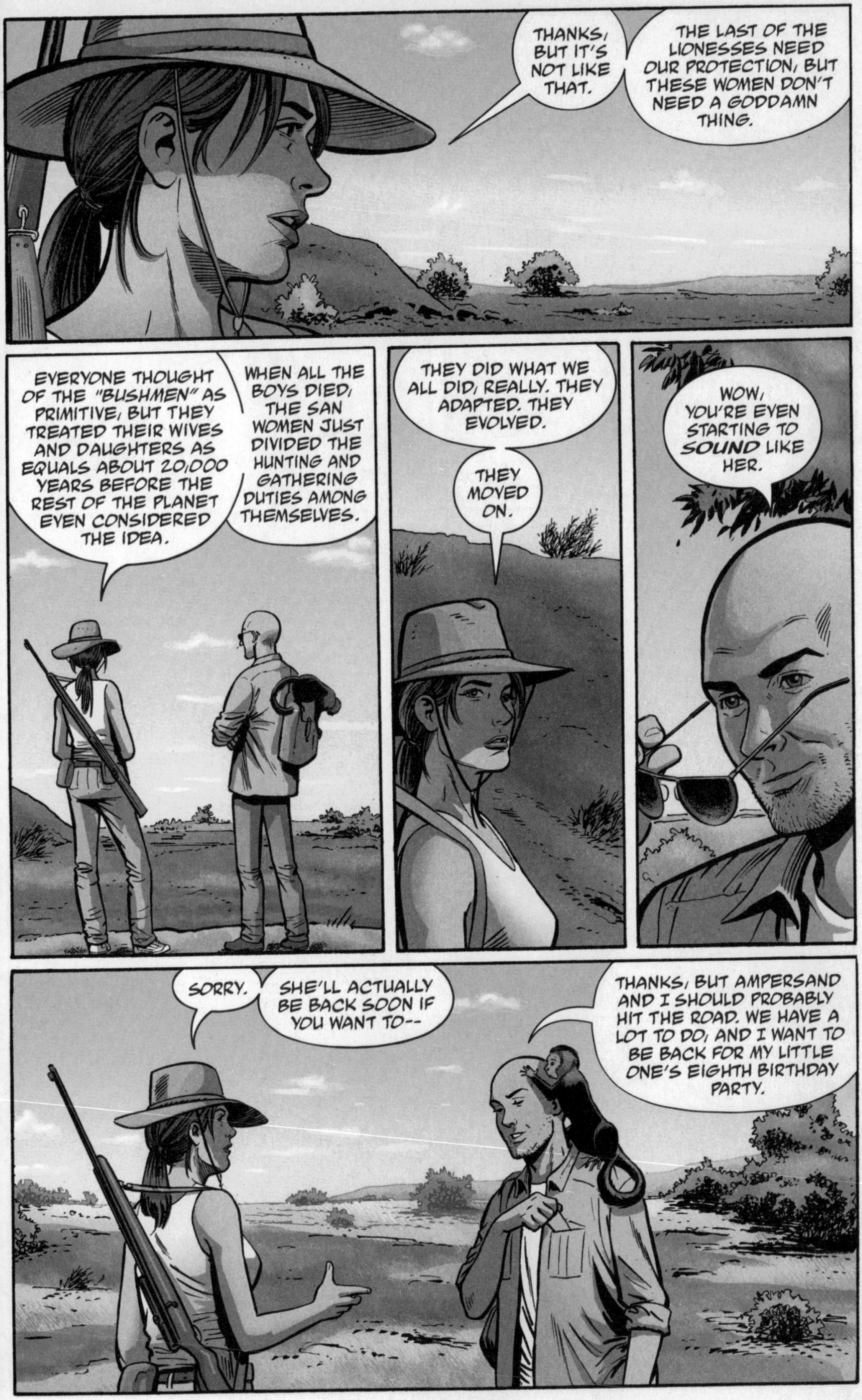
THANKS, BUT IT'S NOT LIKE THAT.
THE LAST OF THE LIONESSES NEED OUR PROTECTION, BUT THESE WOMEN DON'T NEED A GODDAMN THING.
EVERYONE THOUGHT OF THE "BUSHMEN" AS PRIMITIVE, BUT THEY TREATED THEIR WIVES AND DAUGHTERS AS EQUALS ABOUT 20,000 YEARS BEFORE THE REST OF THE PLANET EVEN CONSIDERED THE IDEA.
WHEN ALL THE BOYS DIED, THE SAN WOMEN JUST DIVIDED THE HUNTING AND GATHERING DUTIES AMONG THEMSELVES.
THEY DID WHAT WE ALL DID, REALLY. THEY ADAPTED. THEY EVOLVED.
THEY MOVED ON.
WOW, YOU'RE EVEN STARTING TO SOUND LIKE HER.
SORRY.
SHE'LL ACTUALLY BE BACK SOON IF YOU WANT TO--
THANKS, BUT AMPERSAND AND I SHOULD PROBABLY HIT THE ROAD. WE HAVE A LOT TO DO, AND I WANT TO BE BACK FOR MY LITTLE ONE'S EIGHTH BIRTHDAY PARTY.

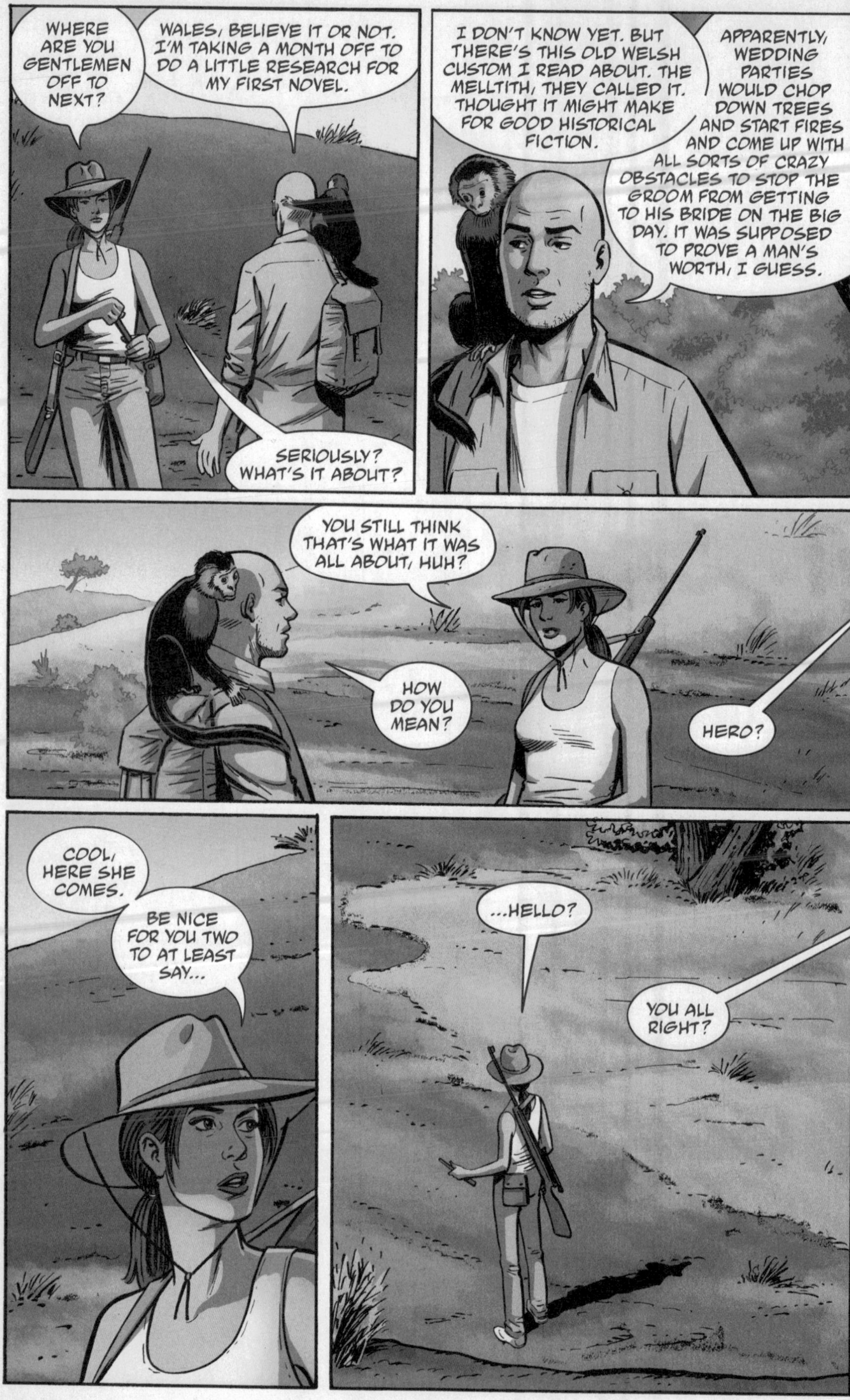
WHERE ARE YOU GENTLEMEN OFF TO NEXT?
WALES, BELIEVE IT OR NOT. I'M TAKING A MONTH OFF TO DO A LITTLE RESEARCH FOR MY FIRST NOVEL.
SERIOUSLY? WHAT'S IT ABOUT?
I DON'T KNOW YET. BUT THERE'S THIS OLD WELSH CUSTOM I READ ABOUT. THE MELLTITH, THEY CALLED IT. THOUGHT IT MIGHT MAKE FOR GOOD HISTORICAL FICTION.
APPARENTLY, WEDDING PARTIES WOULD CHOP DOWN TREES AND START FIRES AND COME UP WITH ALL SORTS OF CRAZY OBSTACLES TO STOP THE GROOM FROM GETTING TO HIS BRIDE ON THE BIG DAY. IT WAS SUPPOSED TO PROVE A MAN'S WORTH, I GUESS.
YOU STILL THINK THAT'S WHAT IT WAS ALL ABOUT, HUH?
HOW DO YOU MEAN?
HERO?
COOL, HERE SHE COMES.
BE NICE FOR YOU TWO TO AT LEAST SAY...
...HELLO?
YOU ALL RIGHT?

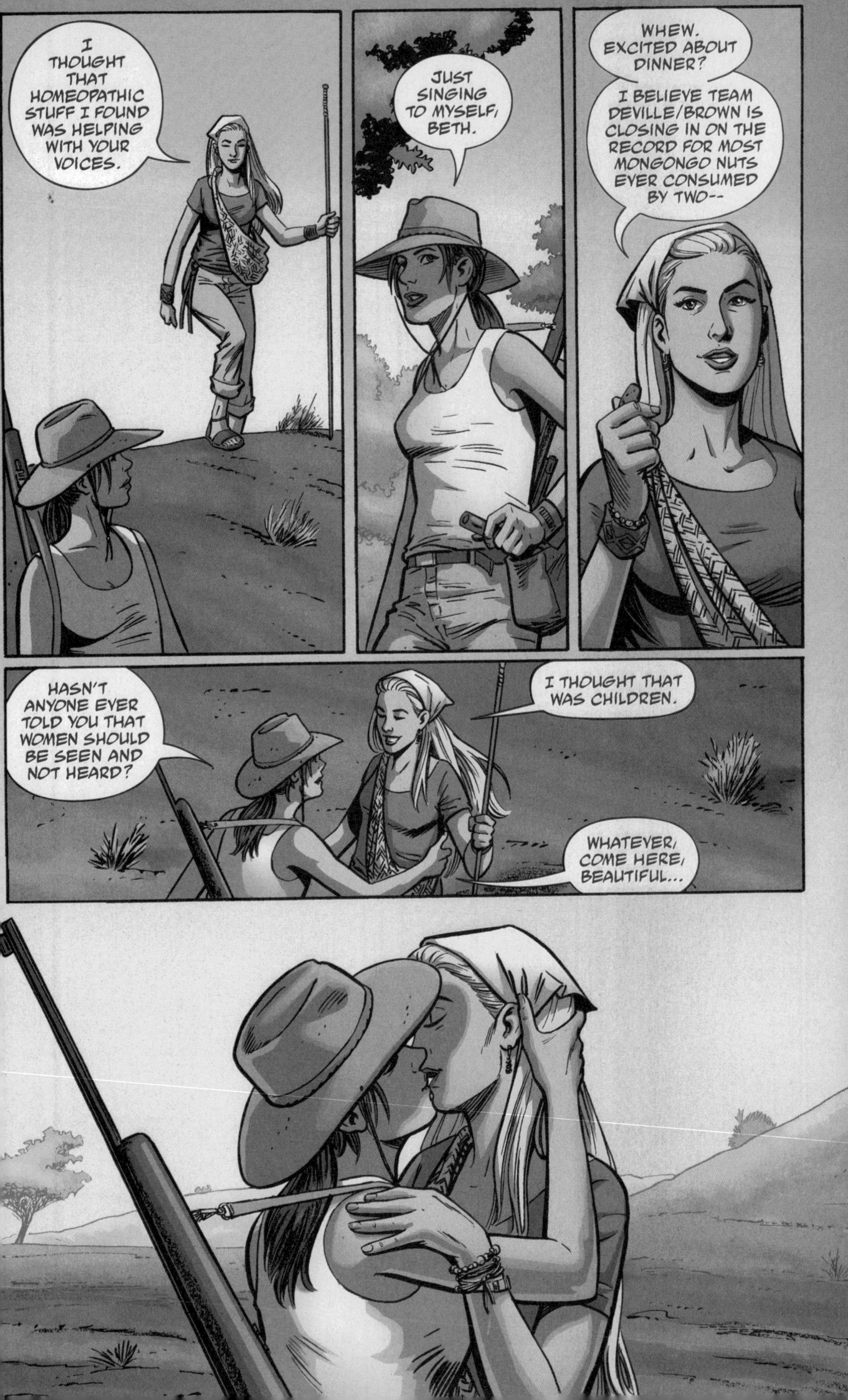
I THOUGHT THAT HOMEOPATHIC STUFF I FOUND WAS HELPING WITH YOUR VOICES.
JUST SINGING TO MYSELF, BETH.
WHEW. EXCITED ABOUT DINNER?
I BELIEVE TEAM DEVILLE/BROWN IS CLOSING IN ON THE RECORD FOR MOST MONGONGO NUTS EVER CONSUMED BY TWO--
HASN'T ANYONE EVER TOLD YOU THAT WOMEN SHOULD BE SEEN AND NOT HEARD?
I THOUGHT THAT WAS CHILDREN.
WHATEVER, COME HERE, BEAUTIFUL...

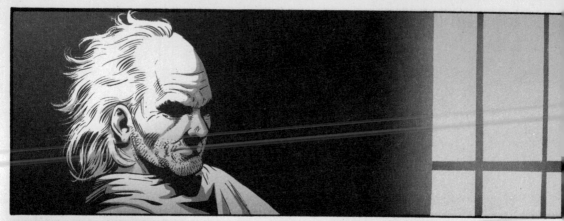

SO, YOU MOVING HERE OR WHAT?

TO GAY PAREE?

NO, I'M THINKING ABOUT RELOCATING TO CANADA. I'M INTERESTED IN LAW, AND ONE OF MY BROTHERS TOLD ME THE UNIVERSITY OF OTTAWA MIGHT BE OPEN TO ENROLLING A MALE STUDENT.

WELL, DON'T FORGET YOUR ENGLISH IN THAT BILINGUAL WASTELAND.

A WHOLE COUNTRY OF WOMEN, AND ONE LITTLE BOY STILL MAGICALLY TRANSFORMS "ELLES" INTO "ILS." IT'S LIKE I TOLD HER WHEN WE MET, FRANÇAIS IS FOR CHAUVINISTS.

WAIT, TOLD WHO?

IT DOESN'T REALLY--

≥HKK≤
≥KOFF≤ ≥KOFF≤
≥KOFF≤
≥HKK≤

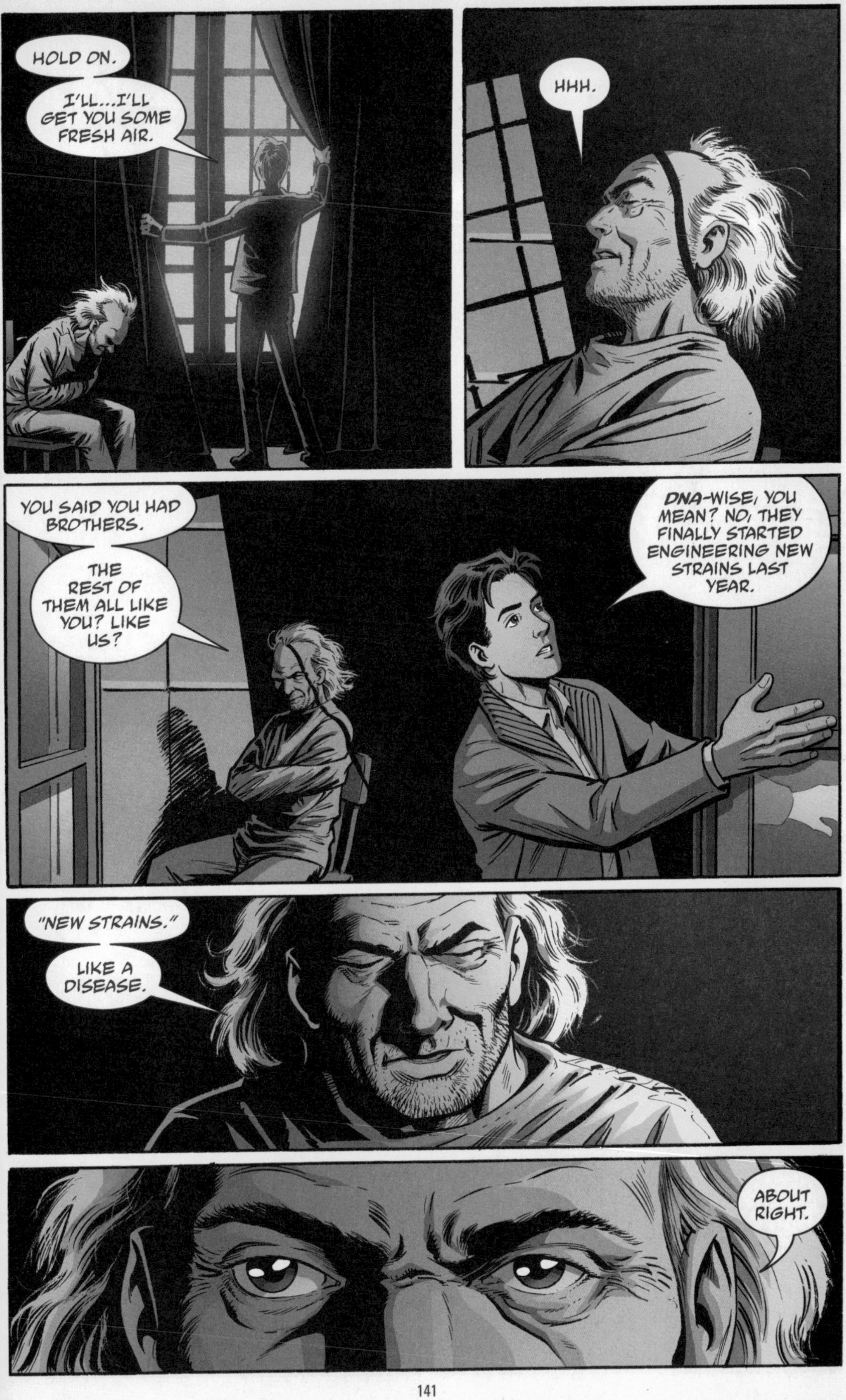
HOLD ON.
I'LL...I'LL GET YOU SOME FRESH AIR.
HHH.
YOU SAID YOU HAD BROTHERS.
THE REST OF THEM ALL LIKE YOU? LIKE US?
DNA-WISE, YOU MEAN? NO, THEY FINALLY STARTED ENGINEERING NEW STRAINS LAST YEAR.
"NEW STRAINS."
LIKE A DISEASE.
ABOUT RIGHT.

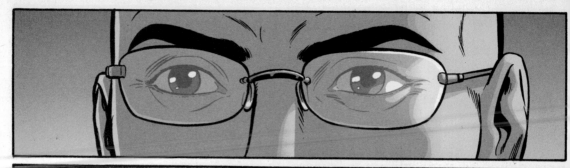

DOC?

DR. MANN?

DON'T MAKE ME SAY "ALLISON."

I STILL CAN'T BRING MYSELF TO CALL YOU--

HELLO, FOUR EYES.

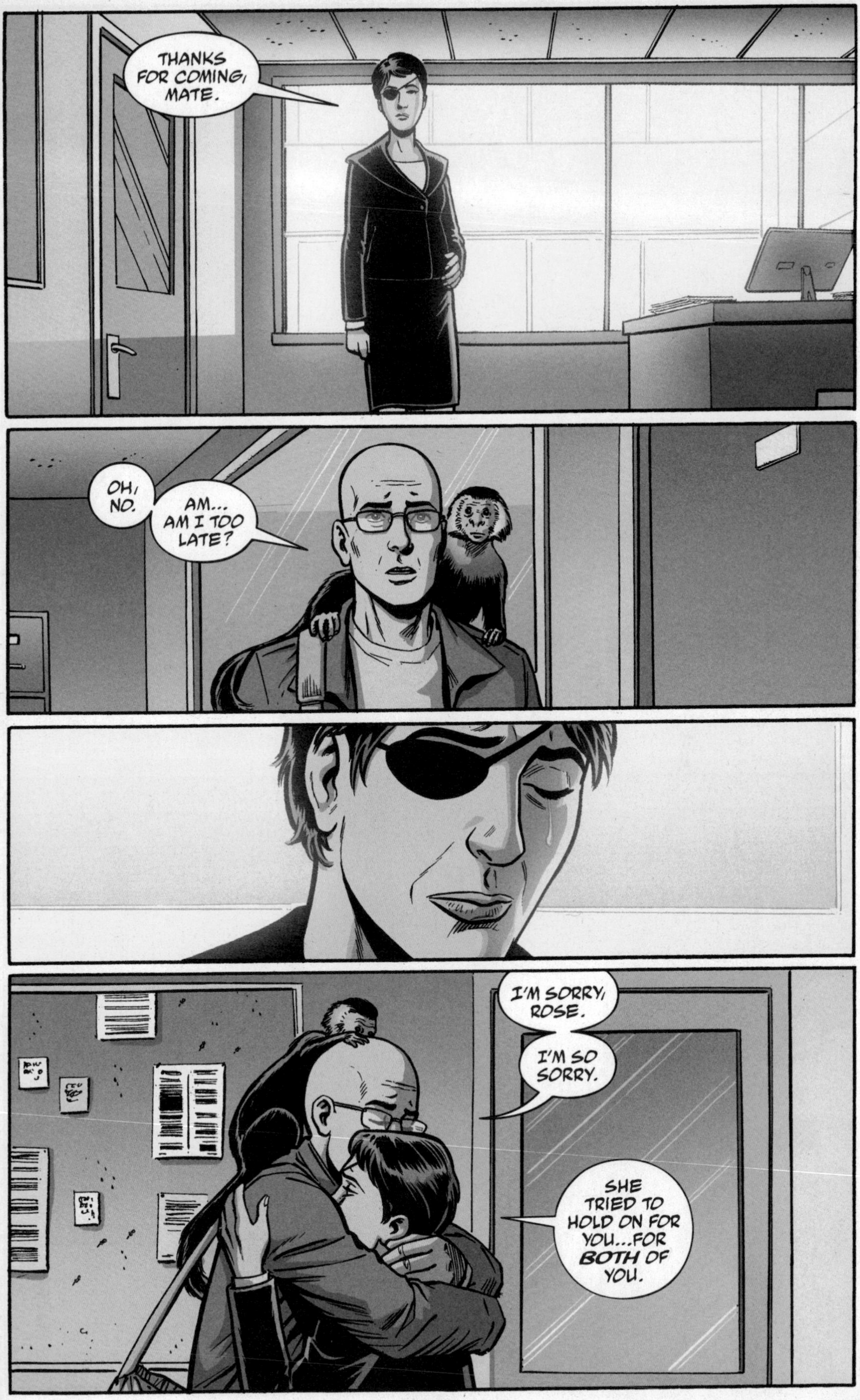
THANKS FOR COMING, MATE.
OH, NO.
AM... AM I TOO LATE?
I'M SORRY, ROSE.
I'M SO SORRY.
SHE TRIED TO HOLD ON FOR YOU...FOR *BOTH* OF YOU.

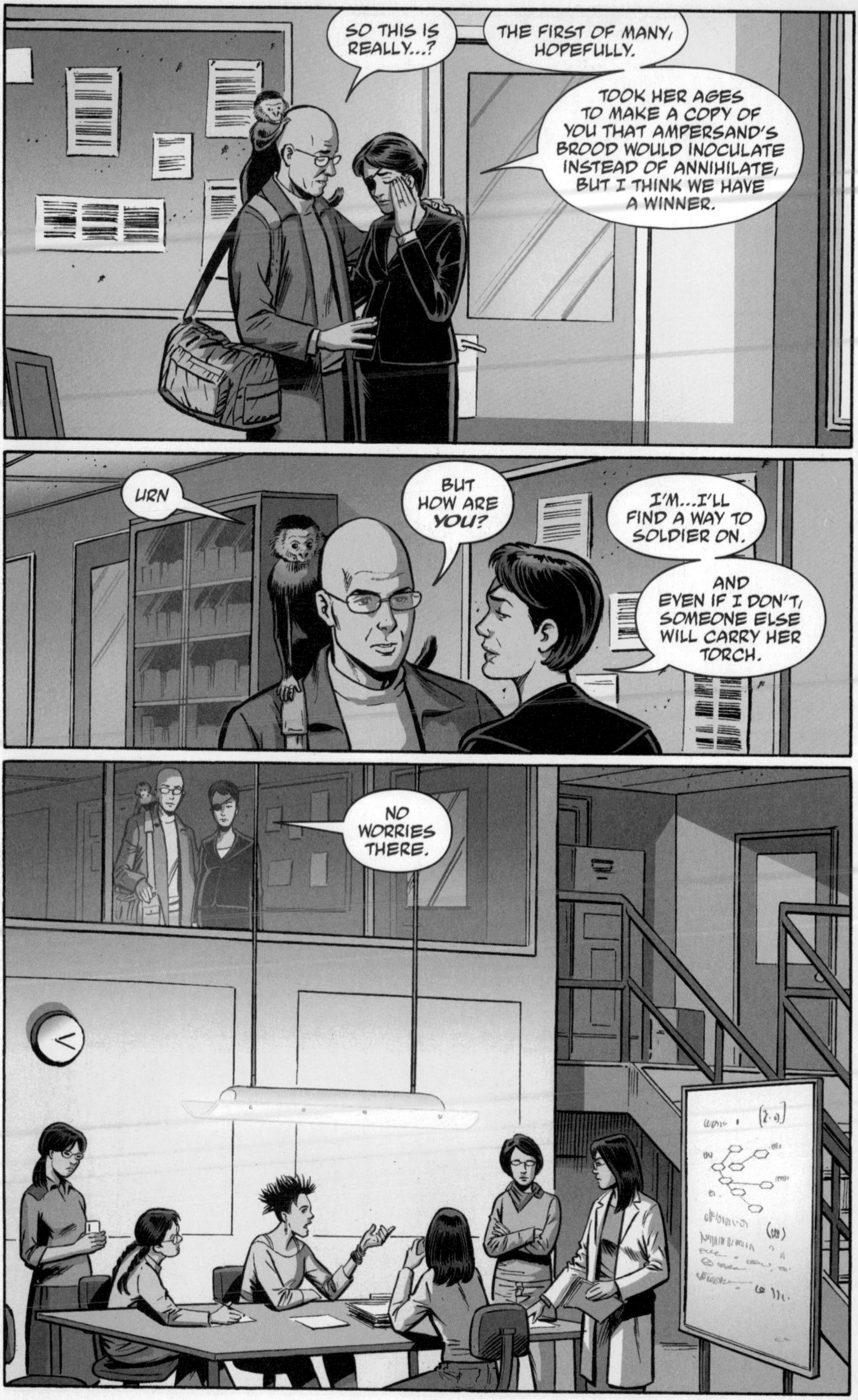
SO THIS IS REALLY...?
THE FIRST OF MANY, HOPEFULLY.
TOOK HER AGES TO MAKE A COPY OF YOU THAT AMPERSAND'S BROOD WOULD INOCULATE INSTEAD OF ANNIHILATE, BUT I THINK WE HAVE A WINNER.
URN
BUT HOW ARE *YOU*?
I'M...I'LL FIND A WAY TO SOLDIER ON.
AND EVEN IF I DON'T, SOMEONE ELSE WILL CARRY HER TORCH.
NO WORRIES THERE.

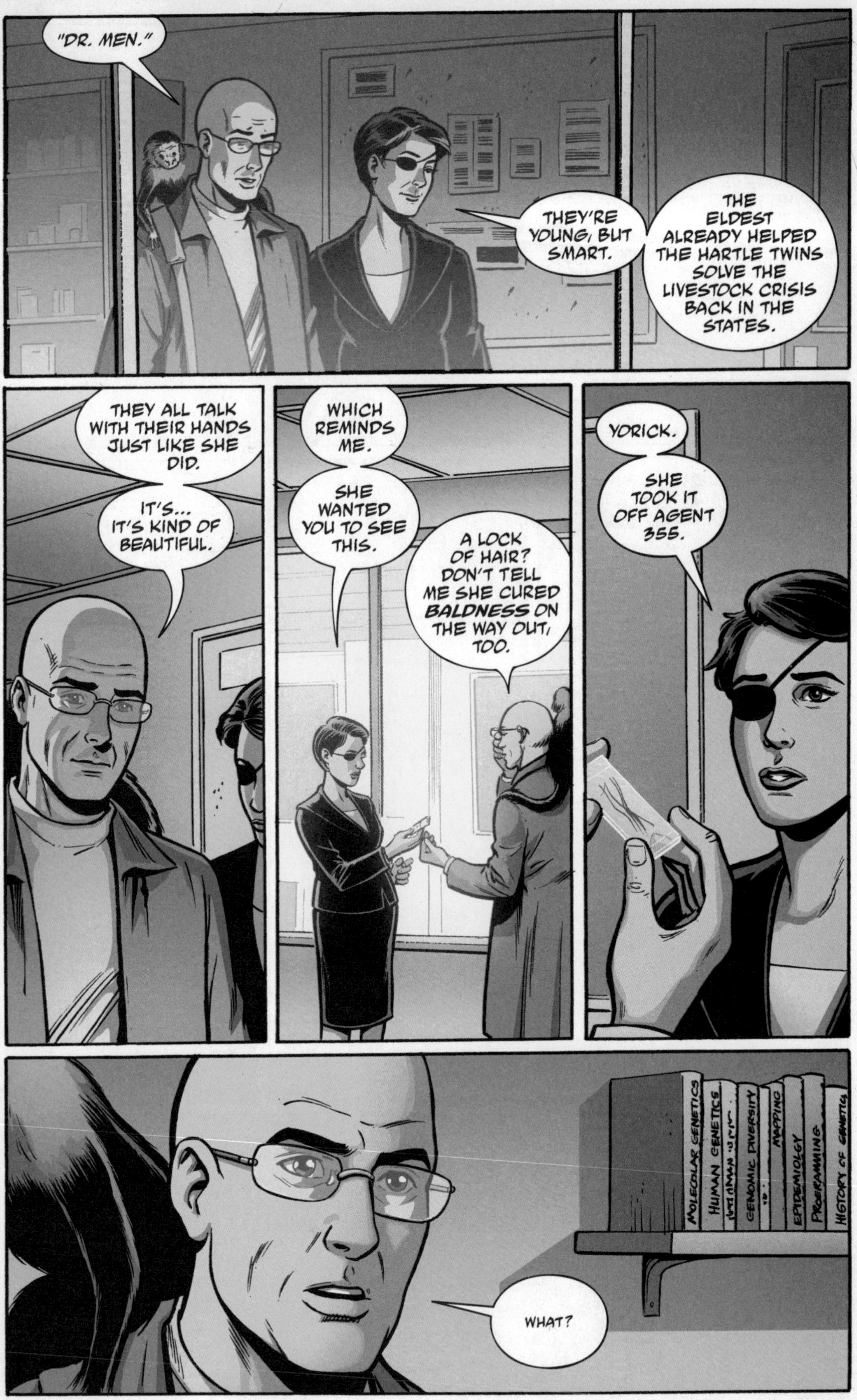
"DR. MEN."
THEY'RE YOUNG, BUT SMART.
THE ELDEST ALREADY HELPED THE HARTLE TWINS SOLVE THE LIVESTOCK CRISIS BACK IN THE STATES.
THEY ALL TALK WITH THEIR HANDS JUST LIKE SHE DID.
IT'S... IT'S KIND OF BEAUTIFUL.
WHICH REMINDS ME.
SHE WANTED YOU TO SEE THIS.
A LOCK OF HAIR? DON'T TELL ME SHE CURED BALDNESS ON THE WAY OUT, TOO.
YORICK.
SHE TOOK IT OFF AGENT 355.
MOLECULAR GENETICS
HUMAN GENETICS
GENOMIC DIVERSITY
MAPPING
EPIDEMIOLOGY
PROGRAMMING
HISTORY OF GENETICS
WHAT?

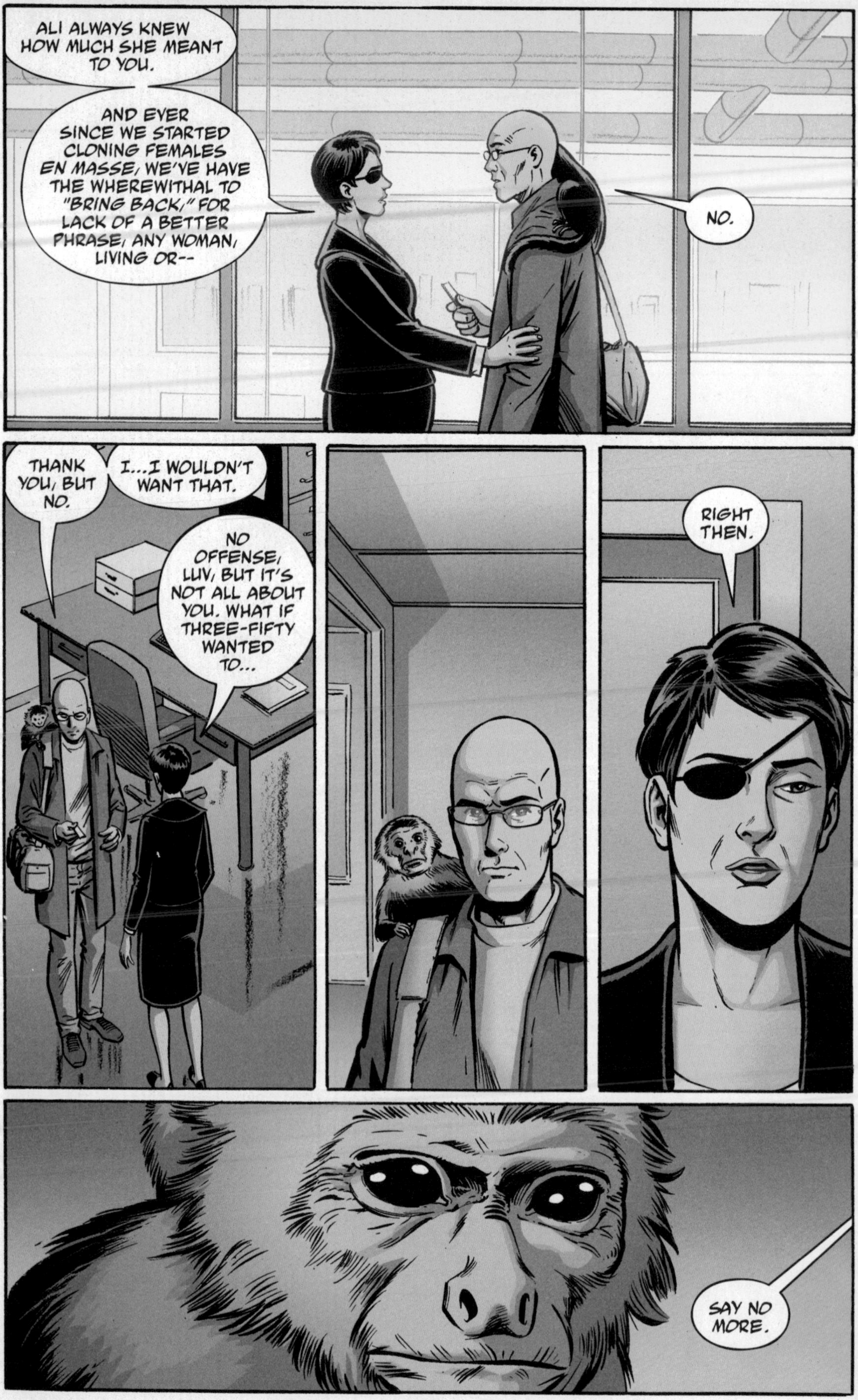
ALI ALWAYS KNEW HOW MUCH SHE MEANT TO YOU.
AND EVER SINCE WE STARTED CLONING FEMALES EN MASSE, WE'VE HAVE THE WHEREWITHAL TO "BRING BACK," FOR LACK OF A BETTER PHRASE, ANY WOMAN, LIVING OR--
NO.
THANK YOU, BUT NO.
I...I WOULDN'T WANT THAT.
NO OFFENSE, LUV, BUT IT'S NOT ALL ABOUT YOU. WHAT IF THREE-FIFTY WANTED TO...
RIGHT THEN.
SAY NO MORE.

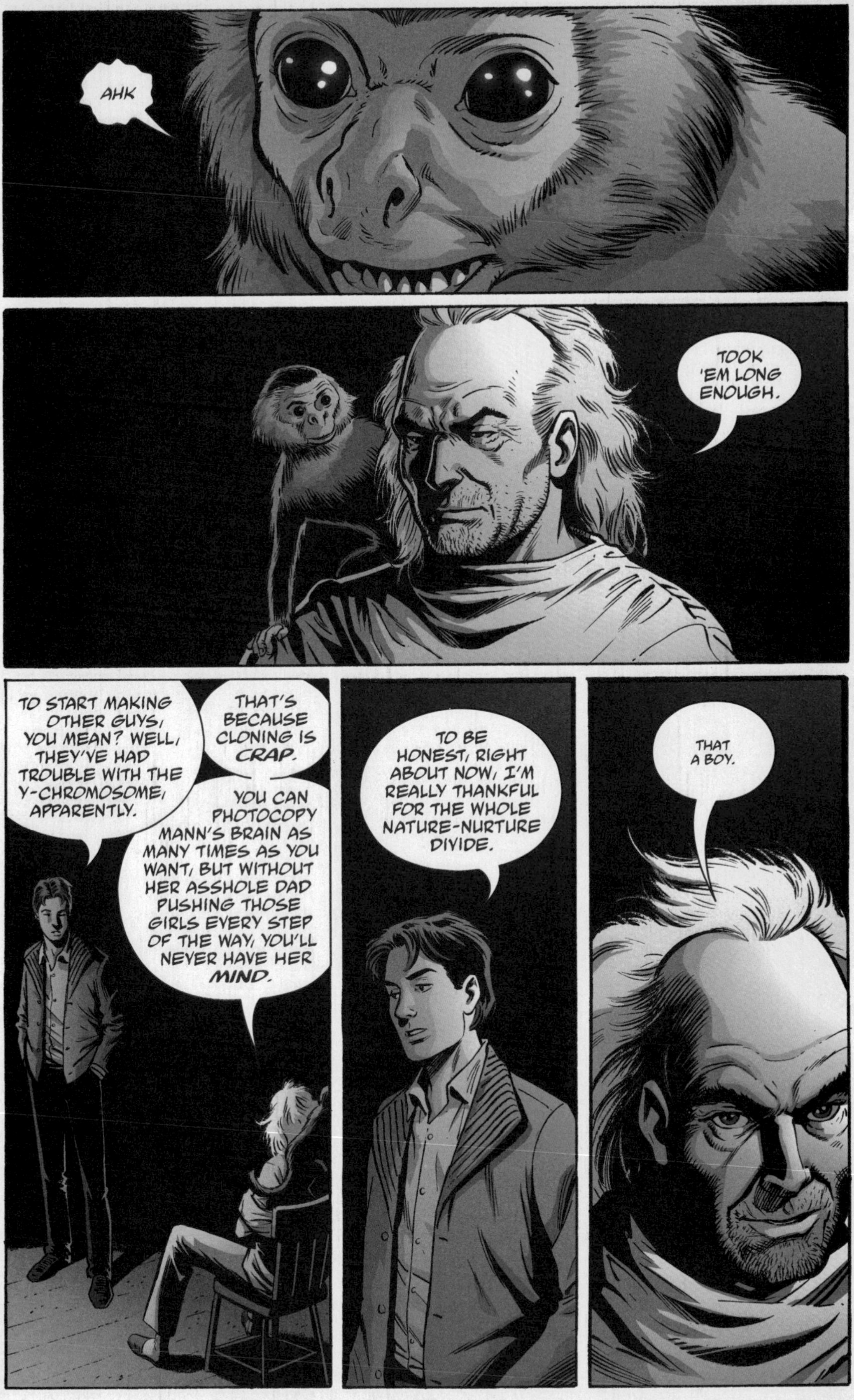
AHK
TOOK 'EM LONG ENOUGH.
TO START MAKING OTHER GUYS, YOU MEAN? WELL, THEY'VE HAD TROUBLE WITH THE Y-CHROMOSOME, APPARENTLY.
THAT'S BECAUSE CLONING IS CRAP.
YOU CAN PHOTOCOPY MANN'S BRAIN AS MANY TIMES AS YOU WANT, BUT WITHOUT HER ASSHOLE DAD PUSHING THOSE GIRLS EVERY STEP OF THE WAY, YOU'LL NEVER HAVE HER MIND.
TO BE HONEST, RIGHT ABOUT NOW, I'M REALLY THANKFUL FOR THE WHOLE NATURE-NURTURE DIVIDE.
THAT A BOY.

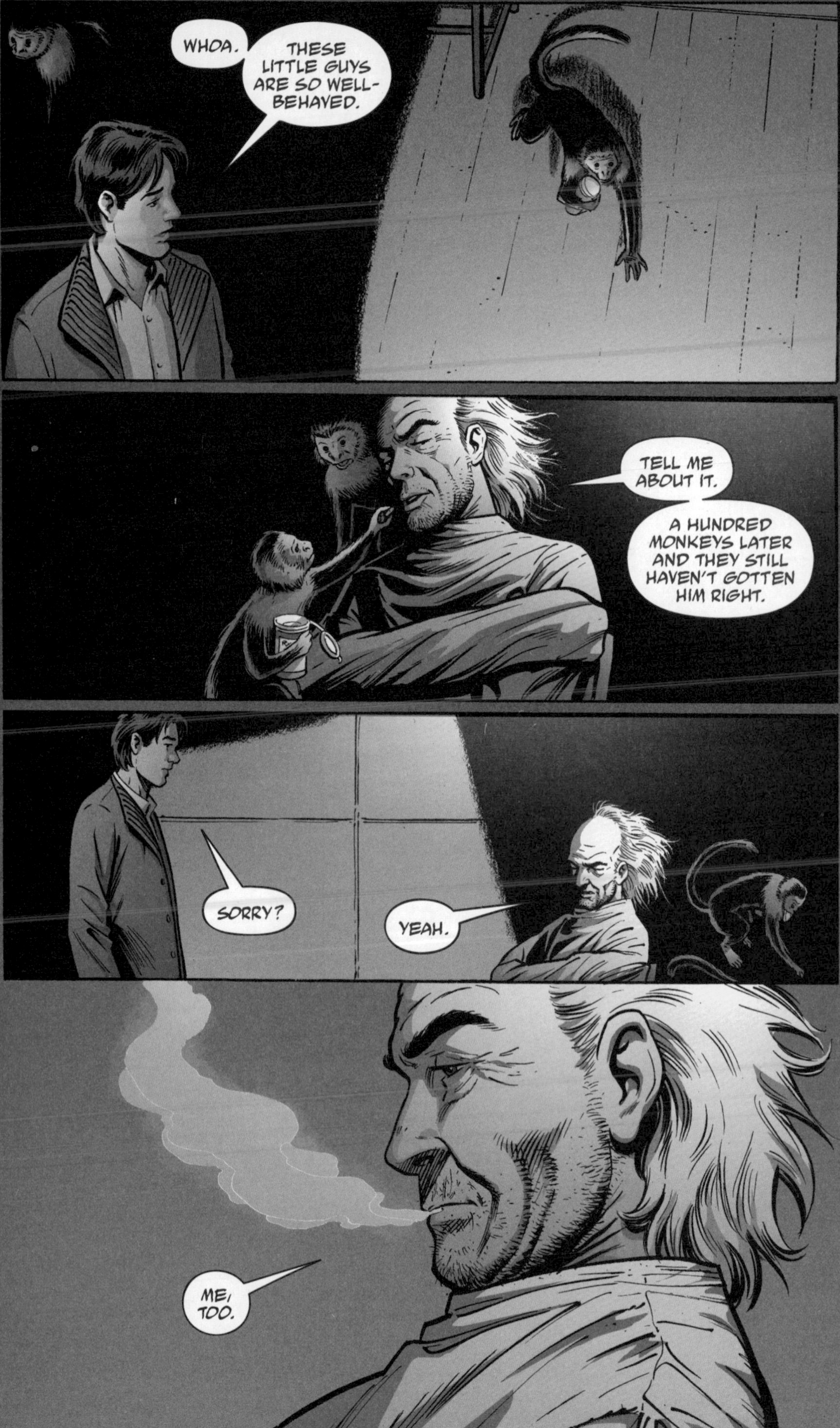
WHOA.
THESE LITTLE GUYS ARE SO WELL-BEHAVED.
TELL ME ABOUT IT.
A HUNDRED MONKEYS LATER AND THEY STILL HAVEN'T GOTTEN HIM RIGHT.
SORRY?
YEAH.
ME, TOO.

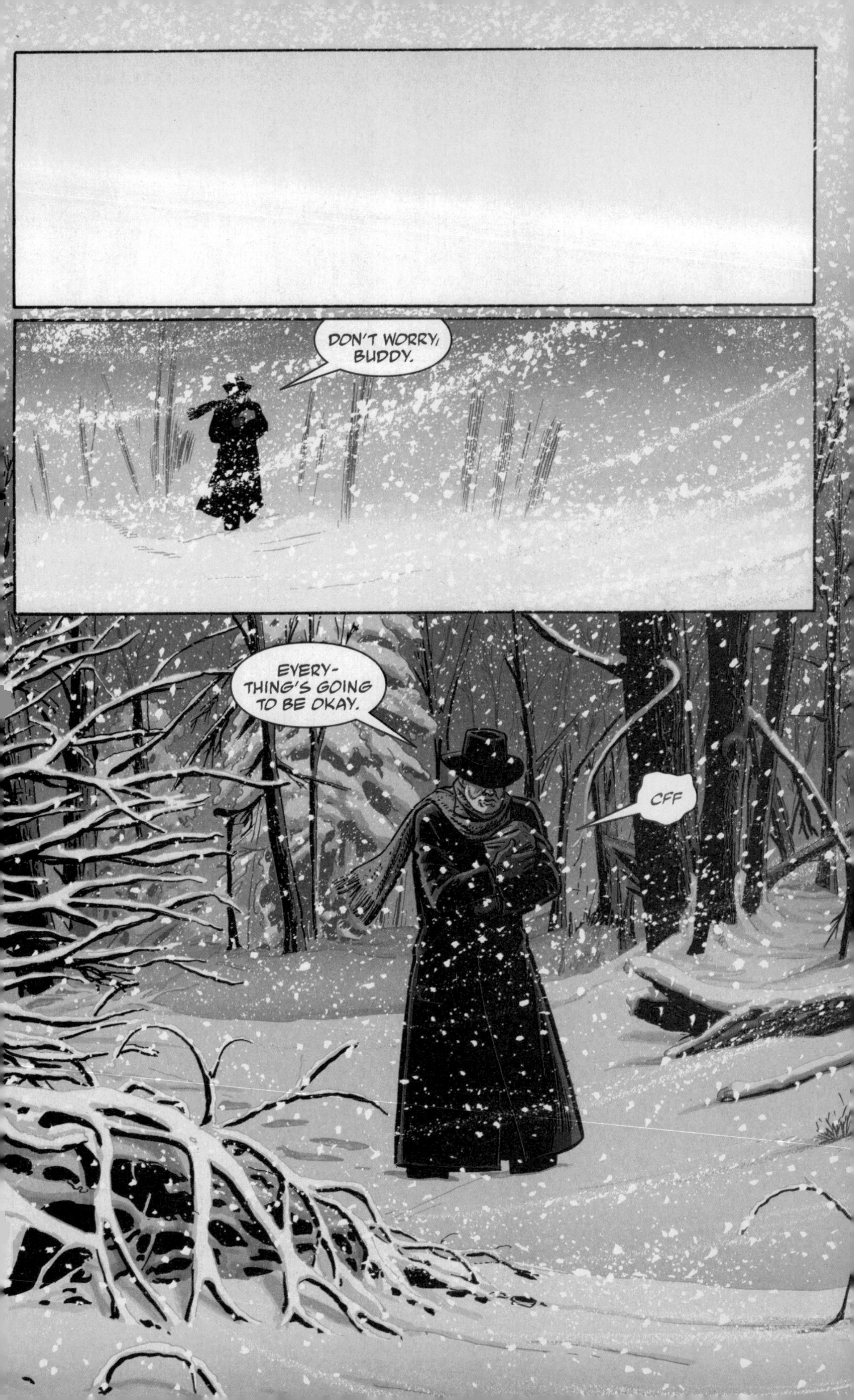
DON'T WORRY, BUDDY.
EVERY- THING'S GOING TO BE OKAY.
CFF

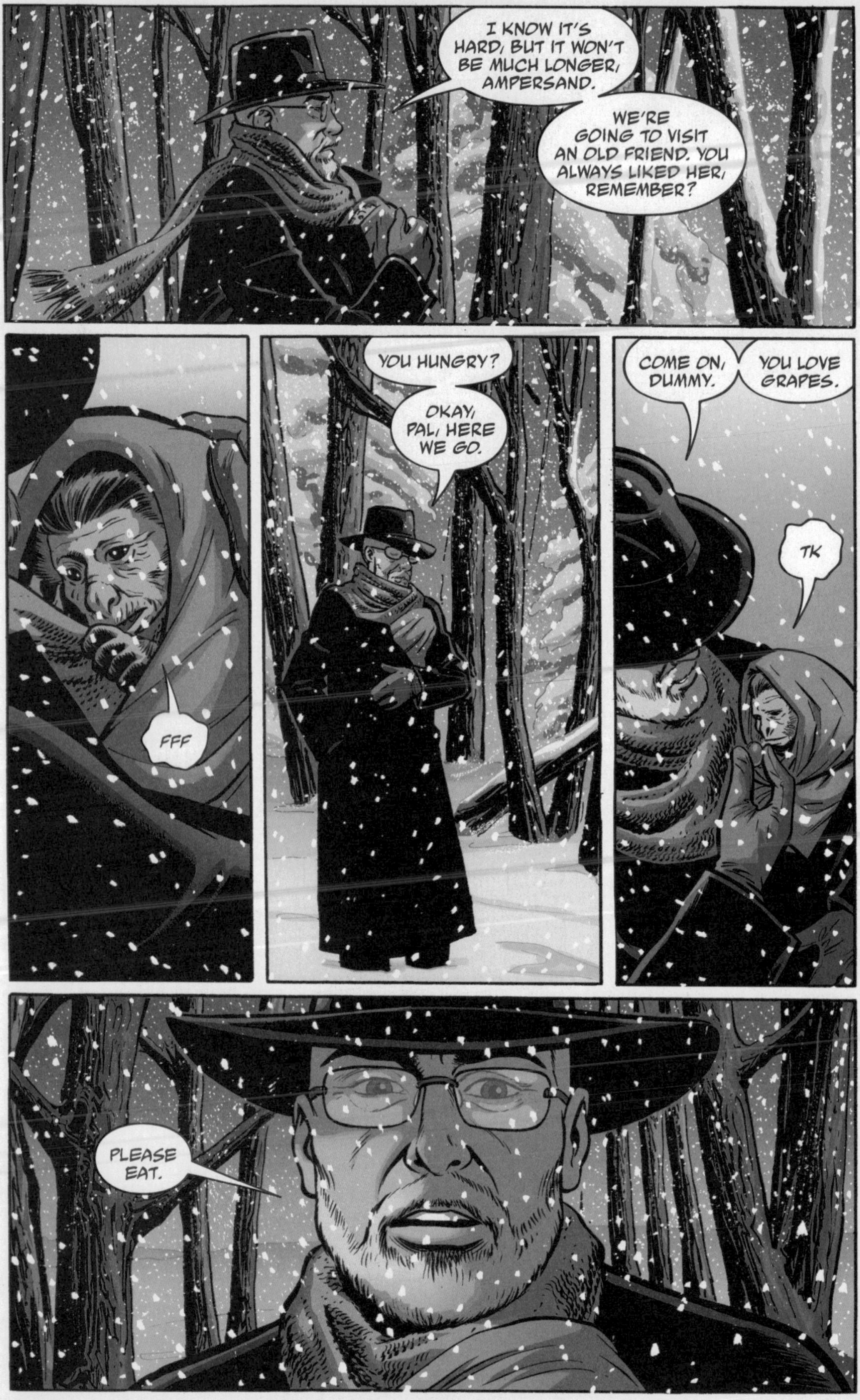

I KNOW IT'S HARD, BUT IT WON'T BE MUCH LONGER, AMPERSAND.
WE'RE GOING TO VISIT AN OLD FRIEND. YOU ALWAYS LIKED HER, REMEMBER?
FFF
YOU HUNGRY?
OKAY, PAL, HERE WE GO.
COME ON, DUMMY.
YOU LOVE GRAPES.
TK
PLEASE EAT.

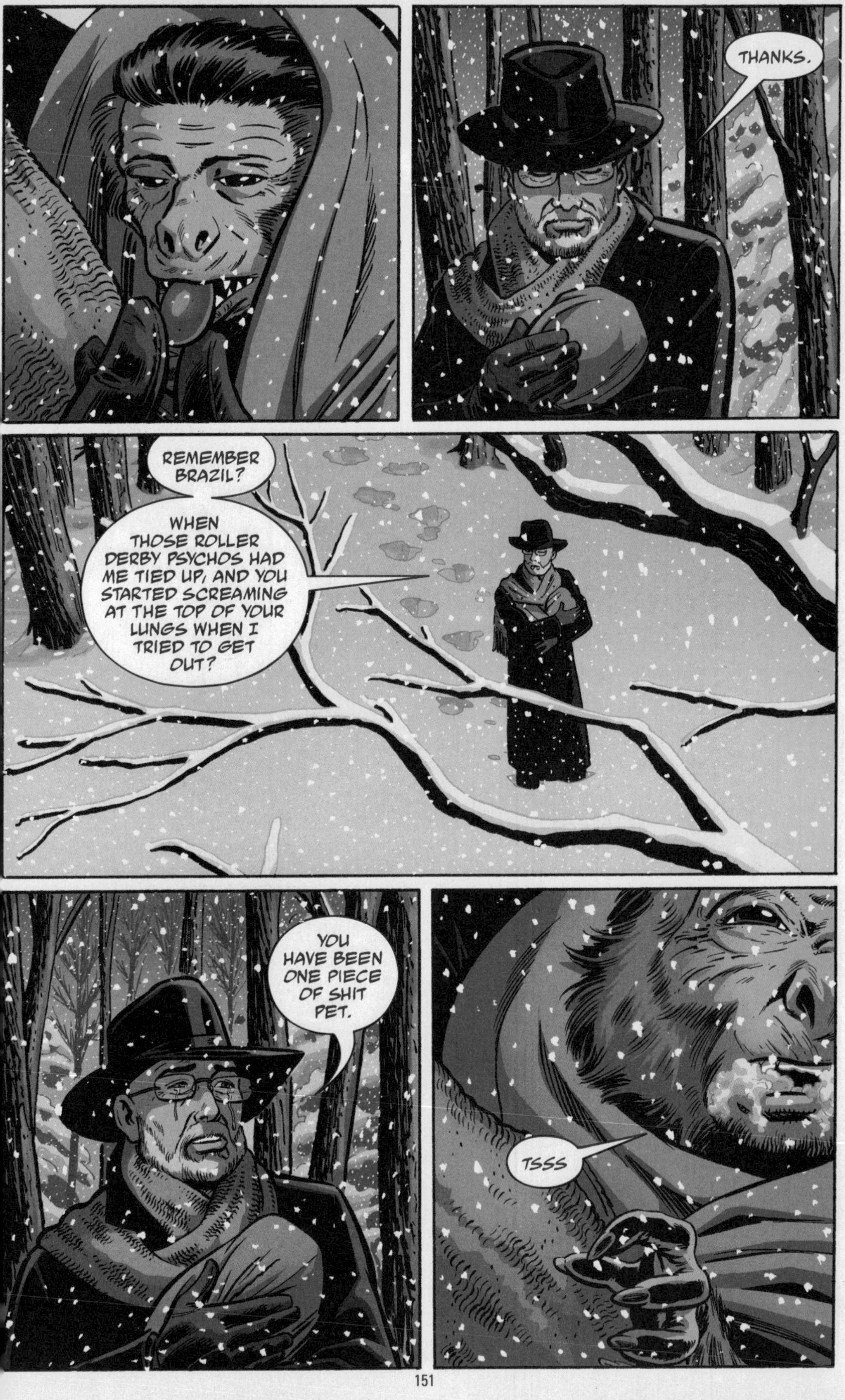
THANKS.
REMEMBER BRAZIL?
WHEN THOSE ROLLER DERBY PSYCHOS HAD ME TIED UP, AND YOU STARTED SCREAMING AT THE TOP OF YOUR LUNGS WHEN I TRIED TO GET OUT?
YOU HAVE BEEN ONE PIECE OF SHIT PET.
TSSS

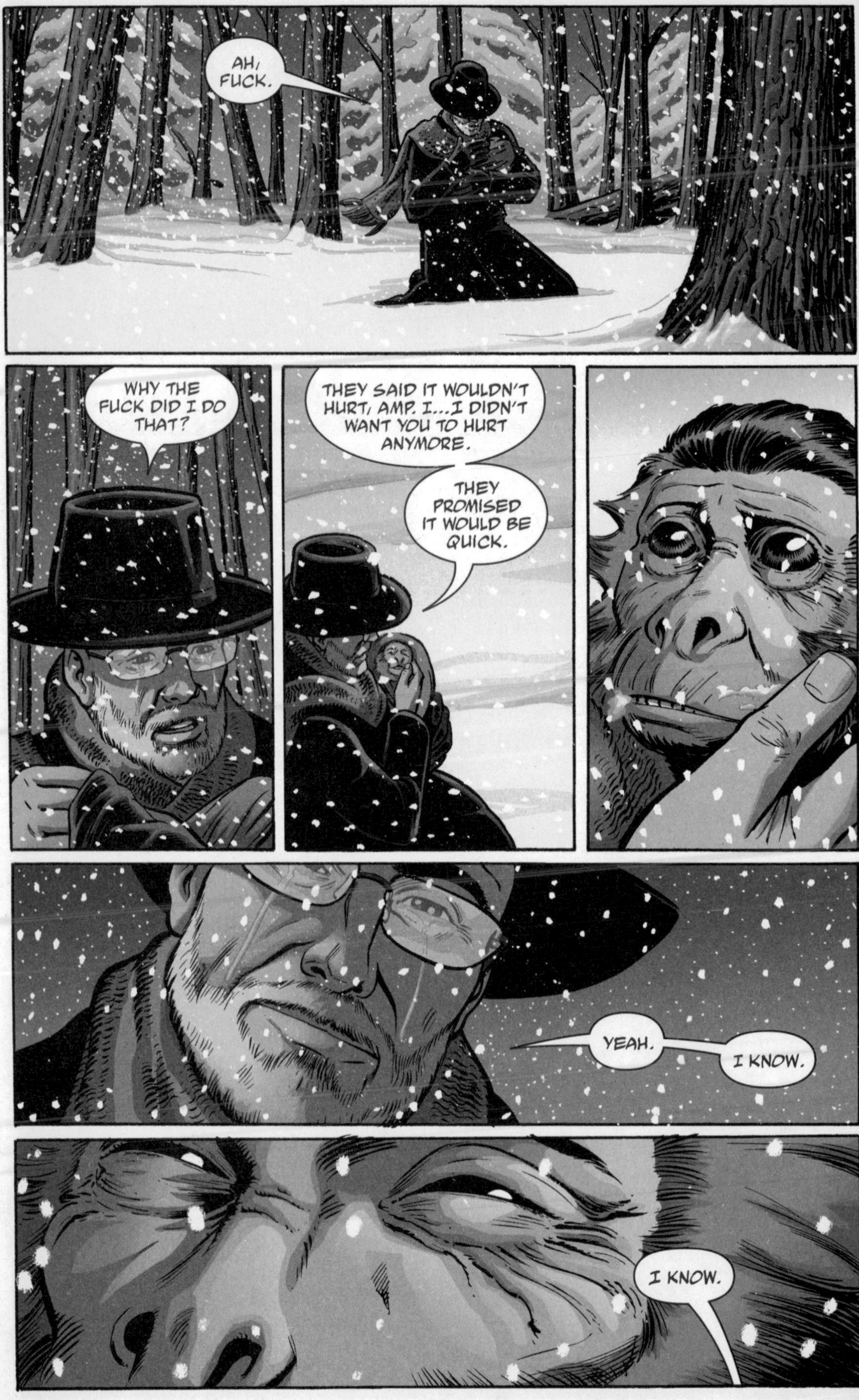
AH, FUCK.
WHY THE FUCK DID I DO THAT?
THEY SAID IT WOULDN'T HURT, AMP. I...I DIDN'T WANT YOU TO HURT ANYMORE.
THEY PROMISED IT WOULD BE QUICK.
YEAH.
I KNOW.
I KNOW.

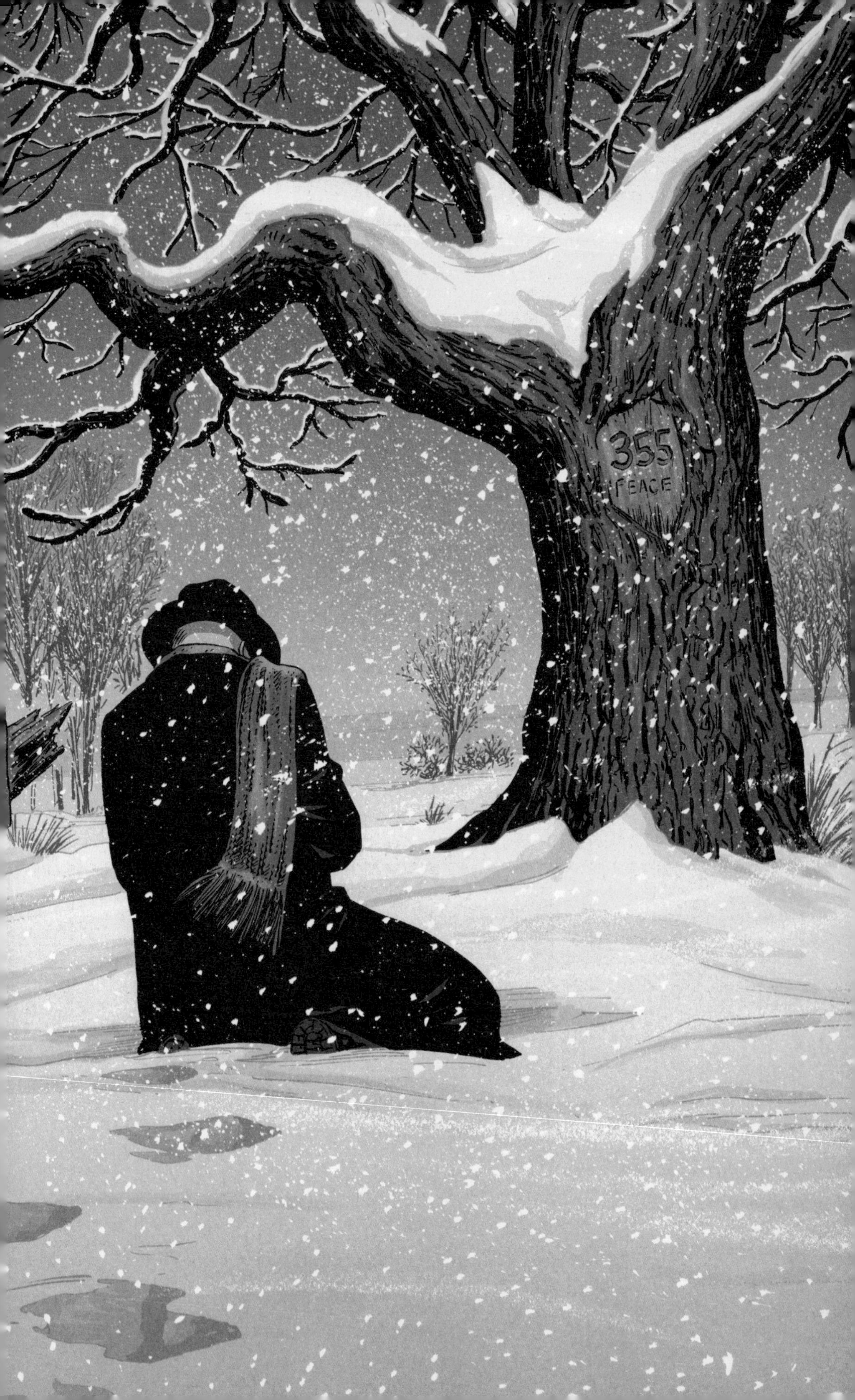
355
PEACE

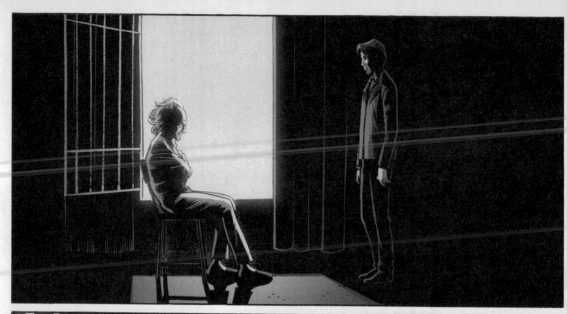

SO THIS IS IT, HUH?

WHAT'S THAT?

YOU KNOW, GROWING OLD. ALL I HAVE TO LOOK FORWARD TO IS PAIN AND MISERY AND...AND HEARTBREAK.

NO.

NO, FIRST COMES *BOYHOOD*. YOU GET TO PLAY WITH SOLDIERS AND SPACEMEN, COW-BOYS AND NINJAS, PIRATES AND ROBOTS.

BUT BEFORE YOU KNOW IT, ALL THAT COMES TO AN END.

AND *THEN,* REMO WILLIAMS, IS WHEN THE ADVENTURE BEGINS.

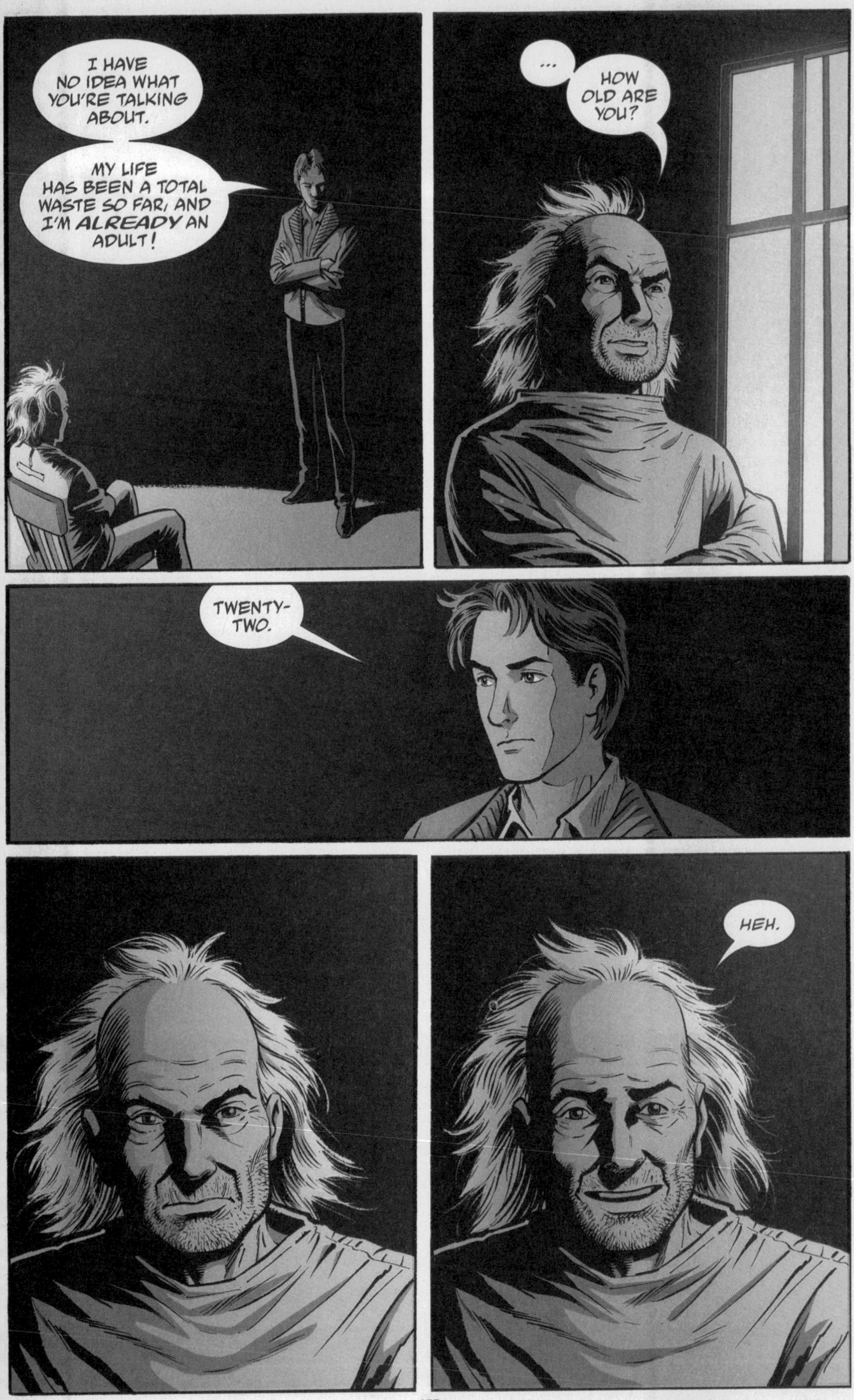
I HAVE NO IDEA WHAT YOU'RE TALKING ABOUT.
MY LIFE HAS BEEN A TOTAL WASTE SO FAR, AND I'M ALREADY AN ADULT!
...
HOW OLD ARE YOU?
TWENTY-TWO.
HEH.

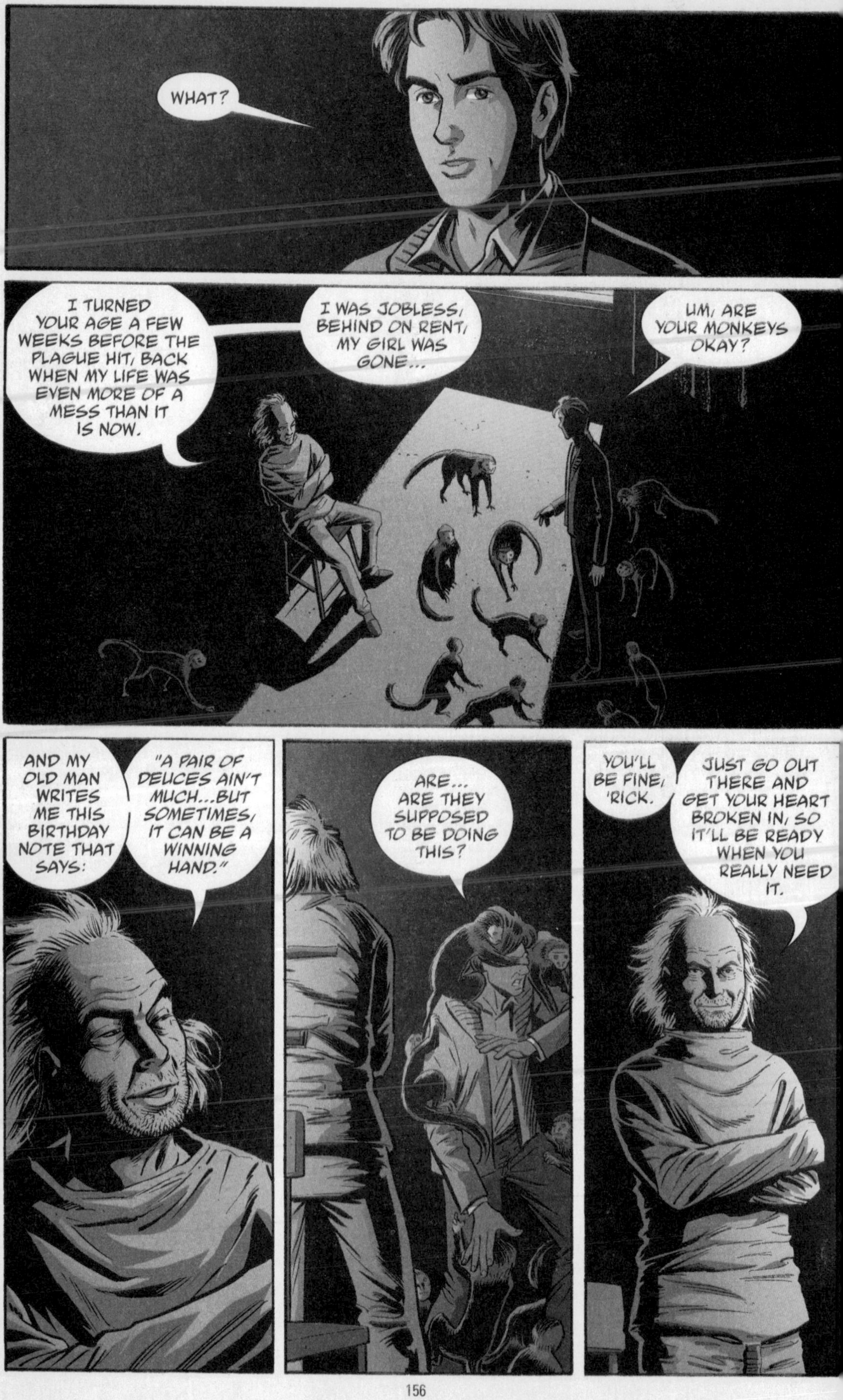
WHAT?
I TURNED YOUR AGE A FEW WEEKS BEFORE THE PLAGUE HIT, BACK WHEN MY LIFE WAS EVEN MORE OF A MESS THAN IT IS NOW.
I WAS JOBLESS, BEHIND ON RENT, MY GIRL WAS GONE...
UM, ARE YOUR MONKEYS OKAY?
AND MY OLD MAN WRITES ME THIS BIRTHDAY NOTE THAT SAYS:
"A PAIR OF DEUCES AIN'T MUCH...BUT SOMETIMES, IT CAN BE A WINNING HAND."
ARE... ARE THEY SUPPOSED TO BE DOING THIS?
YOU'LL BE FINE, 'RICK.
JUST GO OUT THERE AND GET YOUR HEART BROKEN IN, SO IT'LL BE READY WHEN YOU REALLY NEED IT.

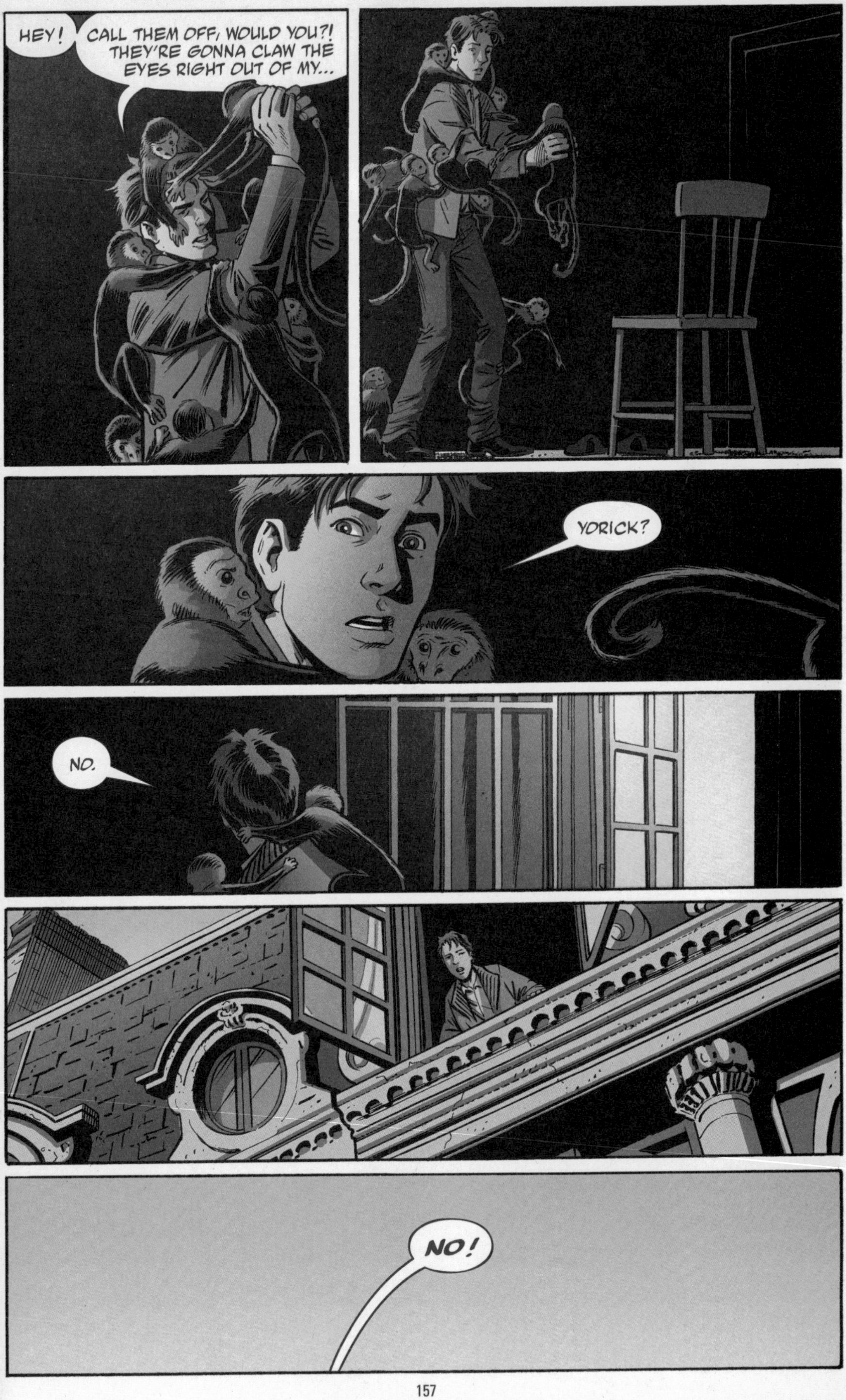
HEY!
CALL THEM OFF, WOULD YOU?! THEY'RE GONNA CLAW THE EYES RIGHT OUT OF MY...
YORICK?
NO.
NO!

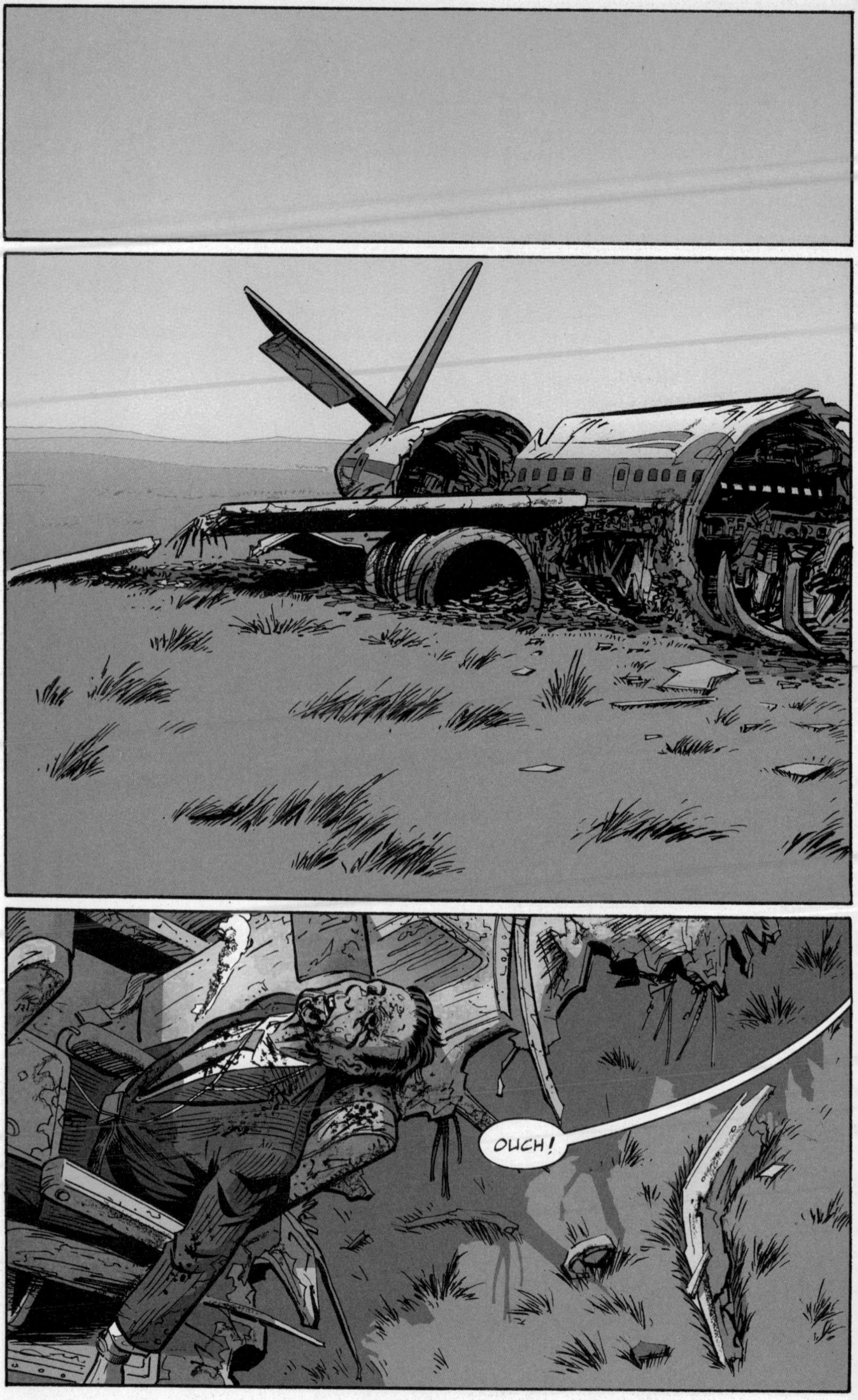
OUCH!

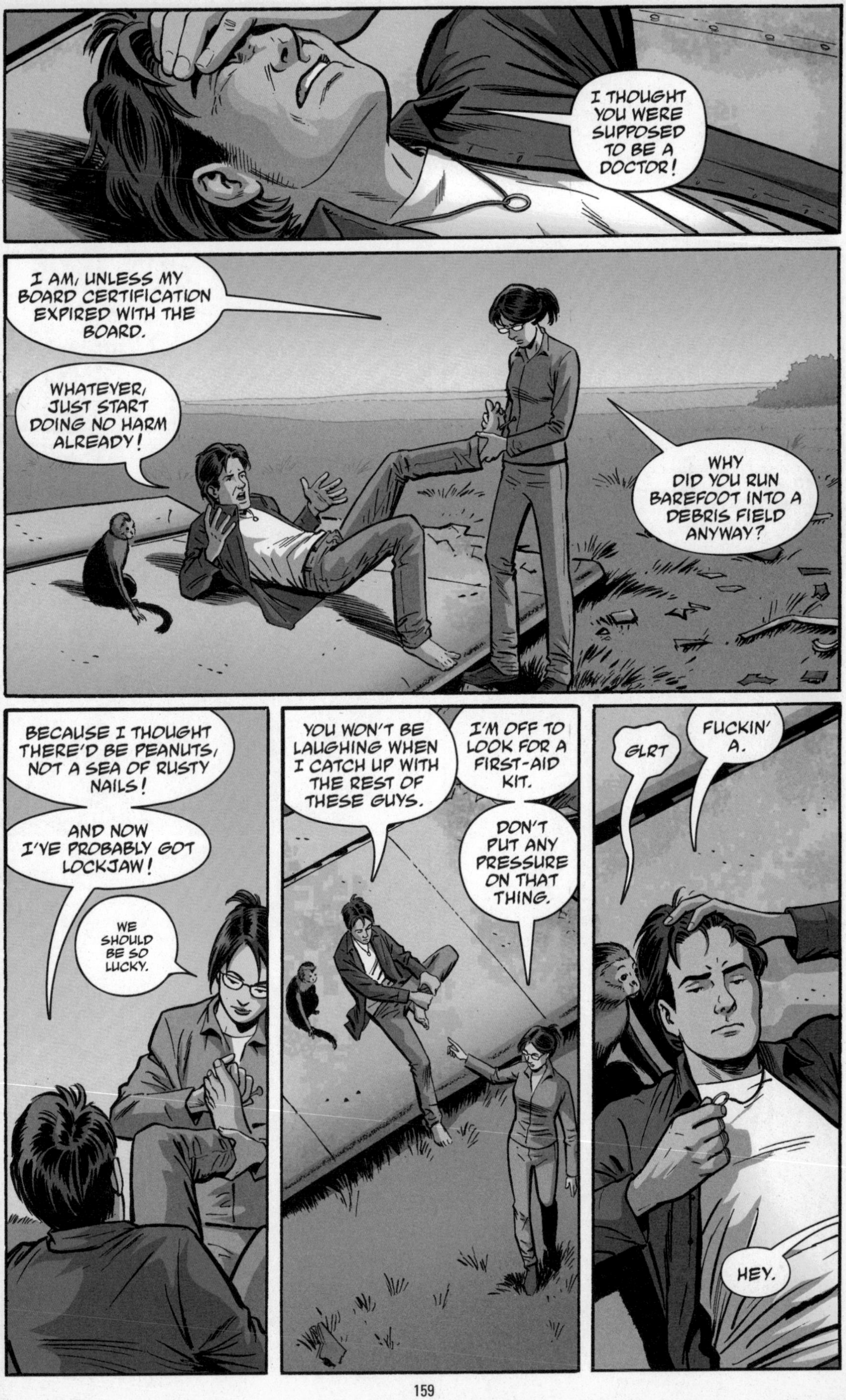
I THOUGHT YOU WERE SUPPOSED TO BE A DOCTOR!
I AM, UNLESS MY BOARD CERTIFICATION EXPIRED WITH THE BOARD.
WHATEVER, JUST START DOING NO HARM ALREADY!
WHY DID YOU RUN BAREFOOT INTO A DEBRIS FIELD ANYWAY?
BECAUSE I THOUGHT THERE'D BE PEANUTS, NOT A SEA OF RUSTY NAILS!
AND NOW I'VE PROBABLY GOT LOCKJAW!
WE SHOULD BE SO LUCKY.
YOU WON'T BE LAUGHING WHEN I CATCH UP WITH THE REST OF THESE GUYS.
I'M OFF TO LOOK FOR A FIRST-AID KIT.
DON'T PUT ANY PRESSURE ON THAT THING.
GLRT
FUCKIN' A.
HEY.

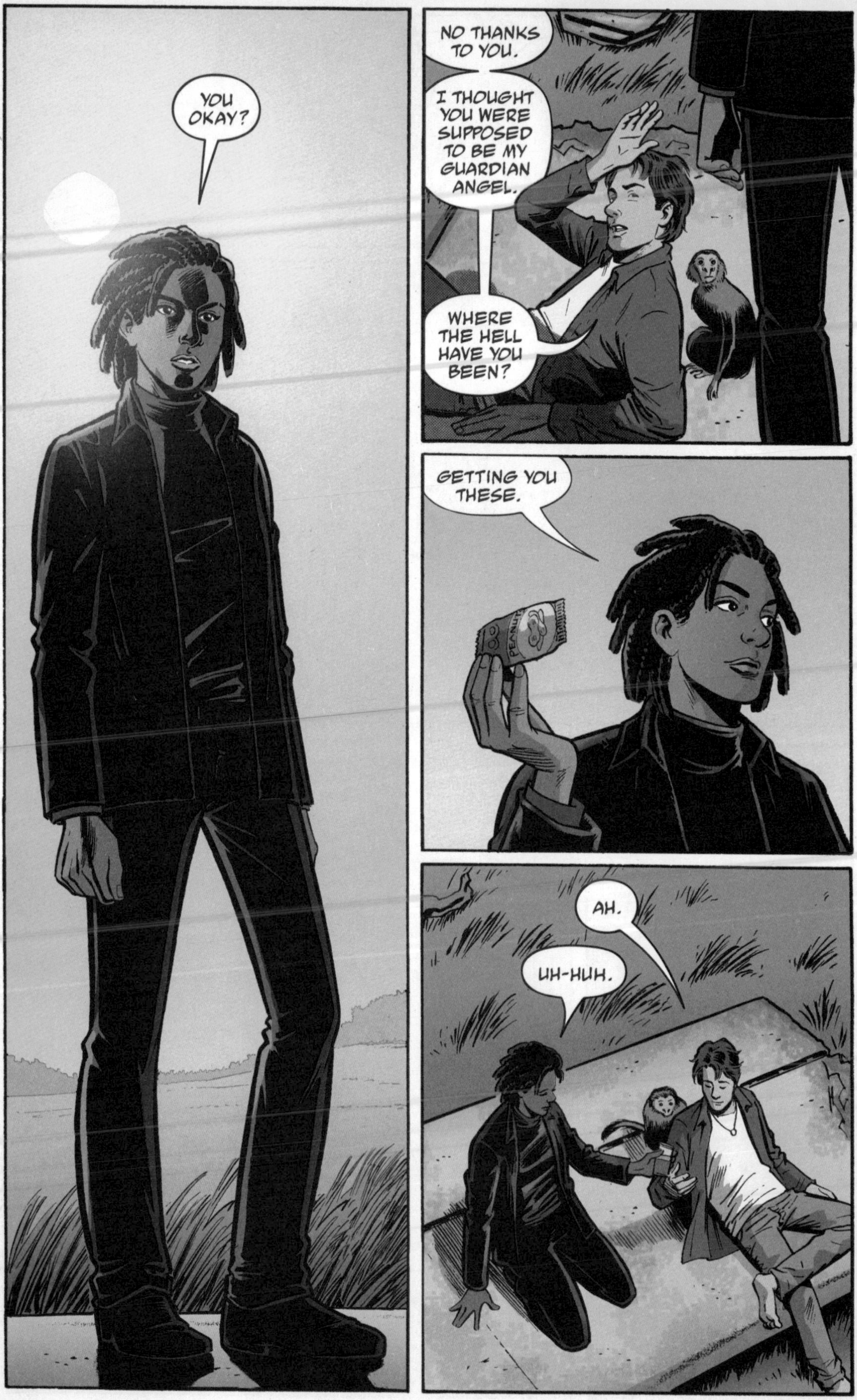
YOU OKAY?
NO THANKS TO YOU.
I THOUGHT YOU WERE SUPPOSED TO BE MY GUARDIAN ANGEL.
WHERE THE HELL HAVE YOU BEEN?
GETTING YOU THESE.
PEANUTS
AH.
UH-HUH.

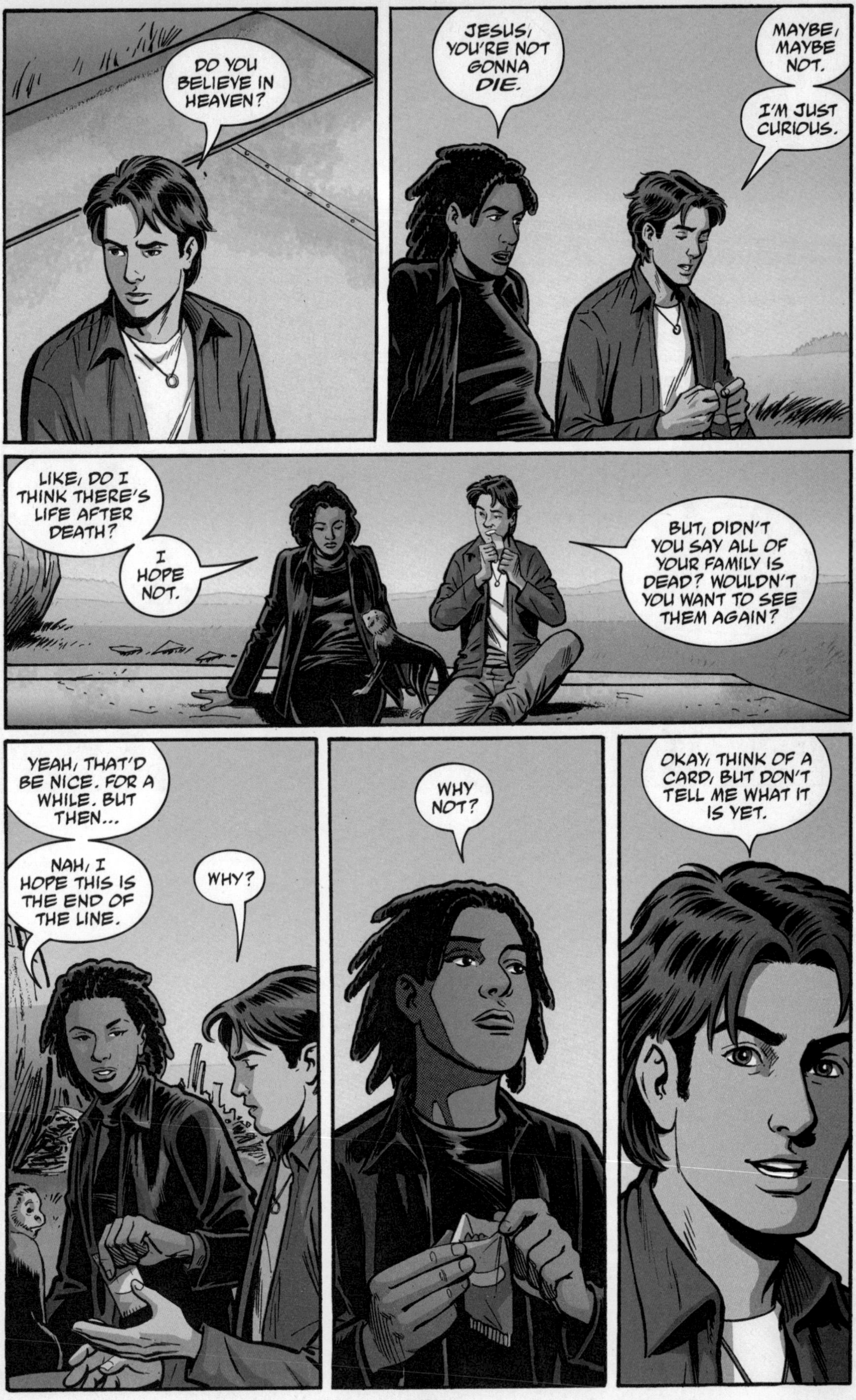
DO YOU BELIEVE IN HEAVEN?
JESUS, YOU'RE NOT GONNA DIE.
MAYBE, MAYBE NOT.
I'M JUST CURIOUS.
LIKE, DO I THINK THERE'S LIFE AFTER DEATH?
I HOPE NOT.
BUT, DIDN'T YOU SAY ALL OF YOUR FAMILY IS DEAD? WOULDN'T YOU WANT TO SEE THEM AGAIN?
YEAH, THAT'D BE NICE. FOR A WHILE. BUT THEN...
NAH, I HOPE THIS IS THE END OF THE LINE.
WHY?
WHY NOT?
OKAY, THINK OF A CARD, BUT DON'T TELL ME WHAT IT IS YET.

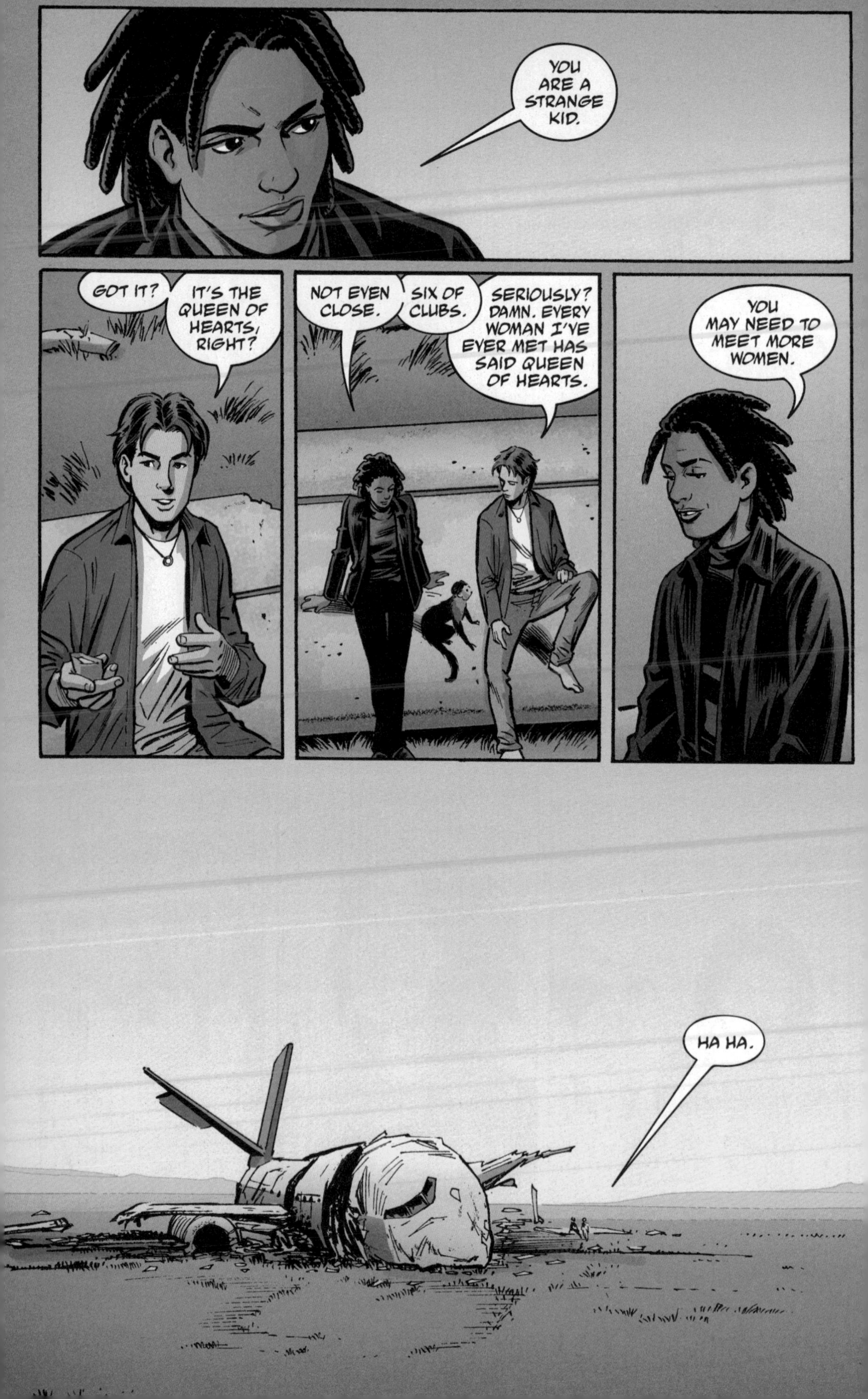

YOU ARE A STRANGE KID.
GOT IT?
IT'S THE QUEEN OF HEARTS, RIGHT?
NOT EVEN CLOSE.
SIX OF CLUBS.
SERIOUSLY? DAMN. EVERY WOMAN I'VE EVER MET HAS SAID QUEEN OF HEARTS.
YOU MAY NEED TO MEET MORE WOMEN.
HA HA.

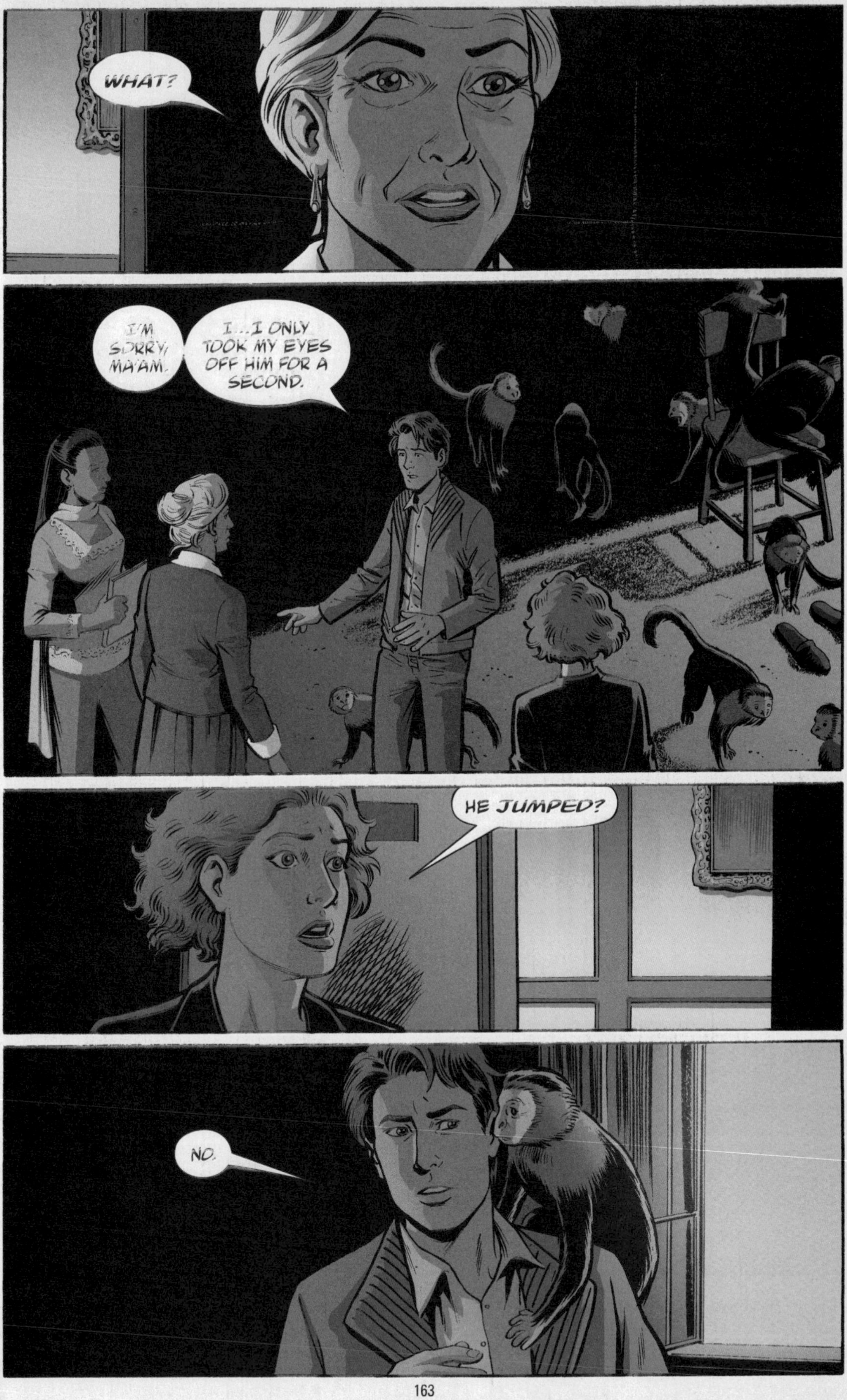
WHAT?
I'M SORRY, MA'AM.
I...I ONLY TOOK MY EYES OFF HIM FOR A SECOND.
HE JUMPED?
NO.

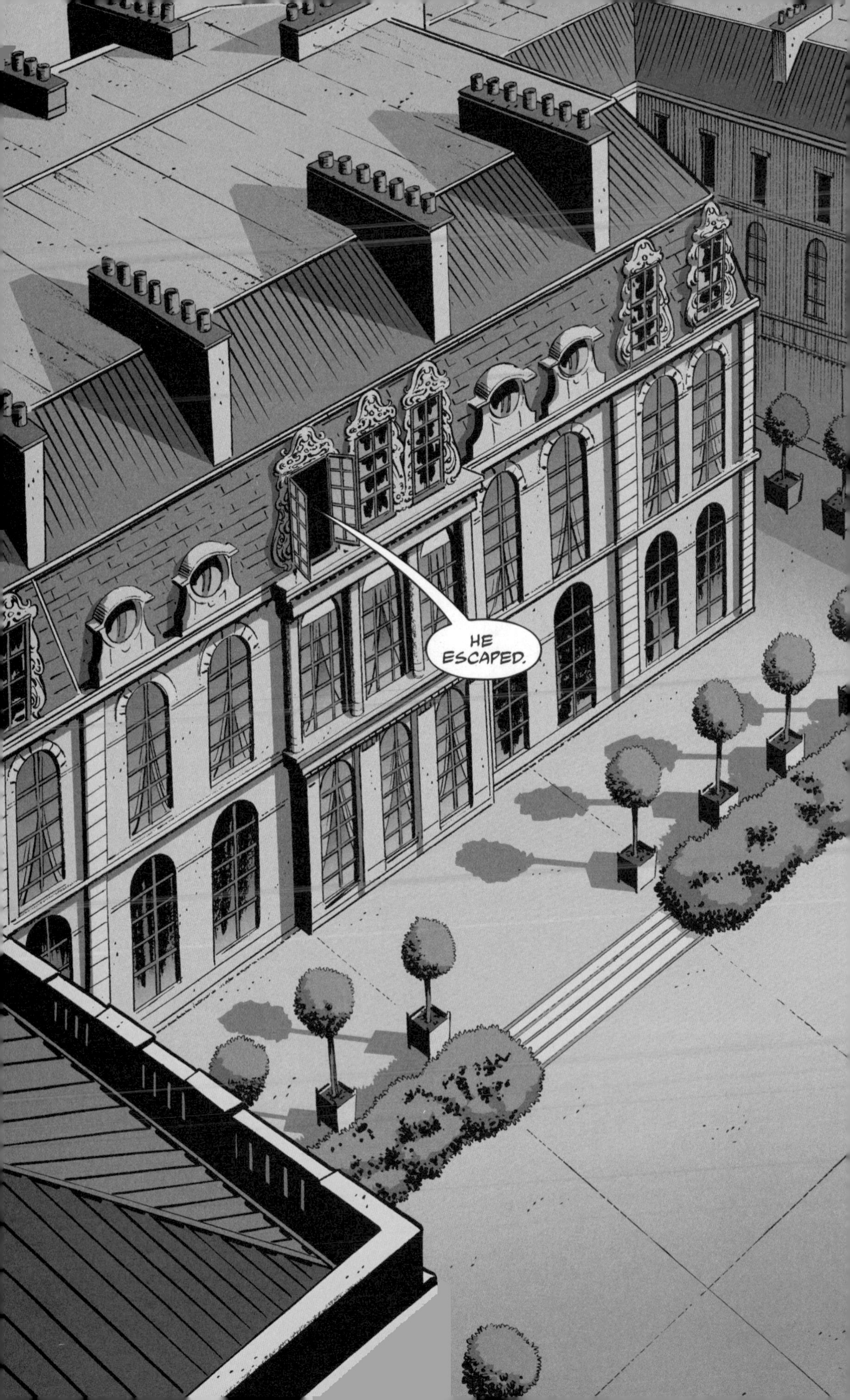
HE ESCAPED.

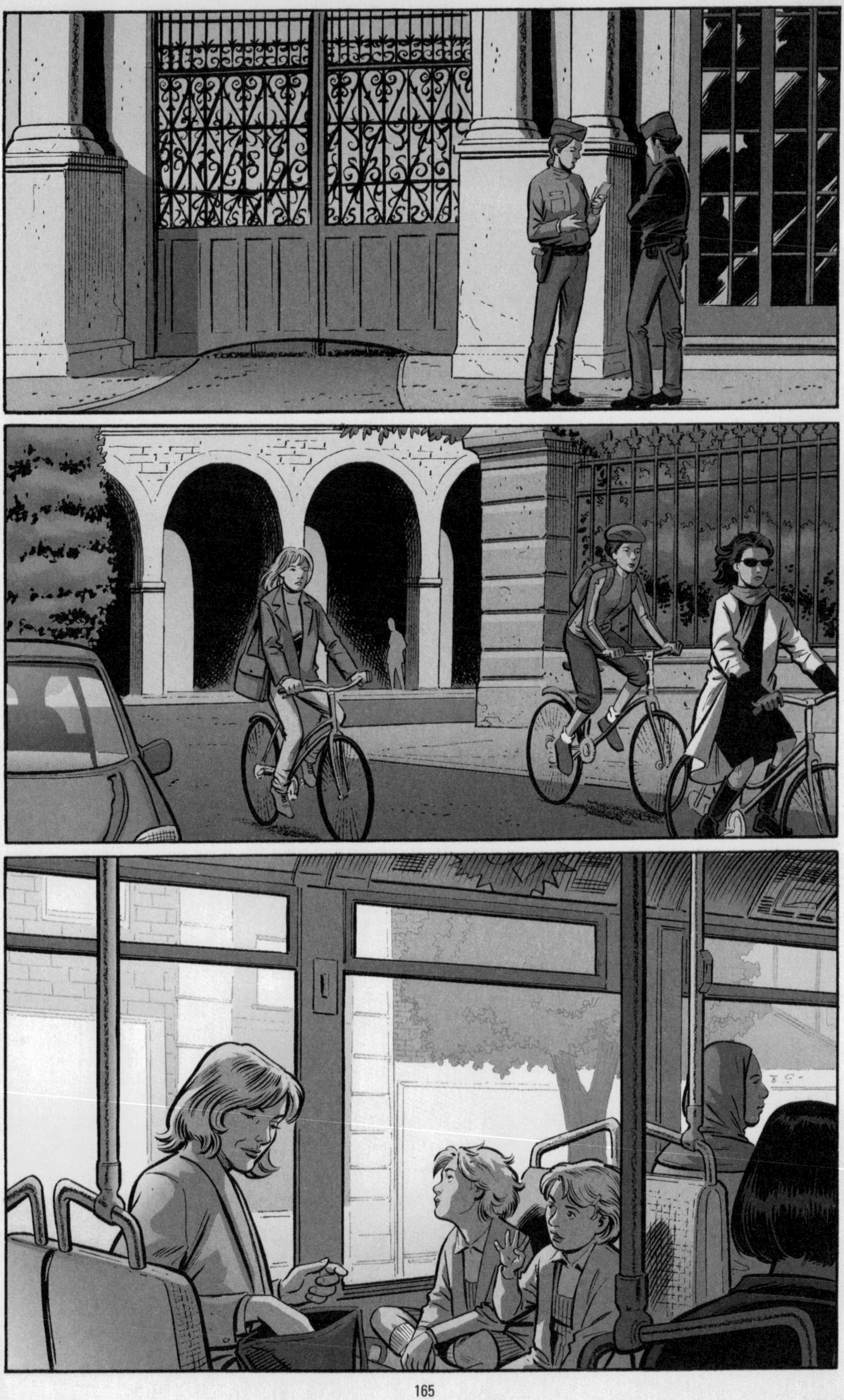

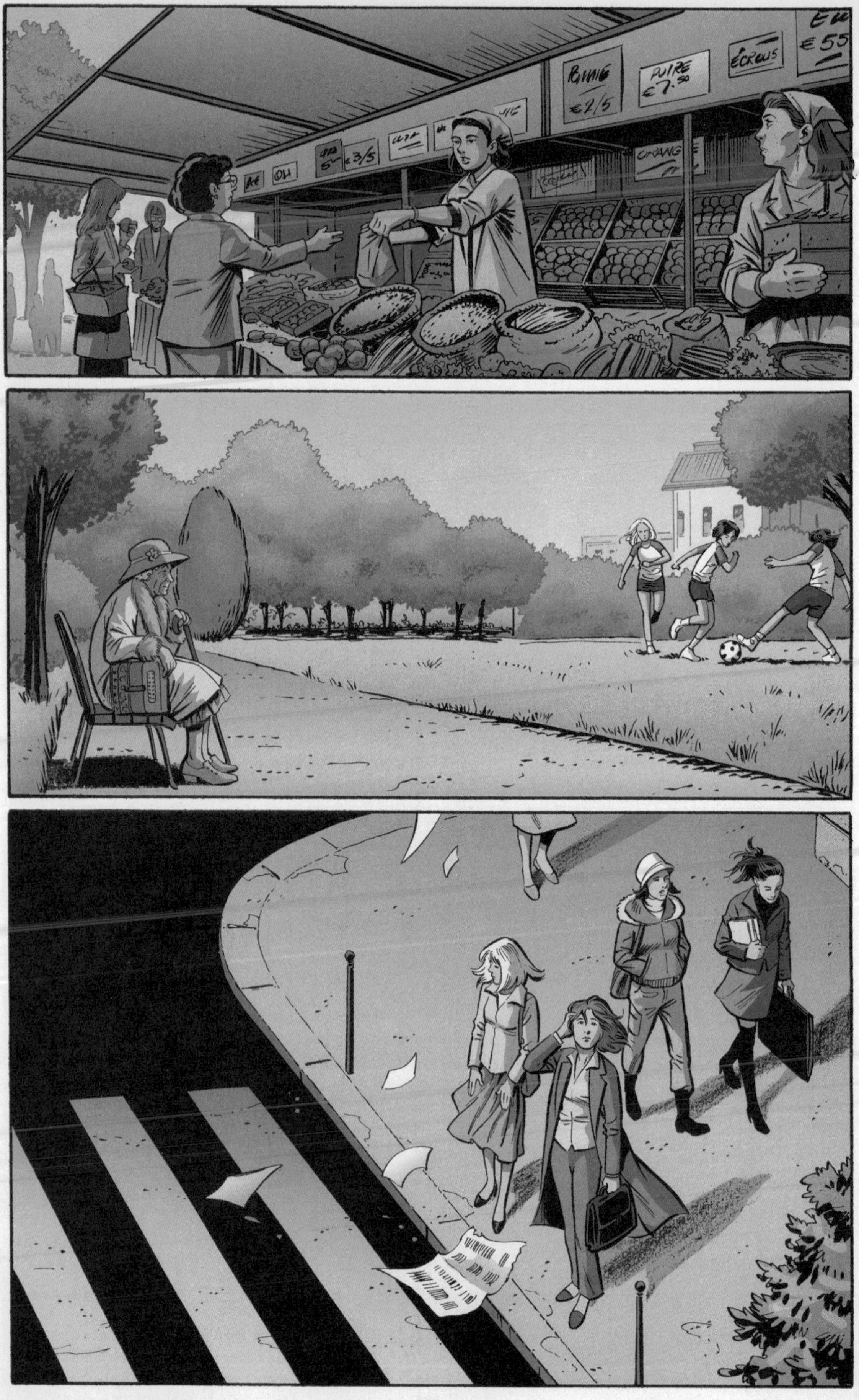
€2/5
€7.50
€55
ORANG

Alas

Brian K. Vaughan
WRITER

Pia Guerra
PENCILLER

José Marzán Jr.
INKER

Lee Loughridge
COLORIST

Clem Robins
LETTERER

COVER ARTIST

ASST. EDITOR

Will Dennis
EDITOR

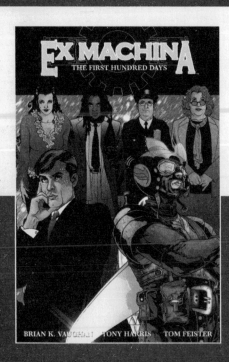